FAITHFUL EDUCATION

FAITHFUL EDUCATION

Madrassahs in South Asia

A L I   R I A Z

RUTGERS UNIVERSITY PRESS
NEW BRUNSWICK, NEW JERSEY, AND LONDON

Library of Congress Cataloging-in-Publication Data

Riaz, Ali.
　Faithful education : madrassahs in South Asia / Ali Riaz.
　　p. cm.
　Includes bibliographical references and index.
　ISBN 978-0-8135-4345-1 (hardcover : alk. paper)
　1. Madrasahs—South Asia.　2. Islamic religious education—South Asia.　I. Title.
　BP43.S68R54 2008
　297.7'70954—dc22   2007039076

A British Cataloging-in-Publication record for this book is available from the British Library.

Map by Anora Wilson

Visit our Web site: http://rutgerspress.rutgers.edu

Manufactured in the United States of America

Dedicated

to the memories of my parents

Mohabbat Ali

Bilkis Ara

CONTENTS

MAP AND TABLES

ACKNOWLEDGMENTS

This book is the result of a long journey––intellectual, temporal, and spatial. It took so many years and so many conversations to gather data and write this book that it is not easy to remember all the individuals who contributed to its content; neither is it possible to recount all the events through which information has been gathered and my ideas have been shaped. From digging out documents to listening to men of wisdom; from formal and informal interactions to unobtrusive observations; from friendly exchanges and heated debates to refusal to talk––all have contributed to this book. My interactions with the people who served as sources of information and ideas took place face-to-face, through regular mail, via e-mail, and over the telephone before, during, and after my field trips. I sincerely thank all the individuals who have shared information and their thoughts with me about South Asian madrassahs since 1999.

I am greatly indebted to my research assistants, Matt McCleary, Daniel Evans, Paula Orlando, and Mina Aitelhadj, who have worked with me closely since I joined Illinois State University. They have made significant contributions at various stages. Among them Mina Aitelhadj deserves special mention. Not only has Mina been engaged in this project for the longest period, she identified sources, kept track of the contemporaneous developments, and helped me gather data. Mina listened to my sometimes incomprehensible ideas with keen interest. Between 2003 and 2007, other research projects had often pulled me in different directions, but Mina kept me focused on this project. She is truly a gifted person with a natural bent for research.

My friend Dr. Marina Carter took special interest in this project, read a number of drafts of each chapter, corrected them with great care, and suggested ways to improve my arguments. I could not ask for more. Margaret Case, who took care of the copyediting of the manuscript, was a blessing for this project.

Her knowledge of South Asian languages and culture helped identify some errors and correct them easily. The comments and suggestions of three anonymous readers were immensely helpful. They not only improved the content of the book but also the presentation of information. I have presented parts of this book at a number of conferences; consequently I have received comments from the discussants and the audiences present. They were invaluable.

I am thankful to Kendra Boileau and Adi Hovav, two editors at Rutgers University Press. Kendra extended her support as soon as she came to know about the project in 2005 and remained supportive until she left the Press in 2007. She has an enviable quality of patience and was always ready to accommodate. I took advantage of both. Adi's support was key in getting the book out to the readers. She ensured that it received due attention. Thanks are also due to Marilyn Campbell, Katie Curran, and Alicia Nadkarni for taking care of the production process. My sincere gratitude to Ershad Ahmed for permission to use the photograph featured on the cover of the book. Thanks also to Routledge for allowing me to use some materials from my book *Islamist Militancy in Bangladesh: A Complex Web*.

Finally, thanks to my wife Shagufta Jabeen and our daughter Ila Sruti. By now they must have become tired of listening to my incessant discussion of madrassah, and my erratic work schedule. Yet they never tired of extending their support in completing the book.

FAITHFUL EDUCATION

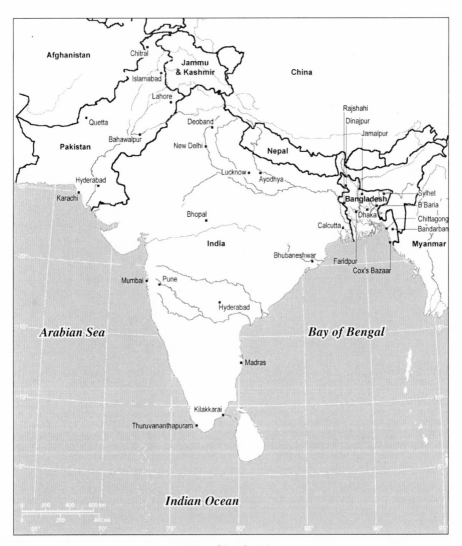

Map of South Asia

WHY STUDY MADRASSAHS?

UNDERSTANDING THE IMPORTANCE
OF ISLAMIC SEMINARIES

Educational institutions called madrassahs have been a feature of Muslim societies for centuries, yet the word *madrassah* was almost nonexistent in the Western lexicon, particularly in public discourse, until September 2001. After 9/11 the U.S. media took special interest in madrassahs, and referred to these institutions as citadels of militancy, or factories of jihad. In a very short time, a once unknown word gained familiarity and notoriety at once. Media coverage of madrassahs, particularly during the U.S. military operation in Afghanistan, was frenzied, to say the least. What became known to the media audience was that the madrassah is a special kind of educational institution that teaches Islamic thought and that provided training to the then ruling regime of Afghanistan—the Taliban. Some media reports provided an element of context, informing readers that the madrassahs were also the recruiting centers of the Afghan *mujahideens* or holy warriors, who fought against the Soviet Union in the eighties. In this highly skewed coverage, vital questions have been overlooked: What do we know about madrassahs? Why and how have Islamic educational institutions whose traditions date back hundreds of years been transformed? Is there any connection between the so-called global jihad and the madrassahs? Is there a need to reform the madrassahs? Should Western policy makers be alarmed by the recent increase in the number of madrassahs in Muslim countries, particularly in South Asia?

This book aims to explore these questions through examination of the madrassahs of three South Asian countries, namely Pakistan, Bangladesh, and India. I shall attempt to define the tracts and territories of thoughts and ideologies, deliberations and practices, debates and conflicts on these issues rather than give a set of ready-made answers. But before we begin our exploration it is necessary that we understand what a madrassah is, what the significance of these institutions is, and what the importance of South Asian madrassahs is. In this introduction I will deal with these three aspects and provide an outline of the chapters that follow.

What Is a Madrassah?

The word *madrassah* is an Arabic word whose literal meaning is "school." The word comes from the same Arabic root as *dars,* which means a lesson or an instruction. In Arabic-speaking regions, it does not specifically refer to a religious seminary; instead schools of various levels are referred to as madrassahs. However, in non-Arabic speaking societies this word has assumed a different meaning, and is often understood to designate a special kind of institution for the training of *ulama* (literally scholars, plural of *alim*). In the South Asian context, madrassah means an educational institution that offers instruction about the Qur'an, the sayings (*hadith*) of the Prophet Muhammad, jurisprudence (*fiqh*), and law. In other words, schools that promote Islamic curricula are called madrassahs. Although the word *madrassah* is used as a generic description of educational institutions covering elementary to university-level education, to Muslim scholars they represent the primary and secondary level of education through tenth grade. Educational institutions offering curricula equivalent to eleventh and twelfth grades are called *darul uloom* (literally, abode of knowledge), and *jamia* offer curricula equivalent to college and university. In this study, I use the term *madrassah* to identify all of these educational institutions. The Arabic plural form of *madrassah* is *madaris,* but for the sake of clarity I have used the English equivalent plural form *madrassahs* throughout the book.

Why Study Madrassahs?

While the rise of the Taliban in Afghanistan and post-9/11 security concerns have thrust the issue of the madrassah into the foreground of public discourse, the urgency to examine the madrassahs stems from four needs; first, to investigate the sources and the veracity of the widely held opinion that madrassahs are a threat to global security; second, to understand Muslim societies, particularly the role of traditional social institutions in the face of the rise of political Islam; third, to reassess the role of educational institutions in the struggles between various groups and classes within society; and finally, to appreciate a social institution that provides a safety net to the poor segments of the society and provides free education, including literacy and valuable cultural skills, to vast numbers of children from poor families who cannot afford expensive private education.

GLOBAL SECURITY AND THE MADRASSAHS

Since the frightful events of 11 September 2001, allegations abound that madrassahs in Muslim countries are indoctrinating young men who wage jihad against the Western world on a global scale. Within this frame of discussion, global jihadists, as they have been referred to in the media, pose a clear and present danger and therefore should be confronted with lethal force. But these discussions not only obscure the long history of these institutions but also are deficient in empirical data to support the argument that madrassahs have produced leading members of the international terror networks. On the contrary, studies published between 2004 and 2006 demonstrate that the connection between madrassahs and international terrorism is tenuous at best and probably nonexistent.[1] How, then, have such allegations become common knowledge? And does this point to a larger problem in regard to understanding Muslim societies and their sociopolitical dynamics?

It is also necessary to be cognizant of the differences between transnational terrorists with a global agenda and militants with circumscribed goals of establishing Islamist states, or pursuing sectarian objectives. While the former purposefully construct and consequently target a common enemy at the global level, the latter aim for far smaller achievable goals. Certainly the former constitute a threat to global security in general, particularly to Western countries; but the latter are not an imminent threat. Under such circumstances, it is legitimate to question whether they should be viewed through the same security lens. Both these groups may, and often do, use similar repertoires and frames of reference from Islamic traditions, but within distinctly different contexts and with different intentions. While available data, to date, has put the veracity of the nexus between madrassah and international terrorism in question, the connection between the madrassah and militancy has remained unexplored. Unfortunately, at times these two are blended together in a generalized fashion. A comment of Samina Ahmed and Andrew Stroehlein after the London bombings in July 2005 illustrates this point: "Jihadi extremism is still propagated at radical madrasas in Pakistan.[2] These religious schools still preach an insidious doctrine that foments the sectarian violence that is increasingly a threat to the stability of Pakistan. And now, it seems, the hatred these madrasas breed is spilling blood in Western cities as well."[3] There is no doubt that sectarian violence and militancy are a menace to society, and various social institutions, including madrassahs, can and in the case of Pakistan do create and perpetuate sectarianism, but sectarianism and militancy do not necessarily pose a threat to global security.

Orthodoxy and reliance on dated curricula are two important features of madrassahs. Orthodoxy is reflected in madrassahs' preoccupation, almost to the verge of obsession, with rituals, personal laws, and individual behavior including dress codes. This orthodox mindset is, indeed, inimical to the mental development of the students and a key obstacle to any productive role of these institutions in modern society; but it should, at least in theory, serve as an impediment to engagement with a global network and therefore participation in the "global jihad." Orthodoxy, be it religious or secular, and narrow-mindedness are two sides of the same coin and influence the cognition of the individual, usually breeding intolerance. Sectarianism, denominationalism, and parochialism of various kinds, all of which have been accompanied by hatred and violence, are telling examples of this phenomenon. Madrassahs are no exception. Violence and militancy can result from the parochial and insular nature of madrassah education.[4] But the nature and scope of the militancy and the targets of violence are neither predetermined nor exclusively influenced by any global agenda; instead the sociopolitical surroundings of these institutions play the decisive role. There is no "one-size-fits all" formula to understand this phenomenon. An a priori conclusion that madrassahs are by nature the training center of "global jihad" is not helpful in this regard.

TRADITIONAL INSTITUTIONS AND POLITICAL ISLAM

In recent decades countries with Muslim majority populations have witnessed the rise of Islam as a political ideology and Islamists as formidable political forces in their domestic political arenas. Ascendancy of these religiopolitico forces has generated many questions. including that of their relationships with traditional institutions. Over the years, societies with a Muslim majority have experienced occasional Islamic revivalist movements that emphasize the need for the spiritual purification of the adherents, but Islamism is distinctly different from this resurgence, and has far-reaching consequences. Islamism is "a form of instrumentalization of Islam by individuals, groups and organizations that pursue political objectives" and which "provides [a] political response to today's societal challenges by imagining a future, the foundations for which rest on reappropriated, reinvented concepts borrowed from the Islamic tradition."[5] Islamism, therefore, is inherently a political phenomenon and by no means simply an Islamic one. Islamists exclusively emphasize specific courses of action to improve their political power, and adopt various strategies to assert themselves on the social and political plane. In sharp contrast to the fundamentalists, who are concerned first with the erosion of religion and its proper role in society, Islamists focus on politicoeconomic interests.[6] "They draw on Islamic referents—terms, symbols, and events taken from the Islamic tradition—in order to articulate a distinct political agenda,"[7] but these signs and symbols are reconstituted, traditions are reworked, and norms are redefined.[8] To them "Islam is more a political blueprint than a faith, and the

Islamist discourse is to a large extent a political discourse in religious garb."[9] For Islamists, "a true Islamic society—and flowing from this, a just, prosperous and strong one—is not simply comprised of pious Muslims; it requires an Islamic state or system."[10]

It is necessary to be reminded that Islamism, interchangeably used with political Islam, is not an antimodern phenomenon; neither is it an antimodernist movement advocating retreat to a "glorious past." It is not "harking back to the essential verities of the faith" but an attempt to redefine the present and the future in light of both domestic and global politics.[11] Domestic contexts play the key role and provide legitimacy to this ideology, but the shadow of global politics always lurks behind the process. Salwa Ismail is correct in saying that "the contemporary Islamist movements, much like other political developments, are not the expression of continuity and of persistent themes of Islamic history. Rather they are constituted as political forces shaped by socioeconomic and political contexts in which they operate."[12]

In this regard Islamism is a mirror image of any and all other religiopolitical forces, as noted by Aziz al-Azmeh: "Islamists use much the same political language and make similar use of archaic political iconography as do the Serb nationalists of Karadzic, their notion of authenticity is analogous to the Hinduttva of the communalist Right in India, and they combine together the political mysticism of the secular Zionist Right with a mild form of the doctrine of divine election propounded by Jewish fundamentalism."[13]

Islamism, therefore, is simultaneously an endogenous and an exogenous phenomenon. Furthermore, spatio-temporal aspects shape it. Paraphrasing François Burgat, we can say that as a political discourse Islamism is active in two areas: in internal contestation (that is, domestic political orders) and, internationally, in the context of East-West relations.[14]

Within domestic politics, the rise of political Islam presents challenges to two constituencies: first, to secularist politics, both ideologically and in electoral terms; and second, to the traditional orthodox/conservative schools of thought within the Muslim community.

This new ideology demonstrates that the hegemony of the ideology of secularism is not eternal; instead it can be taken to task. The causes of and conditions for such challenges and degree of their success vary according to political topography and temporal juncture. But oft-cited causes include the lack of performance legitimacy of the ruling elites (that is, the inability of the secular elites to deliver common goods); the brutal authoritarianism that results in an erosion of the civil society and hence leaves the mosque as the only viable public space; uneven economic development including urbanization; rupture in the hegemony of secularist politics; and the politics of expediency of secular parties, to name but a few.[15] These factors are not mutually exclusive, and their simultaneous occurrence is not necessary.

Until recently, the electoral victory of the Islamic Salvation Front (known by its French acronym FIS) in Algeria in 1991 was the only example of the Islamists' electoral success, but after a long hiatus, 2005–2006 has produced more examples. The surprise victory of Hamas in the Palestinian election in January 2006 can be identified as a part of a trend reflected in elections held in various countries in the Middle East and Gulf since early 2005. In that year, Islamist candidates did well in the first very limited municipal polls in Saudi Arabia, Hizbollah emerged as the preeminent representative of Lebanese Shi'ites, and the Muslim Brotherhood won 88 out of the 150 seats it contested in the Egyptian legislative assembly election, with close to one-third of the popular vote. In the parliamentary election of Iraq, the votes were not only cast along sectarian lines but also went to those who favored a role for Islam in politics. For example, the United Iraqi Alliance, backed by Shi'a clerics, obtained almost 80 percent of the seats for Shi'a community; similarly, the Islamic Iraq Party won 80 percent of the places to which the Sunni minority is entitled. These examples demonstrate successes of the Islamists on their own; elsewhere they have joined alliances that brought them power through elections. The 2001 parliamentary election in Bangladesh, which brought two Islamist parties to power as members of a four-party alliance, is a case in point. The coalition, led by the Bangladesh Nationalist Party (BNP), includes two Islamist parties: the Jamaat-i-Islami and the Islami Oikyo Jote (IOJ, Islamic United Front). Jamaat was opposed to the emergence of Bangladesh in 1971 and was banned until 1979. This group also overtly expresses support for an Islamic revolution. The other partner of the alliance, IOJ, is small in size and more radical, having expressed solidarity with the Taliban regime in Afghanistan. For example, on 8 March 1999, Fazlul Hoq Aminee in unequivocal terms stated in a public meeting in Dhaka, "We are for Osama [bin Laden], we are for [the] Taliban and we will be in government by 2000." The leading partner of the alliance, the BNP, views Islam as an integral part of the sociocultural life of Bangladesh. In the most populous Muslim country, Indonesia, the party that has been gaining strength in recent years is the Prosperous Justice Party (PKS). In 2004, the party increased its share to 7.5 percent from 1.4 percent in 1999, and secured 25 percent of the popular vote in the capital, Jakarta, the largest share any single party commands. The PKS now hold a small number of seats (forty-five seats) in the parliament, but their party members have grown to almost a half a million, from 60,000 in 1999.

Comprehending the emerging row between the Islamists and the conservative/orthodox Muslim authorities within the domestic political arena requires dispensing with a homogenous view of Islam. Rather, Islam should be understood as, following Talal Asad, a "discursive tradition," which assumes different meanings in different sociocultural milieus and is open to contestations.[16] Understanding the nature and scope of the contestations between these forces also requires mapping out the fundamental distinctions between them.[17] Following Ismail, we can identify differences between these forces in three spheres: strategies and modes of actions, contents of the respective ideologies, and their location within the overall political configuration, particularly their relationships with the state and other political groups.[18] Although orthodox/conservative Muslims view Islam as a complete code of conduct and underscore the need for revival of religious values, they are primarily interested in strengthening traditional institutions and spreading spiritual messages through existing social institutions. Therefore, they favor the status quo, remain oblivious to politics, and shun violence. Islamists, on the other hand, extend their sphere of action beyond social institutions, are more concerned with the political realm, and do not hesitate to espouse violence, should they deem it necessary.

The differences in terms of respective ideologies are striking and have an immense impact on those societies in which they play a key role. Key to these differences is the concept of sovereignty. The Islamists insist on *al-hakimiya*, or a total sovereignty and rulership of Allah as opposed to the sovereignty of human beings. In addition, to them society can be either of two kinds—Islamic or *jahiliya* (belonging to the age of ignorance, marked by barbarism and unbelief, a pre-Islamic state of society). They view the present state of society as jahiliya, and insist that jahiliya cannot be reformed but needs to be destroyed, if necessary through violent means (through jihad or through *qital fi-sabillah*, armed struggle in the name of Allah) to establish an Islamic state where Allah's sovereignty (*al-hakimiya*) is supreme.[19] The orthodox strand does not share this ideological stand and remains committed to spirituality and salvation through piety, and practice of traditional rituals.

The third important difference between them involves their relationship to the state and other political parties. As Islamism is not a monolithic and homogenous ideology and the Islamists are not one single entity, the ideal disposition of the state remains a matter of contention within various strands. Yet there are some broad agreements within the Islamist camp with regard to the nature of the state. The origins of these ideas can be traced back the Islamist ideologue Abul Ala Maududi (1903–1979). According to Maududi, the founder of Jamaat-i-Islami in India and Pakistan, in the Islamist state "no one can regard any field of his affairs as personal and private." He had no problems in drawing parallels between his vision of state and the Fascist state: "the Islamic state bears a kind of resemblance to the Fascist and Communist states." Maududi emphasized the importance of one-party rule, which is the very antithesis of Western democracy.[20] Orthodox Muslims, while believing that the existing sociopolitical system causes moral degradation and is inimical to spiritual salvation, do not question the legitimacy of the state and seldom challenge societal arrangements. To reform, not to destroy, is their goal, and they believe that this can be achieved through various sociopolitical organizations. Therefore the relationship between orthodox Muslims and the existing political parties is not (generally) one of hostility.

These differences between the Islamists and the orthodox Muslim authorities are not exhaustive but are fundamental and instructive in understanding their attitudes toward sociopolitical issues and institutions. They also serve to demonstrate some of the defining characteristics of the Islamists. We should add the teleological aspect of Islamist movements, which bears close resemblance to similar religiopolitical forces originating in other religions. The Hindu nationalist movement under the leadership of the Bharatiya Janata Party (BJP) and its like, commonly referred to as Sangh Parivar, is a case in point. Drawing on Thomas Hansen's fine exploration of this movement, we can see that religiopolitical movements construct a paradoxical dual teleology:

> One the one hand, history is invoked to justify the movement and its objectives. The movement is but a realization of inevitable historical development, and individuals in the movement are merely inconsequential actors in a great, unfolding drama.... On the other hand, the founding myth almost always revolves around a notion of self-birth, self-celebration, depicting the founding of the movement in an extraordinary situation by farsighted individuals who, through extraordinary difficulties, succeeded in creating the present movement. Due to their intervention the course of history will be altered as the movement will gradually realize its vision.[21]

Islamist movements, wherever they have embarked on this journey to capture the state, have trodden the same path. Examples include the Iranian revolution in 1979, the Muslim Brotherhood (al-Ikhwan al-Muslimun) in Egypt, FIS in Algeria, and the Sudanese Islamic Brotherhood under the leadership of Hasan al-Turabi.

In recent days, as the Islamists gain ground in Muslim societies, particularly within the domestic political arena, evidenced in the election results previously mentioned, it has become imperative that we understand these features and their implications.

In the face of the growing strengths of the Islamists, the traditional interpretations of texts, doctrine, and acceptable behaviors offered by conservative/orthodox Muslim religious authorities and institutions have become vulnerable, since the Islamists intend not only to seize governmental power but also to bring fundamental changes to "power structure and social controls that legitimize and regulate knowledge and meaning in the society."[22] Locally rooted understandings of Islam, or in other words, a socially negotiated meaning of Islam, produced and accepted over centuries by traditional institutions, face a challenge because of "rival and alternative articulations of belief and practice" presented by the Islamists. These new forces foreground and question the existing practices, and change the balance between competing religious authorities.[23] Under such circumstances, all traditional social institutions face the possibility of being contested. But perhaps educational institutions, particularly madrassahs, face this threat more than others, due both to the importance of education in any society and the specificity of Muslim societies.

EDUCATION: AN ARENA OF STRUGGLE

Education, as the etymology of the word suggests, is to lead someone away from ignorance, a passage from nature to culture, and therefore is a cultural program rather than a conceptual tool in understanding the process of learning.[24] Not so clearly implicit in this meaning of education are two related issues: knowledge and power, and Michel Foucault reminded us that knowledge is one of the manifestations of the presence of power.[25] Thus modes of the selection, classification, distribution, transmission, and evaluation of educational knowledge in a society are manifestations of power relationships within that society and means of social control. Control over knowledge goes further: it provides an unchallenged legitimation for certain hegemonic versions of truth, and it allows the presentation of specific forms of consciousness, beliefs, attitudes, values, and practices as natural, universal, or even eternal. Educational institutions, to echo Louis Althusser, are apparatuses: "what the bourgeoisie has installed as its number-one, that is, as its dominant ideological State apparatus, is the educational apparatus, which has in fact replaced in its functions the previously dominant ideological State apparatus, the Church."[26] But this is not to say that these institutions are free from contestation. Instead, education reflects the struggles between social classes for dominance in the form of debates on curriculum, contents, and pedagogy.

Although these struggles are universal, two aspects of education in Muslim societies further complicate the situation with regard to the madrassah. They are: the position of religious educational institutions vis-à-vis state-sponsored secular educational institutions; and the emerging struggle between orthodox and Islamists to control the "true" meaning of Islam.

Contacts with the West through colonialism in the eighteenth century, or modernization schemes in the postcolonial era, particularly in the fifties and sixties, replaced religious educational institutions with secular educational institutions. In the latter cases schools were viewed as agents of development and modernization, and governments introduced centralized, secular, and homogenized systems of education with an emphasis on imparting skills to the students and reproducing the vision of a secular nationhood. The objectives of the education include transforming the individuals who constitute the community, and transmitting a particular interpretation of history and ideology. This policy is an integral part of the secularization of the society. Secularization, within this context, is a combination of what G. Moyser described as constitutional secularization (that is, "whereby religious institutions cease to be given special constitutional recognition"), institutional secularization (that is, "when religious structures lose their political saliency"), and ideological secularization (when "the basic values and belief systems used to evaluate the political realm and to give it meaning cease to be couched in religious terms").[27]

One of the significant, and perhaps most controversial, aspects of secularization of society is its emphasis on the presence of two contending spheres—private and public, and its placing of religion in the private sphere. Secularization, therefore, privatizes religion. In Muslim-majority societies, the privatization of religion undermines the Islamic scholarly tradition and consequently alienates Muslim communities. However, in the realm of education these two contending spheres intersect, as the primary function of the education is to preserve and transmit tradition—in this case Islamic tradition as opposed to the secular tradition. This makes the education a critical battlefield. Here two contending visions face each other; they concern the identity of the community or nation, and the future of the nation. Control of education, in terms of both content and pedagogy, therefore, is sine qua non for these contending visions.

Marginalized by the state policies of secularization and challenged by the state-sponsored educational institutions, ulama find it necessary to maintain the madrassahs as the primary institutions for the preservation and transmission of Islamic tradition. Furthermore, this places the madrassahs in opposition to state-sponsored education. Madrassahs find themselves at variance with the hegemonic ideology, and the existence of the madrassahs itself becomes a challenge to the dominant ideology.

The modern state, either colonial or postcolonial, views education as a vertically organized system to transmit a unitary body of knowledge, as opposed to the idea of segmented and relatively autonomous sources of knowledge and life-wisdom, which the madrassah system represents. Faced with this situation, madrassahs have further embraced traditional values and have largely refused to reform their curricula and pedagogy, because any reform implies a departure from tradition, and a betrayal of the role history has bestowed on them. The roots of the orthodoxy of madrassahs lie here, but this is also becoming the source of contention between the Islamists and the conservative/orthodox Muslims who have maintained their control over the madrassahs. On the one hand, Islamists stand against conformity, thus favoring reforms. But on the other hand, they subscribe to a totalizing ideology.

One important aspect of this totalizing ideology is the discourse of the "Other." How the Other is constructed and what narrative is employed in depicting the confrontation between Islam and the Other illustrates the political projects of the Islamists. Islamist literatures—ranging from the pamphlet to newspaper articles to academic research—speak of a moral decay within Muslim societies and continuous attacks on the Islamic way of life. While apparently they are two separate topics—the former is endogenous to Muslim society and the latter exogenous—they are connected through seamless arguments of the presence of the Other—the demonic other, the enemy—who is by nature a threat to Islamic ideals. These two issues are intermingled in various combinations, adapted to their audience and circumstances, but all revolve around the narrative of constructing an antagonistic and powerful evil. The discourse of moral decay emanates from the idea of jahiliya, even if jahiliya is not referred to. This moral decay is a result of the ignorance of the Muslim community, on the one hand, who expect to be shepherded back to an idealized state of society; while on the other hand, it may be viewed as the consequence of the invasion and challenges of the immoral Other, the West, which needs to be confronted. The invasion takes various forms, from the physical presence of the West in Muslim societies, to the imposition of Western concepts and ideologies, to the proliferation of cultural products, while challenges include the undermining of Muslim societies and denigration of Muslims on the global scene.[28] Islamists claim a moral high ground by virtue of the moral superiority of Islam. "Within this perspective, Islam's superiority is tied to the moral corruption of the West, itself a cause of its supposed deterioration, bankruptcy, and inevitable collapse."[29] Furthermore, the enemy is not a fixed entity but a shifting notion—the West is construed as both a geographical entity and a concept synonymous with non-Islamic. Under this canopy of "the West" an array of forces can be accommodated: the religious other, the ideological other, the near-enemy and the distant-enemy, and so on.

For Islamists, the interpretation of Islam comes from their ideologues with an embedded political agenda and political strategies to achieve the goals. The political strategies call for a relentless struggle at all levels and at all times, and for adherents to remain on guard against the infiltration of the Other, particularly through various institutions, including those in the educational sphere. Quite correctly, they see all social institutions as ideological apparatuses and understand that without being in command of social institutions no political force can exercise its power to its fullest. The roles of Islamic educational institutions, within this schema, are twofold: to offer moral education, and to provide an alternative to a corrupt education system. In this endeavor, controlling madrassahs is more than a necessity; it is imperative. This makes the madrassahs suitable tools to achieve political goals. Whether the Islamists would succeed depends on sociopolitical dynamics and the location of the madrassahs in a society.

MADRASSAHS AND THE UNMET DEMANDS OF EDUCATION

The presence of madrassahs in Muslim societies is also closely related to the issue of access to state-supported education, which has a class dimension. For decades, access to education, particularly by the poorer section of the society, has been a major concern in developing countries. Although there has been relative progress in this regard, thanks to initiative of international organizations and national governments, universal access is yet to be the norm. This has left a huge gap between the demand and supply of educational facilities at the elementary level. Bangladesh, which has made remarkable progress over the last decades, is a case in point. The gross enrollment in primary level has increased from 61 percent in 1980, to 72 percent in 1990, to 96 percent by 2000, and to 106.34 percent in 2002.[30] In terms of absolute numbers, between 1991 and 2003 enrollment increased from 12.36 million to 17.46 million. Yet about 4.47 million children aged six to ten years are not attending school.[31] Additionally, gross enrollment varies among poor and nonpoor on the one hand, and urban and rural population on the other. Gross enrollment of poor children is about 16 percent less than of nonpoor children, and the disparity between urban and rural is about 20 percent, favoring urban population. The Education Watch Survey 2001 also identified villages in remote areas where the primary net enrollment is rate was as low as 20 percent, and among the children not enrolled in schools 88 percent live in rural areas. These figures assume greater significance if we take into account that almost 80 percent of Bangladeshi population lives in rural areas. Similar problems are identified in case of India: "In the face of growing cohorts of school-age children, there are too few government schools and teachers to meet the potential demand. Rural schools in particular remain insufficient in number, and their buildings and teaching materials are more inadequate than in urban schools. Rural primary schools are least well resourced. . . . In other words, state and non-state schools have marked class and urban biases."[32] The situation of Pakistan can be understood by looking at the province of Sindh. According to official statistics, out of 8.9 million school-aged children (five to fourteen years), 5.2 million remained outside school in 2002.[33]

The most significant policy response to these problems has been the denationalization of education sector—that is, to allow unlimited expansion of private educational institutions. It was argued that having educational institutions outside the state sector would compensate for the shortfall and address the unmet demands. Such expansion was also predicated on the growing liberalization of the economy as part of further integration into the global market. Pakistan and Bangladesh began pursuing this policy in the late seventies, while India joined in the mid-eighties. But to date equitable access is a distant goal: the privatization of education has not been successful in reaching out to the rural poor segments of the society, as cost and spatial location remain major obstacles. The experience of India, summarized by Dreze and Gazdar, is equally true of other countries of the region: "private and government-aided schools are few and far between in the rural areas."[34]

This created a void and pushed the community to find local solutions. In societies such as Bangladesh, where "primary education had been entirely a local effort" until the nationalization of community-based primary schools,[35] it is not surprising that local people came forward with an indigenous solution, that is, to establish schools with limited resources and on the basis of available infrastructure, which is often the mosques and orphanages. What has made these institutions attractive to the poorer segments of the society is that they offer, in adition to education, lodging and food, two major costs for large families. Data from surveys in Bangladesh demonstrate that deficit in food consumption is a major factor in nonenrollment and dropouts at the primary level.[36] Availability of food, therefore, has been a major incentive to send the children to madrassahs. Additionally, often families see these institutions, particularly the disciplined life imposed on the students, as a positive factor, because otherwise these children might become engaged in unsocial and criminal activities. It is this aspect of the madrassah that is highlighted by many observers who describe madrassahs as "institutions of caretaking and education."[37]

THE MADRASSAH CURRICULUM

There is agreement among observers that, barring a few exceptions, madrassahs in South Asia follow obsolete curricula, impart superstitious concepts, teach antiquated social values, and produce a workforce without the skills necessary to become active participants in society. William Dalrymple, who has highlighted the role of madrassahs in Muslim tradition and who insists that madrassahs play a significant role in providing education to poor children of Pakistan, also contends that "many madrasas in Pakistan have an outdated curriculum: some still teach geometry from Euclid and medicine from Galen. Emphasis is put on the rote learning rather than the critical study of the Koran, and considerable prestige is still attached to becoming a hafiz––knowing the Koran by heart. Deobandi madrasas teach that the sun revolves around the earth and some even have special seating for the invisible Islamic spirits, the djinns."[38]

Similar arguments have been advanced by Imtiaz Ahmad in the context of India, while Jeffery et al. disagree.[39] In any case, the texts that are taught, the methodology that is adopted, and the management that is carried out in madrassahs, particularly in South Asia, contribute to the shaping of young minds and social dynamics, and hence are important elements in understanding these societies.

Being aware of these factors, one must look beyond the security considerations that have prompted the immediate interest in madrassahs and examine these institutions within larger contexts, addressing the issues accordingly.

WHY SOUTH ASIAN MADRASSAHS?

Although institutions providing Islamic education, known by different names, can be found in many Muslim countries (for example, *pesantren* in Indonesia), South Asia, the home of the largest Muslim population in the world with a long tradition of madrassah education, has drawn more criticism than any other region in recent years. The negative media coverage and pointed disparagement of madrassahs by Western policy makers is one of the factors that prompted this study; the other factor is the enormous significance of madrasshs in understanding Islamic institutions and practices in South Asia.

Available statistics suggest that over recent decades there has been a dramatic increase in the number of madrassahs in South Asia, particularly in Pakistan and Bangladesh. Although India has not experienced a spectacular rise in numbers, the role of madrassahs in India has changed significantly and madrassahs have acquired greater visibility. Yet no study has assessed these institutions comparatively.

Heated and polemical debates on Pakistani madrassahs have generated some policy-oriented prescriptive reports in the past five years, but they can hardly claim to be a rigorous examination of these institutions vis-à-vis the socioeconomic dynamics of the country. Bangladesh remained below the radar until a series of bomb blasts on 17 August 2005. These bomb blasts were linked to a clandestine organization called the Jamaatul Mujahideen Bangladesh (JMB, Organization of the Holy Warriors) and their networks within the privately operated madrassahs throughout the entire country. Although a nexus between the Indian madrassahs and militancy has been alleged in some quarters, to date hard evidence to that effect is nonexistent. But as the Muslim minority population face systemic discrimination and periodic pogroms in India, these educational institutions have assumed greater significance as providers of education and social institutions within the Muslim community. These countries, now separated by contrived borders, belonged to a single political entity for centuries, share deep historical and cultural ties, and are inheritors of common traditions and heritage, of which the madrassah system is one. It makes sense to explore them together.

In South Asia, the madrassah is an important social institution in the Islamic tradition practiced by the millions of Muslims and is inseparable from any discussions in Islam in South Asia. Jamal Malik aptly noted:

> If one talks about Islam in South Asia, the role of madrasas in any such discussion can hardly be overemphasized. Madrasas have been central to any religious imagination of the Ulama: in terms of denominational debates or over the question of reform. In fact most religious movements of renewal developed networks of madrasas or tried to do so in an effort to institutionalize their ideas and precepts. On the one hand, it seems that

similarity of pedagogical practices have given these madrasas some kind of a pan South Asian grid which could be made use of in terms of a crisis. On the other hand, as a basic building block of any "Islamic society" madrasas present an important case to start a discussion about Islam, in this case in South Asia.[40]

ORGANIZATION OF THE BOOK

This book is organized into seven chapters. The first chapter examines the portrayal of madrassahs in Western academic and popular discourses, and policy statements both before and after 11 September 2001. In pre-9/11 academic and policy discussions, the issue of the madrassah was marginal and appeared largely in the context of the relationship between Islam and terrorism, particularly in regard to efforts to understand the causes of terrorism. I have categorized these discussions into five perspectives: know your enemy, Muslim exceptionalism, clash of civilizations, blowback, and the weapons of the weak. The examination of media reports, books, journal articles, and policy statements reveal that two perspectives—know your enemy and clash of civilizations—have influenced general perceptions of these institutions. In the post-9/11 period the coverage of madrassahs in the media experienced a dramatic surge and consequently a radical shift in Western attitudes, from outright neglect to fearful suspicion. These institutions were seen through the security lens, judged by recent history—almost in unison—from the mass audience to the media pundits and policy makers. The most striking shortcomings of these perceptions are that they are ahistorical and decontextualized. With very little information at hand, these institutions have been characterized in no uncertain terms as schools of jihad. The policy makers of the United States have reproduced this characterization without questioning its validity. Given that post-9/11 discussions of the madrassah were directly tied to Afghanistan, especially the Taliban regime (a product of madrassahs in Pakistan), policy statements particularly focused on the madrassahs in the latter country. Examination of the coverage of Pakistani madrassahs in eleven major news media outlets—nine from the United States and two from the United Kingdom between 12 September 2001 and 31 March 2005—reveals a pattern: the presentation of these institutions as a security threat and a breeding ground of international terrorists.

To address one of the weaknesses of the media coverage and policy discourses in the United States—the lack of historical understanding of these institutions, I present, in the second chapter, a historical narrative of madrassahs, particularly South Asian madrassahs. This narrative begins with a discussion on the genesis of the madrassahs in Arabia in the early days of Islam, and examines the driving forces behind founding madrassahs in quick succession during the eighth through to the eleventh century. The history of the emergence and spread of madrassahs in South Asia shows that they were very much a part of the indigenous education system of precolonial India, and particularly thrived during the Mughul era (1526–1761). Royal patronage was to have a significant impact on the future of these institutions. New madrassahs were modeled after Arabian madrassahs, and made an important contribution to South Asian society throughout the entire precolonial period.

British colonial rule, as we know, had far-reaching consequences for the Indian subcontinent, and has in many ways transformed the societies of the region. Education was one of the arenas where we witness the direct intervention of the colonial power. The introduction of English as the official language and the subsequent establishment of new educational institutions are perhaps the most conspicuous examples of these interventions. However, interestingly, traditional educational institutions such as the madrassah not only survived but also received support from the British colonial administration. An intriguing question is: Why did the colonial power help maintain and at times establish new madrassahs in India? Support of the colonial administration helped one type of madrassah to flourish, but concurrently encouraged the development of madrassahs opposed to colonial subjugation. The Darul Uloom of Deoband is a case in point. Established in 1867, ten years after the first Indian nationalist uprising, commonly referred to as the Sepoy Mutiny, it became a hotbed of anticolonial political activism as well as the citadel of sectarian indoctrination.

Nowhere is this link between political activism and madrassahs more evident than in present-day Pakistan (that is, Pakistan after 1971, following the secession of its eastern province, which created an independent Bangladeshi state). The underlying argument of the third chapter is that understanding the madrassahs in Pakistan requires an understanding of the Pakistani political economy, on the one hand, and sectarianism, on the other. There is considerable disagreement as to the exact number and rate of growth of madrassahs in Pakistan, but it is generally agreed that the country has seen a phenomenal increase in madrassahs since independence in 1947. Although the causes of this growth warrant attention, it is also important to mention that there has been a change in the nature of these institutions: they have evolved from seats of higher learning to citadels of militancy. Does the militancy propagated by these madrassahs teaching the lessons of global jihad? Despite obvious links between madrassahs and militancy, there is no dearth of supporters of madrassahs in Pakistan, and perhaps among observers of Pakistani society. They argue that madrassahs are providing a decent education to the poor of the country. This raises the question: what exactly are these institutions teaching? Pointing to the fact that the Pakistani madrassahs, at the prodding of the United States, played a pivotal role during the Afghan war (1979–1989), it is often argued that the United States itself should be blamed for the current situation. Although no one can discount this fact, questions need to be asked as to how these madrassahs survived after U.S. involvement was terminated in the early 1990s. I argue in this chapter that although encouragement from successive regimes, an unremitting flow of foreign funds (especially from Saudi Arabia), and the absence of governmental supervision are principal factors in the dramatic rise in numbers, the transformation of madrassahs into schools of militancy, and to some extent into the recruiting ground of global jihadists is intrinsically linked to the sectarianism prevalent in Pakistani society. Sectarianism has been encouraged by various regimes over the last three decades and, since 1979, has received substantial support from outside as a result of events beyond the borders of Pakistan—the Iranian revolution and the Soviet invasion in Afghanistan, to name but two. The menace of sectarianism has not only made the country ungovernable but has also increasingly turned it into a breeding ground for transnational terrorists. If intolerance and violence permeate various social and political institutions, can educational institutions remain immune?

Bangladesh, in its early days of independence, succeeded in circumventing the explosive mix of religion and politics, giving rise to the hope that secular Bengali nationalism had done away with this phenomenon for good. Interestingly, this was not the result of any policy intervention but of a social transformation developed from within as a part of the decades-long Bengali nationalist movement. The course of this transformative process came to an abrupt halt as the nation slid into authoritarianism, particularly military rule in 1975. Subsequently Islamism became a dominant political ideology, and ossified institutions like madrassahs acquired a new lease of life. The sites of reproduction of social orthodoxy became the recruiting centers for ultraconservative confessional political forces. The fourth chapter examines these transformative processes. Over the last three decades the madrassahs in Bangladesh have undergone a dramatic transformation, both in terms of numbers and their roles in the society. Official statistics show that between 1972 and 2004, the number of government-supported (Aliya) madrassahs has increased to 11,746 from 1,412—a phenomenal 732 percent increase. The number of privately managed (Qwami) madrassahs is reported to have grown to 60,000. The increased number of institutions does not necessarily mean an increase in the enrollment, and indeed dependable data are sorely lacking in this regard (which by itself is an issue of serious concern). But it cannot escape even casual observers of Bangladeshi society that madrassahs are now a significant part of the educational scene of the country, and the students of these institutions are active participants in Bangladeshi politics. If domestic factors, especially the lack of funding for secular education, changes in state ideology, and Islamization of the society, are identified as important catalysts of these changes, external factors, especially the rise of political Islam as an ideology and Bangladesh's interaction with the global economy, have not been far behind in driving the nation in this direction. They have, indeed, acted in unison. Among the latter set of factors, short-term migration of Bangladeshis to the Gulf and Middle East was instrumental. The most disturbing trend over the last decade, however, has been the growing nexus between these madrassahs and militant Islamist groups. I document in this chapter how the militant networks spread to various parts of the country after 1996, and how the students of madrassahs, especially the unregulated privately managed Qwami madrassahs, are becoming the foot soldiers of these networks.

Independent India has inherited both the traditions and institutions of madrassahs established centuries ago, but the madrassahs have experienced a change in the community they serve. Despite the fact that the Indian Muslim community is larger than the number of Muslims in Bangladesh and almost equal to the number of Muslims in Pakistan, Indian Muslims are a minority. Therefore, the situation called for a different role. Indian madrassahs have, discussions in chapter five show, demonstrated both rigidity and innovativeness in the face of changing circumstances. In the main, however, these institutions have demonstrated their capacity to adapt to the new situation. What made this possible? The situation becomes even more puzzling when one takes into account the fact that the number of madrassahs in India is three times greater than that of Pakistan. I argue in this chapter that the Indian madrassahs need to be examined in the context of the predicament of the Muslim community in India and within the political economy of the Indian education system. The failure of the Indian education system to provide for basic education to marginalized communities, including the Muslims, and the state's inability to accommodate the concerns of the minorities—religious or otherwise—have significantly affected the nature and scope of the madrassahs. The persecution of Muslims, owing to the rise of the Hindutva ideology and the militant groups associated with this ideological bent on the one hand, [41] and the structural elements of the Indian political system on the other, have influenced Muslim consciousness, but have yet to have a decisive impact on the madrassahs. Interestingly, while the limited opportunity for Muslims to enter mainstream education has contributed to the continued existence and growth of madrassahs in India, a significantly small proportion of Muslims send their children to them. The chapter also examines the recent unsubstantiated allegation that Indian madrassahs are citadels of militancy and the consequences of this deliberate campaign to malign the Muslim community.

The sixth chapter examines the necessity of and progress toward the reform of madrassahs. Since the much-publicized speech of Pervez Musharraf on 12 January 2002, when he promised an overhaul of the Pakistani madrassahs, "madrassah reform" has become a buzzword. The general impression provided by the media is that Musharraf's initiative is unprecedented. But in fact, as I demonstrate in this chapter, attempts to reform madrassah education are nothing new in South Asia. Almost all Pakistani rulers since 1958 have attempted to bring about changes in madrassah education. Some of these efforts have merely served to strengthen these institutions and their supporters. The experiences of Pakistani rulers in this regard are similar to those of leaders elsewhere in the region. In this chapter, I examine the history of reform measures during the colonial and postcolonial eras in these countries, presenting a detailed discussion of various reform initiatives in Pakistan and Bangladesh. The chapter places reform in a historical and comparative perspective, but also documents ongoing efforts to deal with madrassahs in Pakistan.

The concluding chapter of the book summarizes the common issues that have emerged from discussions on the South Asian madrassahs. I also try to identify what states and civil societies can do to address these issues, and what role the international community needs to play in making these changes possible.

A Note on Transliteration

The word *madrassah* has been spelled in many different ways; for example, madrasa, madrassa, and madrassah. This is primarily due to different approaches to transliteration of the Arabic language in English. I have used the spelling madrassah, as this is the most commonly used spelling and is closest to the original pronunciation. However, others' spellings have been preserved in direct quotations. Similarly, I have used Qu'ran as opposed to Koran, while the latter spelling is as common as the former. Since 11 September 2001, Usama bin Laden's name has featured quite regularly in media, books, and public discourse; two spellings have been very common: Osama and Usama. The latter is closer to the original Arabic pronunciation and has been used throughout the book. As a general rule of thumb, in transliterations of Arabic words I have opted for anglicized versions of them.

CHAPTER 1

MADRASSAHS

LITTLE KNOWN, MUCH DISCUSSED

Although none of the nineteen hijackers who rammed passenger planes into the World Trade Center and the Pentagon on 11 September 2001 came from Islamic educational institutions, media attention turned to madrassahs immediately after the terror attacks. The U.S. media insisted that Islamic religious schools were partly to blame, for they instill hatred in the minds of young people who later become the recruits of terrorist organizations. The so-called War on Terrorism launched by the U.S. administration in response to the tragic events of 9/11 instantly identified madrassahs as one of the principal battlegrounds. Thomas Friedman, a *New York Times* reporter and analyst, after visiting the now-infamous madrassah in Peshawar where Taliban leaders including Mullah Omar had been schooled, wrote on 13 November 2001 that "the real war for peace in this region . . . is in the schools."[1] George Tenet, then director of the CIA, commented on 9 March 2002 before the Senate Armed Services Committee that

> All of these challenges [the connection between terrorists and other enemies of this country; the weapons of mass destruction they seek to use against us; and the social, economic, and political tensions across the world that they exploit in mobilizing their followers] come together in parts of the Muslim world, and let me give you just one example. One of the places where they converge that has the greatest long-term impact on any society is its educational system. Primary and secondary education in parts of the Muslim world is often dominated by an interpretation of Islam that teaches intolerance and hatred. The graduates of these schools—madrasas—provide the foot soldiers for many of the Islamic militant groups that operate throughout the Muslim world.[2]

In a similar vein, Defense Secretary Donald Rumsfeld asked in a memo on 16 October 2003, "Are we capturing, killing or deterring and dissuading more

20

terrorists every day than the madrassas and the radical clerics are recruiting, training and deploying against us?"[3] Rumsfeld's concerns were echoed by his deputy Paul Wolfowitz in the same week. In a speech at Georgetown University on 30 October 2003, Wolfowitz described madrassahs as "schools that teach hatred, schools that teach terrorism" while providing free, "'theologically extremist' teachings to 'millions'" of Muslim children.

The above comments of three prominent U.S. officials demonstrate that the link between madrassahs and terrorism has become a matter of serious concern for the administration. They also demonstrate that the relationship between madrassah education and terrorism is being viewed in a very simplistic manner, drawing on perceptions derived from "generalisations and oversimplifications of a complex phenomenon."[4]

The most obvious link between terrorism and madrassah education came from the then ruling regime of Afghanistan—the Taliban, who were the products of this type of Islamic education and had been providing a safe haven to Usama bin Laden and his transnational terror network al-Qaeda at the time of the terrorist attacks on the United States. The Taliban, described as followers of an extreme-conservative variant of Islamic thought, grew out of the madrassah education system in Pakistan during and after the civil war in Afghanistan.[5]

In late 2001, as U.S. forces were driving the Taliban from power in Afghanistan, discussions on the means to prevent a recurrence of this phenomenon became a staple of the media. Reporters from around the globe descended on remote places of Pakistan and India to look for the birthplace and spiritual home of the Taliban, and analysts never tired of recommending actions to combat them in the long run.[6] This led to extensive media reporting on madrassahs, but in similar fashion, with nearly identical description of the madrassahs and their students: "Spartan classrooms in which children rocked back and forth reciting passages from the Koran" and "common to most of these schools . . . [are] students' and teachers' unwavering support for Osama bin Laden, and their hostility toward the West, Jews, Hindus, and particularly the United States."[7]

Thus, in the post-9/11 period, previously little-known educational institutions called madrassahs became a significant part of the public discourse, thanks to extensive media coverage. These institutions were now seen through the lens of global security and judged by recent history—almost in unison from common people to media pundits to policy makers—to be breeding grounds for terrorism. But how did the U.S. policy makers, reporters, and media pundits reach these conclusions? How was this perception about madrassahs set in the minds of so many people? What specific images of madrassahs were created, reproduced, and used for making policy decisions? In contemplating these questions, it is useful to examine the portrayals of South Asian madrassahs in the Western academic and popular discourses, and in policy statements, both before and after 11 September 2001.

Although scant attention was paid to madrassahs per se in the West before the 9/11 attacks, references were made to these institutions in the context of the relationship between Islam and terrorism. Attitudes of academics, policy analysts, and journalists toward madrasahs and their portrayal of them were dependent on their view of the causes of and the conditions for the rise of "Islamic terrorism." Five perspectives can be identified in discussing the growing trend of militancy within the Muslim world. These perspectives can be categorized as: know your enemy, Muslim exceptionalism, clash of civilizations, blowback, and the weapons of the weak. Although these perspectives have their origin in pre-9/11 discourses, especially in the post-cold war policy-making environment, they have remained undisturbed to date.[8] These dominant perspectives are reproduced on an everyday basis in the media and shape the public perception and the public agenda. It is therefore necessary to discuss the salient features of these perspectives to comprehend the tone and tenor of these discourses.

FIVE PERSPECTIVES

The "know your enemy" perspective has been the most common approach throughout the eighties and nineties in academia and the media. The adherents of this school have asserted that a global crisis was brewing: that the rise of "Islamic fundamentalism" was on the horizon. In the words of newspaper columnist Charles Krauthammer, a global Islamic threat of "fundamentalist Koran-waving Khomeniism" led by Iran was imminent.[9] Therefore it was necessary to know the enemy. The identification of such an enemy was simple, at least according to the description of the *Economist*:

> It is the mightiest power in the Levant and North Africa. Governments tremble before it. Arabs everywhere turn to it for salvation from their various miseries. This power is not Egypt, Iraq or indeed any nation, but the humble mosque. Over the past year or so, for the first time in a decade, Islamic fundamentalism has become the principal threat to the survival of regimes throughout the Arab world. Because this is an argument about how people think and live, not merely about lines on maps, its outcome may do much more than either the old conflict with Israel or the new one between Iraq and its neighbours to shape the Arab future. . . . Like most big social movements, the expanding power of the mosque is a complicated affair. It takes different forms in different countries and its consequences are graver in some places than in others. But the threat is real enough.[10]

It is this mindset that led the policy journal *Foreign Affairs* to hold a debate in spring 1993 with the title "Is Islam a Threat?"[11] Proponents of this approach argued that they were trying to understand the "roots of the Muslim rage."[12]

However, the nature of the threat was already known to some: "It should now be clear that we are facing a mood and a movement far transcending the level of issues and policies and the governments that pursue them. This is no less than a clash of civilizations—a perhaps irrational but surely historic reaction of an ancient rival against our Judaeo-Christian heritage, our secular present, and the worldwide expansion of both."[13]

They insisted that the growing anti-American and anti-West sentiment in the non-Western Muslim societies was linked to the demise of Islamic civilizations and the failure of the Muslims to adapt to new political realities. While they claimed that they were looking for the causes, their writings tend to be prescriptive of strategies for dealing with the terrorism, which is, in their opinion, Islamic. Often these authors focused on tactics to combat the enemy instead of redressing the causes of and conditions for the grievances. It is fair to say that the leading authors of this school were searching for weaknesses of the enemy in order to exploit and defeat them.

The best-known and much-discussed approach has been the "clash of civilization" thesis. It draws its name from Samuel Huntington's oft-quoted essay and subsequent book.[14] While Huntington's name has come to epitomize this approach, it had been invented by Bernard Lewis as early as 1964, and has been in vogue since the demise of the Soviet Union.[15] Francis Fukuyama's "end of history" thesis is a case in point.[16] Similarly, President Bill Clinton, in his address to the United Nations on 27 September 1993, noted that one of the twin challenges to national governments and international institutions is: "resurgent aspirations of ethnic and religious groups." The principal argument of this approach is that the West has a long history of struggling with the East for political, cultural, military, and economic dominance. This is a power struggle between Islamic Eastern culture and secular Western culture, and a clash is inevitable and almost cosmic, proponents argue. This clash has been referred to in other terms as well; for example, "Jihad vs. McWorld."[17] In this frame of mind and from a Western vantage point, "Islamic civilization" is the adversary and thus should be confronted.[18]

A less popular, but distinctly identifiable trend is the "Muslim exceptionalism" approach. The most generalized account of this argument is that Muslim countries are hopelessly backward and their cultures are unfit for democracy, capitalism, and human rights. Often Muslim is interchangeably used with Islamic in this framework, although experts of the Middle East or Arabic-speaking world have tried to limit it to the Arab world. In either form, it is argued that the Muslim world cannot coexist peacefully with the West and will become increasingly aggressive as globalization increases Western influence. The most succinct description of this exceptionalism comes from Martin Kramer in a debate with Natan Sharansky, a former Soviet dissident and political prisoner, on 23 February 2005 at Tel Aviv University. Kramer argued that the reason the Middle East remains the last redoubt of tyranny and despotism

> has to do with a certain understanding of Islam, sometimes called Islamism. Muslims who are under its sway uphold divinely-revealed Islamic law as the blueprint for the just society. I will spare you the details, but this law is not compatible with democracy, or even with a plural society. It is predicated on a set of dichotomies, primarily between believer and unbeliever, secondarily between men and women. Some of its provisions are open to interpretation, but it is not infinitely elastic. Most importantly, Islamic law does not recognize the autonomous sovereignty of man, only that of God. And Islamists are largely indifferent to the means by which they would establish Islamic law and the regime to implement it.[19]

The most unapologetic argument for Muslim exceptionalism in recent years comes from Robert Spencer and Kenneth Timmerman.[20] Spencer argues that "freedom is under attack by the warriors of Jihad and the battle does indeed resemble the theme of the Cold War, a fierce division between the West standing for freedom and the East standing for totalitarian society." He feels that Sharia "has not been reformed and by its nature cannot be, as it is commanded by Allah himself. Any group that wishes to restore Islamic purity and has the power to do so would institute the institutionalized humiliation and oppression that are mandated by the Sharia."[21] Spencer feels that Muslim ideology is incapable of finding accommodation with Western values. Timmerman argues that the Muslim world is saturated with anti-Semitism and anti-Americanism. He states that "it is a simple and deep-seated hatred and denial of the other that has clear historic precedents and has found fertile ground in the Muslim World." He feels the long support for Israel as well as the general policies of the United States have welded anti-Americanism to anti-Semitism, meaning that hatred for the Jews is always closely followed by hatred for America. Timmerman asserts that "when the hateful fantasy is turned against America (global) 'jewry' is replaced by 'imperialism' and 'globalization.'"[22] He contends that this hatred drives terrorism and undermines any efforts to find common ground between the West and the Muslim world.

While the three perspectives described above place the blame for the growing threat of terrorism squarely at the doorstep of the "Muslim world," others take critical views of the situation. In some ways, they attempt to turn the tables. Among these, the most prominent is the blowback theory, first articulated by Mary Ann Weaver and later developed by Chalmers Johnson in his book *Blowback*.[23] The term, however, originated in a CIA document in 1954 as a metaphor of unintended consequences. This was used to describe the failed attempt to overthrow the government of Mohammed Mossadegh in Iran in 1953. This school of thought argues that Western policies in the Middle East, particularly the American-Israeli relationship and U.S. support for oppressive regimes in the Arab World, have angered Muslim countries and consequently created support for terrorism. Although this approach has attained a remarkable audience in recent years, especially after the Iraq invasion in 2003, there were discussions along this line for quite some time. However, blowback is generally considered a partial cause of the growing terrorism instead of the principal reason.

The fifth distinctly discernable approach is the "weapons of the weak" argument. This approach asserts that intractable social, political, and economic problems in the Muslim World have led to despair, anger, and desperation. These social, political, and economic problems are seen by people in the Muslim World as the outcome of a system dominated by the West. This in turn has motivated terrorist attacks against the West. Edward Said has made that point on various occasions, including an article after 9/11:

> Anti-Americanism in this context is not based on a hatred of modernity or technology-envy: it is based on a narrative of concrete interventions, specific depredations and, in the cases of the Iraqi people's suffering under US-imposed sanctions and US support for the thirty-four-year-old Israeli occupation of Palestinian territories. Israel is now cynically exploiting the American catastrophe by intensifying its military occupation and oppression of the Palestinians. Political rhetoric in the US has overridden these things by flinging about words like "terrorism" and "freedom" whereas, of course, such large abstractions have mostly hidden sordid material interests, the influence of the oil, defence and Zionist lobbies now consolidating their hold on the entire Middle East, and an age-old religious hostility to (and ignorance of) "Islam" that takes new forms every day.[24]

These five perspectives differ at various levels, but interestingly there is one fundamental similarity that warrants our attention: their proclivity toward a binary division of the world. They tend to present the world as a dichotomy— West versus the rest, Islam versus West, and so on. They impart the idea, both implicitly and explicitly, that the "Muslim world" should be seen as a homogenous entity sharing a similar ethos and with a unanimous political agenda, and similarly that "the West" is a single unit. Kellner rightly questioned the validity of such bifurcation, describing these theories as

> analytically suspicious in that they homogenize complex civilizations and cover over differences, hybridizations, contradictions, and conflicts within these cultures. Positing inexorable clashes between bifurcated blocs a la Huntington and Barber fails to illuminate specific discord within the opposing spheres and the complex relations between them. These analyses do not grasp the complexity in the current geopolitical situation, which involves

highly multifaceted and intricate interests, coalitions, and conflicts that shift and evolve in response to changing situations within an overdetermined and constantly evolving historical context.[25]

Kellner's points are in some ways an amplification of Said's arguments: "much as it has been quarrelled over by Muslims, there isn't a single Islam: there are Islams, just as there are Americas. This diversity is true of all traditions, religions or nations even though some of their adherents have futilely tried to draw boundaries around themselves and pin their creeds down neatly. Yet history is far more complex and contradictory than to be represented by demagogues who are much less representative than either their followers or opponents' claim."[26]

This mindset of seeing the complex world through a binary lens led to the use of a series of oppositional conceptual categories in understanding Islam. They are: on the one hand rational, humane, developed, and superior, and on the other hand aberrant, underdeveloped, and inferior. In popular press and public discourse, the former attributes are associated with the West while the latter are the inherent qualities of Islam.[27] Such binary division is not limited to juxtaposing Islam with the West, but is also used in portraying Islam and the Muslims. Discussions on Islam often present a "dual vision" of Islam, meaning contradictory images of the religion and its adherents: "Islam is monolithic but sectarian. It is fixed and an excuse to adapt what is outside Islam, which allows Muslims to be seen as manipulative. Islam is a threat but inferior."[28] In similar vein, Muslims are perceived as of two varieties: good Muslims and bad Muslims. Mamdani, in his exposition of this reductive portrayal, noted: "even the pages of the New York Times now include regular accounts distinguishing good Muslims from bad Muslims: good Muslims are modern, secular, and Westernized, but bad Muslims are doctrinal, antimodern, and virulent."[29]

The other feature of this dualistic exposition has been the insistence on a nexus between Islam and violence. Many authors, for example John Esposito, have been pointing to the contrary, saying that "to equate Islam and Islamic fundamentalism uncritically with extremism is to judge Islam only by those who wreak havoc—a standard not applied to Judaism and Christianity. The danger is that heinous actions may be attributed to Islam rather than to a twisted or distorted interpretation of Islam."[30] These voices, however, were drowned by the loud assertions made by authors like Daniel Pipes that "The Muslims Are Coming! The Muslims Are Coming!"[31]

Nevertheless, these perspectives, or some variants of them, have found their expression in publications on Islam, terrorism, and war on terror for decades.[32] Therefore, there is no paucity of literature on these topics. However, as noted before, there are very few writings that referred to or imparted some ideas about madrassah education before 9/11. Before examining them in detail, I would like to draw attention to the fact that these small number of articles and media reports that referred to madrassahs usually highlighted the conflict between state agencies seeking to exert greater control over these schools and local groups resisting that power. The articles that went beyond this narrow focus highlighted one of two themes: the lack of quality instruction on secular subjects, or the radical tenor of the Islamic views being taught. There were, of course, some articles alluding to the pivotal role of madrassahs in the rise of the Taliban. But these articles were not intended either to look at the role of madrassahs in Muslim societies in general or to examine the transformation of the madrassah system in South Asia.[33]

Pre-9/11 Dominant Discourses

Although the Afghan resistance movement in the eighties, especially the social context of the movement and the social background of the leaders, provided an excellent opportunity to discuss the roles of madrassahs in Muslim society, Western academics and official documents, to a great extent, did not venture into that realm. Olivier Roy is one of the very few scholars who contextualized the crisis and highlighted the roles of madrassahs and the religious elites in Afghan society in the mid-eighties in his book *Islam and Resistance in Afghanistan*.[34] Roy, describing Afghanistan as a fragmented state, argued that tribal and local ties are very strong and that the traditionalist ulama have a tight hold over the people and the exercise of law. Significantly, Roy traced the relationships between the orthodox Deoband madrassah in India and the Afghan ulama over centuries.[35] The Afghan state tried to intercede in this relationship by establishing state madrassahs that would train modern religious leaders who would therefore be indebted to the state. This process only succeeded in creating a deeper stratification between urban and rural Afghanistan. The dependence on the rural ulama only strengthened as their madrassahs provided young men to participate in the jihad against the Soviets. In an essay written in 1988, Roy also noted the influence of Wahhabism and its link with the madrassahs in Pakistan serving the Afghan refugees: "The prospects for the traditional clerics are also dim. Most of the new madrassas built in Peshawar are wahhabi-sponsored. Wahhabis generally despise traditional Afghan Islamic culture, considering it to be full of ignorance and superstition."[36]

The close and intricate relationship between the madrassahs and political developments in Afghanistan came to public knowledge in 1998, thanks to an article by Ahmed Rashid, whose thorough and detailed study in 2000 is perhaps the most comprehensive and accessible resource on the Taliban to date.[37] The fact that Taliban "were full or part-time students at madrassahs" modeled after the Deoband school of thought was not a revelation, but Rashid's study established it authoritatively.[38] Furthermore, it demonstrated how regional and global politics played critical roles in changing the traditional schools into citadels of militancy.

By late 1998, with Kabul under the control of the Taliban, policy makers in Washington started to realize that the nexus between madrassah and militancy in South Asia posed a serious danger to them. It was not unknown to the U.S. policy makers that a significant number of madrassahs in Pakistan had already undergone a transformation during the Afghan resistance, because they had deliberately encouraged them throughout the eighties, but now they were trying to halt the process. This concern began to appear in policy statements. For example, on 2 November 1999, Michael A. Sheehan, coordinator for counterterrorism at the Department of State, informed the Senate Foreign Relations Committee that the United States had "urged Islamabad to close certain madrassas, or Islamic schools, that actually serve as conduits for terrorism." About six months later, on 12 July 2000, Sheehan went further in his statement before the House International Relations Committee:

> Pakistan's political and economic difficulties and the resultant damage to Pakistan's institutions have provided fertile ground for terrorism. One of the great failures has been in education. Pakistan's government-sponsored educational system has been unable to meet the needs of Pakistan's people. As a result, many poor Pakistanis are drawn to free education provided by madrassas, or religious schools. Many of these schools perform a needed service in imparting such education. Some schools, however, inculcate extremism and a violent anti-Americanism in their students. In these schools, a rigid condemnation of Western culture, coupled with the local conditions of failing societies, produces young men inclined to support the same causes championed by Usama Bin Ladin and other terrorists. The Government of Pakistan is aware of this problem and has stated that it intends to ensure that madrassas provide a proper education for their students.

To policy makers, these madrassahs were what Huntington described as Qur'anic study centers and part of "an extreme network of Islamic organizations filling a vacuum left by government."[39] Furthermore, from the Huntingtonian point of view, this was the unifying structure for a new multinational Islamic civilization.

The emphasis on madrassahs in policy-making circles was matched by academic interest and discussion. Gilles Kepel's book *Jihad: A Trail of Political Islam* addresses the madrassah issue more seriously than most of the contemporary books. Kepel argued that a void created in the Muslim world due to the decline of nationalist ideology had been filled by the Islamists, who drew their inspiration from Abul Ala Maududi (1903–1979) and Syed Qutb (1906–1966), two of the most radical Islamist thinkers of the twentieth century. Their ideas were propagated through an array of sociopolitical organizations, including traditional educational institutions such as madrassahs. They came at a time when Saudi Arabia was providing enormous sums of money to spread the Wahhabi version of Islam. This new resource has empowered traditional ulama, who have used madrassahs to construct a constituency of young radicals.

Discussions on madrassahs in the popular media followed an identical pattern in the nineties. Most of the references to madrassahs came in the context of Afghanistan. The Soviet withdrawal in December 1989 and the downfall of the Najibullah government in 1992 led to a waning of media interest in Afghanistan. This is not to suggest that the international media did not report events in Afghanistan. The infighting among the mujahideen and resulting chaos did make their way into the news now and then. But compared to the early years, it was negligible. In November 1994, when a band of young militants captured Kandahar, a southern city, and continued advancing toward Kabul, it became known that these youths had come from traditional schools called madrassahs. In the following two years, until the capture of Kabul in September 1996, news reports on the Taliban had mentioned madrassahs only to identify these new militants. Interestingly, the capture of Kabul did not draw enough media attention, as noted by a reporter from the *Economist*:

> Of the two bloody episodes that disfigured south-Western Asia a week ago, the fighting between Israelis and Palestinians won far more headlines than the capture of Afghanistan's capital by a murky army of Islamic militants who call themselves the Taliban, "the Seekers." Yet what has happened in and around Kabul is much the bloodier of the two stories, and it may matter at least as much to the rest of the world. Afghanistan is the third country to pass into the hands of an Islamic-revivalist government after Iran and Sudan; and the Taliban's victory in Afghanistan is the first to have been achieved by straight force of arms. This is not a purely local affair. Its causes lie, in part, outside Afghanistan; so, quite possibly, will its consequences.[40]

The reporter went on to explain the genesis of the Taliban and their connections to the madrassahs:

> The Taliban had their origins in the chaos which outsiders' manipulation of local politics has created in Afghanistan. . . . In the summer of 1994, a convoy was stopped by bandits on the road north of Kandahar. The convoy's owners, influential Pakistanis, begged their government to do something. The Pakistani government could not intervene openly. Instead, it encouraged a band of Afghan madrassas (religious schools) run by the fundamentalist Jamiat-e-Ulama Islam on the border with Afghanistan to organise themselves for action.

Concerned with the future of Afghanistan, the report focused on how the United States would react to this new development and whether the new rulers of Afghanistan would export their brand of religious uprising to the neighboring Central Asian region. It is not difficult to work out that the report's motivation was to understand a potential (or perhaps a real) enemy. The *Economist* articulated this concern not only in the Afghan context but also beyond. For example, in 1992 a report discussed the role of the madrassah in the conflict over governing principles in Uzbekistan. This report noted the political conflict over the role of religion in governance and the reopening of madrassahs as a central issue for those who "are keen to build an Islamic Republic."[41]

The *Guardian* (London), in its report on 8 April 1995, focused on Pakistan and stated, "a new Islamic force is emerging in Pakistan—the students of the madrassahs, or Islamic schools. They have become so powerful [that] they threaten to shake the influence of the religious groups which participate in parliamentary politics." The report drew a grim picture of these madrassahs, mentioning that some children were put in leg irons to prevent their escape. But reporter Kathy Evans remained focused on the political picture. The report indeed mentioned that madrassahs had produced the Taliban and that the madrassahs were fiercely protected by religious groups in Pakistan.[42]

The renewed interest of the U.S. media in Pakistani madrassahs may be attributed to the arrest of Ramzi Ahmed Yusef, a mastermind of the World Trade Center bombing in 1993. Yusef was reported to be one of the students of the University of Dawa and Jihad, a madrassh-cum-training center in Peshawar established in 1985 with Saudi funding. He was arrested on 7 February 1995 in Karachi and whisked away to the United States by FBI agents for trial. Mary Anne Weaver traced Yusef's footsteps in her investigative piece entitled "Children of the Jihad" published in the *New Yorker* on 12 June 1995. Weaver provided an exceptionally moving and very vivid description of the institution, but it was not the madrassah that she was interested in; her objective was to trace the footsteps of one of the masterminds of the WTC bombing. The Afghan war, the CIA's role in creating these "nostalgic jihadis," and their journey to the United States to wreak havoc at the WTC were the foci of the report.[43]

Within Pakistan itself, the debate on madrassah education in early 1995 was due to the growth of sectarian violence and the contributions of the madrassahs in providing foot soldiers to militant sectarian groups. The government, in an effort to curb the influence of these madrassahs, proposed a ban on direct financial assistance to religious schools. Although the Agence France-Presse (AFP) reported the story, it received very little attention in the U.S. media.[44] In 1998, soon after the U.S. cruise missile attack on the alleged base of Usama bin Laden in Afghanistan, there were a few reports in the U.S. press that highlighted the support Usama received from students of madrassahs across Pakistan. A report in the *Philadelphia Inquirer* informed its readers,

Darul Uloom Haqqania is to the Taliban as Harvard was to the Kennedy administration. The Taliban's supreme leader, Mullah Mohammad Omar, attended the school. So did a famous mujahideen commander, Jalaluddin Haqqani, who was one of the first to join the Taliban in 1995. The school's campus, a hodgepodge of two- and three-story white stucco buildings surrounding a mosque embellished with ornate blue tiles, has seen reduced attendance in recent weeks. Samiul-Haq said most of the seminary students were away, fighting for the Taliban in Afghanistan where an offensive is under way in the north.[45]

By 1999, concerns regarding madrassahs, both in Pakistan and as a general phenomenon, began to appear in the media and, as noted before, in the statements of U.S. policy makers. Pakistani madrassahs were placed in the spotlight when the new military ruler of the country, General Pervez Mussharaf, declared in 1999 that he intended to reform the centuries-old madrassah system to make it more compatible with the demands of the future.[46] (Discussion of Pakistani madrassahs in the U.S. media is presented later in this chapter, a detailed history of Pakistani madrassahs is presented in chapter 3, and critical examination of the reform measures is presented in chapter 6).

Amid the allegations that the Pakistani madrassahs were serving as training centers for Kashmiri militants and a recruitment center of the Taliban, the government began treading cautiously. This later became an issue within Pakistan when parents complained that their sons had been sent to Afghanistan to fight alongside the Taliban.[47] Between 12 October 1999 and 10 September 2001, news items on Pakistani madrassahs were primarily related to these allegations and the proposed reform measures. For example, a wire service report filed from Islamabad on 10 October 1999 published in various newspapers in the United States quoted the interior minister, Chaudhry Shujaat Hussain, as denying that there would be any government crackdown on madrassahs for "training religious terrorists." The report also quoted him as saying that no military training had been found in the madrassahs. The article notes that Islamic political parties had strongly opposed any interference with the madrassahs.[48] The same wire service reported on 24 August 2001 that the government had announced a new policy under which all madrassahs were supposed to register voluntarily with the government. The report stated that the Religious Affairs Minister Mahmood Ghazi had assured the press that this move was neither a prelude to government takeover of madrassahs nor a reaction to "pressure from Western countries which consider the existing madrassahs nurseries of Islamic militancy."[49] Many of the articles discussing madrassah reform describe these schools, directly or implicitly, as being anachronistic in their curricula. These articles depict madrassahs as teaching few marketable skills, with particular deficiencies in science and technology. Similarly, the *New York Times* reported on 10 June 2000 that the new Pakistani government had begun a campaign to curb militancy, and "identifying thousands of religious schools, which typically have not been regulated, and imposing standards on them."[50]

From 1999 on, news stories regarding the madrassah-terrorism nexus outside Pakistan began to appear as well. For example, the AFP news agency reported on 29 January 1999 from Dhaka about the suspected use of Bangladeshi madrassahs as offices for a terrorist organization. This report alleged that an organization of "Moslem extremists with suspected links to alleged terrorist mastermind Osama bin Laden" named Harkatul Jehad distributed funds to madrassahs to gain their assistance in recruiting new members. Similarly, reports from Russia reaching Western Europe and North America through local television stations and the Interfax news agency began asserting that madrassahs had become dens of militants. For example, it was reported from Tajikstan that the government had closed down a madrassah because of "suspicion of training religious extremists." The reporter described the school as "a center for brainwashing" and circulating the ideas of "Islamic extremist organizations."[51] The Russian news agency Interfax reported on 6 July 2000 that the supreme mufti of Russia and European countries proclaimed that some madrassahs are "breeding grounds for terrorists." He stated that the Wahhabi brand of Islam is taught in these schools, and this is meant to radicalize young Muslims.[52]

It was against this backdrop that three essays published in 2000 had a significant impact on subsequent discussions concerning madrassahs. These were Jessica Stern's "Pakistan's Jihad Culture" in *Foreign Affairs,* Jeffery Goldberg's report in the *New York Times Magazine* titled "Inside Jihad University: The Education of the Holy Warrior," and Stephan P. Cohen's article "Pakistan Fear of Failure" in the *Asian Wall Street Journal.* Goldberg termed the Pakistani madrassahs a means of "education of the holy warrior," a "jihad factory," and stated that "in a Pakistani religious school called the Haqqania madrasa, Osama bin Laden is a hero, the Taliban's leaders are famous alums and the next generation of mujahedeen is being militarily groomed." Stern described these schools as emblematic of "Pakistan's jihad culture." She insisted that

[In the eighties] many madrasahs were financed by the *zakat* (the Islamic tithe collected by the state), giving the government at least a modicum of control. But now, more and more religious schools are funded privately—by wealthy Pakistani industrialists at home or abroad, by private and government-funded nongovernmental organizations in the Persian Gulf states and Saudi Arabia, and by Iran. Without state supervision, these madrasahs are free to preach a narrow and violent version of Islam. . . . Most madrasahs offer only religious instruction, ignoring math, science, and other secular subjects important for functioning in modern society.[53]

In contrast to Stern's indictment of Pakistani culture generally for the growing militancy, Stephen Cohen, who had previously worked for the State Department as an expert on Pakistan, expressed cautious optimism. As for the madrassahs, Cohen insisted that "while some madrassas, or religious schools, are excellent, others (estimated at 12 percent of the total) are hotbeds for jihadist and radical Islamic movements." Cohen and Stern agreed on one point, however: the need for assistance to be given to Pakistan's educational system. "The most important contribution the United States can make, then, is to help strengthen Pakistan's secular education system," writes Stern. In Cohen's view, "the positive dimension of America's Pakistan policy should concentrate on two areas. The first is the provision of assistance to Pakistan's educational system." Evidently Stern and Cohen's contrasting positions demonstrate how one can generalize from a small sample. Goldberg's dramatic description of Darul Uloom Haqqania, a madrassah that has featured in some ways in almost every news report on Pakistani madrassah, has been extrapolated to the level of national culture by Stern and subsequently made an object of attack.

Post 9/11 Discourses on Madrassahs

Goldberg and Stern's characterization of madrassahs became the dominant perspective in the wake of 9/11. Their arguments shaped both academic and public discourses and perhaps influenced policy makers as well. The comments of George Tenet, Donald Rumsfeld, and Paul Wolfowitz, quoted earlier, demonstrate that in the minds of U.S. policy makers the relationship between terrorism and madrassahs was obvious. These statements have been echoed at different times at different levels. Colin Powell, for example, denounced madrassahs in Pakistan and several other countries as breeding grounds for fundamentalists and terrorists. Responding to a statement by Congresswoman Marcy Kaptur in the House Appropriations Subcommittee that unless modern education was imparted in these institutions, they would cause multiple cloning of militants throughout the region, Powell said the "U.S. had held several discussions on the issue with the countries concerned and was in the process of introducing education programmes which would shift such madrassas' focus to providing 'useful education.'"[54] Two points warrant attention: first, Powell's assertion that these schools create "terrorists"; and second, the contention that this also holds true for madrassahs beyond Pakistan. This shift from particular examples of Pakistani madrassahs to a more general understanding of the madrassah as an undesirable institution seems to have taken place without any specific information. Implicit is the idea that students of madrassahs are becoming transnational terrorists, although evidence was wanting. U.S. Senator Charles Schumer, in a letter to the Saudi ambassador

on 4 December 2002, linked the widespread anti-American sentiment in the
Middle East with the madrassahs:

> While I appreciate the intent of the white paper your government issued
> this week, it fails to attack the root of anti-American sentiment in the
> Arab world: the madrassahs. Islam is an admirable and peaceful faith that
> embraces tolerance, morality and charity, but the madrassahs distort this
> message by preaching hate, violence and intolerance toward the Judeo-
> Christian world. These teachings have created a "lost generation" in the
> Middle East, where thousands of young people are being indoctrinated with
> the idea that terrorism is an acceptable way to articulate their Islamic beliefs.
> In order for your government to be a true partner in the war on terror, it
> must denounce the teachings of those schools which preach extremism and
> must stop funding them.[55]

Schumer also commented, "when Americans ask how is it that there is a generation of Muslim men that hates us, it's because of these madrassah schools that
have hijacked Islam and preached extremism and violence."[56] On 26 June 2003,
Schumer in his statement at the hearing at the Senate Judiciary Committee's
Subcommittee on Terrorism, Technology, and Homeland Security reiterated
the link between global terrorist violence and madrassahs:

> But if they [Saudi Arabia] truly want to stop the violence that led to 9/11 and
> to the recent attacks in Riyadh—going beyond simple band-aid action—they
> must repudiate the Wahhabi extremism that is the source of this violence.
> This means shutting down the extremist madrassahs, purging the hate-filled
> textbooks that populate Saudi schools, and putting an end to the extremist
> Wahhabi preaching that takes place in their mosques. If the Saudis do not
> end the funding and teaching of extremism, the cycle of terrorist violence
> wracking the globe will never end.[57]

As discussions on the war on terror took the center stage of academic discourse after 9/11, identifying madrassahs with global terror become a common
feature. Jessica Stern's essay in November 2001 and book in 2003 are at the forefront of this line of argument.[58] She is, however, not alone; one can easily find
dozens of books dealing with terrorism or global security published after 9/11.
The preponderance of these works demonstrates that among the five perspectives described earlier, "know your enemy" became the most popular. Stern
not only states the familiar fact that the Taliban leadership was born from the
madrassah system but also claims to have met children in Pakistani madrassahs
from Afghanistan, Bangladesh, Burma, Chechnya, Kuwait, Mongolia, Nepal,
Russia, Tajikstan, Turkey, Uzbekistan, and Yemen.[59] In her opinion, "the most
important aspect of training these militants is mental training" and at these
schools "children are taught about hate." She further states, "they [students of

the madrassahs] are susceptible to their teachers' message that the best way to fulfill their religious duty is to fight on behalf of the Taliban or so-called jihadi groups."[60] Stern intends to help devise a better counterterrorism policy, thus economic and social factors that breed terrorism are secondary to her. As for the primary factor, Islamic "seminaries are often fertile grounds for recruitment" of terrorists and therefore should be dealt with immediately.[61]

David Benjamin and Stephen Simon also underscore the importance of education in understanding the ideological aspect of the East-West conflict, and note that "religious education is supplanting public education and creating a generation of zealots" in the Muslim world.[62] They argue that governments in Islamic countries try to supplement their ruling values with radical Islamic beliefs. "Every flanking movement [of this kind] undertaken by these regimes validates the Islamist agenda," state Benjamin and Simon. They identify the ulama and Islamist political parties as agents of the radicalization of madrassahs, stating that "the religious parties that subsidize these schools use them to propagate the faith and punish opponents."[63]

Identifying schools as future battlegrounds in the war on terror was first articulated by Thomas Friedman immediately after 9/11 but gained currency in later years.[64] Over time, it transcended the particularity of Pakistan and took a generalized form. The schools have been characterized as sites of indoctrination, and therefore, roots of terror.[65] Dore Gold, former Israeli ambassador to the United Nations, suggests that "the ideological sources for terrorist organizations have been overlooked in the West." He cites Mohammed Chafri, former education minister of Tunisia, who states that "Sept. 11, seems to have been a product of schooling. While Saudi Arabia is obviously a moderate state allied with America, it also has been one of the main supporters of Islamic fundamentalism because of its schools."[66]

How is the indoctrination for a cause translated into day-to-day teaching? This is a question that many authors have not addressed in their discussions. Bruce Hoffman and Gordon McCormick, however, see this as vital in comprehending the transformation of an individual into a terrorist. They assert that the madrassah perpetuates the cycle of terrorism by providing a forum where the accomplishments of martyrs may be praised and the sentiments that drive terrorism recycled. The authors claim "the heroic and selfless character of the martyr's sacrifice is the subject of sermons and discussions in the mosques and madrasas. The details of the attack are then reenacted in school playgrounds and in the streets thereby validating the actions of the martyr and bringing greater attention to his cause."[67]

These discussions and the policy-making process in the United States went hand in hand. This is reflected in the report of the National Commission on Terrorist Attacks upon the United States, commonly referred to as the 9/11 Commission. The report of the bipartisan commission, published in July 2004, focuses on tactics, threat assessment, the details of the attacks, and potential strategies to combat terrorism. It also brings together a number of the dominant perspectives. It briefly addresses the roots of terrorism and the underlying relationships between the religious schools, frustrated youth, and terrorism: "a large, steadily increasing population of young men without any reasonable expectation of suitable or steady employment—a sure for social turbulence. Many of these young men, such as the enormous number trained only in religious schools lacked the skills needed by the society." It traces the indigenous roots of fundamentalism in South Asia to Deoband and "the Wahhabi school of Islam . . . nurtured by Saudi-funded institutions." "Over time," the report insists, "these schools produced large numbers of half-educated young men with no marketable skills but with deeply held Islamic views." As for the Pakistani madrassahs, "Pakistan's endemic poverty, widespread corruption, and often ineffective government create opportunities for Islamist recruitment. Poor education is a particular concern. Millions of families, especially those with little money, send their children to religious schools, or madrassahs. Many of these schools are the only opportunity available for education, but some have been used as incubators for violent extremism."[68]

The issue of nonavailability of education in Pakistan, particularly to the poor rural population, has been highlighted by some academics and researchers, including P. W. Singer and Robert Looney.[69] Singer insists that it is the state's failure to provide education to the poor people that is the primary factor in the proliferation of madrassahs in Pakistan: "With no better options, poor parents send their sons to Madrassahs, where they receive at least some education. Some Madrassahs provide food and clothes, and even pay parents to send their children, further increasing their enticement." Singer holds that "the primary worry with the explosion of [the] Madrassah system is not with the schools in general, but the implications of the radical minority of them. Around 10–15 percent of the schools are affiliated with extremist religious/political groups, who have co-opted education for their own ends."[70] Looney, however, believes that "a number—probably a significant fraction—of these schools have built extremely close ties with radical militant groups. In this capacity they have increasingly played a critical role in sustaining the international terrorist network."[71] These aspects, important as they may be, have been kept on the margin of discussions on madrassahs, particularly in the popular media.

Two Shortcomings

One can easily identify two serious shortcomings of popular and academic discourses on madrassahs in both the pre-9/11 and post-9/11 discourses. They are the absence of context and the lack of historical background. What I mean by the absence of context is that madrassahs are rarely seen as part of a social whole. Madrassahs are social institutions like any other educational establishment. Therefore, they operate within the norms and practices of a society, play certain social roles, and interact with political institutions. Societal norms and practices, along with various political forces, influence the orientation and functioning of these institutions. Add to this the role of the state. In the developing world, even in its weakest form, the state plays a dominant role and intervenes in almost every sphere of social activity, such that the madrassahs are subject to the influence of the state.[72] Furthermore, where the state itself is a site of incessant battle between ideologies, the social institutions it influences are bound to become instruments of ideological indoctrination and thus the battleground. In the existing literature on madrassahs this aspect has largely remained unexplored.

The lack of historical background is even more striking than the absence of context. More often than not, discussions on madrassahs refer to the Deobandi tradition that began in 1867 and the Afghan resistance, particularly the role of the United States in the eighties. This is as much as we get in terms of historical background. These discussions provide an impression that Deoband is the only tradition of madrassahs in South Asia, if not in the entire Muslim world. The other traditions of madrassahs, which predate Deoband in South Asia and in other parts of the world, remain unexplored. This provides a partial, if not distorted, account of the history; and fails to appreciate the transformation in the nature and scope of madrassahs.

While these two limitations are common to almost all discussions on madrassahs, the post-9/11 deliberations have acquired another problem: insisting on an implicit or explicit nexus between madrassahs and terrorism. The definition of terrorism is contentious and the term is often used imprecisely, but in the contemporary context it points to acts that transcend national boundaries, are international in scope, target a global power, and are motivated by a universal ideology.

Perceptibly missing in this understanding of terrorism is the role of the state as a perpetrator—both within its own borders and at the global level—and its implication in engendering radical politics and violent responses. Throughout the cold war era states not only actively engaged in terrorism to counter legitimate grievances of disenfranchised and marginalized citizens but also legitimized these actions under various names such as national security and protecting territorial integrity, and thus justified labeling their opponents as terrorists. This remains true to date, and examples abound. The ongoing war between the Russian military and the Chechen guerrillas, between the Tamil separatists and the Sri Lankan government, and the Palestinians and the Israeli state are the clearest examples in this regard. While the Chechens, the Tamils, and the Palestinians are often portrayed in media and in the policy discourses as terrorists, none have transcended national boundaries, targeted a global power, or been motivated by any universal ideology. This is far more significant in the present context, due to the rise of the United States as an imperial power and its policy of waging imperial war.

Nevertheless, in common understanding terrorism is synonymous with international terrorism and those who want to attack the United States. Within this framework, terrorism is larger than a strategy; it is an ideology by itself. This mindset has propelled the statements of the U.S. policy makers that I have referred to at the beginning of this chapter. But interestingly the connection is more an assumption than a conclusion derived from data. Instead, data suggest that "there is little or no evidence that madrassas produce terrorists capable of attacking the West."[73] Peter Bergen and Swati Pandey, after examining the educational backgrounds of seventy-five terrorists behind the most significant terrorist attacks against the Westerners, found that

> a majority of them are college-educated, often in technical subjects like engineering. In the four attacks for which the most complete information about the perpetrators' educational levels is available—the World Trade Center bombing in 1993, the attacks on the American embassies in Kenya and Tanzania in 1998, the 9/11 attacks, and the Bali bombings in 2002—53 percent of the terrorists had either attended college or had received a college degree. As a point of reference, only 52 percent of Americans have been to college. The terrorists in our study thus appear, on average, to be as well educated as many Americans.[74]

This conclusion is consistent with Marc Sageman's study on the members of terror networks. Sageman, using a larger sample, examined, among other things, the educational backgrounds of the terrorists. "Of 137 terrorists, only twenty-three (17 percent) had an Islamic religious primary and secondary education. The rest went to secular schools," writes Sageman. It is also interesting that "half (eleven) of those who had an Islamic religious education were Indonesians who went to private Islamic boarding schools," specifically to two schools infamous for their alleged connection to international terror networks; and the other half "went to madrassas, because they seemed to be the only available school for poor people in their area of the world (sub-Saharan Africa and the Philippines)." Furthermore, Sageman's study also shows that of 132 cases where the level of education was known, "over 60 percent had at least some college education, which makes them, as a group, more educated than the average person worldwide, and especially more educated than the vast majority of people in the third world."[75]

These findings were not available until 2004 and 2005, by which time the tone and tenor of discussions on madrassahs had already been set by the media, academia, and the government; consequently policies were made and actions were under way. The perspectives and patterns identified in the foregoing discussion shaped these actions. The country that immediately came under the spotlight was Pakistan, for good reason, particularly owing to its geopolitical importance. With the invasion in Afghanistan in 2001 to dislodge the Taliban regime, a product of madrassahs located in Pakistan, the media paid particular attention to Pakistani madrassahs. Understandably, the events influenced the agenda of the media, but was there any identifiable pattern in the portrayal of Pakistani madrassahs?

PAKISTANI MADRASSAHS IN THE WESTERN MEDIA AFTER 9/11

The coverage of the Pakistani madrassahs in nine media outlets between 12 September 2001 and 31 March 2005 was examined to answer these questions. Of these, seven are from the United States and two from the United Kingdom. Although during the period under review there have been ample references to Pakistani madrassahs in the context of the U.S. invasion of Afghanistan in 2001, the U.S. invasion of Iraq in 2003, and the war in terror in general, focus was placed on those news items that exclusively discussed the madrassahs in Pakistan. The objective was to find out how the madrassahs have been portrayed in these media and what information has been provided to the audiences. Forty-two news stories that directly dealt with the Pakistani madrassahs were identified. Eleven of these stories were published in British media and thirty-one in the U.S. media. The seven U.S. media outlets examined are the *New York Times*, the *Chicago Tribune*, the *Los Angeles Times*, the *Boston Globe*, the *Christian Science Monitor*, the *Philadelphia Inquirer*, and the *Washington Post*. These newspapers represent a wide variety of political persuasions, and cover almost the entire continental United States. From the United Kingdom, two media outlets were chosen, the British Broadcasting Corporation (BBC) and the *Financial Times*. All but one medium chosen for the review were print media. The print media were selected because of the permanency of the message. For BBC outputs, their Web site was examined so as to conform to the other samples. The selection of the BBC was based on two considerations: the size of the operation and the high degree of reliability with which it is credited around the world.

Four electronic data bases, *LexisNexis*, *EBSCO*, *ProQuest*, and *World News Source* were searched with one keyword. Given the variation in spelling of *madrassah*, we used three commonly used spellings: *madrassa*, *madrassah*, and *madaris*. After generation of an initial list from these sources, the archives of the respective media were searched to cross-check. In the event of unavailability of the full text on the Web, hard copies of the newspapers were consulted from the archives of the Milner Library at Illinois State University, and the University of Illinois at Urbana-Champaign.

Analysis of the contents of the news items shows that three issues have dominated the coverage of madrassahs. They are: the number of madrassahs and of the students attending these institutions, characterization of these seminaries as incubators of terrorism, and the reform measures initiated in early 2002, especially the lack of progress in reform measures.

These reports provide a wide range of numbers about the total madrassahs in Pakistan—from 5,000 to 10,000. Similarly, the number of students given varies from 700,000 to 1.8 million. The sources of these figures are vague, yet most of the reporters have accepted them uncritically. This is equally true of other media outlets that are not included in our sample. For example, NBC News reported that there are "an estimated 8,000 to 10,000 madrassas in Pakistan," CNN reported that there are 10,000 madrassahs and over a million students, the *Detroit Free Press* enumerated 6,000 madrassahs teaching hundreds and thousands of students, and Fox News cited an Associated Press report saying that "more than 700,000 boys—and some girls, in separate classes—study at 7,000 to 8,000 religious schools."[76] There are some semantic variations in the characterization of the madrassahs in Pakistan. But in the main, these media portrayed them as places where "jihadi ideology"—shorthand for anti-American, anti-Western, hateful, Islamist terrorism—was being imparted to the children. Barring a few exceptions, there was very little discussion as to the causes of the proliferation of madrassahs in recent years. The sorry state of Pakistani public education, an issue that reared its head here and there in the coverage, did not receive much attention, although readers were often told that the madrassahs offered education, food, and shelter for the poor segment of the society that otherwise would have been abandoned by the Pakistani state. In regard to the background, insofar as these reports are concerned, the Afghan war in the eighties is where the history lesson begins and often ends. The declaration of intent by the Pakistani president Pervez Musharraf on 12 January 2002 to bring about a historic change in the madrassahs received a euphoric reception in the press, followed by dismay and frustration.

Analysis of the salient features of the coverage and the differences within the five selected media outlets that have extensively covered the Pakistani madrassahs during the period under study (12 September 2001–31 March 2005) is presented below. Two thematic similarities were identified with regard to the portrayal of madrassahs among a large number of media within our sample. These two features—depicting children as an enemy-in-the-making, and framing the madrassah environment as repressive—have important significance and warrant further discussion. There is a question of whether there is a similar pattern in media in general, and these findings follow the discussion on the five media.

The Chicago Tribune

Evident in some of the headlines of the reports in the *Chicago Tribune* is the slant of the newspaper: to highlight the role of madrassahs as the center of indoctrination of the children. The headlines—"Schools Indoctrinate Young Radicals,"[77] "Classes, the Koran and Jihad: Religious Schools in Pakistan Teach Extremist Islam,"[78] "Schooled in Jihad"[79]—also demonstrate that this position remains unchanged over more than three years.

The report published on 28 November 2004 was the lead item of the day, presented as a special report called "Struggle for the Soul of Islam" and with a special note from the editors. The note quoted the September 11 Commission report and claimed that "Tribune reporters traveled to the secretive classrooms that are often breeding grounds for those who view Western governments, particularly American, as mortal enemy."[80] In a section entitled "a rare glimpse inside a madrassa," reporters described their visit to the Darul Uloom Haqqania as "a rare visit," although hundreds of reporters had already visited the place since 9/11.[81] The reporters insisted that the reform measures initiated more than two years earlier had failed: "little has changed inside the Darul Uloom Haqqania madrassa where Maulan Samiul Huq still preaches the same anti-American rhetoric and praises Al Quaeda leader Osama bin Laden."[82]

The reports in the *Chicago Tribune* avoided referring to any specific numbers of madarssahs and students. However, on two occasions, in 2001 and in 2004, they quoted government sources putting the numbers of madrassahs at 7,000 and 8,000, respectively.

The Los Angeles Times

Although the reports in the *Los Angeles Times* sought to demonstrate that the madrassahs had been engaged in militant activities and had "turned Pakistan into a factory for moujahedeen, or holy warriors," they often also drew attention to issues beyond the madrassahs.[83] The report of David Lamb on 3 January 2002 is instructive in this regard. The central point of the report is that the danger of madrassah teaching does not lie in what they teach, for they only teach the recitation of the Qur'an, but who the teachers are—the religious fanatics, and what the motive of these teachers is—indoctrination. Furthermore, Lamb writes: "The madrassas do not offer military training but in a country where anyone can buy a Kalashnikov rifle on the open market for $250, that instruction is readily available elsewhere. What they do offer is such an unworldly and narrow view of life that students invariably consider anything non-Muslim as anti-Islam and godless. This leads to cries for jihad."[84]

Unlike the *Chicago Tribune*, headlines in the *Los Angeles Times* are not value-laden: "Rounding out the Seminary Curricula," "Pakistan Pledges to Curb Militants," "Radical School Reform," and "Dollars to Help Pupils in Pakistan."[85] The last headline was followed by an explanatory sentence—"The Asian nation's educational system is in shambles. Islamic schools are a mainstay, but some are said to foster radicalism."

David Lamb's report on 3 January 2002 and Chris Kraul's report on 14 April 2003 follow a similar pattern. Unlike others, they highlight madrassahs that are accommodative to newer ideas and do not identify themselves with militancy. Kraul's report, dealing with the allocation of a $100 million grant from the U.S. Agency for International Development (USAID) to Pakistan for its education sector, put the total number of madrassahs at 10,000 and reported that these schools educated about 10 percent of all Pakistani students—thereby helping readers to understand that the religious schools are "embedded . . . in the country's social and political fabric."[86]

The Christian Science Monitor

The stories in the *Christian Science Monitor* provide a picture of the extent of the madrassahs in Pakistan, and address the problems faced by the Pakistani regime in reforming the madrassahs since Pakistani military ruler Pervez Musharraf declared his plan in January 2002. The reporters reiterated the cliché of Deobandi tradition, often in an over-dramatic fashion. For example, Robert Marquand in his report of 18 October 2001 presents a simplistic connection between Deobandism and the culture of Peshawar: "Peshawar was the place where sweet Pakistani 'milk tea' and an ethnic Pashtun brand of Islam, Deobandism, were served. Deobandism is a nineteenth century Indian school of Islam that was tied closely to the anti-British movement, and that had always been more severe and strict than the milder south and Southeast Asian Islamic variants."[87] His understanding of Deobandi tradition as an "ethnic brand of Islam" is flawed to say the least, and raises more questions than it answers.

However, occasionally the newspaper did delve into social factors in explaining the causes of the proliferation of madrassahs. Scott Beldauf's report on 3 October 2001 is a case in point. Beldauf informs us, "for more than a generation, Pakistan's social divide has been drawn in this Muslim nation's schools. Westernized middle- and upper-class families send their children to private schools like St. Paul's which, despite its name, is nondenominational. The poor attend either inadequately funded public schools or the madrassahs. And this gap that marks Pakistan's social divide is turning into a chasm."[88] This report is also notable for drawing attention to the fact that not all madrassahs are engaged in teaching intolerance. He refers to one of the moderate madrassahs, the Anjuman Faizul Islam in Rawalpindi. Boys and girls, 700 of who are orphans, attend this school, the report states. They study together until fifth grade and then continue their studies separately. In this madrassah, "the library is full of books in English and the National language, Urdu. Islamic studies are a part of the curriculum however the aim is achievement not militancy."

By 2002, the focus shifts to the reform measures, particularly the resistance to them from understanding the causes of the proliferation of the madrassahs. The reports of Philip Smucker on 2 July 2002 and Owasis Tohid on 24 August 2004 underscore the fight between religious leaders and the government, and highlight U.S. support, particularly the $34 million grant for reform initiatives.[89]

What is intriguing in these reports is the number of madrassahs and students: each report seems have a different number, and they vary widely. Baldauf, quoting an Indian source, claims the number of madrassahs at 15,000 and of students at between 600,000 and 700,000, while Smucker suggests a smaller number of madrassahs—8,000. Two years later, Tohid suggests a new set of numbers—20,000 madrassahs and 1.5 million to 1.8 million students. These are the highest numbers we came across in our sample.

The Washington Post

All of the six articles—five news reports and an op-ed piece—of the *Washington Post* included in our sample were published in 2002 and in large measure are concerned with the reform initiatives, particularly its effectiveness. However, the reporters of the *Washington Post* link the proliferation of madrassahs with two factors: poverty and the lack of educational infrastructure. The primary focus of the report of Paul Blustein on 14 March 2002, for example, is the abject poverty of the rural Pakistani population and the dismal failure of foreign assistance to bring about a change. His argument that money cannot do everything, illustrated by a comparative table which demonstrates that countries receiving less foreign assistance than Pakistan between 1960 and 1988 are ahead of the country in combating illiteracy, infant mortality, and access to sanitation is forcefully presented. This report addresses an issue that has not been argued with such potency in other newspapers, although there have been ample references to the role of poverty. Furthermore, Blustein relates the Pakistani situation to the larger global picture when he states: "The abysmal state of Pakistan's education system is the sort of problem that must be addressed if the international community is to wage a successful war on terrorism by attacking the root causes, according to many experts and world leaders, including United Nations Secretary General Kofi Annan and World Bank President James D. Wolfensohn."[90]

In similar vein, John Lancaster reports on 14 July 2002: "the rapid growth of the madrassa system in recent years reflects, in many respects, the dismal state of Pakistan's public education system." Lancaster is one of the very few reporters who clearly mentioned that the statistics related to the numbers of schools and the students are somewhat unreliable—"most estimates put the figures at around 10,000, with a student population of perhaps 1.5 million."[91]

British Broadcasting Corporation (BBC)

The coverage of the Pakistani madrassahs in BBC reports between 2001 and 2004 have largely been driven by the events on the ground. Although this resulted in lack of depth and probing analysis, it also kept subjective judgments

at bay. The deficiency in the news reports can be explained by the fact that
the BBC regularly broadcast analytical programs. The issue of the madrassah,
for example, was addressed within the larger context of Pakistani culture in a
six-part series called "Muslims in the Modern World" in July–August 2002.[92]
But occasionally news reports have contained reporters' opinions, although
they are presented as facts. Owen Benett-Jones's comments that "the Americans may be able to topple the Taliban leader Mohammad Mullah Omar but,
in one form or another, the Talibs will surely remain a force to be reckoned
with," and "Pakistan's middle classes have keenly supported Pervez Musharraf's plan to rid the country of religious extremism" are examples of such
instances.[93] As a rule of thumb and due to the nature of the media (that is,
both Web site and audio-visual media), BBC reporters illustrate their reports
with anecdotes, interviews, and comments of people, which allows inclusion
of a variety of opinions in the news report. The reports included in the sample
are full of such examples. In contrast to the most of the U.S. media, the
BBC has avoided a wholesale characterization of madrassahs; therefore, any
reference to the connection between madrassahs has been usually qualified
and guarded: "some of Pakistani madrassas have clearly been seen as training grounds for Islamic militants" and "the bad image of madrassas is not
entirely deserved" demonstrate this caution.[94] In instances when a reporter
used the oft-used characterization, for example, "the university of holy war,"
to describe the Darul Uloom Haqqania, it is attributed to the students and
principal of the madrassah.[95] Interestingly, barring one exception, throughout
the period BBC reporters have avoided estimating any specific number of
madrassahs and students. The only reference came on 13 October 2001: "It is
reckoned that between 600,000 and 700,000 people are currently studying in
Pakistan's Madrassahs."[96]

Two Themes—One Message?

Equally important as the differences in terms of tone, tenor, and orientations
among the sample media, particularly the five media discussed above, are the
two thematic similarities easily discernable across media in the United States
and the United Kingdom. These two similarities are portrayal of an "enemy-
in-the-making," and constructing an image of repression.

   One of the central features of the portrayal of madrassahs in popular media
after 9/11 has been the use of anecdotes, at random and often without any context, to illustrate that children as young as six years old are being indoctrinated
by a special kind of school—madrassah—to fight the "infidel" America. Children, who remained unnoticed for years and whose lives otherwise had very
little to offer to the U.S. media, came under the spotlight almost overnight, and
have been characterized as Taliban-in-the-making—a dangerous development

that cannot be ignored. As Tina Babarovich put it in her commentary on ABC television a month and a half after 9/11, "This small boy [Hamidullah] is, in one colleague's words, an angry puppet. His thoughts are not his own; they belong to those men who are grooming the next generation to carry on their radicalism, their fight against 'the infidels.'" These young children are puppets yet they cannot be exonerated, because "the anger Hamidullah feels toward Americans is real. But he has no understanding as to why he feels that way," and "I had such foreboding that we would hear Hamidullah's voice again, years from now, speaking to a crowd with the same venom and hatred as he did when he was six."[97] In each of these reports there is always a child who speaks maliciously against the Jews or the United States—whether it is in a story by Rob Gifford reporting for NPR on 19 September 2001 from Peshawar, Tim Butcher reporting for the *Telegraph* of London on 27 September 2001 from Quetta, Peter Fritsch reporting for the *Wall Street Journal* on 2 October 2001, Rick Bragg reporting for the *New York Times* on 13 October 2001 from Peshawar, Thomas Friedman writing for the *New York Times* on 13 November 2001 from Peshawar, Lisa Anderson reporting for the *Chicago Tribune* on 23 December 2001, Doug Struck reporting for *Washington Post* on 20 January 2002 from Rawalpindi, Ron Moreau and others reporting for *Newsweek* on 1 December 2003, or Christine Lamb writing for the London *Sunday Times* on 17 July 2005. In identical fashion, reporters have told their audience the stories of children—the enemy in-the-making. The story of Abdul Bari, narrated in the *Newsweek* in 2003, is an archetype:

> Abdul Bari's school day begins at 4 A.M. The freckle-faced, outgoing nine-year-old, an Afghan poppy farmer's son, wakes up on the tile floor he shares with four dozen other students at the Jamia Uloom Islamia religious academy, in the untamed mountains of Pakistan's tribal areas. After morning prayer services, he fixes tea for the older boys and himself, eating a bit of bread before classes start at daybreak. Students spend most of the day reciting the Qur'an; memorizing every one of its 6,666 verses is the main requirement for graduation. . . . Abdul is an eager learner. He dreams of enlisting in the jihad against Afghanistan's U.S.-backed president, Hamid Karzai. "Karzai is a killer of Muslims," the boy says. "When I grow up I'll fight him, and then we'll see who's a man and who's a woman."[98]

This mode of portraying madrassahs assumes a greater significance if we consider that in the wake of 9/11 the representation of Islam in U.S. media has been closely associated with unfavorable characteristics. The negative portrayal of Islam and Muslims in the U.S. media, however, is not a post-9/11 phenomenon. Studies have consistently shown that the Western media, particularly the U.S. media, have a tendency to "highlight stereotypes which conflate Islam, Arabs, violence, and terrorism into a single, undifferentiated phenomenon."[99] Edward Said pointed out that the portrayal is peppered with clichés, misrepresentations, stereotypes, ignorance, and demonization.[100] Others have also documented a similar pattern.[101]

Martin and Phelan have demonstrated in their study of the contents of five U.S.-based television networks and the CNN messageboard during the first week after 9/11 (that is, 11 September to 16 September) that Islam has been depicted in a stereotypical fashion, with remarkable negativity and at times with virulence. In television, about 35 percent of the references to Islam were associated with negative noun phrases; on the CNN messageboard the corresponding figures were about 40 percent. They conclude, "our findings indicate a strong cross-media collocation of 'Islamic' with a litany of definers as unfavorable as terrorist(s); militant(s); fundamentalist(s); radical(s); jihad; struggle; extremist(s); militant(s). It is a characterization of Islam that is particularly evident in a messageboard context, where it is even more frequently collocated with negative evaluative terms such terrorist(s), extremist(s), fundamentalist(s), fundamentalism and jihad, radicalism."[102]

Martin and Phelan's study also found that the media representations of Islam were polarized between our American Muslims and an international Islamic axis. With "television's insatiable desire to frame news in confrontational terms" this polarization soon takes the shape of us versus them in the messageboard. "Any official deployment of an 'us and them' rhetoric generates dangerous implicatures, which, though they aim for a different target, will invariably be used by many to defame a whole cultural entity or entities, and crystallize a popular view of Islam that has little, besides our own, to redeem it," write Martin and Phelan.[103]

A news story published in a U.S. newspaper and the consequent discussion in internet message groups vindicates this conclusion dramatically. The report, headlined "Trainees Eager to Join 'Jihad' against America," was published in *USA Today* on 27 September 2001. In this report, Jack Kelley, a reporter with a twenty-one-year career with the newspaper, who was nominated five times by the newspaper for the prestigious Pulitzer Prize, claimed that he met three students at the Darul Uloom Haqqania in Peshawar. One of them who had "just attended" one of bin Laden's training camps carried a manual with him instructing how to bomb U.S. embassies and economic interests. After reading this section to Kelley, the student says,

> "That's what I will do to you and your country. I will get your children. I will get their playgrounds. I will get their schools, too. I will get all of you."
> ... Tempers then flare. Several students begin yelling at once, pointing their fingers and gesturing wildly. One yells out the name of Mohammed Atta, an alleged bin Laden associate believed to have hijacked one of the two jets that crashed into the World Trade Center. Another says he will "kill more than

Atta." A third student then unfolds a picture of the Sears Tower in Chicago. "This one is mine," he says.[104]

This report was immediately copied into or hyperlinked in a number of Web sites and forums for discussions. In one of those forums, Bressler.org, the immediate comment of a member named Laurie from Minnesota was,

> These people are far worse than any depiction I have ever had of the devil. While reading this article, I felt my heart rate quicken . . . out of anger, but more so out of fear. These people, for lack of a better word right now . . . are just fucking insane. The more information I read on this whole thing we call terrorism, the more frustrated I get. These people are sociopaths with no regard for human life. What God approves of the killing of innocent children? (as quoted by the monster in this article) I've kept intermittently quiet about the actual military aspect of this situation . . . but I can't hold back after reading this tidbit of information. I'm frightened for my children. I want them all dead. Earth is no place for monsters like these. I hope these fucking bastards burn in hell. I hope I can watch on TV the destruction of it all. I hope . . .

This was followed by SSG Rock from Fort Leavenworth, Kansas: "I don't fear death either. God dammit, get me on the first thing smoking to afgahnistan!."[105]

In another forum, littlegreenfootballs.com, Josh commented on 2 October 2001, "There is obviously no option but to kill those people. I am a pretty mellow individual, but 'we will kill your children'?!!! There can be no argument against it, anyone who says that has forfeited their right to live on this earth."[106]

More than two years later, in early 2004, *USA Today* admitted that the story was one of eight major fabricated stories written by Jack Kelley. An investigation conducted by a team of journalists assigned by the newspaper "found that Kelley quoted a Darul Uloom Haqqania student named Hussain Zaeef. School officials said their records show no one by that name ever enrolled. They also said they did not see a student display a picture of the Sears Tower in Chicago and say 'this one is mine,' as Kelley wrote."[107]

The second significant feature of the portrayal of the madrassah is the description of the surroundings: dungeon-like, exclusionary, and repressive. Samples drawn from a number of sources between 1998 and 2005 quoted below show how identical they have been:

> Samiul-Haq's Islamic seminary [is] located behind whitewashed walls off a highway outside this town in Pakistan's North West Frontier Province. . . .
> The school's campus, a hodgepodge of two- and three-story white stucco buildings surrounding a mosque embellished with ornate blue tiles. . . .
> The school's offices are stacked with yellowed religious tracts bundled with

twine. The classrooms are spare. In one auditorium, students sat on floor cushions and paged through Koranic texts placed on small pine tables while stand-mounted fans moved the humid, 90 degree air.... Many of the students have wispy pubescent beards, in keeping with belief that beards should never be shaved. Students typically attend for eight years before they become *maulvi fazil*—religious scholars—about age sixteen. Some older students, who appear to be in their twenties with thicker builds and beards, attend the school for advanced religious training.[108]

With their austere dormitories, disciplinarian teachers and awful food, the madrassahs of Quetta might seem like Islamic versions of Oliver Twist's workhouse.... Behind the high walls that surround the city's 500 madrassahs young boys receive a strict Muslim education. They enter as six-year-olds and emerge as men in their twenties steeped in the lore and traditions of the type of Islam that sponsors the college. The day is long, starting with pre-dawn prayers and finishing at about 11 P.M. The year is also long, with short holidays and tough exams.... One solitary eight-year-old sat cross-legged in a classroom, poring over some Koranic scripture.... The classrooms were austere: just a cushion for the teacher and a mat for the pupils with a low bench on which to prop their reading material as they squatted on the ground.... On the walls were Koranic verses and a picture of Mecca: outside was the sound of older boys playing, occasionally chastised by bearded teachers not afraid to use the palm of their hand as discipline.... The under-10s were so tightly crammed into their dormitories that their metal tuck boxes, the only private property allowed for each pupil, were stacked in the corridor outside.[109]

In his [Asif Qureishi, head of the Darul Uloom Ashrafia madrassah in Peshawar] tiny office, a bag of rice rests against a wall. Outside the door, a student hefts the carcass of a slaughtered goat.... In the madrassas, students ranging in age from seven or eight to men over twenty are taught a strict interpretation of the Koran, including the duty of all Muslims to rise up in jihad. There are no televisions and some madrassas do not even allow transistor radios. There are no magazines or newspapers except those deemed acceptable by the elders. The outside world is closed to them, and many of the students seem puzzled when asked if they mind that. Their teachers, most of them respected elders, tell them what they need to know, the students said.[110]

The air in the Koran class was so thick and stale you could have cut it into blocks and sold it like ice. A sign on the wall said this room was "A gift of the Kingdom of Saudi Arabia." The teacher asked an eight-year-old boy to chant a Koranic verse for us, which he did with the beauty and elegance of an experienced muezzin. What did it mean? It was a famous verse: "The faithful shall enter paradise and the unbelievers shall be condemned to eternal hellfire."[111]

Jamiat-Ul-Arabic Al Islamia, [is] a school housing 150 boys, ages five to eighteen, in a walled compound on the edge of [Quetta]. . . . [Here] the boys sleep together like sardines—side-by-side and head-to-feet on thin mats in a series of small, bare-walled bedrooms. . . . The classroom is one large, drafty room with six teachers for 150 students. Outside, on the staircase up to the second-floor classroom each step is covered with the mostly small sneakers and sandals of the students. The concrete floor is covered with oriental rugs on which the students place blue and cream-colored mats. For hours, they sit barefoot at low wooden lecterns, their Korans open before them.[112]

Mohammed Adil's storefront school . . . has one classroom that doubles as a boy's dormitory. Four open latrines with six cold-water faucets serve as a lavatory and laundry area. There is no furniture, and students sit on worn prayer mats, listening to hours of recitation by teachers as their slim torsos bob to the cadence of verse in Arabic.[113]

The students live six to a room in a hostel or a nearby mosque, where neighbors cook their meals as a form of charity. The students attend classes in airless classrooms from 7 A.M. until noon, sitting on tattered straw mats with their Korans propped open on wooden reading stands.[114]

It was a chill autumn day and a strange murmuring sound was coming from inside the building. At first I thought it was the wind that was whipping up angry columns of dust around the white arched courtyard. . . . Then the teacher let me peer through the door to see hundreds of boys in white pajamas and prayer caps [who] sat on the floor hunched over large books and rocking back and forth. The sound was their muttering as they tried to memorize all 77,934 words of the Koran.

This was Darul Uloom Haqqania or House of Knowledge, one of Pakistan's leading madrasahs based in Akora Khattak in the North West Frontier Province. The Eton of budding Islamic warriors, its 2,500 places are heavily oversubscribed. Upstairs in the hall leading to the Library of Fatwas, a roll of honour lists most of the Taliban leadership as alumni as well as an honorary degree for Mullah Omar. . . . For one used to a Western lifestyle, the students—aged from five to their twenties—seemed to inhabit an almost prison-like life. Up at 4am for the first of five prayers a day, they sleep on thin mats on the floor in unheated dormitories. . . . Greying washed shirts hung stiff on a line outside. The only posters on the walls were of a Kalashnikov-wielding Osama Bin Laden on a charging white horse. A large boom box stood on the floor but the tapes alongside were of sermons from radical imams.[115]

It is not my intention to question the veracity of these descriptions, but to draw attention to the point that their repeated presentation leaves an indelible mark in the minds of the readers and therefore on their judgments about the society as a whole. Images and messages, particularly those repeated by various media outlets, influence readers at very subliminal levels of consciousness. These subtle influences mold sensitivity, awareness, and attitudes toward a specific event or subject. Whether or not the media intend this is a different question altogether. But knowingly or unwittingly, they create or at least contribute to the construction of a "common wisdom," which is devoid of any knowledge of the society and which lacks a specific context. Repeated presentations of certain images, in the long run, become the sources of off-the-shelf judgments, of preexisting sentiments, and a perception of the other cultures as threatening.

CONCLUSION

The foregoing discussion maps the dominant discursive paradigms articulated by policy makers, media, and academia in understanding the role of madrassahs in general, and the South Asian madrassahs in particular. The discussion demonstrates that after the tragic events of 9/11, we have witnessed a dramatic shift—from sheer neglect to fearful suspicion. The silence that prevailed over a long time, despite opportunities and necessities to break it, was shattered with a cacophony of repeated presentations of ahistorical and decontextualized understandings of an institution which has existed for centuries and is deeply embedded in Muslim societies. Media pundits and policy makers alike depicted these institutions with limited information and without questioning the validity of their characterizations. Furthermore, these characterizations were colored by dominant perspectives on the perceived nexus between terrorism and Islam. The heightened concerns of policy makers in regard to security of the United States after 9/11 is legitimate, but trying to view any social institutions in the Muslim world through the security lens is flawed, to say the least. It not only inhibits a proper understanding of the phenomenon but also does a disservice to the cause it purports to serve.

Indeed, the Afghan resistance in the eighties, particularly its linkages with the puritan interpretation of Islam advanced by the Deoband madrassah established in 1867, is a watershed in the history of madrassah education in South Asia, but this is just one historical episode of one strand of madrassah education in the region. The strand, we must acknowledge, is small in size. Therefore this connection fails to tell us what role, if any, the other strands of madrassahs play in politics and society. Occasionally we are told that the number of "jihadi" madrassahs is small and that they are training centers rather than schools, but seldom are we told what the others are teaching and what the significance of their education is. Why and how such a small school of thought became influential is a question that cannot be avoided any longer.

The considerable discussion on madrassahs in recent years, however, has had one positive impact—it brought forth the necessity to understand these institutions in greater detail. It has become imperative that we examine their historical backgrounds, their location within the socioeconomic contexts of various Muslim societies, their interactions with the politics of the nation-states, their roles as both educational and social institutions, and their future.

CHAPTER 2

THE GENESIS AND
THE TRAJECTORIES

Educational systems do not emerge abruptly. It takes centuries for a system to appear, grow, spread, institutionalize, and thrive. This is particularly true of the madrassah education system, for three reasons: first, because of its intrinsic link to Islam—a universal religion that spread through various means to a vast area over hundreds of years. In the process there appeared many schools of thought and denominational differences within Islamic theology, which produced a long-lasting impact on the system of education. Inseparability between Islam and the madrassahs is also due to the centrality of knowledge (*'ilm*) in Islam, reflected in the fact that 'ilm is the third most used term in the Qur'an, and by the repeated insistence on the lifelong pursuit of learning as fundamental to piety.[1] Second, because of its relationship with political institutions; madrassahs were either patronized or were opposed by the political authorities. The nature and scope of the political authorities influenced the relationship and consequently the impact of madrassahs. Third, because of the innate flexibility of the madrassah education system, which allowed these institutions to interact with local cultures and evolve according to the customs and practices of the host society. These interactions have not been limited to that between a model of the madrassah that arrived from outside and the traditional educational system of the host society, but also between models practiced contemporaneously in various parts of the world.

The setting becomes far more complex if we add to these factors the rise and demise of empires and dynasties of Muslim rulers, the proclivities of individual rulers, and societal responses to the system of governance, on the one hand; and discourses on educational theories among Muslim scholars in the medieval period and the rise of Islamic jurisprudence (*fiqh*), on the other.

Although a genealogical connection between the systems of education during the early days of Islam in Arabia beginning with the era of Prophet

Muhammad and the present-day madrassahs in any country can be traced, it is almost impossible to compile a linear historical narrative of madrassahs (say, from 610 C.E. to 2006 C.E.), marked with definite dates, key institutions, and exclusive trends.[2] This is not to say that a historical continuity is absent, but on the contrary, to insist upon the multiplicity of paths traversed by the Islamic education system. Nevertheless, the developments in the early age of Islam help us to identify the similarities and differences between various forms of institution engaged in imparting knowledge and exchanging ideas among scholars. These institutions have inscribed specific characteristics to, and shaped the nature and the scope of, the madrassahs that emerged in later years as organized institutions.

The history of madrassah education in South Asia is connected in many ways to developments outside the region, but the growth and role of madrassahs has been shaped by the historical and social conditions of the region. Many of the precolonial rulers of South Asia, including the Mughals (1526–1857), played key roles in promoting education and providing patronage of various educational institutions, including madrassahs. The policies of British colonial rule (1757–1947), however, made the most indelible marks on madrassah education, not only directly, wherein their policies have impacted on the structure, functions, and curriculum of madrassahs, but also indirectly, through the prompting of responses from the ulama and the Muslim community that determined the contours and the content of madrassah education. These responses, in large measure, revolved around the concept of Muslim identity, and therefore, were laced with political activism.

PRECURSORS OF MADRASSAHS IN ARABIA

When Muhammad received the revelations in the seventh century, organized educational institutions were nonexistent in Arabia. With the Prophet Muhammad beginning to spread the message, the new converts to Islam began meeting in groups to discuss the revelations and learn the rituals from the Prophet and his companions.[3] This gave rise to nonformal educational arrangements, described by historians as *halqa* (study circles, also referred to as *majlish*).[4] Soon this became a model emulated elsewhere. Most of these early study circles were centered on places for prayer—*masjid* (mosque), but some emerged in the homes of the Prophet's companions and new converts.[5] The latter provided residential facilities as well. For example, Arkam bin Abul Arkam, who embraced Islam at a very early phase, dedicated his home to teaching and learning the Qur'an in Makkah at a time when the Prophet and his companions were being persecuted. This tradition of teaching in the residence of Arkam bin Abul Arkam continued even after the Prophet migrated (*hijra*) to Yathrib (320 km. north of Makkah, later named Madinat un-Nabi, commonly known as Medina) in 622 CE.[6] Soon after entering Medina, the Prophet built a mosque (later came to be known as al-Masjid an-Nabawi, the Mosque of the Prophet) which included facilities for learning and teaching.[7]

This pattern of education, particularly teaching the Qur'an and the practices of the Prophet (*sunnah*), continued throughout the era of four Caliphs (632–661) who succeeded the Prophet as the spiritual and temporal leaders of the Muslims.[8] Over time, education became linked to two institutions—halqa and mosques. The former used to be created around one or more scholars, while the latter was centered around the mosques where illustrious teachers would spend time with the eager students.

INSTITUTIONALIZATION OF MADRASSAHS

The exact time of the establishment of the first madrassah as a separate, distinct, and exclusively educational institution is contentious. The most widespread narrative claims that the madrassah established in Baghdad in 1067 (known as Madrassah al-Nizamiya) by Nizam ul-Mulk Tusi (1018–1092), the *vizir* (prime minister) of the Seljuk Turk Sultan Alp Arslan, was the first institutionalized madrassah.[9] But available historical accounts show that madrassahs began to be established during the reign of Abbasyaid Caliph al-Ma'mun (786–833).[10] Some historians suggest that "both as term and as institution, the madrasah existed before Nizam was born."[11] Leaving aside the establishment of al-Azhar in Cairo in 975 by the fourth Fatmid Caliph al-Muiz li Dinullah (also known as al-Muizz Abu-Tamim Mu'd), educational institutions called madrassahs were established in other cities contemporaneously. Ibn al-Imad al-Hanbali mentions a madrassah founded by al-Imam abu Bakr bin Faurik al-Isfahani, who died in 1014, in Nishapur (currently located in Iran).[12] Therefore, the madrassah in question was established well before the Nizamiya madrassah in Baghdad and around the time when al-Azhar was founded. In Nishapur, local people are reported to have built a madrassah for Abu Ishaq Ibrahim Asfaraini in the late tenth century. Asfaraini died in 1027. He was succeeded by Allama Baihaqi, who continued teaching in the madrassah until his death in 1065.[13] "The Turkish ruler Sultan Mahmud (971–1030) is said to have established a madrasa at Ghazni in present-day Afghanistan in the early eleventh century."[14] Furthermore, Said Amir Arjomand suggests that the Nizamiya madrassah was probably not the first madrassah founded by Nizam ul-Mulk; instead he started establishing madrassahs "during the first year of his vizierate of Khurasan (1058)."[15]

These accounts demonstrate that although a watershed in the history of Islamic education, the Madrassah al-Nizamiya, which later became a model for other madrassahs, is not the first institutionalized madrassah. Instead, "the pattern for the emergence of madrasah, or its counterparts, was long in the making. Far from being an innovation, it was a natural development of the practice of the preceding centuries."[16] This tradition helped the spread of madrassahs throughout the regions under Muslim rule (Iran, Iraq, Anatolia, Syria, and Egypt). Nizam ul-Mulk alone is credited with founding madrassahs at least in "eleven cities including Isfahan, Balkh, Herat, and Marv in northeastern Iran and Basra and Mosul in Mesopotamia."[17]

Here it is also necessary to mention another educational institution that existed throughout the four centuries following the commencement of Islamic education (that is, seventh through tenth centuries) in Arabia. That is the *maktab*, also called *kuttab*. The maktab was "for removal of illiteracy and the teaching of reckoning, grammar, poetry, history (*akhbar*), and above all, the Qur'an. . . . The maktab could be held in a private house, shop, or any other place and was presided over by a *mu'allim* [teacher]."[18] There is general agreement among historians that "most of those who sought education stopped at the first stage. Thereafter the seekers after knowledge pursued different courses in the circles of traditionalists,

TABLE 2.1

ORGANIZATIONS OF MUSLIM EDUCATION, 750–1350

Known as maktabs or kuttubs (writing schools)	Known as 1) mosque schools (*masjid*) 2) mosque circles (*halqha*) 3) madrasahs, outside of mosques, offering both secondary and college disciplines	1) bait-al-hikmas (houses of wisdom) 2) bookshops as centers of research 3) literary salons as centers of exchange of views and disputation of issues
Ages 5 or 6 to 14 elementary mostly outside the mosque in shops or tutors' houses	Ages to 18 and above secondary—college The transition from secondary to college was flexible and based upon individual initiative	University education and postuniversity education 4) public libraries, semi-public libraries, and private libraries in homes of scholars, as centers of research and scholarship higher education also was carried on in some mosques exclusively, such as al-Azhar

Source: Nakosteen, *History of Islamic Origins of Western Education: A.D. 800–1350*, 45.

Note: The mosque circles (*halqha*) varied in content and approach; individuals belonged to the circles according to the extent of their education. The standard depended on the quality of the teacher. Students were mobile in circles, looking for the right teacher and leaving when he could not offer further enlightenment. Preschool education was accomplished in the home, sometimes under private tutors or moral guardians. There was no formal preschool organization.

linguists, mystics, philosophers, etc."[19] Mehdi Nakosteen provides a similar picture in his discussion of educational organizations in the Muslim world between 750 and 1350 (Table 2.1).[20]

Thus, the madrassahs that emerged over the first four centuries or so were primarily designed to cater to the needs of these seekers of knowledge rather than providing basic knowledge related to Islam, the Qur'an, and/or Sunnah.

MADRASSAH AS A SITE OF CONTESTATION

Although the pursuit of knowledge was a factor in the spread of madrassahs in the tenth through twelfth centuries, often described as "the golden age of the madrasa," it was not the only motivation for founding madrassahs in quick succession.[21] The patronizing of madrassahs by various ruling dynasties and their officials, either as private citizens or as representatives of the state, was also associated with Shi'a–Sunni rivalry, contention between various *madhabs* (schools of thought) within the Sunni Islam, and philosophical debate between the rationalist Mutazilites and orthodox Asharites.[22]

Notwithstanding the theological differences, political, military, and intellectual rivalry between the Sunnis and Shi'as reached a high point in the eleventh century as the Shi'as firmly established their rule through the Fatimid Dynasty (910–1171) in present-day North Africa and Egypt. Fatimids are known to have established "various centers for teaching and preaching as well as centers for study and research."[23] The establishment of al-Azhar in 975 and contemporaneous intellectual developments posed a threat to the Sunni rulers as great as the military might of the Fatimids, which prompted the Abbasid Empire to consider the dissemination of Sunni Islamic thought through networks of educational institutions. Nizam ul-Mulk "used the foundations of the madrasas as an instrument of the policy of strengthening Sunni Orthodoxy against the serious threat of Isma'ili Shi'ism."[24] Similar measures by contemporary rulers prove that Nizam ul-Mulk was not alone in this regard. For example, Dominique Sourdel's study demonstrates that the ruler of Aleppo founded a college in 1120 to combat Shi'ism.[25]

Alongside the rivalry with Shi'as, debate intensified within the Sunni community in regard to various interpretations of Islamic jurisprudence (*fiqh*). "As Islam spread to new areas, Muslims were confronted with new situations for which neither the Qur'an nor the Hadith contained any specific advice. This led, from the middle of the eighth century onwards, to the founding of a number of schools (sing. *mazhab*, pl. *mazahib*) [also spelled *madhab*] of Islamic jurisprudence or fiqh."[26] Although the initial number of madhabs within the Sunni sect was in the hundreds, over time they dwindled to just four (the Hanafi, the Maliki, the Shafi'i, and the Hanbali, named after their progenitors Abu Hanifa al-Numan, Malik ibn Anas, Muhammad ibn Idris as-Shafi'i, and

Ahmad ibn Hanbal, respectively). Similarly, one school of thought emerged within the Shi'a fold, the Ja'fari school (named after Ja'far as-Sadiq). The rise of various madhabs indicates scholarly debates between learned persons and within the Muslim community at large, and the practice of *ijtihad* (creative interpretation of the original Islamic laws) as opposed to *taqlid* (accepting and following the verdicts of expert scholars of Islamic fiqh in their exposition and interpretation of Islamic law).[27] But it also brought forth denominational differences and thus created schisms within the community. Followers of these schools often established institutions, including madrassahs, to propagate their interpretations.

This is not to say that all madrassahs were exclusive in nature; indeed, many madrassahs taught various madhabs, but the madrassahs did become a vehicle for the dissemination of denominational teachings. George Makdisi argued that the relationship between educational institutions and the various madhabs was cyclical—from unrestricted *jami* (place of worship) that served all madhabs, to exclusive masjids and madrassahs each serving a particular madhab, to finally unrestricted madrassahs, particularly those founded by the Abbasid Caliph al-Muntasir (1226–1242).[28] The presence of this cyclical trend has been contested by some historians, but one must acknowledge that such differences contributed to the rise of madrassahs in great numbers. Typically the patron's affiliation with a particular madhab decided the nature of the madrassah, but when many patrons adhering to different madhabs were involved, tensions ensued. The Madrassah al-Nizamiya in Baghdad is a case in point: the caliphs were followers of al-Shafi'i, the sultans were followers of Abu Hanifah, and the Nizam a follower of al-Shafi'i. But the Nizamiya madrassah, ultimately, was at the forefront of popularizing the teachings of Shafi'i madhab.

The third most influential factor in the proliferation of madrassahs throughout the region was the theological battle between the Mutazilites and the Asharites. The former, which emerged in the eighth century as a result of the strong impact of Greek philosophy, challenged the dominant notion that the Qur'an was the eternal word of God. The Mutazilites emphasized reason and justice, and relied on a synthesis between reason and revelation in regard to the interpretation of the Qur'an. This was countered by the group of ulama who would later be named Asharite (after the founder Abu al-Hasan bin Isma'el al-Ash'ari, 873–935). The Asharites' view was that comprehension of the unique nature and characteristics of God was beyond human capability. They undermined the role of human free will and insisted on a literal interpretation of the Qur'an.[29] In the face of growing challenges from the Mutazilites, the rulers of the Abbasid Empire took a special interest in advancing the Asharite theology. Nizam ul-Mulk's decision to appoint al-Ghazali, the most prominent Asharite theologian, initially at the madrassah in Nishapur and later as the chair of law at Nizamiya in Baghdad is a testimony to this effort.

MADRASSAHS IN SOUTH ASIA
The Beginning

Until the rise of the Mughal Empire in 1528, Islamic educational institutions including madrassahs were founded in India without any discernable pattern. The nature, scope, and role of the madrassahs varied according to region, and depended on the mode of interactions between the Muslims and the local community, for Islam reached India through a variety of ways—trade, migration, preaching, and military invasions. The northern parts of the subcontinent, for example, were invaded by Muhammad bin Qasim in 711 and Mahmud of Gazni in the early eleventh century. The invasion of Sind by bin Qasim was prompted by an attack on Arab trading ships by pirates, evidence of trading contacts long before the military conflict. On the other hand, in the eastern parts of India, particularly in Bengal, Sufis, saints, and holy men began arriving as early as the late seventh century.[30]

Some historians contend that following bin Qasim's invasion, Arab scholars migrated to well-known cities in Sind such as Debal and new cities such as Mansura, founded between 728 and 738.[31] According to some accounts, madrassahs were founded where "scholars delivered lectures on Hadiths, Tafsir [Qur'anic commentary], and Fiqh literature, comparable with Damascus."[32] But little detail is available to support this claim. Muhammad Ghori, who laid the foundation of Turkish rule in India in the late twelfth century, is credited with establishing a madrassah in Ajmer in 1191, considered the first institutionalized madrassah in South Asia.[33]

When Gazni was seized by the Turks in 1153–1154, large numbers of the elite fled from Gazni and Khurasan, and migrated to the city of Lahore. The refugees included scholars. Their presence influenced the local culture and education.[34]

Many of the rulers belonging to the Delhi Sultanate, which existed between 1201 and 1528 under various dynasties, displayed admiration for education and religious learning. A number of them built mosques and religious learning centers, and some built madrassahs in the areas they ruled including the capital, Delhi. The first madrassah in Delhi was founded by Shams-ud-din Iltutmish (or Altamash, 1211–1236) in the early years of his reign and was named Madrassah-i-Muizzi. Among the rulers of the Tughluq Dynasty (1290–1302), Muhammad bin Tughluq (1325–1351) was the most enthusiastic founder of madrasshas. There were nearly one thousand madrassahs in Delhi during his rule.[35]

Although these madrassahs were not established by a single ruler, they generally served a similar purpose—educating people for state employment—and their pattern closely followed that of the well-established madrassahs in the Muslim world. "The important subjects of study, broadly speaking, were 1) grammar, 2) literature, 3) logic, 4) Islamic laws and its principles, 5) Qur'anic commentary, 6) hadiths, 7) mysticism, 8) scholasticism (religious philosophy). The books listed contained many of the original texts from the Baghdad schools, but also contained texts from the later scholars of Bukhara, and Khwarizm in Central Asia."[36]

The curricula of these madrassahs, particularly those located in the north, were influenced by the scholars who migrated to India following the demise of the Abbasid Dynasty, when the Mongols ransacked the main centers of Islamic rule and madrassahs. A significant number of these scholars belonged to the Hanafi school of thought, and thus established the character of many madrassahs.[37] But this cannot be said of India as a whole, because, as noted earlier, the nature of madrassahs varied widely by region.

A number of regional kingdoms with distinct characteristics emerged as the Delhi-based rule weakened over time. In the south, the independent Muslim kingdom of Deccan was founded. The Bahmani Sultanate (or Bahmanid Dynasty), located in the northern Deccan, lasted for almost two centuries beginning 1347, and is known for establishing a number of madrassahs. The first of these madrasshs was built in 1378 by Mahmud Shah.[38] The most prominent of the madrassahs was built in Bidar in 1472, under the direction of Khwaja Mahmud Gawan, the prime minister of Shams-ud-din Muhammad Shah Bahmani (also known as Muhammad Shah III Lashkari, 1463–1482). The reputation of this madrassah attracted the most eminent theologians, philosophers, and scientists. An interesting aspect of this madrassah was that, unlike most of those elsewhere in India, it was built to reaffirm Shi'ism, which received state patronage. The madrassah, named after Mahmud Gawan, was the embodiment of the excellence of Persian architecture. The curriculum of the madrassahs in the south, various accounts indicate, included both religious and secular subjects. This is largely due to the rulers' patronage of education in general. For example, the first madrassah established by Mahmud Shah provided education to orphans; expenses for lodging and food were borne by the state, and government subsidies were provided to other educational institutions.

In Bengal, the institutionalization of Islamic education began during the period of the Delhi Sultanate, but its foundation was established in earlier days with the arrival of Sufis and saints. Sufis and saints used to travel from outside the region, and usually formed organized centers of learning in their *khanqas* (that is, their place of worship and residence).[39] These gatherings, akin to the halqas in Arabia in the early days of Islam, were primarily for adults and particularly to discuss the teachings of the Qur'an and Sunnah. These were not intended to provide literacy in any language, nor designed for elementary education. Lack of support from the rulers made these khanqas entirely dependent on individual Sufis and saints and support from their local followers; therefore, if the Sufi or saint moved, the khanqas, especially the educational gatherings, often ceased to exist in one place and began in another. Over time, some of these khanqas began to resemble regular centers of elementary education, called maktabs. Maktabs were also organized at mosques, and at the homes of Muslims who could afford to provide space.

It is worth mentioning that, prior to the introduction of maktabs, an indigenous system of education was thriving in Bengal. The institution central to the elementary education system was the *toll*, primarily to teach Hindu religious practices. These institutions were a community response to the needs of literacy and religious education of the children. Each of these institutions was organized around one person called a *guru* (teacher, in Sanskrit), and the students were supposed to spend a considerable time learning Sanskrit. The students of these tolls generally came from the higher social classes. Another institution that emerged after the twelfth century in Bengal was the *pathshala*. The pathshala curriculum was relatively secular: designed to teach language, basic mathematics, and skills related to agriculture, boat making, and the like. Some historians argue that, generally, the pathshalas spread in the sixteenth and seventeenth centuries, and that students of these institutions came from all social strata.[40] By the fifteenth century, the Bengali alphabet had been formalized and the pathshalas became the principal institutions of learning in the Bengali language.

Thus maktabs and subsequently madrassahs were established in various parts of Bengal well before the Bengali learning institutions came into existence. The maktabs and madrassahs remained community-based and community-supported institutions until they began to receive the support of the rulers, which occurred after Ikhtiyar bin Bakhtiyar Khilji's military expedition reached Bengal in 1197. Bakhtiyar Khilji, after expanding his rule in Bengal, founded a new city called Rangpura, where a number of madrassahs were established within a short span of time.[41] His successors followed the practice and founded a number of madrassahs and extended support to various maktabs.[42]

The preceding discussion demonstrates that Islamic educational institutions, which began to spread under the rulers of the Delhi Sultanate, continued despite the gradual weakening of the sultanate and the emergence of various political structures. Patronage from regional Muslim rulers was one of the reasons for the expansion, but not the only reason. In some instances madrassahs emerged due to the presence of preachers, and in other situations as a community response to the needs of providing education to the children.

It is noteworthy that no single model of madrassah was replicated, that these madrassahs enjoyed autonomy in their operation, and that they had complete freedom in deciding their curriculum. Additionally, "both 'transmitted' as well as 'rational' sciences were taught at the madrassahs, for the notion that the two were somehow opposed to each other or that there was a clear distinction between religion and the secular world was, as in other contemporary Muslim societies, quite foreign to the medieval Indian Muslim educational system."[43] Emphasis on both sciences helped the madrassah graduates acquire employment in royal courts and various branches of administration. In addition to the madrassahs, the opening of maktabs has also been discussed. These institutions were equivalent to preschools or kindergartens, but usually taught only the memorization of the Qur'an.

Madrassahs under the Mughals (1556–1858)

The number of madrassahs increased manyfold during the Mughal Empire (1556–1858), which was at its height for almost two centuries and was spread through an area no smaller than a continent. This was primarily due to the support provided by the royal courts, irrespective of the ruler. Two other factors contributed to the growth of the educational institutions under the Mughals, especially in the sixteenth century; first, the political stability owing to the consolidation of power at one center, resulting in a centralized bureaucracy; and second, the growing influence of the ulama vis-à-vis the Sufis as the dominant religious figures. These factors are connected to each other in many ways. Although the influence of the ulama on Mughal courts did not undermine the authority of the emperor or the general bureaucracy, the ulama were immensely important: "it was they who were responsible for the education of the entire nobility, who staffed the various levels of judiciary; and who oversaw the whole charitable establishment of the empire. . . . A career as 'alim in this period was seen as a route to prestige, or, at least respectability."[44] Therefore, madrassahs received patronage and respect from the emperors and common people alike.

Two features characterize the Mughal period, however—the presence of two conflicting trends within the education sector, and the consolidation of one tradition within the madrassah curriculum. Within the education sector one trend was to expand educational opportunities for a large number of members of the society while the other was to isolate itself from contemporaneous developments in technology elsewhere, particularly in Europe. Within madrassah education, the tradition of *manqulat* (revealed/transmitted knowledge) was consolidated over time at the expense of the tradition of *maqulat* (rational sciences). Interestingly, in the early days of the empire, it was the study of maqulat that spread widely.

Dominant historical narratives suggest that spreading education was high on the agenda of the Mughal rulers. Narendra Nath Law, in his seminal work on education under Muslim rule in India, concluded that "almost all the Mughal Emperors took much interest in the education of the people and the diffusion of learning."[45] Educational institutions of various levels were founded by these rulers. Royal documents of Babar (1526–1530) reveal that education was considered a duty of the state to its subjects. Akbar (1556–1605) was at the forefront of making education available to a large number of people; he established a "department dispensing state patronage to educational institutions" and embarked on significant educational reforms (to which we will return soon).[46] Jahangir (1605–1627) introduced a law that stipulated that if a rich man or a rich traveler died without heir, his property would be transferred to the crown and be utilized for building and repairing madrassahs and monasteries.[47] Jan Jahan Khan in his *Tarikhi-Jan-Jahan* states that Jahangir repaired "even those madrassahs that had for thirty years been the dwelling places and birds and beasts, and filled them with students and professors."[48] The most celebrated act of Emperor Shahjahan (1627–1658) in the field of education was the establishment of the Imperial College in Delhi, around 1650.[49] During Mughal rule, the royal support for education was matched by individuals belonging to the nobility and by well-to-do members of the society. Thus, educational institutions grew phenomenally and the ulama held a respected position in the royal courts. Often scholars accompanied emperors on their military expeditions.[50]

The close relationship between the state and the ulama was not unique to the Mughal Empire but was also a characteristic of the Ottoman and Safavid empires, and neither was it solely due to the emperors' proclivities for patronage. The ulama were also interested in being a part of the state, not only to have successful careers but also to oversee the implementation of their religious ideas and interpretations.[51] This is not to say that the relationship was always comfortable; indeed, occasionally tensions between the ulama and the emperor surfaced.

Although patronage to education, arts, music, and architecture was the hallmark of the Mughal emperors, they seem to have been reluctant to embrace new knowledge and technology, and lagged behind in the adoption of contemporaneous inventions. Saiyid Naqi Husain Jafri insists, "in so far as reception of new ideas and technologies was concerned, the Mughals . . . were not much interested."[52] The examples Jafri cites in support of his argument are the refusal of Akbar to adopt a printing press when a delegation of Portuguese missionaries presented printed papers, and Jahangir's indifference to a mechanical clock presented to him by the French royal delegation. "These two instances have been cited only to suggest how the rulers and powers that be guided and shaped the priorities of a nation."[53] Jafri believes that this was a serious anomaly compared to earlier Muslim rules elsewhere:

> Unlike the earlier examples of the centers of learning in Damascus Baghdad, and later in Toledo, Granada, and Cordoba, when Arabs mastered the Syriac, Greek, and Coptic languages, the Muslims of later ages, particularly

in Ottoman, Safawid Iran and Mughal India showed no, or at the most little, interest in acquiring any competence in foreign languages (in this case, European languages). . . . Muslims not acquainted with any of the European languages did not know the pace and scope of scientific thought.[54]

Thus despite the expansion of education during the Mughal Empire, the content did not reflect available up-to-date knowledge, especially in technology, primarily owing to the educational institutions' reluctance to teach European languages.

Equally important is the trend that the royal patronage of education for all in the early days of the Mughal Empire changed over time and became skewed toward coreligionists in the late Mughal period. "We see in Akbar, perhaps for the first time in [Indian] history, a Muslim monarch sincerely eager to further the education of the Hindus and the Muhammadans alike."[55] Akbar created and supported institutions, including madrassahs, where Hindu and Muslim children learned together. Systematic policies were followed by the royal court to ensure that Hindu children and youth were educated about their religion and culture. Hindu scholars received royal patronage almost in equal measure with Muslim scholars. These actions were consistent with Akbar's other policies and his attitude toward religion; for example, the abolition of pilgrimage tax on Hindus, and of *jizya* (per-head tax on non-Muslims), and the encouragement of debates among scholars of various religions in the Ibadat Khana (House of Worship) founded by him. Akbar's attempt to introduce a new religion called the Deen-i-Ilahi (Divine Faith) indicates his desire, among others, to bridge the differences between Hindus and Muslims.[56]

Changes in the educational curriculum, particularly the emphasis on rationalist content, continued under Jahangir's rule; but faced resistance from orthodox ulama. Some ulama, for example Shaikh Abd ul-Huq during Akbar's reign, attempted to revive the *manqulat* tradition. Shaikh Abd ul-Huq later fled to Hijaz "to escape the lax atmosphere of Akbar's court."[57]

In contrast with Akbar and Jahangir, Aurangzeb's rule reveals a less tolerant face of the Mughal Empire. Aurangzeb not only cared little about the education of Hindus but also ordered the provincial governors to destroy Hindu schools and temples in 1669.[58] He eagerly tried to foster the education of Muslim youth and spread Islamic learning.[59] Muslim students received royal support in the form of stipends, and the emperor provided monetary help to educational institutions, sometimes in the form of jagirs for perpetual support of the institution. Aurangzeb, known for his dissatisfaction with the education imparted by his teachers, founded innumerable madrassahs during his reign.[60]

The most significant steps in the education sector during the reign of Akbar were changes in the learning method at the elementary level, and the revision of the madrassah curriculum under the auspices of Mir Fateullah Shirazi. The former was intended to shift the focus of education in maktabs from rote memorization to learning by practice. Akbar proposed a system which gave emphasis to understanding: "Care should be taken that he [student] learns to understand everything himself, but the teacher may assist him a little."[61]

The reform of the madrassah curriculum was chiefly the contribution of Mir Fateullah Shirazi, a scholar who initially migrated to one of the southern Muslim sultanates from Shiraz, a town in Iran, sometime in the mid-1500s. He provided services to Sultan Ali Adil Shah, but was later incarcerated after his patron was murdered and political changes ensued in the sultanate. He was freed at the request of Emperor Akbar and brought to the royal court in 1583. Subsequently he occupied various important positions within the administration (for example, the *amin-ul mulk*, the trustee of the empire, and *sadrus sudur*, the head qadi (judge) and made his mark in education reform. He, however, maintained a distance from the religious matters of Akbar's royal court.

As a result of the revision, the madrassah curriculum included courses on ethics, mathematics, astronomy, agriculture, medicine, logic, and government; the study of Sanskrit including *vyakaran* (grammar), *vidayanta* (philosophy), and the teachings of Patanjali (yoga) was prescribed.[62] Eighteenth-century historian Ali Azad Bilgrami states that after Shirazi's arrival in Akbar's court, "the study of maqulat took great strides towards popularity," and according to Ikram, "during Akbar's reign the 'mental sciences'—logic, philosophy, and scholastic theology—had taken on new importance."[63]

The tradition of syncretism promoted by Akbar was reversed by Aurangzeb during his rule, as he tried to conduct the affairs of state according to traditional Islamic policy, and "in some of his letters written during the struggle for the succession he claimed that he was acting 'for the sake of the *true faith* and the peace of the realm'" (emphasis added).[64] Yet a development during the reign of Aurangzeb provided a leap to the tradition of studying rational sciences: the establishment of Farangi Mahall in Lucknow as an institution of learning.[65] The building in which it was housed, previously owned by a European merchant, was donated by Emperor Aurangzeb to the family of Mullah Qutubud-din Sihalwi. Sihalwi, a leading scholar of rational sciences, was consulted by the royal court on many occasions. After he died as a result of a land dispute in the late seventeenth century, the emperor bequeathed the compound to his family. The third son of Sihalwi, Mullah Nizamuddin Sihalwi, turned the place into a seat of learning in the early eighteenth century. Mullah Nizamuddin laid down a curriculum, later named Dars-i-Nizami, which made the study of rational sciences central to education. Robinson underscores the salient features of the Dars-i-Nizami, saying that: "By encouraging students to think rather than merely to learn by rote the syllabus enabled them to get through the usual run of madrasa learning with greater speed, while they came to be noted for their capacity to get to the heart of the matter, to present an argument, and to be flexible in their approach to jurisprudence."[66]

Two points are worth noting here. First, Farangi Mahall was not organized as a madrassah (until 1905); instead, the members of the Farangi Mahall families "simply taught in their homes those who came to them."[67] And second, revealed knowledge—manqulat—was not excluded from the curriculum, but "the religious part of the curriculum consisted of classical texts."[68]

Considering Aurangzeb's avowed adherence to a puritanical version of Islam, his support for the establishment of Farangi Mahall is intriguing, to say the least. Equally remarkable is the role of the nawabs of Awadh, who made the continued existence of the Farangi Mahall and particularly the adoption of the Dars-i-Nizami curriculum possible. It is well to bear in mind that the nawabs were Shi'a. It must also be acknowledged that Aurangzeb's initial support was pivotal in bringing the institution to life, and that the lodging expenses of students who studied in the Farangi Mahall were paid by the Mughal emperor.

By the early eighteenth century, the Farangi Mahall had become one of the largest centers of learning in India, and students from outside Lucknow were attending this institution in great numbers. Throughout the eighteenth and early nineteenth centuries the rationalist tradition, espoused by the Farangi Mahall, spread, and the Dars-i-Nizami became the de facto standard syllabus of madrassah education. Barbara Metcalf correctly noted, "the most important measure of the Farangi Mahalli ulama was their systematization of a new curriculum which, with modifications, has dominated religious teachings in South Asia to the present."[69] The wide acceptance of the Nizami syllabus since its inception was due to two factors: first, that it enabled the students to gain employment, especially in government—"the skills it [Dars-i-Nizami] offered were in demand from increasingly sophisticated and complex bureaucratic systems of seventeenth- and eighteenth-century India"; and second, that members of the Farangi Mahall families traveled throughout India "from court to court, from patron to patron, in search of teaching opportunities" and devoted themselves to teaching. This increased the number of students exponentially.[70]

The popularity of the study of rational sciences began to wane in the later days of the Mughal period, and the manqulat tradition—the tradition of emphasis on revealed sciences—began to regain its position in the eighteenth century. This was, in large measure, a contribution of the thought of Shah Waliullah Dehalvi (1703–1762) and the Madrassah-i-Rahimia, a madrassah where he taught for more than twelve years.[71] The madrassah, however, attracted attention when Shah Abd al-Aziz (1746–1823), son of Shah Waliullah, became its head.

Shah Waliullah devoted himself to the study of Islam from childhood under the guidance of his grandfather Sheikh Wajihuddin, a warrior turned scholar, and his father Shah Abd ar-Rahim, an eminent scholar who established the Madrassah-i-Rahimia and taught at this institution. After his father's death in 1719, Shah Waliullah took charge of the madrassah at the age of seventeen. Shah Waliullah was capable of being the head of the institution at such an early stage of his life because by then he had demonstrated high qualities of scholarship. After completion of his elementary education, Shah Waliullah acquired the knowledge of logic, fiqh, hadith, *tib* (Eastern medicine), algebra, mathematics, and oratory from his father.[72] After twelve years of teaching, he went to Arabia in 1731, where he stayed for about two and a half years and studied under Medinese hadith scholar Muhammad Haya al-Sindi (d.1750).[73] Upon his return to India, Waliullah taught at the Madrassah-i-Rahimia for about three years before devoting himself to writing.

Waliullah was a product of the Madrassah-i-Rahimia, but it was his ideas that shaped the madrassah's curriculum and made indelible marks on the Muslim scholarship of his time and beyond. He is one of the few scholars whose ideas are debated among both Islamic activists and scholars to date. Waliullah's primary concern was the decline of the Muslims, moral and political, in his time. Waliullah viewed the disintegration of the Mughal Empire after Aurangzeb, the rise of smaller states, the invasion of Nadir Shah (1739), and the lack of religiosity among Muslims as a crisis of the Muslim community, and examined the causes of this decline. He wrote extensively on issues related to jurisprudence, Sufism, hadith scholarship, and the relationships between the scholars (*ulama*) and the state, to name but a few subjects.[74] He also translated the Qur'an into Persian.

One of the central themes of Waliullah's writing was the disunity among Muslims and, therefore, political issues featured significantly in his work.[75] "His success, however, rested neither in curricular and institutional innovation nor in the compilation of mere commentaries, but rather in his major individual effort at intellectual synthesis and systematization, an unprecedented *tatbiq* of the whole range of Islamic knowledge."[76] Yet his insistence on studying hadiths, his complete rejection of maqulat, criticism of the influence of Greek philosophy on the ulama, criticisms of the local customs of Muslims as *bida't* (wrongful innovations) strengthened the study of revealed sciences among his followers and in the Madrassah-i-Rahimia under the stewardship of his son Abd al-Aziz, who declared India under British rule a Darul Harb (abode of war).

Thus, by the end of Mughal rule, the tradition of manqulat within the madrassah education curricula had regained its dominant position. This is not to say that the maqulat tradition was obliterated, for the Farangi Mahall existed and variations of Dars-i-Nizami curriculum were followed by many madrassahs, but Shah Waliullah's ideas began to find more adherents within the Muslim community. It is, however, necessary to acknowledge that the madrassahs and ulama during Mughal rule made a remarkable contribution to the discipline of revealed knowledge; "their contribution is indeed significant in the Islamic world."[77]

Madrassahs under British Colonial Rule

The nature, scope, and role of madrassahs in colonial India were significantly shaped by the colonial administration's policies toward education, endeavors of Muslims to locate their position within the changing political structure after the demise of the Mughal Empire, and the rise of identity politics within the Muslim community in India. Therefore, the history of madrassah education in India under British colonialism is inextricably linked to the political dynamics of the country, particularly of the nineteenth century, and must be discussed in the context of these three factors.

The British East India Company assumed political power in Bengal in 1765, nine years after the Battle of Plassey, which saw the defeat of the nawab of Bengal at the hands of British soldiers led by Robert Clive and marked the beginning of British colonialism in India.[78] After the death of Aurangzeb in 1707, the Mughal Empire centered in Delhi was in serious decline and was virtually ineffective as a political power, owing to the rise of various non-Muslim powers (for example, the Jats, the Marathas, the Sikhs) in areas previously under Mughal rule and the growing strength of the British East India Company. Additionally, the invasion of Nadir Shah (1739) from Persia and the subsequent sacking of Delhi weakened the material base of the Mughal Empire forever. Thus, the East India Company's policy measures, initially effective for the eastern part of India (Bengal, Bihar, and Orissa), lay the groundwork for future rule throughout India.

Although the colonial administration's direct and protracted involvement in education began in 1813 with the Charter Act, it came after considerable debate and various other measures. The Company's policy of maintaining distance from the educational sector in the early days of its power allowed the continuation of traditional educational institutions such as pathshalas, maktabs, and madrassahs established during Mughal rule with state patronage, and as community responses outside state involvement. There were also initiatives to introduce new educational institutions. These initiatives largely came from the Christian missionaries. For example, first missionary school was established in Calcutta in 1702, before the East India Company emerged as a formidable political entity. Soon after the Battle of Plassey, Robert Clive invited a missionary activist from Madras to open a school in Calcutta. The number of students of the school rose to 174 in the second year, in 1759, from 48 in its first year.[79]

However, the East India Company maintained a distance from missionary activism, opposed proselytizing, and restricted missionary activities within Company-controlled territory.[80] Missionaries not only needed permission from the Company to conduct their activities but were also discouraged through various means. Undoubtedly this policy was deliberate: "Afraid of the reaction that meddling in the religious beliefs of its Indian subjects might provoke, the East India Company made it clear to these subjects as well as to its own British officials that it was not in India to challenge or undermine existing religious beliefs."[81]

Nevertheless, the missionaries influenced educational policies in later years, especially with regard to the medium of instruction. Additionally, the presence and activities of these missionaries engendered reactions from both Hindu and Muslim communities, and helped reform movements to gather pace.

Despite the pronounced religious neutrality of the Company, the first direct involvement of the Company in education came at the auspices of Warren Hastings, the governor general of Bengal, in 1780 with the establishment of the Calcutta Madrassah. Hastings's statement delineating the rationale for the establishment of the madrassah indicates that political consideration was the driving force behind the decision. The madrassah was established "to conciliate the Mahomedans of Calcutta . . . to qualify the sons of Mahomedan gentlemen for responsible and lucrative offices in the state, and to produce competent officers for Courts of Justice to which students of the Madrassah on the production of certificates of qualification were to be drafted as vacancies occurred."[82]

The decision to establish the Calcutta Aliya madrassah followed the decision to employ different laws for Muslim and Hindu communities. In 1772 Warren Hastings and William Jones had decided to apply "the laws of Koran with respect to Mohammedans and that of the Shaster with respect to Hindus."[83] Jones's effort to stratify society along religious lines may have its origin in the intention to divide and rule, or may have grown out of a "civilizational perspective," but it also had an impact upon the educational policies of the administration, with far-reaching consequences.[84]

The Calcutta Aliya madrassah adopted the Dars-i-Nizami curriculum and continued to follow the curriculum until 1790. Adoption of the Dars-i-Nizami in the Calcutta Madrassah was a vindication of the utilitarian value of the curriculum introduced by Farangi Mahall in the early eighteenth century. In 1791, however, with the dismissal of the first principal, changes were made in the curriculum. The company also provided support to the establishment of the Sanskrit College in Benaras in 1791, and Fort William College in Calcutta in 1800.[85] These measures were not official requirements for the East India Company.

The responsibility of education of Indian subjects was included in the renewed charter of the East India Company in 1813, which stipulated that although not a replacement for indigenous languages, English would be taught in the Indian education system. The expectation was that English would coexist with Oriental studies as a means by which moral law could be reinforced.

This inclusion was the result of Charles Grant's study conducted in 1792 entitled "Observations on the state of society among the Asiatic subjects of Great Britain, particularly with respect to morals, and the means to improving it" (published in 1793). Grant, in his report, insisted that darkness had fallen on India, and Hindus (by which he meant Indians) were to be blamed for their plight. Grant suggests, "the communication of our light and knowledge to them would prove the best remedy for their disorders." By "light" Grant meant Christianity, and by "knowledge" English education. Thus, his suggestions included the introduction of English as the medium of instruction, establishment of schools to provide education to local elites who would then pass on the education to the commoners, and the replacement of Persian with English as the official language.[86]

Although the Board of Directors of the East India Company entrusted the responsibility of providing education to the Indian subjects of the Company, Grant's proposals were not approved by the directors. One of the key elements of Grant's proposals, the theory of "downward filtration," was, however, adopted and followed until 1854. The encouragement to the establishment of the Hindu College in 1817 and the Sanskrit College in 1824 in Calcutta—both to attract the children of elites and to teach English, among other subjects—reflects the policy of filtration. The decision to introduce an English course in the Calcutta Aliya madrassah in 1824 (which was implemented in 1826) demonstrates the administration's gradual move toward introduction of English in schools. The Calcutta Aliya madrassah continued to offer an English course until 1851.

The proposals presented by Charles Grant finally became a reality in 1835, thanks to Thomas Macaulay's Education Minute. Of course, the Education Minute also resulted from the broader Anglicist/Orientalist controversy, marking the victory of the Orientalists.[87] Two central issues of the debates were the system of education (local versus Western) and the medium of education (local languages versus English). The minute favored Western education and English. It clearly stated the goals of administration with regard to education: "We must at present do our best to form a class who may be interpreters between us and the millions who we govern; a class of persons, Indian in blood and colour, but English in taste, in opinion, in morals, and in intellect."[88] The minute was approved immediately by Governor General William Bentinck, making 1835 a watershed in the history of education in India.[89] The immediate consequence of the adoption of this policy was the discontinuation of government support to madrassahs and other traditional educational institutions.

But the most serious blow came when English replaced Persian as the official language and medium of the higher courts of law in 1835, and regional languages became the medium of the lower courts in 1837. These two decisions in succession reduced the employability of those educated in Persian in madrassahs. In 1844, when Governor General Henry Hardinge declared that only those with Western-style education and knowledge of English were eligible for government employment or for a career in public life, the utility of Persian ceased immediately, and the employability of madrassah-educated youth became almost nonexistent. This decision came despite William Adam's three-volume survey report on the state of education in Bengal and Bihar in 1838, which recommended strengthening the existing local educational institutions including pathshalas and madrassahs, and using local languages as a medium of instruction for better education.[90]

With little success in spreading education among the elites, let alone the common people, the policy of filtration came under scrutiny in the 1850s, and a shift ensued. In the wake of the renewal of the charter of the East India Company in 1853, the British Parliament conducted an enquiry into the state of Indian education, the first of its kind. This resulted in Wood's Despatch of 1854. Wood's Despatch, named after Charles Wood, the president of the Board of Control for India, not only expressed dismay at the limited success in the education sector, but also recommended a scheme for education from the primary school to the university level. The proposed scheme suggested an end to the filtration policy, recommended that the government take responsibility for education at all levels, and proposed a transformation of the indigenous schools into Western-style institutions through grants-in-aid to private schools.[91] These recommendations were implemented without much delay, and they transformed the education landscape of India. The Westernization of education became the "public agenda" rather than a "government initiative," English education proliferated, and the structure of educational institutions changed. These changes marginalized the traditional educational institutions, particularly madrassahs, because eligibility for grants-in-aid "required adoption of a curriculum focused on math, science, and language, and removal of all reference to religion to a discrete 'religion' class. It also required that educators receive formal teacher training, which gradually shifted teaching from respected local figures, often religious authorities who did not teach as a primary occupation, to full-time educators with teaching certificates issued by colonial authorities."[92] In the early years, however, the lion's share of the new grants-in-aid went to the missionary schools, which posed another kind of threat to the madrassahs.[93] This was particularly important because missionary schools were functioning as secular institutions. It is now well documented that missionary activists deeply believed that "education might serve to prepare young minds for a conversion."[94] In other words, to the missionaries, education was a *praeparatio evengelica*. It is understandable why the missionary schools would hope to spread the Word of God, but importantly, nonmissionary secular schools were not too far behind. Macaulay, a year after his historic Education Minute, said, "It is my firm belief that, if our plans of education are followed up, there will be no single idolater among respectable classes in Bengal thirty years hence."[95] Such optimism was based on the fact that English literature courses were designed "to convey the message of the Bible."[96]

The decision to introduce English education is indicative of the influence of the missionaries on the administration's education policy. Alexander Duff of the Church of Scotland, after his arrival in Calcutta in 1830, insisted on English as the medium of education and was critical of rote learning. The school founded by him, which eventually developed into the Scottish Church College, not only set the standard for other missionary schools but also influenced the decision of 1835 to devote state funds to Western education through the medium of English.

In the long run, the education policies of the colonial administration, especially its insistence on Western education (labeled as secular education), had an impact in two ways: first, it bifurcated education into two realms—secular and religious. By instituting what Yoginder Sikand has aptly called educational dualism, religion was pushed to the private sphere and was identified as a "distinct sphere of life and activity, neatly separate or separable from other similarly defined spheres."[97] By implication, the madrassah was consigned to provide religious education as opposed to general education. This bifurcation—religious versus secular—was also interpreted as sacred versus profane, and within the discourse of the ulama this translated into education of *deen* (religious/sacred) and *duniya* (temporal). It is interesting to note here that essentially both the colonial administration and ulama subscribed to the post-Enlightenment Western approach of rigid compartmentalization between these two, although in reverse order of importance. But for ulama this was also a mode of resistance to colonialism: "the din-duniya separation should be construed as a form of cultural resistance, an effort to protect the 'inner world' from Western intrusion."[98] The defense of the inner world is based on an understanding of its superiority, it sovereignty, and its primacy in life. This attitude has remained unchanged to date throughout South Asia.

The second impact is the creation of a new social space for religiopolitical activism. The marginalization of religious education and the exclusion of overt religious texts in schools created a space for religious movements to reach a new public through their own educational institutions. Vickie Langhour, in her perceptive articles, has demonstrated that this came to pass both in Egypt and Punjab under the British, and in Indonesia under Dutch colonial rule.[99] The transformation of traditional kuttubs under the auspices of the Muslim Brotherhood in Egypt, the establishment of schools and colleges called Dayanand Anglo-Vedic (DAV) institutions by the Arya Samaj in Punjab, and the Muhammadiya school system in Indonesia bear testimony to this fact. In the nineteenth century, madrassahs played a similar role in the identity politics of the Muslim community.

The question of identity as a distinct issue appeared at the middle of the nineteenth century in India, as a section of the Muslim community began to lament the disintegration of the Mughal Empire and to endeavor to locate their position within the changing political structure. In many ways, the process began with the intellectual tradition of Shah Waliullah, but gained salience within the Muslim public discourse as a result of the failure of the Mutiny of 1857. Even for those who disagreed with the approach of Shah Waliullah and approached the issue from an entirely different position, the questions were similar and simple: why has Islamic rule collapsed? How to regain the "lost glory of Islam"? These questions privileged religion in general and particularly Islam as identifier and social demarcator of identity, but this was nothing exceptional; because, "times of crisis breed religious reform movement, as people ask why the temporal glories of their religious community have faded."[100] These reform movements often take various shapes and employ various methods. In the case of nineteenth- (and twentieth-) century India, the Muslim reformist movements took the shape of sectarian and revivalist activism, and educational movements, among others.[101] These movements were connected in many ways, but for our purposes the educational movement, particularly madrassahs, as a vehicle of Muslim awakening and identity politics, is important.

Although the founding of the Calcutta Aliya madrassah in 1780 can be described as the beginning of the modern era of madrassah education in South Asia, its role in producing Muslim consciousness and encouraging political activism was limited, especially in comparison to other community-initiated madrassahs such as the the Deoband Madrassah and the Darul Uloom Nadwatul Ulama, established in the mid-nineteenth century in north India. The primary objective of the Calcutta Madrassah, as discussed previously, was to enable Muslims to join the colonial administration. Since its inception, the madrassah followed the curriculum known as Dars-i-Nizami. Some changes were made in the curriculum in 1853 following the recommendations of an inquiry committee appointed by the government to look into its management; but in the main the focus remained the same, leaving very little room for the institution and its ulama play any role in social activism.

Four other madrassahs replicating the Calcutta Madrassah were established in the later part of the century—at Hughli in 1871, and at Dhaka, Chittagong, and Rajshahi in 1873. In the early twentieth century, the number grew significantly. Primarily as a result of the drive to include English in the school curriculum and to continue providing financial support to these madrassahs, there was a major change in their curriculum in 1915—inclusion of English as a mandatory subject, replacing Persian, and the introduction of mathematics, geography, history, and physical education to the curriculum. Madrassahs that adopted the reformed curriculum were called reformed (or new-scheme) madrassahs. This change created two separate trends within the institutions that followed the Calcutta Madrassah curriculum as the old-scheme madrassahs and the new-scheme madrassahs followed different curricula. The government policy was to assist the new-scheme madrassahs with financial aid (see chapter 6 for further details on the reform measures).

These changes, however significant they may be, were received with very little enthusiasm by the ulama, because by then a distinct tradition of the madrassah with an agenda of Muslim consciousness, empowerment, and activism, which originated in Deoband, had already made its mark.

Darul Uloom, commonly referred to as the Deoband Madrassah, was founded in Deoband, a small town about a hundred miles north of Delhi in 1866—ten years after the historic rebellion against British colonialism. Maulana Muhammad Qasim Nanautawi (1833–1877) and Maulana Rashid Ahmed Gangohi (1829–1905), two founders of the institution, reportedly participated in the rebellion, and viewed this effort as their new means to counteract the debilitating effect of the colonial education system and uphold traditional Islamic education. In large measure, the establishment of the Deoband Madrassah in 1866 and raising it to an uloom in 1867 were calculated responses of the orthodox ulama to contemporaneous politics. Although the madrassah adopted a revised version of the Dars-i-Nizami curriculum, it was intended to continue the intellectual tradition of Shah Waliullah and therefore emphasized the manqulat (revealed knowledge) rather than maqulat (rational sciences) in its curriculum; "fiqh formed the core of the curriculum."[102] Whether Deobandi ulama were opposed to modern education, especially English, is a matter of debate, but what is beyond doubt is that they were not willing to compromise the integrity of what they considered "Islamic education." Like all other contemporary reform movements, perhaps more than others, the objective of the Deobandis was the "correction of [the] defective state of Islam and Muslim life in India," but they insisted that it must begin with the revival of faith and piety.[103]

The Deoband Madrassah was founded with modest financial contributions from a small group of people who envisioned a spiritual awakening of individual Muslims as well as a politically emancipatory movement for the community at large. Scripturalist in their orientation, the ulama of Deoband considered that the Muslim community was facing threats from the colonial power as much as from the within the community. The modernist efforts of the Anglo-Mohammedan College at Aligarh, founded by Sayyed Ahmad Khan, and the growing influence of reformist liberal Muslim leaders who favored English education and closer cooperation with the British colonial administration was viewed as one of these challenges. Additionally, Deobandis were opposed to folk Islam, including Sufi tradition, and the Shi'as. The founders of Deoband, Nanautwi and Gangohi, challenged the veracity of the Shi'a faith on many occasions and wrote extensively against it. The ulama of Deoband not only adhered to the Hanafi school, but also insisted that any deviation from taqlid was a serious matter of concern and must be confronted because it was no less than bida't (innovation). To the Deobandis, the gates of ijtihad were firmly closed. One important issue that made the Deobandi ulama distinctly different was their position in regard to local practices: "the Deobandis opposed folk Islam in which intercession by saints occupied a major place, seeking initiation in a mystic order was considered the path to salvation, and miracles and other such phenomena were seen as the crucial and defining attributes of saints and prophets. They did not oppose mysticism altogether but did argue that adherence to the Islamic law (sharia) was the path to mystical exaltation."[104]

Whereas earlier madrassahs were loosely organized, Deoband had an elaborate administrative setup: a rector (sarparast), a chancellor (muhtamim), and a chief instructor (sadr mudarris).[105] The adoption of a hierarchical structure within the madrassah demonstrates the triumph of Western ideas of education. The presence of a planned curriculum, set requirements for admission and graduation, organized examinations, a building of its own (as opposed to being part of a mosque), and a well-structured bureaucracy to serve the managerial needs were inconsistent with the spirit of the archetypical medieval madrassahs that Deoband aspired to emulate. One can point fingers at Dars-i-Nizami for the structural dimensions, but it is well to bear in mind that the ulama of Farangi Mahall never organized their activities as an institution, and that the Deoband Madrassah was founded in opposition to the colonial educational system, not to replicate it. But these characteristics can also be interpreted as the capacity of the ulama to adapt to changed circumstances. Indeed, they helped the Deoband to emerge as the leading Islamic educational institution, serving a wide audience.

In the early days of its existence, the Deoband Madrassah did not generate much activism, but with Maulana Mahmud ul-Hasan (1851–1920) at its helm, the institution placed itself at the forefront of sociopolitical movements. Maulana Hasan, the first student of the madrassah, often called the Shaikhul Hind (the Leader of India), established an organization called Samaratut Tarbiyat (Results of Training), organized the Jamiat ul-Ansar for armed uprising against the British, and was deeply involved with an abortive attempt to internationalize the independence movement. In 1919 the Deoband Madrassah was also instrumental in founding the Jamiat-i-Khilafat-i-Hind (All-India Khilafat Conference), and Jamiat-i-Ulama-i-Hind (Association of Religious Scholars of India), two very active political organizations.[106]

Activism aside, the reputation of the Deoband Madrassah spread over time, attracting students from far and wide, and the madrassah was replicated in many places. Metcalf noted that the Deoband Madrassah and its close replication in Shahranpur, twenty miles from Deoband, drew students in great numbers from as far as Bengal.[107] But the madrassah also drew criticism from various quarters of Sunni Muslim community because of its austere measures, the Deobandi ulama's strict stance on taqlid, their puritanism, and their insistence on the correctness of their interpretation of religious texts. Differences on the immediate sources of the "threat to Islam," a matter of serious concern to the Muslim community at large, was one of the factors that led to the emergence of various others schools of thought and subsequently new madrassahs.

The emergence of the Ahl-e-Sunnat wa Jama'at (People of Sunnah and the Community), commonly referred to as Barelvis, under the leadership of Maulana Ahmed Riza Khan (1855–1921) in the late nineteenth century, is a case in point.[108] Maulana Ahmed Riza Khan was born in Bareilly in northern-central India (currently in Uttar Pradesh), undertook the traditional Dars-i-Nizami courses under the supervision of his father Maulana Naqi Ali, a scholar of hadith, and never attended any structured madrassah. At the age of fourteen he assumed the responsibility from his father for writing fatwas, and continued to do so for the rest of his life. He performed the hajj twice. Since his childhood, Riza Khan had demonstrated unique qualities, including an outstanding capacity for memorization and scholarship. In 1900, Maulana Ahmed Riza was proclaimed a *mujaddid* (renewer) of the fourteenth-century Hijri by like-minded ulama meeting in Patna. After several failed attempts to establish a madrassah, he succeeded in founding the Madrassah Manzar al-Islam in Bareilly in 1904. Another school, Darul Uloom Numaniyyah of Lahore, established in 1887, shared his thought and identified itself as Barelvi.

The defining characteristic of the Ahl-e-Sunnat wa Jama'at, as the name suggests, is the claim that it alone truly represents the *sunnah* (the Prophetic tradition and conduct), and thereby the true Sunni Muslim tradition. Despite the fact that Barelvis are adherents of the Hanafi madhab, like the Deobandis, they differ on issues such as the acceptance of Sufi tradition, respect for the saints, and traditional practices. While Deobandis are opposed to these, Barelvis encourage these practices: "A major part of the theological literature of Ahmad [Riza] Khan was directed at proving that the mystical practices of the Barelwis as spiritual mentors and guides (*pir*) were in consonance with Islamic law or prophetic tradition."[109]

The differences of opinion turned into a bitter fight in the late nineteenth and early twentieth centuries, when Deobandis and Barelvis engaged in a fatwa war. In 1906, Ahmed Riza issued a fatwa accusing leading figures at Deoband—including the founders of the madrassah, Rashid Ahmed Gangohi, Muhammad Qasim Nanautawi, and Ashraf Ali Thanvi—of being leaders of *kafir* (infidel or nonbeliever, pl. *kuffar*). They were also termed Wahhabis (the followers of the Arabian puritanical reformer Muhammad ibn Abd al-Wahhab). The Deobandi's countered Ahmed Riza's fatwa with one of their own, testifying that the Deobandis were the only Hanafi sunnis. Barlevis' vehement opposition to Deobandis and other contemporary reformists led Barbara Metcalf to conclude that the Barelvis were "an oppositional group as much as they were reformers."[110] In their madrassahs, Barelvis followed the Dars-i-Nizami curriculum, but added a significant number of texts on sufi tradition. Insofar as national politics are concerned, the Barelvis acted quite conservatively. While they opposed British colonial rule, they distanced themselves from mass movements such as the noncooperation movement of the 1920s supported by the Deobandis. The positions of Barelvis and Deobandis remained divergent and oppositional to each other in later years as well. Deobandis opposed the Pakistan movement, while Barelvis extended their support to the Muslim League.

The acrimonious relationship and high-profile debates, at times not so civil in nature, between the Deobandis and the Barelvis demonstrates that in the late nineteenth century a schism had become obvious within the Muslim community. Educational institutions became vehicles of incessant quarrel as much as they were places of intellectual endeavor toward a "true path." The primary objective of these madrassahs, therefore, was to define the true Muslimness and the role of the Muslim community at a critical juncture of history. Definitely the madrassahs were contributing to this redefinition and denominational differences, but that was not the only role played by the madrassahs. Instead, efforts were made to reconcile the differences and adopt a centrist path.

The most significant example of an effort to reconcile differences, to bring together various strands of intellectual accomplishments, and to transcend the denominational differences was the establishment of an association of scholars—Nadwatul Ulama (the Council of the Ulama) in 1893 under the leadership of Maulana Muhammad Ali Mungari (1846–1927).[111] Among the primary objectives of the council were reforming the curriculum and pedagogy of madrassahs, uniting the Muslim community on the basis of common concerns, and raising awareness of Muslim identity. The beginning was truly auspicious and unifying, as the council brought together representatives of almost all shades of opinion including the Shi'as, who otherwise were left out of Sunni initiatives of any kind. The organizers expected the council to be the bridge between the old ideas and the new realities, and thus create a common ground of activism for the entire community. But the hope of unity faded soon, as many groups parted, and Barelvis began a scathing attack on the council and its ideas. Undeterred by these criticisms, the leading members of the council decided to establish a madrassah in 1896, thus the Darul Uloom Nadwatul Ulama (in short Nadwa) came into existence. Later Shibli Numani, an eminent scholar who taught at the Muhammedan Anglo-Oriental College (commonly known as Aligarh College) for more than a decade, joined the Nadwa in 1905. Shibli Numani joined the madrassah almost ten years after its founding, but is considered the inspiration behind the council and the madrassah.

Although the Nadwa maintained a close relationship with the Deobandi ulama and expected to have active support from the Western-educated elites, the institution did not succeed in becoming the all-inclusive institution the founders wanted it to be. The Nadwa was successful in rekindling interest in Arabic as a medium of instruction, as opposed to Urdu—a language popularized by the Deoband Madrassah. The Nadwa's efforts to underscore the importance of Arabic were due to its connections with the Arabic-speaking ulama, particularly the Egyptian reformists. Numani, during his trip to the Middle East and North Africa in 1892, met these reformists. It is often argued that his idea of educational reform was influenced by Muhammad Abduh (1849–1905), a prominent Salafist.[112] Nadwa's connection with Salafists continued even after Numani left the school. In the mid-twentieth century, the Nadwa collaborated with the Egyptian Salafists in bringing out an Arabic journal to record their contribution to the ideals of Salafiyya.

The library built for the Nadwa, and its rich collection, were testimony to an emphasis on the intellectual tradition of Islamic knowledge more than on activism. Despite, or perhaps because of, the ambitious nature of the project it did not succeed as well as was expected.

The curriculum and pedagogy of the Darul Uloom Nadwatul Ulama incorporated many of the changes the reformist ulama were arguing for. Inclusion of modern history, spoken Arabic in the curriculum, and encouragement of intellectual debate instead of memorization and blind adherence to the teachers' views were among these changes. However, "the outlook remained largely conservative and modestly open."[113] The reform measures faltered and finally came to a halt after the departure of Shibli Numani in 1913, although the madrassah continued to exist and enjoy a certain degree of respect and influence in India.

CONCLUSION

The preceding historical narrative demonstrates that madrassah as a concept and as an institution has traversed a long way, that its contents and contours have undergone changes, and that as an institution it largely remained embedded within the society. The demands of the Muslim community, depending on time and location, have played a significant role in the making of the madrassahs. The history of South Asian madrassahs reminds us that there is no single pattern of interaction between the madrassah and the state and/or society; for example, madrassahs have received state patronage at one point and the wrath of state power on another.

Since their inception as distinct institutions, madrassahs have been sites of contestation, primarily between denominational differences within Islamic thought—whether between Shi'a and Sunni, or between various madhabs of Sunnis. In late-nineteenth-century India, the debate further narrowed to various subgroups (or *mashlaks*, paths) within the same madhab (for example, the debate between Deobandis and Barelvis, who belonged to the same Hanafi school of thought). The acrimony notwithstanding, some kind of dynamism, that is, continuous efforts to keep the institution relevant to the contemporaneous intellectual debates and offer interpretation of the classical texts in light of the new situation, was evident.

The lessons from the history of madrassah in South Asia during the colonial era are instructive in many ways. Their nature and scope was shaped not only by the internal dynamics of the Muslim community, but also by the policies of the colonial administration, the challenges from other communities—such as Christian missionaries and the Arya Samaj—and the desire of the Muslim community to be part of the emerging political system, to name but a few.

Political activism of the madrassahs and the ulama, the products of the madrassahs, were driven by the urge to define and redefine the identity of the community, especially under adverse circumstances. Aside from their success or failure, these developments created the background against which came the independence of India in 1947. The change also partitioned the subcontinent, and a new country—Pakistan—emerged. In the following chapters I examine the trajectories of the madrassahs in three successor nation-states: Pakistan, India, and Bangladesh after 1947.

CHAPTER 3

PAKISTAN

THE MADRASSAH AS A MIRROR OF SOCIETY

The defining features of madrassahs in contemporary Pakistan are their close connections with political activism, their transformation into institutions of indoctrination from predominantly educational institutions, and their interplay with national and international politics. An intimate relationship between madrassahs and politics is not new in South Asia, as the history of madrassah education discussed in the previous chapter has demonstrated. Since the late nineteenth century in colonial South Asia, madrassahs have played a significant role in the political process, including the anti-colonial struggle; but the tie between politics and madrassahs as witnessed in Pakistan over the last three decades is not a continuation of this tradition; instead, it has taken a new shape. This relationship has been forged under different circumstances and has been propelled by varied dynamics almost three decades after the country came into existence. Therefore, understanding Pakistani madrassahs—their nature, scope, and roles—requires closer examination of domestic political dynamics and the interaction of the Pakistani state with the global political system. Domestic constraints, the external compulsions imposed on the Pakistani state, the choices made by the elites of the society, and the ulama's perception of their roles have shaped the contours and the content of madrassahs in Pakistan. Thus, the interplay of the madrassah and politics in Pakistan is multilayered and multifaceted.

CATEGORIES AND ORGANIZATION OF MADRASSAHS

Madrassahs in Pakistan usually come into existence as a result of local initiatives, often by local devout Muslims and philanthropists, and tend to center on mosques, but that does not mean that they remain completely autonomous. Instead, most of the madrassahs are affiliated with one of the five national boards (*wafaq*). Of these, four are organized according to sects and schools of thoughts, while the fifth board is associated with the prominent Islamist political party—the Jamaat-i-Islami Pakistan (JIP). Based on their affiliation, the madrassahs in Pakistan can be categorized into five types.

There are three Sunni madrassah boards: the Wafaq al-Madaris al-Arabia (Deobandi tradition, established in 1955), the Tanzim al-Madaris al-Arabia (Barelvi tradition, established in 1959), and the Wafaq al-Madaris al-Salafia (Ahl-e-Hadith tradition, established in 1959, initially named the Markaz-e-Jamiat-Ahl-e-Hadith). Shi'a madrassahs are under the Wafaq al-Madaris (Shi'a) Pakistan (established in 1959, originally named the Majlis-e-Nazarat-e-Shi'a Madaris-e-Arabia). The fifth board—the Rabat al-Madaris al-Islamia (established in 1983)—is a suprasectarian umbrella organization.

Until the early eighties, the affiliation of madrassahs with one or another board was a matter of choice. Since 1983/84, it has become a de facto requirement, because without affiliation a madrassah cannot award an officially recognized *shahadah al-alamiyaah* degree. Although the lower degrees awarded by madrassahs have not been recognized as equivalent to any general education degrees, in 1982 the University Grants Commission (UGC) recognized the shahadah al-alamiyaah as equivalent to a master's in Arabic or Islamic Studies.[1] It is worth mentioning that the UGC has little control over these boards with regard to the curriculum and texts used in the courses.

Table 3.1 documents the number of madrassahs affiliated with these boards in 1988. As is evident from these figures, Deobandi madrassahs were high in number, and spread throughout the country, with the largest numbers of the Deobandi madrassahs located in North West Frontier Province (NWFP). The largest concentration of the Barelvi madrassahs was in the Punjab. The pattern is still true to date.

The salient feature of these boards is that while national in scope, with one exception they are organized along strict denominational lines. These educational boards are meant to design curricula and syllabi for affiliated institutions, to conduct examinations, and award the *sanads* (diplomas) to the graduating students of these madrassahs, but these are often treated as secondary responsibilities. In practice, their primary responsibility lies with representing the interests of madrassahs at the national level, particularly in relation to state policies that may have a bearing on them, and fostering denominational or sectarian interests within society.

The denominational nature of these boards can be traced back to the circumstances of their emergence. Three of the boards emerged as a direct response to the government's reform initiatives in the late fifties (see details in chapter 6), but their emergence is also linked to their goal to define and preserve their own distinct identity vis-à-vis other madrassahs. The emergence of the board representing the Deobandi madrassahs in the mid-fifties, the first of

TABLE 3.1

CLASSIFICATION OF MADRASSAHS BY REGION AND SECT IN PAKISTAN, 1988

	Deobandi	Barelvi	Ahl-e-Hadith	Shi'a	Other	Total
Punjab	590	548	118	21	43	1,320
NWFP	631	32	5	2	8	678
Sindh	208	61	6	10	6	291
Balochistan	278	34	3	1	31	347
A.J. Kashmir	51	20	2	—	3	76
Islamabad	22	20	—	2	3	47
Northern areas	60	2	27	11	2	102
Total	1840	717	161	47	96	2861

Source: Government of Pakistan, *Deeni Madaris Pakistan ki Jam'e Report 1988*.
Madrassahs listed under "other" include but are not limited to the Jamaat-i-Islami-
affiliated madrassahs.

its kind, was in some measure an attempt to gain a foothold within the newly
founded country. It is well to bear in mind that the Deobandi ulema opposed
the Pakistan movement.

Close observations of the operation of these boards reveal that they gener-
ously bestow degrees on students of their own sects and usually degrees are
awarded without any examination.[2] The requirements for affiliation include
the payment of a small fee (between 500 and 2000 Pakistani rupees) and a
letter of declaration from the manager of the madrassah. There is no institutional mechanism within these boards for regular monitoring of these affiliated madrassahs.

CURRICULUM OF MADRASSAHS: DIFFERENCES AND SIMILARITIES

The common understanding that the madrassahs in Pakistan follow the traditional Dars-i-Nizami curriculum is only partially true. This is because on the
one hand the Dars-i-Nizami curriculum itself has undergone some revisions
over time, while on the other, the Pakistani madrassahs do not strictly follow
a standardized curriculum. However, the essential elements of the curriculum
adopted by a large number of the madrassahs can be identified as variants of
the Dars-i-Nizami.

Madrassahs in Pakistan offer an eight- or sixteen-year course of study. The
length depends on the level at which the student is enrolled. The curriculum is
commonly divided into six stages (see table 3.2).

TABLE 3.2

STAGES OF MADRASSAH EDUCATION AND GENERAL EDUCATION IN PAKISTAN

Level in madrassah system	Duration	Sanad (diploma)	General education grade/certificate
Ibtidayee (Nazara)	4 to 5 years	Shahadatul Tahfeez ul-Qur'an	primary, 5th grade
Mutawawassat (Hifz)	3 years	Shahadatul Mutawassat	middle, 8th grade
Sanawiya Amma (Tazvid, Qeerat)	2 years	Shahadatul Sanawiya ul-Amma	matric, 10th grade
Sanwiya Khasa (Tahtini)	2 years	Shahadatul Sanawiya Khasa	intermediate, FA
Aliya, Mohafequl Khasa wa Sada	2 years	Shahadatul Aliya	bachelor's, BA
Alamiya, Daura-e-Hadith Sabia wa Saniya	2 years	Shahadatul Alamiya	master's

Source: C. Christine Fair, "Islamic Education in Pakistan."

The primary stage is often taken care of by the maktabs, which may or may not be a part of a madrassah offering higher stages. In the primary stage, the students are introduced to recitation of the Qur'an and encouraged to memorize important verses. Some maktabs/madrassahs also teach basic literacy to the students. Traditional and less institutionalized maktabs/madrassahs, however, concentrate only on recitation. The memorization of the Qur'an in its entirety is the principal task in the *hifz* or *mutawawassat* stage. In recent years, some madrassahs have introduced courses on Pakistan studies, history, geography, and similar subjects. Most of the madrassahs do not have any infrastructure to teach science subjects. *Tazvid* and *qeerat* are various modes of Qur'an recitation. The latter comprises seven standardized modes of recitation. Successful completion of these seven modes of recitation makes one a *qari*, which offers a career and prestige.

While the six-stage madrassah system is predominant, some madrassahs divide these stages differently. The Jamia Binoria, SITE Town in Karachi, is a case in point. Established in 1978, the madrassah has eighteen branches in Karachi and another in the United States.[3] The Jamia has adopted the system shown in table 3.3.

Since the early eighties, various madrassah boards have included some "secular" subjects in their curricula. For example, the Wafaq al-Madaris

TABLE 3.3

LEVELS OF DEGREES AND COURSES OF STUDIES
AT JAMIA BINORIA, SITE TOWN, KARACHI

Level	Duration	Degree	Equivalence
Basic level of learning by heart (Hifzul A'dadia)		witness of learning	primary level
Level Tajveed-ul-Qur'an (reading the Holy Qur'an with proper phonetic sounds)	1 year	certificate of tajveed	basic level
Middle	1 year	degree/ certification: witness certificate of middle.	middle/lower secondary level
Lower-middle secondary	2 years	certificate of secondary (general)	matriculation/ secondary level
Intermediate special	2 years	certificate of intermediate special-higher secondary	higher secondary/ intermediate level
Higher (graduation-bachelor)	2 years	certificate of graduation	bachelor's degree
Post-graduate	2 years	certification of alimia in Arabic and Islamic science	master's degree

Source: Personal communication with Jamia Binoria, SITE TOWN, Karachi, 2007.

al-Arabia curriculum requires its students up to grade eight to learn Urdu, social studies, and arithmetic. The Tanzim al-Madaris al-Arabia requires history, geography, arithmetic, geometry, and astronomy to be taught at various levels in madrassahs. The Wafaq al-Madaris al-Salafia curriculum lists English, Pakistan studies, general science, and general mathematics courses as requirements for its students up to grade ten. In the level equivalent to FA (grades eleven and twelve leading to a diploma commonly referred to as intermediate), the students are required to take courses on economics and civics, and in the level equivalent to the bachelor's degree, the students are required to complete a course on political science. According to the documents of these boards, madrassahs are supposed to use the books prescribed by the national textbook board in teaching these secular subjects, to ensure that the students are acquiring knowledge equivalent to the government-run schools. Although these requirements are listed on paper, small madrassahs, particularly those which offer up to *tahtini* (intermediate/FA) level seldom offer these courses.

Some observers of Pakistani madrassah education insist that "after passing the mutawawassat-level, students have studied not just those subjects that are taught to their peers up to the matric level in government-run and private schools but have also acquired additional education in Islamic Studies and Persian."[4] Attainment of this level of education from madrassahs in Pakistan is the exception rather than the rule.

Notwithstanding the variations, the typical curriculum of the Pakistani madrassahs has some common elements. An eight-year curriculum includes the subjects shown in table 3.4. Through the entire period of study, up to the master's level, the subjects covered are as follows: Qur'anic studies (*uloom ul-Qu'ran*),

TABLE 3.4

TYPICAL CURRICULUM OF A PAKISTANI MADRASSAH

Year 1	biography of the Prophet (syrat), conjugation-grammar (sarf), syntax (nahv), Arabic literature, chirography (khush-navisi), chant illation (tajvid)
Year 2	conjugation-grammar, syntax, Arabic literature, jurisprudence (fiqh), logic, chirography (khush-navisi), chant illation
Year 3	Qur'anic exegesis (analysis of text), jurisprudence, syntax, Arabic literature, hadith, logic, Islamic Brotherhood, chant illation, external study (Tareekh Millat and Khilafat-e-Rashida—these are Indian Islamic movements).
Year 4	Qur'anic exegesis, jurisprudence, principles of jurisprudence, rhetoric, hadith, logic, history, chant illation, modern sciences (sciences of cities of Arabia, geography of the Arab Peninsula and other Islamic countries)
Year 5	Qur'anic exegesis, jurisprudence, principles of jurisprudence, rhetoric, beliefs (aqa'id), logic, Arabic literature, chant illation, external study (history of Indian kings)
Year 6	interpretation of the Qu'ran, jurisprudence, principles of interpretation and jurisprudence, Arabic literature, philosophy, chant illation, study of Prophet's traditions
Year 7	sayings of the Prophet, jurisprudence, belief, responsibility (fra'iz), chant illation, external study (Urdu texts)
Year 8	Ten books by various authors focusing on the sayings of the Prophet

Source: Uzma Aznar, "Islamic Education: A Brief History of Madrassas with Comments on Curricula and Pedagogical Practices," 15–16.

studies related to tradition, that is, hadith (*uloom ul-hadith*), phraseology of hadith (*mustalih al-hadith*), Islamic jurisprudence (*uloom ul-fiqh il-Islami*), principles about the jurisprudence of Islam (*uloom ul-usool ul-fiqh*), studies of faith about hidden facts (*uloom ul-kalaarn*), life and character of the Prophet (*uloom ul-seerat un-nabawiyyah*), Islamic history (*uloom ul-tareekh ul-Islam*), Arabic literature (*uloom ul-adab il-arabi*), etymology and syntax (*uloom ul-nahw was sarf*), meaning and rhetoric (*uloom ul-ma'aani wal balaaghah*), comparative study of religions and sects (*uloom ul-maqarinat ul-adiyaan wal firaq*), arithmetic (*'ilm ul-hisaab*), economics (*uloom ul-ma'aashiyaat*), political science (*uloom us-siyaasiyaat*), etc.

The list of the subjects mentioned above is provided by the Jamia Farooqia of Karachi. The Jamia, established in 1967, is considered an important Islamic educational institution within the country. It has about 2,300 students and is headed by Shiakhul Hadith Maulana Salimullah Khan. Maulana Salimullah Khan, a graduate of Deoband, is also the president of the Wafaq al-Madaris al-Arabia Pakistan. Thus, there are a number of madrassahs that replicate the syllabus followed in this institution. The fundamental elements of their curricula, according to authorities of the Jamia, are "the education of Qur'an, hadith, and fiqh."

Some well-known jamias offer studies beyond the master's level and describe them as "specialization." "The 'specialization' system has not yet come under the wifaq" and has no standardized curriculum.[5] The programs vary in terms of length of study and focus. The Jamia Farooqia of Karachi, for example, offers two of these specialized curricula. They are called *takhassusaat* (specialization in various fields, for two years); and *ma'had* (a separate system of Islamic studies in Arabic language, for six years).

The Jamia Binoria, SITE Town, Karachi, has a sixteen-year curriculum that includes various "secular" subjects including English and mathematics (table 3.5).

Although most of the Pakistani madrassahs use Urdu as the medium of instruction, some variations are present: in the Pashto-speaking parts of North West Frontier Province (NWFP), Pashto is used, while Sindhi is used in the madrassahs of Sindh. However, as Tariq Rahman underscored in his study of language teaching in the Pakistani madrassahs, Arabic and Persian, particularly the former, have a special place in madrassah education. These languages are taught because they facilitate mastery of the religion and because they are necessary for an alim. Rahman further states, "the Arabic books are often those which were used in the medieval age and were prescribed later by Mullah Nizamuddin Sehalvi in the middle of the 18th century. . . . The oldest books are in Arabic, then come books in Arabic with an explanation in Persian and the most modern texts explain in Urdu."[6] It is well to bear in mind that languages taught in the madrassahs, whether Arabic or Persian, are not taught

TABLE 3-5

EDUCATIONAL COURSES AT JAMIA BINORIA, SITE TOWN, KARACHI

	the Holy Qur'an	teachings (diniyat)	writing	arithmetic/mathematics	English
1st year	the Holy Qur'an: Noorani Qaida: Yesernal Qur'an, Islamic	teachings (diniyat): first kalima (kalima tayyaba), second kalima (kalima-e-shahadat), sana (eulogy) with translation	writing (hand writing): Urdu qaida, Urdu kitab, Urdu for Jamat Awal	arithmetic: units writing, numbers writing up to 100	English alphabet: ABC
2nd year	the Holy Qur'an: recitation of the last section (paragraph); learning the last ten chapters by heart	Islamic teachings (diniyat): nimaz (prayer).	Urdu writing: Urdu kitab class 2	Arithmetic: compound number writing, class 2 mathematics	English: *My Children* (book).
3rd year	the Holy Qur'an: recitation of the first 5 sections (paragraphs)	Islamic teachings (diniyat): Hanifite prayers except sermons and verses	Urdu writing.	arithmetic: dictation of compounds, mathematics class 3	English: Faisal/English books #1
4th year	the Holy Qur'an: from section 6 to 15 recitation	Islamic teachings: teachings of Islam (taleem-ul-Islam) part 1	Urdu writing: Urdu book class 4	mathematics: writing words; mathematics for class 4	English: Faisal/English books #2
5th year	the Holy Qur'an: from section 16 to the last, recitation	Islamic teachings: teachings of Islam (taleem-ul-Islam) part 2	Urdu writing: Urdu book for class 5, dictation and oral	mathematics: mathematics for class 5	English: Faisal/English books #3

	Qur'an exercise	Islamic teachings	Urdu	Persian	math	social science	English
6th year	Exercise in learning of the Holy Qur'an: Section one—derivation of basic roots	teachings of Islam part 3; Arabic book for class 6 Islamic teachings and Arabic language	Urdu writing: Urdu book for class 6; writing from Urdu book for Islam	Persian: *Rehbar Farsi* (guide to Persian); *Karima*		social science: social science for class 6	English: English for class 6
7th year	exercise in the Holy Qur'an and phonology: from section 11 to 20; property of words	Islamic teachings and Arabic: teachings of Islam part 4, Arabic book for class seven	Urdu writing: Urdu book for class seven; dictation from Urdu book	Persian: *Pundnama Gulistan-e-Sa'adi* chapters 1 to 4		social science: social science for class 7	English: English for class 7
8th year	exercise in the Holy Qur'an and phonology: from section (paragraph) 21 to the last: explanation of hidden meanings	Islamic teachings: character and language Arabic, *Behashti Gohar*, personality of the Prophet in Urdu, Arabic book for class 8	Urdu writing: Urdu book for class 8, dictation from Urdu book	Persian: *Gulistan Sa'adi*, chapters 7–8, *Bostan* chapter 1	math: math for class 8	social science: social science for class 8	English: English for class 8
9th year	exercise and phonology: beauties of the Holy Qur'an (*jamal-ul-Qur'an*) section 30 last quarter; exercise in phonetic recitation: section 30 the last quarter	traditions and personality of the Prophet: benevolent for the words (Rahmal-ul-Al-ameen)	grammar: statement of grammar	syntax: syntax *mir*, explanation (guide) *Maat-al-Amil* Arabic language and essay writing; modern style/present style.		tamreen: *Seeghoon ki Tamreen*	English: English for classes 9 and 10

(continued)

Table 3.5. Educational Courses at Jamia Binoria, SITE Town, Karachi *(continued)*

10th year	exegesis and phonology: translation and explanation of section 30, Makkimerits *(Fawaidal Makkia)*: exercise section 30 third quarter	traditions of the Holy Prophet: *Zadal-al-Talibeen*	*al-Qural ul-Rashida*: Arabic language and essay writing		part 1: essay teacher *(Moalim-ul-Insha)*, part 1	grammar: gift of grammar *(Hadyat-ul-Neyhave)*	logic: *Teeseer-ul-Muntaq, Essem Ghoti; Marqat.*
11th year	explanation of the Holy Qur'an and traditions of the Holy Prophet: translations and explanations from chapters. The Spider al-Ankabut # 29 to # 77; those sent forth al-Murslat; *Riyaz-ul-saleheen, kitab al adab, kitab al fasail*	jurisprudence: *Kinaldeqaiq*	principles of jurisprudence; principles of al-Shathi grammar; *Kafia, Sharan ibn Aqeel*	logic: *Sharah Tahzeeb*	Arabic language and essay writing: *Nafhat-ul-Arab*	*Moalim-ul-Insha*, part 2	phonetics: *Muqadmat-il-Jazriah*
12th year	exegesis of the Holy Qur'an from chapter 10: Jonah-Yunus to the Spider #2 (al-Ankabut); the traditions of the Holy Prophet; *Riyaz-ul-*	jurisprudence: guide *Waqiah Awalain*	principles of jurisprudence: *Noor-ul-Anwar* to Qiyas	grammar: guide *Jami* to *Mubniyat*	logic: up to *Aske-Nageidh*		Arabic language and essay writing: *Muqamat-e-Harari* (10 essays); *Moalim-ul-Insha*, part 3

Saleheeem (Kitab-ul-Dawa, Kitab-ul-Azkar).

13th year	exegesis of the Holy Qur'an from chapter 1: the opening al-Faleha to Jovah; jurisprudence: *Noor-ul-Anwar* from (conceiving) Hasami (kitab *Sunnat-ul-Ajmal*).; eulogy: short meanings; logic: *Salam-ul-Aloom*; *Tawwarat*; Arabic language: collection of mutnab up to the end of *Qafia ul Haya*
14th year	exegesis: *Galaleen Sharif* (complete); traditions of the Holy prophet: *Kitabul Asars*; jurisprudence: *Hadiayah*, vol. 2; principles of jurisprudence; philosophy and faith: *Maybaz*, *Shaht-ul-aqaid*; Arabic language and al-Faroodh: collection of *Hamsa*, around the circle
15th year	exegesis: *Tafseer-e-Baidhavi* (commentary by Baidhavi), part 1, first quarter.; principles of exegesis: *al-Fauzal Kabir*; hadith: *Mishkat Sharif*; principles of hadith: *Nakhkat-ul-fikr*
16th year (hadith only)	hadith: *Bukhari Sharif* (complete); hadith: *Muslim Sharif* (complete); hadith: *Tirmizi Sharif* (complete); hadith: *Abu-Dand Sharif* (complete); hadith: *Nisai Sharif*, *Ibn-e-Majh*, *Shamial Tirmizi*; jurisprudence: (a) *Hidayah*, vol. 3; (b) *Hidayah*, vol. 4; hadith: *Tahavi Sharif*, *Muta Imam, Malik*, *Muta Imam Mohammad*

Source: Personal communication, Jamia Binoria, SITE TOWN, Karachi, Pakistan, 2007.

as a living language, but rather through rote memorization of texts written a long time ago:

> The student is made to memorize the rhymed couplets from the ancient texts as well as their explanations. As the explanations in a number of texts are in Persian, which is also memorized, the student generally fails to apply his knowledge to the living language. Some ancient texts, such as the *Mizbah-ul-Nahv*, are explained in Urdu. But in this case the Urdu is much Arabicized. The explanation is scholastic and would not be understood by, let alone convince, somebody who is not familiar with the special branch of medieval Islamic philosophy on which it is based.[7]

The use of Arabic language and memorization of classical Arabic and Persian texts are common to madrassahs of all sects.

THE NUMBER OF MADRASSAHS: KNOWN, UNKNOWN, AND UNKNOWABLE

On 20 March 2003, Christina Rocca, assistant secretary of state for South Asian affairs, and Wendy J. Chamberlin, assistant administrator of USAID, appeared before the U.S. House of Representatives' Committee on International Relations to discuss the U.S.-Pakistan relationship. During the hearing the issue of Pakistani madrassahs came up, and the following exchanges took place between Representative Nick Smith of Michigan, Ms. Rocca, and Ms. Chamberlin.

> MR. SMITH: Specifically, are there still madrasas out there? How many of them are there? How is that changing? I know it is a long process, but are we making progress?
> MS. ROCCA: There certainly are madrassas out there. There are, I believe, 600, and somebody can jump on me if there are more than that.
> MS. CHAMBERLIN: Thousands.
> MS. ROCCA: Thousands in Pakistan? Okay. There are thousands in Pakistan, and they are still operating, and it is still a problem.[8]

This conversation, particularly the huge difference between two U.S. officials in regard to the estimated number of madrassahs in Pakistan, is indicative of the problem one faces in ascertaining the exact number of madrassahs in Pakistan. The numbers of madrassahs and of students enrolled in these institutions have been a matter of serious contention, and consequently the rate of growth has been debated at various levels.

The total reported number of madrassahs has varied widely: from an unbelievable low of 600 to a highly exaggerated 50,000.[9] Media reports (discussed in chapter one) and various studies since 11 September 2001 have either uncritically accepted a number reported by others or invented a new set of numbers.

Therefore, the total number of students enrolled in these institutions and their share of the total school-going population has also varied. Reports have suggested the total number of students from 650,000 to 7.5 million, and their share of total enrollment from 10 percent to 47 percent.

The most quoted numbers since 2002 have been drawn from the International Crisis Group (ICG) report, which estimated 10,000 institutions, and between 1 million and 1.7 million students enrolled in these madrassahs.[10] Based on their computation that 1.7 million students were enrolled in the mainstream educational institutions, the report concluded that between 33 percent (1 million/2.9 million) and 47 percent (1.7 million/3.6 million) of the school-going population are enrolled in madrassahs. The number of madrassah students was provided by the minister for religious affairs, and the number of total students in the country was derived from Finance Ministry documents. But it was later discovered that the total number of students enrolled, according to the Finance Ministry documents, is 19.2 million. Thus the share of the madrassah students, when the error was corrected, came down to 8 percent at the high end (1.7 million/20.9 million) or 5 percent at the low end (1 million/20 million).

In 2005, three years after the ICG report was published, Andrabi et al. questioned the reliability of these estimates of students enrolled. Using four sets of data derived from the 1998 Census of Pakistan and three waves of Pakistan Integrated Household Surveys (PIHS, conducted in 1991, 1998, and 2001) they concluded that the total enrollment is close to 1 percent of total school-going children in Pakistan, roughly about 475,000 students.[11]

The study by Andrabi et al., despite attracting enormous media coverage and public attention, presented a figure that is unrealistic, to say the least, and close reading of the study reveals that the number is bound to be higher. The reasons are as follows: first, none of these surveys (census and PIHS) was designed to gather data on madrassah enrollment. The census survey asks about the "field of education" of the respondent but not the specific nature of students' institutions. Second, Christopher Candland rightly noted that the base figure of total students (19 million) provided in government documents should be treated with caution, because it fails to take into account dropouts, which is as high as 50 percent by grade five. Additionally, the household surveys are open to statistical manipulation.[12]

In addition to the four secondary sources, Andrabi et al. used their own survey of three districts in Punjab (Learning and Achievement in Punjab Schools, LEAPS survey). The data from these three districts show the enrollment as high as three times that shown in the households and census surveys. "Their survey was restricted to areas served by public schools and thus probably underestimates madaris enrollments for Pakistan as a whole, which is poorly served by public schools."[13]

There are several reasons for the discrepancy in reported numbers. First, madrassahs in Pakistan are privately operated institutions. As noted before, they are supervised by five boards with very little monitoring by the government. Record keeping of these boards is not free from errors. Moreover, these numbers may be inflated by the respective boards to demonstrate their appeal to the students. Second, until recently there has been almost no academic interest in these institutions.[14] Discussions on madrassahs have been limited to Islamists and ulama, who tend to generate polemical literature, primarily in defense of these institutions. Thus there has been very little empirical data available. Third, government surveys on madrassahs have been sporadic and inconsistent (recent surveys include a 1979 survey by the Ministry of Religious Affairs, and two surveys—in 1988 and in 2000—by the Ministry of Education). Not only has the reliability of these data been suspect, none of these survey reports referred to previous reports to illustrate any trends. Additionally, these numbers present a skewed picture because they only represent the madrassahs registered with the government, whereas most madrassahs are not registered with any government agencies. Fourth, as registration of madrassahs takes place at the district level, using forms only available in paper copy format, the data regarding the registered madrassahs are not available at the national level––there is no central database of registered madrassahs.[15]

These shortcomings and the recent controversy notwithstanding, one can discern a pattern of growth in madrassahs from various reported figures over time. Given enormous interest in this issue after 9/11, a tendency to exaggerate the figures on the part of the popular media is understandable. But closer examination of various sources—before and after 2001—reveals some consistency among these figures and a trend depicting a high rate of proliferation.

The areas that constitute present-day Pakistan had 137 madrassahs before the independence of the country. According to one account, the number of madrassahs in 1947 was 245. In any case, the number began to climb after 1947. Throughout the sixties, while the country was ruled by military ruler Ayub Khan, often credited for having a secular outlook, there was a remarkable increase in the number of madrassahs, which reached 908 in 1971.[16] The increase in the population and consequent demand for Islamic education, particularly in the rural areas, provide a plausible explanation to this growth. But it still had taken more than a decade for the number of madrassahs to almost double, from 472 in 1960 to 908 in 1971. In 1979 the total number was 1,745, more than double what it had been in 1975, when the total number was 868; and the most dramatic increase occurred after 1979. The corresponding figures for 1988 and 1997 are 2,861 and 5,500, respectively. The 2003 figure stands at 7,000 (table 3.6). Clearly, there has been a phenomenal increase in madrassahs since independence. Between 1947 and 2001, a 2,745 percent increase over 55 years, or

TABLE 3.6

MADRASSAHS IN PAKISTAN, 1947–2006

Year	Number of madrassahs
Pre-1947	137
1947	245
1950	210
1956	249
1960	472
1971	908
1975	868
1979	1,745
1980	2,056
1982	1,896
1984	1,953
1986	2,261
1988	2,861
1995	3,906
1997	5,500
2000	6,761
2001	6,870
2002	6,582
2003	7,000
2006	13,500

Sources: Pre-1947 statistics are from Hafiz Nadhr Ahmad, "A Preliminary Survey of Madaris-e-Deeniyah in East and West Pakistan"; 1947, 1988, and 2000 figures are from the Institute of Policy Studies, "Pakistan: Religious Education Institutions, An Overview"; 1947, 1988, 2001, and 2003 figures are from Hasan Mansoor, "Pakistan Sees 2745 Percent Increase in Seminaries since 1947"; 1950, 1960, 1971, 1984, and 1986 figures are from Mumtaz Ahmad, "Madrassa Education in Pakistan and Bangladesh"; 1975 figure is from Nasir Jamal, "Religious Schools: "Who Controls What They Teach?"; 1979 and 1982 figures are from Jamal Malik, *Colonization of Islam: Dissolution of Traditional Institutions in Pakistan*, 180; and 1995 figure is from International Crisis Group, *Pakistan: Madrasas, Extremism and the Military*; 2006 figure is from "Most Madrasas Now Registered, Says Aziz".

(continued)

Table 3.6. Madrassahs in Pakistan, 1947–2006 *(continued)*

Notes: In 2002, a press report suggested the number of registered madrassahs as 6,582 (Zulfiqar Ali, "EU Ready to Help Madrassas"), but Tariq Rahman insists that the total number is 9,880 (Tariq Rahman, *Denizens of Alien Worlds: A Study of Education, Inequality and Polarization in Pakistan*, Annexure 4, 190–191), a figure close to the government sources provided to the International Crisis Group (*Pakistan: Madrasas, Extremism and the Military*, 2). As for 1996, Nasir Jamal ("Religious Schools: "Who Controls What They Teach?") reported the total number at 8,000. Of 13,500 madrassahs, by mid-2006 a total of 12,176 were registered with the government, according to the Ministry of Religious Affairs (*Year Book 2005–2006*, 18).

on average 120 schools per year, came into existence. From 1988 to 2000, the number has increased by 236 percent.[17]

By Ahmed Rashid's account, whereas 870 madrassahs were set up in the first twenty-eight years of independence (1947–1975), about 1,700 new madrassahs came into being in the fourteen years between 1976 and 1990.[18] A. H. Nayyar, however, provides different figures.[19] According to his account, between 1947 and 1960 the number of new madrassahs established was 488; between 1960 and 1980 the number was 1,445, and between 1980 and 1987 the number was 684 (table 3.7).

The regional breakdown shows that the largest number of madrassahs is located in the province of Punjab, while North West Frontier Province

TABLE 3.7

NEW MADRASSAHS IN PAKISTAN, 1947–1987
(Numbers in parentheses show the average number of new madrassahs per year.)

	1947	1947–1960	1960–1980	1980–1987
Punjab	121	195 (15)	620 (31)	384 (55)
NWFP	59	87 (7)	426 (21)	106 (15)
Sindh	21	66 (5)	156 (8)	48 (7)
Balochistan	28	131 (10)	131 (5)	57 (8)
"Azad" Kashmir	4	4 (.3)	39 (2)	29 (4)
Islamabad		1	26 (1)	20 (3)
Northern areas	12	4 (.3)	47 (2)	40 (6)
Total				

Source: A. H. Nayyar, "Madrassah Education Frozen in Time," 232.

(NWFP) and Balochistan, two provinces bordering Afghanistan, have substantial numbers of madrassahs. The latter two provinces have seen more madrassahs established between 1979 and 1988. In NWFP, the number has increased from 218 in 1979 to 678 in 1988. Corresponding figures for Balochistan are 135 in 1979 and 347 in 1988 (table 3.8).

These figures support the conventional wisdom that the support of American and Pakistani security services for the Afghan mujahideen was a major driving force in the proliferation of madrassahs in Pakistan during the eighties. Andrabi et al., who are highly skeptical of the number of madrassah students suggested in various media, concur with this finding:

> The notion that the madrassa movement coincided with resistance to the Soviet invasion of Afghanistan is supported by the 1988 data from the population census. The increase in the stock of religiously educated individuals starts with the cohort that came of age in 1979 (the year of [the] Soviet invasion of Afghanistan) and the largest increase is the cohort co-terminus with the rise of the Taliban. Combined with the fact that the largest enrollment percentage in Pakistan is in [the] Pashtun belt bordering Afghanistan, this suggest events in neighboring Afghanistan influence madrassa enrollment.[20]

This development was funded by the U.S. taxpayers and the closest ally of the United States at that time—Saudi Arabia. Material support and encouragement

TABLE 3.8

REGIONAL BREAKDOWN OF MADRASSAHS IN PAKISTAN, PRE-1947–2000

	Pre-1947	1950	1979	1982	1988	2000
Punjab	87	137	1,012	910	1,320	3,153
NWFP	20	31	218	572	678	1,281
Sindh	19	25	380	277	291	905
Balochistan	7	11	135	59	347	692
"Azad" Kashmir	4	6	—	12	76	151
Islamabad	—	—		34	47	194
Northern areas	—	—		32	102	185
Total	137	210	1,745	1,896	2,861	6,561

Sources: Jamal Malik, *Colonization of Islam: Dissolution of Traditional Institutions in Pakistan*, 180, except figures for 1988 and 2000. For 1988 and 2000 figures, see Hasan Mansoor, "Pakistan Sees 2745 Percent Increase in Seminaries since 1947."

Note: In 2000, the total figures were reported to be 6,761. But 200 madrassahs remain unaccounted for in the regional breakdown.

came from the United States via the Pakistani government, especially its intelligence agency ISI (Inter Services Intelligence), and Saudi funds were disbursed through government channels and various nongovernmental organizations.

But these statistics also raise three pertinent questions. First, why has there been a progressive growth of madrassahs in Pakistan throughout its entire history? Second, does the U.S. support for the Afghan war alone explain the growth of madrassahs during the eighties? Third, how and why did the trend continue after the CIA abandoned its Afghanistan operation following the Soviet withdrawal in 1989?

Answers to these questions are far from simple––on the one hand they require an examination of the education sector of the country, while on the other hand the global politics that thrust the Pakistani state into a frontline position in turn led to these educational institutions that performed a particular role consistent with that of the state. The growth of madrassahs in Pakistan and the dramatic shift in their nature from seats of higher learning to citadels of militancy are related to a combination of factors. The convergence of the Iranian revolution and Soviet intervention in Afghanistan in 1979, the subsequent CIA-ISI nexus to create a band of militant Islamists, the Islamization program of the military regime of Zia-ul Huq (1977–1988) that began before these events took place in and around Pakistan, and the unremitting flow of external funding for ideology-based religious education that continued well after these events subsided are important in understanding the phenomenon. Add to these the sectarian nature of madrassah education in Pakistan, which provided the groundwork for this transformation. Here it is necessary to point out that relationships between these factors are by no means one way; instead they are symbiotic. Once they came in contact with each other, a new dynamic emerged that allowed mutual reinforcement, enabling the process to gain further momentum.

The Education Sector: Fragmented and Failed

The education system in Pakistan is broadly divided into five stages: primary, middle, secondary, higher secondary, and tertiary. Primary education is provided by primary-level institutions, and the total length of study is five years (grades one to five). Middle schools are of three years' duration (grades six to eight). Secondary education is imparted by high schools with grades nine and ten. At the end of this stage, the students sit for a standardized test, and successful candidates receive a degree called matric. This is followed by two years of higher secondary education, upon completion of which the students are awarded an intermediate degree. The tertiary or higher education level begins with the bachelor's degree, which can be earned after two years of college/university education. In the final stage, students can earn a master's degree from universities. Opportunities to move toward vocational or technical education start at intermediate level. At the bachelor's level, students can pursue engineering, medical, and other degrees.

All pre-university curricula are designed by the Federal Curriculum Wing of the Federal Education Ministry. The curriculum wing also issues guidelines to textbook writers and school teachers. The provinces have their own bureaus of curricula, which are primarily responsible to train school teachers. The provincial textbook boards publish and distribute textbooks and prepare the prescribed textbooks in the provinces under the guidance of the central government. The contents of textbooks must receive approval from the curriculum wing before being printed and distributed.

Out of the 153 million citizens of Pakistan, it is estimated that 60 million are children of school-going age.[21] The latest available figures, of 2002–2003, show that 23.945 million children are enrolled in public, private, and community schools.[22] This means that about 40.12 percent of children are currently attending school. In the age group that should start school, that is ages five through nine, the percentage of children out of school is comparable. Of a total 23.9 million children of this age group, only 9.6 million attend any school, leaving the remainder 14.3 million, a staggering 60 percent, without access to education.

The numbers, as they are, present a very dismal picture, yet they tell only one part of the story. The situation is worse for the poorer segment of the society. The education sector of the country reflects the stark inequality prevalent in Pakistan. To understand this disparity, three aspects of school enrollment should be borne in mind: first, the rate of enrollment is not evenly distributed among the social strata, and among the poor it is markedly lower; second, the rate is significantly lower in rural areas, where most of the Pakistani population lives; and third, enrollment figures for girls are particularly low.

The statistics provided by the Pakistan Integrated Household Survey (PIHS, 2001–2002) show that only 27 percent of children from the poorest segment of society, described as the first quintile (that is, with a per capita monthly income of 621 Pakistani rupees or below), go to school, while the share among the richest, described as the fifth quintile (that is, having a per capita monthly income of 1,255 Pakistani rupees and above), is 56 percent. Thus, the children of the poorest segment of society are much less likely to have access to education. For girls the likelihood of being deprived of education is far greater.

The World Bank in early 2007 pointed to these features, particularly in the context of the lack of gender parity:

> Gender gaps remain in schooling, largely due to the rural areas where only 22 percent of girls above age ten have completed primary level or higher schooling as compared to 47 percent boys. While the PSLSMS [the Pakistan Social and Living Standards Measurement Survey] indicates an improvement in Net Enrollment Rate (NER) and Gross Enrollment Rate (GER) from 42 to 72

percent respectively in 2001/02 and 52 percent to 86 percent respectively in 2004/05, it still indicates that almost half of the primary school age cohort is currently out of school. While elementary education GER has increased from 41 percent in 2000/02 to 46 percent in 2004/05, it remains far below the targets. Moreover, gender gaps remain large, especially for rural females. While the NER shows an insignificant gender gap in urban areas, NER for rural girls at 42 percent trails behind rural boys' NER of 53 percent.[23]

The picture becomes gloomier if the dropout rate by grade four, which is "nearly 40 percent of children belonging to the poorest quintile" is taken into account. "The comparable figure for children belonging to the richest quintile is only 12 percent."[24] What these statistics reveal is that poor children may not be able to go to school in the first place, and even if they begin they may soon be out of school. This is not incongruent with the overall thrust of the education system of the country.

Partly due to the colonial legacy and partly owing to the choice of the Pakistani political elites, both military and civilian, three streams of education have persisted in Pakistan since the inception of the country. They are: Urdu-medium mainstream public schooling, English-medium private education, and the madrassahs. These three streams cater to three distinctly different classes of the society: the Urdu- (and Sindhi-) medium public education serves the educational needs of the lower middle class and working classes, the English-medium schools are for the upper-middle class and the rich, and the madrassahs are for the rural poor class.[25] These streams, in large measures, remain separated throughout the rest of the education lifecycle, which consequently affects job prospects. Mashood Rizvi, the director of programs for the Sindh Educational Foundation, summarized this succinctly: "There are schools for the elite, and there are schools for the poor. The products of elite schools go back to elite circles, and the products of public school go back to the underprivileged classes. There is no possibility of traversing these [boundaries]."[26]

The cost of education and low budgetary allocation to education throughout the entire history of the nation are testimony to the fact the policy makers have opted for an educational system whereby only the rich can enjoy the benefits of modern education while the poorer sections are marginalized. Take the case of cost, for example. On average the annual tuition cost per student in Urdu-medium public schools is 2,265 Pakistani rupees, which is borne entirely by the state; the comparable figures for an elite English-medium school is 96,000 rupees, to be borne by the parents; and for cadet colleges or public schools it is 90,000 rupees, of which the state bears 15,000 rupees.[27] By contrast, for madrassah students the state contributes less than 2 rupees per student per year, while the remainder— 5,700 rupees (including lodging and food)—is borne by the madrassahs with contributions from religious organizations and philanthropists.[28] Except in the case of madrassahs, these figures are only for tuition fees. The numbers become much higher when the other expenses such as stationary, books, uniforms, and transport are added. Under these circumstances, the madrassahs, which provide not only schooling but also lodging and food, have seemed an attractive alternative, particularly for poorer families with a number of children.

Public investment in human capital—health and education—has always been a low priority for the Pakistani ruling elites, both military and civil. Between 1955 and 1960, the government allocation for education was on an average 4 percent of the budget, while the defense expenditure was on an average 60 percent.[29] Throughout the eighties, for example, expenditure in the education sector remained below 2.5 percent of GNP, less than half of defense expenditure. In the early eighties, the share was significantly lower—less than 2 percent (table 3.9). Owing to chronic economic crises and high defense expenditure, successive regimes have cut back on public education, while the population has grown at a high rate. Therefore, educational opportunities have remained beyond the reach of the majority of the population, especially those who live in rural areas and are economically disadvantaged.

The effects of this meager allocation are felt by the students who are "fortunate" enough to go to the public schools. A survey conducted by the Karachi-based Social Policy and Development Center (SPDC) in 2002 revealed that 16 percent of these public schools are without any building, 55 percent do not have a boundary wall because they are located in a corner of farmland or the premises also serve as a thoroughfare, 79 percent do not have electricity, 44 percent are without water, and 60 percent are without any restrooms.[30]

The policy of miserly public allocation for education came under severe criticism from the international community, particularly after 9/11. In response, the Pakistani government has in recent years increased the allocation, and a number of international bodies such as the European Commission and the World Bank have provided funds for the restructuring of the education sector. The budget allocation for 2002–2003 was increased to 111,475 billion rupees. Although the number is ten times higher than in earlier years, it is still extremely low in terms of the GNP (a mere 2.29 percent), and small compared with other South Asian nations.[31]

Instead of pressing ahead with its constitutional responsibility to provide education to all sections of the society, the government is increasingly relying on the private sector to provide education, resulting in a significant growth in private schools. According to the PIHS, in 2000 a total of 26.1 percent of children at primary level attended these private schools. Importantly, in the rural areas the percentage was 17.1 percent—less than half of the urban enrollment. Obviously, the cost and the location of these schools prevent children from the poorer sections of society enrolling and thus contribute to the stark disparity akin to an educational apartheid.

TABLE 3.9

PUBLIC EXPENDITURE IN EDUCATION AND DEFENSE
IN PAKISTAN, 1981/82–1989/99
(as a percentage of GNP)

Year	Education	Defense
1981/82	1.4	5.7
1982/83	1.5	6.4
1983/84	1.6	6.4
1984/85	1.8	6.7
1985/86	2.3	6.9
1986/87	2.4	7.2
1987/88	2.4	7.0
1988/89	2.1	6.6
1989/90	2.2	6.8
1990/91	2.1	6.3
1991/92	2.2	6.3
1992/93	2.4	6.0
1993/94	2.2	5.6
1994/95	2.4	5.5
1995/96	2.4	6.2
1996/97	2.5	6.5
1997/98	2.3	6.9
1998/99	2.2	7.1

Sources: Economic Survey of Pakistan, various volumes.

The impact of this apartheid-like policy is aptly summarized by Ian Talbot: "the collapse of the state educational sector and the lack of access, for all but the rich, to the burgeoning English language private sector, left the madrasa as the only schooling option for large numbers of people."[32] Hence, the proliferation of madrassahs throughout the history of Pakistan.

ISLAMIZATION OF PAKISTAN AND THE MADRASSAHS

The discussion on the growth of madrassahs demonstrated that the number has increased remarkably since the late seventies. This growth was indeed partly driven by events outside the boundaries of Pakistan (to which I will return below), but also due to changes in domestic politics, particularly the Islamization policy of the Zia-ul Huq regime (1977–1988). Even before the events in neighboring countries—Iran and Afghanistan—began to unfold, domestic political processes were unleashed that created a conducive environment for the Islamists, the ulama, and madrassah education.

The Islamists in Pakistan showed their mobilizational capacity in 1977 when they joined the anti-government coalition and shaped the opposition alliance's political agenda by inserting their demand for the Nizam-e-Mustapha (the system of Prophet Muhammad). What began as a movement for democracy against the populist authoritarian regime of Zulfiqar Ali Bhutto (1973–1977), which blatantly rigged the national election, was transformed into a movement for an Islamist state, in spite of the fact that the Pakistan National Alliance (PNA), a combine of nine disparate parties, had more secular parties in its fold. This popular discontent paved the way for the military coup that brought Zia-ul Huq to power and served as the foundation of the Islamization project of the military regime. The Bhutto regime's wavering between socialist rhetoric and Islamic symbolism, reflected in the land reforms and nationalization of certain industries on the one hand, and declaring Pakistan an Islamic Republic, Islam a state religion, and Ahmadiyyas non-Muslim on the other, also helped the Islamists gain power and colonize the political arena.[33]

The Islamization program of Zia-ul Huq began in earnest in 1977, soon after the military regime came to power (for example, a martial law regulation in July 1977 decreed the imposition of "Islamic punishment" for crimes like theft, robbery, and robbery by a gang).[34] Zia strengthened the Council of Islamic Ideology (CII) in 1977, revitalized the religious ministry, appointed the leaders of Jamaat-i-Islami as his advisors in 1978, and declared himself the "soldier of Islam." The Islamization program comprised four areas—judicial reform, implementation of the Islamic penal code, economic activity, and education. All of them had long-term repercussions for Pakistani society and created supportive sociopolitical conditions for flourishing madrassahs; the latter in particular had a direct influence.

The regime had a clear agenda with regard to education: to change the nature of education to make it more "Islamic." This prompted Zia-ul Huq to organize a national education conference in 1977. One of the goals of the conference was "to redefine the goals of education." Zia-ul Huq declared in his opening speech that "our curriculum must ensure that our children are brought up educated as good Pakistanis and good Muslims. They must imbibe the lofty ideals and principles of Islam."[35] With this goal in mind, Islamiat (Islamic studies) was made mandatory up to the bachelor's degree, and Arabic was made mandatory in all schools throughout Pakistan. These steps demonstrate the government's proclivity toward Islamic education, and consequently institutions that could offer this type of education were bound to be supported by the government. It should be no surprise to learn that the government recognized shahadah al-alamiyaah as equivalent to a master's degree in 1982.

Zia's Islamization program was both a matter of personal conviction and a project to legitimate his repressive regime. The legitimacy of the regime was in question not only on the grounds that it had diverted the nation from representative democracy but also on constitutional grounds, because the intervention of the military in politics was a violation of a clause of the constitution framed in 1973. Fashioning Islamism as a political ideology for gaining legitimacy was not an exclusive preserve of Zia-ul Huq (as we will see in chapter 4, in the case of post-1975 Bangladesh by his namesake Zia-ur Rahman), but perhaps he took it further than anyone else. In any case, it is important to note that while the Iranian revolution (February 1979) and the Soviet intervention in Afghanistan (December 1979) both had a considerable impact on the nature and pace of Islamization in Pakistani politics, the Islamization program was initiated long before these events. Therefore, it is fair to say that when the ISI-CIA nexus was created after 1979 to build ramshackle schools, akin to military camps, along the Pakistan-Afghanistan border and term them madrassahs, the domestic environment was already prepared.

PAKISTAN AS THE FRONTLINE STATE AND MADRASSAHS AS INSTRUMENTS

Much has been said about the connection between the war in Afghanistan and the madrassahs in Pakistan. It is now a mere cliché to say that the Afghan War, especially the creation of the *mujahideen* (holy warriors) has played a significant role in the proliferation of madrassahs and the militarization of these educational institutions in Pakistan. It is also well known that the mujahideen, the rebel forces who fought against the Soviet invasion, and the Taliban, the most violent products of these schools, are essentially the byproducts of cold war rivalry between the West and the Soviet Union.[36] The emergence of these retrograde bands of armed groups is fundamentally connected to Pakistan becoming the "frontline state" and the proxy of the United States in its war against the Soviet Union. But questions remain as to what prompted the ruling regime of Pakistan to take up this role, and why madrassahs were chosen as the instrument in this war.

Pakistan's alignment with the United States has a long history. A desperate attempt to secure the United States as an ally was initiated by the Pakistani rulers within months of partition in 1947. The United States, however, showed very little interest at that point because of its narrowly defined interests in South Asia.[37] The U.S. policy toward South Asia, throughout the fifties and the sixties, was to treat the region with low priority, and to placate Pakistan at the same time. Pakistan was seen as a strategic bulwark against Soviet expansion, and thus needed to be pampered. These two elements of policy blinded policy makers as to the consequences of their policies on South Asian domestic politics and made them disregard regional concerns in the interests of the broader security issues.[38]

One of the main objectives of U.S. policy toward South Asia during this period was, however, to maintain stability. The bloodshed between the Hindus and Muslims during the partition of India in 1947 and the belligerent postures of these two countries since the 1948 war were sufficient to paint an outlook characterized by perennial acrimony. The United States, deeply engaged in the Korean War in the fifties, and embroiled in the Vietnam quagmire in the sixties, maintained a distance with South Asia. However beneath the apparent indifference was a growing unease with India, owing to its policy of nonalignment under the leadership of Jawaharlal Nehru (1947–1964), the first prime minister of India. This anxiety played a significant role in initiating a closer relationship with Pakistan under the Eisenhower administration (1953–1961). Vice President Richard Nixon, after a trip to Pakistan in 1953, argued for cultivating Pakistan as "a counter-force to the confirmed neutralism of Jawaharlal Nehru's India."[39]

The U.S.-India relationship improved in the sixties, for a variety of reasons. The United States help to India during the Sino-Indian war in 1962, the Kennedy administration's pragmatic approach of not alienating uncommitted nations, and changes in the power balance between China and the Soviet Union are just a few of them. The Johnson administration (1963–1969) maintained a policy of equidistance from both nations, and tried to be evenhanded. The war in Vietnam, and consequent concerns at home and on the military front, compelled the administration to focus on Southeast Asia rather than on South Asia. This diminished U.S. influence in the region and created an environment where both Pakistan and India searched for a closer ally. Pakistan grew closer to China as the latter came forward to help during the Indo-Pak war in 1965; the Soviets emerged as the peace broker after the war.[40] In the late sixties, the United States administration felt the necessity to cultivate closer relationship with Pakistan.

In this context, the Pakistani Army unleashed a genocidal war against the majority Bengali population of the eastern province of the country in March 1971. In the following nine months of crisis, which led to the India-Pakistan war in December and the emergence of Bangladesh, the Nixon administration (1969–1974) stood firmly behind the Pakistani president Yahya Khan. Indeed, a combination of Nixon's emotional attachment to General Yahya, his dislike for Indira Gandhi, Pakistan's role as a conduit of rapprochement with China, and National Security Advisor Henry Kissinger's predilection for power politics and focus on geopolitical concerns greatly influenced the American policy decision in 1971.[41] The geopolitical concern, to be precise, was the role of the

Soviet Union in the region. To the U.S. policy makers, particularly the Nixon White House, the crisis was a part of the global cold war. As India was viewed as a Soviet pawn in the game, Pakistan was to be the standard bearer of the free world. In the long term, the U.S. policy proved to be damaging to its own interests in South Asia. But the administration continued its support for Pakistan.

When Zulfiqar Ali Bhutto came to power in a truncated Pakistan in 1972, the U.S. administration was not very happy, thanks to Bhutto's populist socialist rhetoric, but accepted the reality on the ground. The relationship, however, began to sour in 1974 when Bhutto, in response to Indian's testing of a nuclear device, decided to build a nuclear bomb. Gerald Ford's administration took special note of this move and tried to dissuade Pakistan from the nuclear path, with little success. The arms embargo imposed on Pakistan in 1965 was lifted to demonstrate that the United States was ready to work with Pakistan on its security. But nothing seemed to work. Z. A. Bhutto went ahead with his ambition of a nuclear Pakistan, or for an "Islamic Bomb," as he called it. Bhutto was deposed in a coup by Zia-ul Huq in 1977, arrested, charged with the murder of one of his opponents, convicted in a trial closed to cameras, and hanged in early 1979. Although the followers of Bhutto believe that the coup was supported by the United States due to Bhutto's insistence on making Pakistan a nuclear power, the new regime of Zia-ul Huq continued with the nuclear program anyway.

The Zia-ul Huq regime came under intense pressure from the United States in 1979 to discontinue its nuclear program. In April 1979 President Jimmy Carter imposed unilateral military and economic sanctions against Pakistan under the Symington Amendment to the Foreign Assistance Act after discovering that Islamabad was secretly constructing a facility to enrich uranium.[42] Additionally, it was later discovered that the United States was considering an attack on Pakistani nuclear facilities as an option to terminate the program.[43]

While publicly strong words and tough actions were mounted against the Zia-ul Huq regime, secretly the United States was working with the Pakistani government in arming the opponents of the pro-Soviet government in Kabul. This began soon after President Carter signed the presidential directives authorizing such an operation on 3 July 1979, six months before the Soviet invasion, knowing well that this would provoke a direct Soviet intervention in Afghanistan.[44] With the overthrow of the Shah regime in Iran, often referred to as the U.S. policeman in the Gulf, in an Islamist revolution under the leadership of Ayatollah Khomeini in February 1979, and the U.S.-induced Soviet invasion in Afghanistan in December 1979, the regional political landscape changed radically. The public tough talk of the United States gradually diminished, and the so-called rogue state became the most attractive ally. By the time Ronald Reagan came to power in 1981, Zia-ul Huq was in a position to dictate the terms of extending cooperation to the United States in its fight against the Soviet

Union. The Reagan administration gladly embraced a military regime that had usurped power unconstitutionally, hanged the elected prime minister, and embarked on an Islamization program.

It was a classic marriage of convenience. The Pakistan-United States understanding provided the Zia-ul Huq regime with legitimacy, relieved him from the pressure to terminate the nuclear program, allayed any call for a swift return to democracy, ensured an unremitting flow of funds to pursue his domestic agenda, and provided protection against the Soviet threat. Further, it fitted neatly with Pakistan's strategic interest—to establish a protectorate state in Kabul. With regard to Afghanistan, the Pakistani objectives were: "to break the Kabul–New Delhi axis, to get strategic depth vis-à-vis India, to isolate Iran by strengthening the Sunni specificities of the Islamist movements, [and] to carve out a corridor to Central Asia in case of a collapse of the USSR."[45] For the U.S. administration, there was only one goal: "giving the USSR its Vietnam War."[46]

In the process of institutionalizing cooperation, Pakistan insisted and the United States agreed that no direct contact between U.S. intelligence and Afghan resistance groups would be forged; that all assistance—money, training, and weapons—would be mediated through the Pakistani intelligence agency ISI; and that radical Muslims from all around the globe would be recruited to join the war. The first two conditions were beneficial to the United States, as they gave it plausible deniability of their involvement in the conflict. The third condition was to demonstrate that the conflict was between the Muslim world and the godless communists, rather than between the West and the Soviets.[47]

It is the third element of the understanding that brought the madrassahs into the political equation. Claiming religion as the raison d'etre of the war positioned the religious institutions at the forefront and, therefore, madrassahs inexorably became one instrument in the struggle. The number of madrassahs was already on the rise in the country due to the Islamization program of the regime, so establishing new ones was not considered a departure from the government's policy. Labeling these recruiting centers as madrassahs was to give them respectability, to provide rationales for the influx of foreigners who would come to join the war, and to demonstrate that the Pakistani government was offering not only food and shelter but also education to the Afghan refugees. Although these are important factors, there were deeper issues as well: the historical connections between the Afghan ulama and the Pakistani madrassahs, the militant tradition within the frontier areas, and the rebel leaders chosen to pursue Pakistani strategic objectives.

Connections between Islamic activists and the ulama of India and Afghanistan are too long-running and complex to be recounted within the short space of this section, but suffice it to say that for both scholarly and militant political activism in the name of jihad Afghanistan drew inspiration and leadership from the Indian subcontinent. For example, in the early nineteenth century, Syed Ahmad of Rai Bareilly (1786–1831), a disciple of Shah Abd al-Aziz (1746–1823), launched an armed struggle, calling it jihad against the Sikhs in the frontier region of Afghanistan, and rallying the Pashtun tribes. Ties grew stronger following the establishment of Deoband Madrassah. In the early twentieth century, Abd ar-Razzaq, a former student of Deoband, tried to organize the Pashtun tribes against the British. Such was the reliance on the Indian madrassahs that Afghanistan never had a reputable madrassah, although various rulers of Afghanistan tried to develop one. The other place where Afghan ulama used to go for further studies was Bukhara, but after the Soviet revolution in 1917 Deoband became the only option, and "after partition in 1947 Peshawar became the center where the traditionalist ulama pursued advanced studies."[48]

This connection was at the heart of the decision to utilize the madrassah as the conduit of armed resistance against the occupying Soviet forces in Afghanistan in the eighties. This is not to say that these madrassahs were by nature militarized institutions, but it is well to bear in mind that they are located in a region where violence is an integral part of social life. The naturalization of conflict within the society and the long tradition of armed resistance to outsiders helped immensely in transforming the existing madrassahs and in founding new madrassahs with a goal of producing resistance fighters. This was the result of a deliberate policy, not a natural progression of the educational institution.

This policy was adopted also because the leadership of the resistance preferred by the Pakistani policy makers needed a band of loyal warriors, a band for whom there was no conflict between tribal identity and the cause of the resistance. After the failed uprising in 1975, Afghan Islamists and a few ulama took refuge in Pakistan and received support from the Pakistani government. But by 1978 the Afghan rebels in exile had split into two groups—the Jamaat-i-Islami under the leadership of Borhanuddin Rabbani, a Persian speaker, and the Hizb-i-Islami under the leadership of Gulbuddin Hekmatiyar, a Pashtun. The former, although inspired by the Egyptian Brotherhood and the ideas of Syed Qutb, appeared to be more moderate than the latter. It was Hekmatiyar's followers who insisted on the uprising in July 1975 against the wishes of the Rabbani and his followers. By 1978 the rebels had lost the support of their host and their financial backers. But the situation changed when the communists staged a coup in April 1978. The United States took special note of the coup and began to cultivate relationships with these exiled militants. In the meantime, beginning in July 1978 both spontaneous and organized uprisings in various parts of the country broke out and continued until the Soviet invasion in December 1979. After the Soviet invasion and the U.S.-Pakistan understanding in 1981, the exiled groups were reorganized. In so doing, the Pakistani administration demonstrated a clear preference for the Hekmatiyar faction, though others also received support. Support for Hizb-i-Islami was due to its ethnic identity (Pashtun) and its connection with the Jamaat-i-Islami of Pakistan. The leaders of the Hizb, unlike the Rabbani faction, represented the ulama, pursued radicalism, and were popular among the youth. Hekmatiyar was more comfortable reaching the students because of his political training on the Kabul campus. It appeared to the Pakistani policy makers that the combination of radicalism and ulama support could be combined if the madrassahs were utilized to recruit and indoctrinate the resistance fighters.

Although the U.S.-Pakistan understanding stipulated that the United States would not be directly involved in contacting the Afghan militants, the latter became involved in some educational projects. In the heyday of the Afghan war, USAID funded a project for the writing and printing of elementary schoolbooks established in refugee camps in Pakistan for Afghan children. The University of Nebraska, Omaha, oversaw the $50 million contract with the Education Center for Afghanistan, a group approved by the Pakistani government and various mujahideen factions. These books were then distributed and used by the educators in Pakistan and, after the Soviet withdrawal, in Afghanistan. The books were not only replete with pictures of kalashnikovs but also taught children the Persian alphabet and basic mathematics; in an unusual way. The first-grade language arts books introduced the alphabet: "The letter *Alif* is for Allah [Allah is one]; *Bi* is for baba (father) [Baba goes to the mosque]; ... The letter *Jim* is for jihad [jihad is an obligation. My mom went to jihad. Our brother gave water to mujahideen]." A fourth-grade mathematics textbook posed this problem: "The speed of a Kalashnikov bullet is 800 meters per second. If a Russian is at a distance of 3,200 meters from a mujahid, and that mujahid aims at the Russian's head, calculate how many seconds it will take for the bullet to strike the Russian in the forehead."[49] Thus both the United States and Pakistan engaged the educational institutions, particularly madrassahs, as a site to indoctrinate Afghan youth and train them to participate in a "religious war"—a jihad to fight as a Muslim––rather than a nationalist war to fight as an Afghan.

The so-called jihad in Afghanistan ended in 1989 when the Soviets left the country, and the last phase was completed three years later when the Soviet-backed Najibullah government collapsed. Various factions of the mujahideen captured Kabul and in no time confronted each other violently. The international players of the "great game," having achieved their goal, conveniently forgot both the war-ravaged country and the militants assembled from around the world. Pakistan, however, remained deeply involved because their primary strategic goal—to have a hand-picked government installed in Kabul—was yet to materialize. Thus emerged the Taliban in 1994, under the leadership of

Mullah Omar. The Taliban, which received all kinds of material support from the Pakistani authorities, by then under an elected civilian regime, succeeded in capturing the capital within two years. The foot soldiers of this movement, as their name suggests and as we all know by now, came from the infrastructure created under the name of madrassahs in Pakistan.

Despite the CIA and the Western nations' abandonment of Afghanistan, the training centers, and the foot soldiers of war, the madrassahs in Pakistan associated with militancy continued to grow. The obvious question, therefore, is how and why did the trend continue after 1989 or even 1994? The simple answer to this question is that while U.S. policy makers must be credited with being the midwife for the transformation of these institutions, the distinct honor of being the protector of these transformed institutions goes to the Pakistani political and military establishment. Since 1989, madrassahs have been further radicalized because of their intimate connections with religiopolitical forces, their use as tools to promote sectarian interests through violent means, and government policy toward Indian-administered Kashmir.

Politics, Sectarianism, and Madrassahs: Playing with Fire

Although Pakistan first experienced sectarian violence in 1953 when the Jaamat-i-Islami launched a violent campaign against the small Ahmadiyya community, the relationship between the two major sects of Islam—Sunni and Shi'a, and various denominations within the Sunnis (for example Deobandi, Barelvi, Ahl-e-Hadith), remained relatively amiable until 1979.[50] The Islamization policy of the Zia-ul Huq regime unleashed the forces of sectarianism and helped these forces to spread throughout the country. Subsequent civilian regimes continued exploiting sectarian differences and used militant sectarian groups for their short-term benefit.

Being a minority, the Shi'a population maintained a low profile in the political scene in the early days of the country, but later extended tacit support to the secularist Pakistan People's Party led by Zulfiqar Ali Bhutto. Two major Sunni denominations—Deobandis and Barelvis—organized their political parties in the forties. The Deobandis, who were opposed to the establishment of Pakistan, formed the Jamaat-i-Ulama-i-Hind in 1945 and broke away from their parent organization after 1947 to form the Jamaat-i-Ulama-i-Islam (JUI), while the Barelvis formed the Jamaat-i-Ulama-i-Pakistan (JUP) in 1948. The political influence of these parties was far more limited than their sectarian following. The election results of 1970 bear testimony to this fact—each secured only seven seats. In fact, the results demonstrated that religious or sectarian identity had very little political appeal to the Pakistani population. For example, the nonsectarian Islamist political party, the Jamaat-i-Islami (JI), did not do well, either: it won only four seats.

But the Islamization program of the Zia regime, particularly its insistence on implementing Sunni inheritance laws, making zakat mandatory, giving preference to conservative Deobandi ulama in various government positions, and underscoring Sunni Hanafi theological interpretations on religious matters indicated that, first, the Sunni interpretation of Islam was being presented as universal Islam, and second, a specific denominational interpretation was being privileged.[51] These government steps and the resulting perceptions of other sects and denominations created the backdrop of sectarian tendencies in the society.

The sectarian tendency was also influenced by the Iranian revolution in 1979. This event enhanced the sectarian consciousness of the Shi'a population in Pakistan, helped them emphasize their Shi'a identity, encouraged assertiveness, and emboldened their aspiration to gain political power. Both ideological and material support from Iran began to flow in and influence the activism of the Pakistani Shi'a community.[52]

The demonstration of the newfound power of the Shi'a community was both a defensive act and a preemptive measure. Since the declaration of the Ahmadiyya movement to be non-Muslim in 1973, the Shi'a community feared a similar fate. Thus their show of force was an outgrowth of that fear. It was also a preemptive bid: to create a space in domestic politics. As the political landscape was undergoing a change, the Shi'a community was trying to claim a stake in it. The formation of the Tehrik-i-Nifaz-i-Fiqh-i-Jafria (later named Tehrik-i-Jafria Pakistan—TIJ, Pakistan's Shi'a Movement) and their militant student wing (Ithna Ashariya Student Organization—ISO, Twelver Shi'a Student Movement) in 1979 testify to this. Shi'as in Pakistan successfully challenged the Zia-ul Huq regime on the zakat ordinance and secured a victory when Zia declared that the Shi'a population would be exempted from the mandatory zakat fund. The growing strength of the Shi'a population irked the Sunnis as well as two regional powers—Saudi Arabia and Iraq. Iraq was at that time engaged in a bloody war with Iran with the support of the West, especially the United States. For Saudis, the primary challenge was to contain the Iranian brand of Islamism within Iran by hardening Sunni identity in countries around Iran and through building a "Sunni wall" around Iran.[53] To do so, they began providing funds to madrassahs of the Ahl-e-Hadith persuasion as a counterweight.

The immediate and most violent reactions came from the Deobandis, who founded the Sawad-e-Azam Ahl-e-Sunnat (Greater Unity of the Sunnis) and demanded that Pakistan be declared a Sunni state, and Shi'as non-Muslim. The movement, which encouraged violence against the Shi'as, was institutionalized in 1985 as the Anjuman-e-Sipah-i-Sahaba (ASS, Society of the Army of the Prophet's Companions), later named the Sipah-i-Sahaba Pakistan (SSP).[54] The militant organization was founded in the Punjab with only one objective:

to confront the Shi'a population violently.[55] The virulence of their rhetoric and actions were unprecedented. The SSP, although apparently an independent organization, was closely connected to the Jamaat-i-Ulama-i-Islami (JUI) until 1989. (The SSP entered into mainstream politics in 1990. The organization was renamed Millat-i-Islami after being proscribed in 2002.) During the Zia-ul Huq regime the military establishment extended support to the SSP to counter growing Shi'a political influence, made it an integral part of its anti-Iran policy at home, and engaged it in raising fighters for the Afghan war. The SSP gradually spread to the southern parts of the province from its base in the central region.

The politicians associated with the Ahl-e-Hadith sect organized a militant group in 1988 named Lashkar-i-Tayeba (LT, renamed Jamaat Dawa in 2002 after proscription by the government). The LT, which grew out of the Markaz Dawa-wal Irshad, comprised veterans of the Afghan war and soon became engaged in violence at home and in Kashmir. A spiral of violence was unleashed by the SSP and the LT. This resulted in a backlash from the Shi'a community: a militant group named the Sipah-i-Muhammed (SM, Army of Mohammed in Pakistan) was founded in 1991. As the SSP moved to the mainstream and was trying to tone down its violent rhetoric, a split occurred and some members formed a more aggressive organization called the Lashkar-i-Jhangvi (LJ, the Army of Jhangvi) in 1994. The organization was named after Haq Nawaz Jhangvi, the founder of the SSP, to demonstrate that it is carrying on the work of Jhangvi, who was assassinated by his adversaries.[56] By then the Barelvis had their own militant groups––Sunni Tehrik (ST) and the Anjuman Sipah-i-Mustafa (ASM). The Tehrik-i-Jafria Pakistan (TJP) was banned by the government in 2002, but reincarnated under the banner of Tehrik-i-Islam (TIP). (For a list of the sectarian political parties and militant organizations see table 3.10.)

Throughout the Afghan war, Islamist parties, with their bases in madrassahs, vied for state patronage and financial support. The government-controlled zakat fund and U.S. money was the prize they went after, but to increase their share of the pie they had to marginalize their opponents ideologically, dwarf them numerically, and if necessary, annihilate them physically. Needless to say, all of these groups required foot soldiers, and the madrassahs became the recruiting centers. The growth of madrassahs controlled by sects is one indication of the sectarian organizations' effort to reach out to as many youth possible (table 3.11). A closer look at various regions where madrassahs grew reveals that these militant groups flourished in the same region. Southern Punjab is, perhaps, the most glaring example: "The belt that stretches from Jhang to Dera Ghazi Khan, has the highest rate growth and concentration of madrasas in the province. It is also the stronghold of the Sipah-i-Sahaba and its twin, the Lashkar-e-Jhangvi."[57] In 1996, police in the Punjab reported that at

TABLE 3.10

SECTARIAN PARTIES AND MILITANT GROUPS IN PAKISTAN

Denomination	Deobandi	Barelvi	Ahl-e-Hadith	Shi'a
Political party	Jamaat-i-Ulema-i-Islam (JUI)	Jamaat-i-Ulema-i-Pakistan (JUP)	Jamaat-i-Ulema-i-Ahl-e-Hadith (JUAH)	Tehrik-i-Islami (TII)
Militant organization	Sipah-i-Sahaba (SSP)	Sunni Tahrik (ST)	Lashkar-i-Tayeba (LT)	Sipah-i-Muhammad (SM)
	Lashkar-i-Jhangvi (LJ)	Anjuman Sipah-i-Mustafa (ASM)	Tehreek-ul-Mujahideen (TuM) (LT and TuM also operate in Kashmir)	Ithna Ashari-aya Student Organization (ISO, Twelver Shi'a student movement)
	Jaish-i-Muhammad (JM)			
	Harkat-ul-Mujahideen (HM)			Mukhtar Force Sipah-i-Abbas
	Harkat al-Jihad al-Islami (HUJI)			

Source: Compiled by the author.

Notes: SSP also supports Majlis-i-Tahaffuz-i-Khatme Nabuwat (Movement to Protect Finality of Prophethood). The HM (and its companion organization Harkat ul-Ansar—the HA), primarily operates in Indian-administered Kashmir but is based in Pakistan and has close contacts with other sectarian militant organizations. There are seventeen Ahl-e-Hadith organizations, of which six participate in mainstream politics; JUAH is the most prominent of these organizations, and the other prominent organization is the Jamaat al-Mujahideen Ahl-e-Hadith.

least 746 madrassahs in the province had strong sectarian links; they also said that these madrassahs provided space for clandestine meetings to plan violent acts.[58] In 2000, it was reported in the Pakistani press that intelligence officials had identified 126 madrassahs as having direct links with militant organizations.[59] The connections between the sectarian madrassahs and militancy became conspicuous when the background of leaders of these organizations, particularly their educational background, was examined. For example, Haq Nawaz Jhangvi and Azam Tariq, the two key leaders of the SSP, studied in Binori Town madrassah in Karachi.[60]

By the mid-nineties, communities with sectarian or denominational identity not only had their own political parties but their militant groups as well.

TABLE 3.11

CLASSIFICATIONS OF MADRASSAHS BY SECT IN PAKISTAN, 1960–2002

	Deobandi	Barelvi	Ahl-e-Hadith	Shi'a	JI	Unknown	Total
1960	233	98	55	18	13	55	
1971	292	123	47	15	41	390	
1979	354	267	126	41	57	900	
1984	1,097	557	76	76	107		
1988	1,840	717	161	47	96		2,861
2002	7,000	1,585	376	419	500		9,880

Sources: Total numbers for 1960, 1971, 1979, and 1984 are not consistent with Table 3.1, because these figures are derived from the respective madrassah boards, and the affiliation of a large number of madrassahs remains unidentified. 1988 figures are from Government of Pakistan, *Deeni Madaris Pakistan ki Jam'e Report*, 1988; and 2002 figures are drawn from the report of Sindh Police quoted in the national newspaper Dawn on 16 January 2003.

Consequently, the incidents of sectarian violence have continued to rise since then (table 3.12).

The growth of madrassahs and unabated violence between various sectarian groups have affected mainstream politics as well: Islamist political parties began facing fragmentation, and the monopoly of the JI over Islamist politics was challenged by the JUI.[61] Consequently, the JI intensified its drive to recruit new adherents from madrassahs as well as other educational institutions. Madrassahs supported by the JI also became training centers for the recruits of militant groups operating within the country and elsewhere. Maraz Uloom-i-Deeniyah's Alfalah Academy, Jamiat-ul Ikhwan, and Jamia Darul Islam in Punjab, all connected to the JI, have a track record of association with the Hizbul Mujahideen (HM).[62]

The end of the Soviet occupation of Afghanistan removed the cause célèbre. But by then these political leaders, their followers, and the Pakistani political system had become hostage to this tendency, and the militant groups had learned that the madrassahs could become sources of manpower for an unending war. The infighting among the various groups in Afghanistan after the Soviet withdrawal and the continued struggle of the Taliban for power provided these organizations with much-needed justification and lent legitimacy to their functioning. This is why, despite the end of the Afghan war, these organizations have not only survived but have flourished.

TABLE 3.12

SECTARIAN VIOLENCE IN PAKISTAN

Year	Incidents	Killed	Injured
1989	67	18	102
1990	274	32	328
1991	180	47	263
1992	135	58	261
1993	90	39	247
1994	162	73	326
1995	88	59	189
1996	80	86	168
1997	103	193	219
1998	188	157	231
1999	103	86	189
2000	109	149	NA
2001	154	261	495
2002	63	121	257
2003	22	102	103
2004	19	187	619
2005	62	160	354
2006	38	201	349
Total	1,837	1,668	3,997

Source: South Asia Terrorism Portal, "Sectarianism Violence in Pakistan."

By 1996, when the Taliban came to power in Afghanistan, these organizations, with the active support of the Pakistani government, became the sources of militants for the Kashmir conflict. The success of the mujahideen in driving out the Soviets and the Taliban in capturing the Afghan state created an illusion among a section of Pakistani policy makers that similar success could be achieved in Indian-held Kashmir.

An indigenous uprising for self-rule in Kashmir took a militant shape in 1989.[63] Extra-judicial killings, custodial deaths, excessive use of force, torture, rape, and arbitrary arrests by the Indian forces and the massive rigging of the 1987 legislative elections all contributed to the radicalization of the movement.[64] In the words of Atul Kohli, "The more the democratic political process lost its meaning, the more a full-scale insurgency came to be unleashed."[65]

In the nineties there were remarkable changes in the orientation and nature of the movement for self-rule in Kashmir. The ideological emphasis of the self-rule movement shifted from nationalistic and secularist to Islamist, and the Kashmir conflict became a proxy war between India and Pakistan. The latter was made possible by the availability of a large number of "militant volunteers" after the Soviet withdrawal from Afghanistan, and Pakistan's open patronage of militant groups like Lashkar-i-Tayeba and Jaish-i-Mohammad, among others.

MADRASSAHS AND THE GLOBAL JIHAD?

The relationships forged between the Afghan Mujahideen and the Pakistani militants under the auspices of the United States and the Pakistani government was furthered by the Pakistani authorities when the Taliban was created as a strategic tool for keeping Afghanistan under Pakistani control. The same strategy was abortively pursued in Kashmir after 1989. All of these brought changes in the madrassahs, some of which have been and to some extent are still being used to train militants. This policy spawned sectarian militant groups that fight against each other within the country, with the active support of the Pakistani military establishment.

This has also opened the door to establishing contacts with transnational terrorist groups. Some believe that after 9/11 the goals and objectives of the Pakistani sectarian militants and the transnational terrorists have come closer together than ever before, but for Pakistani sectarian militants the "internal enemy still takes priority over the enemy without."[66] However, it is also true that the issue of global jihad looms large in the discourse of the militant groups, the sectarian political parties, and the madrassahs supported by these parties. This discourse provides an impression that the madrassahs in Pakistan are producing foot soldiers for the global jihad. Despite a rather circumscribed agenda, why "global jihad" features prominently in sectarian militants' discourse is a question one must confront.

The creation and proliferation of these organizations demonstrate that their raison d'etre is sectarian identity. This identity and accompanying discourse cannot be used as an ideology for political mobilization domestically and earn legitimacy from Muslims elsewhere at the same time. Thus their appeal needed to be defined and articulated in a fashion that could appeal to the greater Muslim population—both domestically and internationally. A radicalized Islamism, presented as an anti-Western, anti-American ideology, was therefore constructed. "Thus, for motivation and mobilization, jihad [has been] propounded as a legitimate concept to wage war against infidels."[67]

The "infidels" are defined, discussed, understood, and demonized in madrassahs within the global political frame and in terms of local community relations. This is where the sectarian literature becomes instrumental in Pakistani madrassahs. In the name of refutation (which is called *radd* in Urdu), pungent criticism of other sects, hatred toward other sect members, and a siege mentality are imparted from the very beginning of the schooling. Texts, chosen either as mandatory or supplementary readings, disseminate "opinions against other sects, sub-sects, views seen as heretical by the ulema, Western ideas—may be the major formative influence on the minds of madrassa students."[68] These discourses are then mingled with the concepts of jihad and militancy. Children are taught that Muslims all around the world, especially in Pakistan—a country which has been created as the home of the Muslims—are under siege from sinister forces that they must fight to death.

Conclusion

The foregoing discussion of Pakistani madrassahs has demonstrated that these institutions are shaped by specific factors both within and without. By no means can these institutions be separated from these contexts, and therefore, a one-dimensional analysis of these institutions must be avoided.

The state's failure—deliberate or unwitting—to provide education to a large segment of the society has created opportunities for madrassahs to grow in size and number, and has helped these institutions to assume importance in the lives of many people. The fragmentation of education along social divides has left the poor, particularly the rural poor, with very little option but to send their children to madrassahs that are organized along sectarian or denominational lines. Sectarian madrassah boards accentuate these divisions and cause irreparable damage to the pursuit of universal Islamic knowledge—the primary goal of the madrassah. The political environment of the country beginning in 1977, the Islamization policy of the Zia-ul Huq government, and the encouragement of sectarian militancy by the military establishment vitiated the society at large, and madrassahs did not remain immune to this menace. Indeed, the Islamist political parties, who have very little electoral support, have exploited the situation and exercised great influence on government and politics.

More than two decades of war in neighboring Afghanistan; the involvement of superpowers, especially the United States; and Pakistani governments' decision to exploit the situation to pursue their regional aspirations have transformed the nature of the madrassahs. As the frontline state, Pakistan has used the madrassahs as instruments, and is paying a high social and political price. The future of madrassahs in Pakistan, therefore, is intrinsically tied to the nature of the Pakistani state and the social dynamics of the country.

CHAPTER 4

BANGLADESH

A TALE OF TWO SYSTEMS

Madrassahs have been in existence in Bangladesh for a long time. As discussed in chapter 2, Islamic educational institutions began to emerge with the arrival of Sufis and saints, perhaps as early as eighth century, but the invasion of Ikhtiyar bin Bakhtiyar Khilji in 1197 paved the way for institutionalization of madrassahs. Since then madrassahs have become part of the educational landscape and experienced changes, as in many other parts of India, during colonial rule. After decolonization in 1947, the area that constitutes Bangladesh became the eastern province of Pakistan. After about a quarter of a century and a bloody civil war, it emerged as an independent nation in 1971. Over the last sixty years, socioeconomic conditions, government policies, and political dynamics all have played parts in the proliferation and transformation of the madrassahs in Bangladesh.

Official statistics with regard to the government-supervised madrassahs show that between 1972 and 2004 the number of institutions has grown 731 percent, and the number of students attending these institutions has also increased phenomenally. At the primary level more than four milion children are now enrolled in about seven thousand schools. Beyond the supervision, or even the knowledge, of the government exist thousands of primary-level madrassahs, students of which are often engaged in political activism in support of the Islamist parties. Once located on the margins, madrassahs have become an integral part of the country's education system over the last three decades. Why and how have the madrassahs attained this position? Why should there be any need for these institutions at a time when the country has succeded in expanding access to secular education to a large number of people through formal and nonformal educational institutions? What roles do madrassahs play in the society and politics of Bangladesh? These questions are vital in understanding the future of a nation with 45 percent of population below the age of fifteen years.

Era of Benign Neglect

After the partition in 1947, there were at least five kinds of Islamic educational institutions in East Pakistan: the old-scheme madrassahs, the new-scheme madrassahs, the madrassahs of the Deoband tradition, Hafizia madrassahs, and the maktabs or preprimary institutions.

The Deobandi madrassahs began to appear in rural East Bengal over the course of the nineteenth century, following the demise of two Islamic revivalist movements in Bengal called the Faraizi movement and the Tariqah-i-Muhammadiya. The Faraizi movement, founded by Haji Shariatullah (1781–1840), was a revivalist movement, akin to contemporary Arabian Wahhabism, that spread through a large part of eastern Bengal in the early nineteenth century. After Shariatullah's death, his son Dudu Miyan (1819–1862) succeeded to the leadership of the movement. The Tariqah-i-Muhammadiya movement, pioneered by Shah Sayyid Ahmad (1780–1831) of Rai Barelwi and Shah Ismail (1782–1831), began in northern India and reached Bengal during the 1820s and 1830s. A 'true' interpretation of the Holy Qu'ran was central to the movement and received serious attention. Followers of Tariqah-i-Muhammadiya raised funds and joined the *jihad* waged in the north western frontier region. The most prominent follower of the movement in Bengal was the peasant leader Sayyid Nisar Ali, alias Titu Mir (1782–1831), who fought against the British army and died in battle. The goals of his movement included socioreligious reforms, elimination of the practice of *shirk* (pantheism) and *bida't* (innovation) in Muslim society, and inspiring Muslims to follow Islamic principles in their day-to-day life.

The most notable madrassah of the Deobandi tradition, Darul Uloom Muinul Madrassah, was established on the outskirts of the port city of Chittagong in 1901. The madrassah was first started as a maktab in Hathhazari in 1897 but later moved to the present location.[1] Over the following twelve years, at least three major madrassahs emerged in Chittagong district, especially in the rural areas. Among the madrassahs that came into being in the early part of this century, the Jamia Yunusia Brahmanbaria Madrassah became the best known. Although this madrassah was not formally established until 1914, it was effectively operating from 1907.[2]

The government of Pakistan, especially the provincial government, remained oblivious to the presence of the Deoband madrassahs and focused on the 1,452 madrassahs—378 old-scheme and 1,074 new-scheme—it inherited from the Calcutta madrassah system known as Aliya madrassahs. (Following the partition of India in 1947, the Calcutta Madrassah had been relocated to Dhaka.) In the following quarter century the number of madrassahs in both wings of Pakistan increased slowly but steadily. For example, prior to the independence, besides a few Shi'a madrassahs, there were 137 traditional Sunni madrassahs in what now constitutes Pakistan. According to one account the total number of madrassahs in 1947 was 247. By 1950, there were 210, and the number more than doubled in a decade, reaching 472 in 1960. The number continued to rise, reaching 908 in 1971.[3] In the eastern province of Pakistan, the total number of madrassahs was 1,129 in 1964.[4]

Several commissions on education (for example, the Muazzam Uddin Syllabus Committee of 1946–1947, the Education Reconstruction Committee of 1949, and the East Pakistan Education Reforms Commission of 1957), recommended integration of madrassahs within the general education system. Interestingly, these commission reports hardly recognized or made any specific recommendations in regard to the privately managed madrassahs of the Deobandi tradition then known as Khariji madrassahs.[5] These madrassahs remained outside any supervision of the government or local authorities and were dependent on precarious irregular local donations. Students of these madrassahs received free education and often food and lodging. Despite lack of government support, they survived "because of the spirit of sacrifice of the teachers who worked practically for no pay. Often the madrassahs consisted of a single room and one person taught at all stages of studies."[6] One can therefore conclude that between 1947 and 1971 madrassah education in East Pakistan suffered benign neglect.

Madrassahs after Independence: Integration and Mainstreaming

The decade-long Bengali nationalist movement that led to the emergence of Bangladesh in 1971 was spearheaded by secularists who favored a universal education system. By implication they were against religious education as much as they were against the English-medium privately managed kindergarten system. However, the reality struck them when the first education commission tried to formulate a national education policy in 1974: they were caught between the ideals of secular universal education and the political agenda of a government that was trying to woo the rightist elements to its fold.[7] They also had to assure the new-rich class that the private kindergarten system would remain to serve them. In an effort to strike a balance between these conflicting aims, the Education Policy document of 1974 recommended some changes in madrassah education but not a total elimination of the system. The government also increased allocation for madrassah education to taka 7.2 million in 1973 from taka 2.5 million in 1971. What had been an unstated policy of the Awami League government between 1972 and 1975 became the cornerstone of the education policy of the military regime of Zia-ur Rahman which came into power after the coup d'état of 1975: that is, to integrate the madrassahs into mainstream education. The establishment of a separate directorate within the education ministry in 1977 and of the Bangladesh Madrassah Education Board in 1978 were key steps in furthering the process. Even a cursory look at the existing education system of the country demonstrates that one of the two kinds of madrassahs has now become an integral part of the system.

The education system in Bangladesh is broadly divided into three stages: primary, secondary, and higher education. Primary education is provided by primary-level institutions, and the total length is five years (grades one to five). General nonformal education is part of this stage. Secondary education is imparted by junior secondary, secondary, and higher secondary education institutions, and is all together seven years. Higher education is imparted by degree colleges, universities, and other specialized and professional educational institutions. Primary education (five years, ages six to ten) and junior secondary education (three years, ages eleven to thirteen) is delivered through two systems: formal and nonformal. There are now eleven types of primary schools in Bangladesh. Six of these are considered mainstream schools, that is, they implement the curriculum of and use the books adopted by the National Curriculum and Textbook Board (NCTB). The mainstream schools are: government primary schools (GPS), registered nongovernment primary schools (RNGPS), nongovernment primary schools (NGPS), attached experimental schools (EXP), high school attached primary schools (HSAPS), community schools, and satellite schools. Nonformal system schools include the ibtedayee madrassahs (IM), high madrassah-attached primary schools (HMAPS), and nonformal schools run by nongovernmental organizations (NGOs).[8] The postprimary level in education is divided into four streams in terms of curriculum: general education, madrassah education, technical-vocational education, and professional education.

Categories of Madrassahs

At independence, Bangladesh inherited four types of madrassahs: Aliya madrassahs—government-supported institutions modeled after the Calcutta Madrassah (and later the Dhaka Aliya Madrassah); Qwami madrassahs, privately managed madrassahs modeled after the Deoband Madrassah; Furkania/Hafizia madrassahs—preprimary educational institutions offering basic Islamic education for about four years and exclusively meant for memorizing the Holy Qur'an; and Nurani madrassahs/maktabs, which offered preprimary education—literacy and basic knowledge of Islam. To date, not only have all of these types of madrassahs remained in place but the number and influence of all these institutions has grown remarkably. Also notable is that a new kind of madrassah, more orthodox in character and closely tied to a certain political ideology, has emerged in the nineties. Although these madrassahs are similar in that they provide education based on religious texts, especially the Qur'an and the hadiths, they possess different characteristics.

CHARACTERISTICS OF MADRASSAHS
Aliya Madrassashs

Aliya madrassahs have five stages—from primary education to the level of master's degree. Ibtedayee or primary level is equivalent to five years of primary school, dhakil covers five years of secondary level education, alim—equivalent to higher secondary education—is a two-year curriculum, fazil is equivalent to baccalaureate education and is a two-year program, and kamil is equivalent to a master's degree and takes two years to complete. For a comparison of major curricula of general education in three categories of madrassah, see table 4.1.

At dhakil level, students can pursue one of four sequences: general, science, *tazbid* (proper pronunciation in reciting the Qu'ran), or *hifzul* Qu'ran (memorization of the Qu'ran). At alim level there are three sequences: general, *mujabbid* (Islamic way of life and etiquette), and science. At fazil level, there are two sequences: general and mujabbid; a further third of the curriculum involves subjects such as political science, economics, and so on. Kamil has three sequences: *fiqh* (jurisprudence), *tafsir* (exegesis or commentary on the Qu'ran), and *adab* (etiquette). Terminal examinations of dhakil and alim are overseen by the Madrassah Education Board, established in 1978. Although these madrassahs receive government support, only a minority are directly managed by the government. They are generally administered by management committees selected by the patrons of these institutions.

Qwami Madrassahs

The number of Qwami madrassahs in the country is anybody's guess, and they follow a number of systems. The Bangladesh Qwami Madrassah Education Board, one of the twelve umbrella organizations who claim to represent thousands of Qwami madrassahs, insists that there are three stages in madrassah education: the first stage, considered to be the essential stage and equivalent to primary and secondary stages of general education, consists of ten years; the second stage, considered higher education, spans six years and is equivalent to the baccalaureate degree; and the third stage is research-oriented and takes any number of years.[9] The board also classifies the curriculum into sixteen grades, following the general education system. These grades are then each divided into five stages, determining when the students are supposed to take standardized completion examinations conducted by the board. These five stages are: marhalatul ibtedayee (equivalent to primary); marhalatul mutawassitah (equivalent to secondary); marhala sanubiah ulyia (equivalent to higher secondary); marhalatul fazeelat (equivalent to baccalaureate), and marhalatul taqmeel (equivalent to master's).[10]

However, the systems followed by the Qwami madrassahs can be categorized into two broad strands: one that is subject-based rather than grade-based,

TABLE 4.1

COMPARISON OF THE MAJOR CURRICULUM FOR GENERAL EDUCATION
AND ALIYA AND QWAMI MADRASSAHS IN BANGLADESH

General education	Aliya madrassah	Qwami madrassah
1. Primary	Ibtidayee	Ibtidayee
Bengali, English, mathematics, general science, social science, drawing, religious studies	Bengali, English, mathematics, history, geography, social studies, Qur'an, Arabic, aquaid, fiqh	Bengali, English, mathematics, general science, social science, Arabic, Urdu, Qur'an, fiqh
2. Secondary	Dakhil	Ustaani
Bengali, English, mathematics, general science, social science, social studies, history, geography, agriculture, home economics, history, computer science, basic trade, physics, chemistry, biology	Bengali, English, mathematics, general science, social science, social studies, agriculture, home economics, history, computer science, basic trade, physics, chemistry, biology, Qur'an, Arabic, aquaid, fiqh	history, political science, fiqh, tajweed (recitation), mantiq (logic), Bengali, Arabic, Urdu, Persian
3.Higher secondary	Alim	Sanubi
Bengali, English, civics, economics, computer science, agriculture, home economics, computer science, basic trade, physics, mathematics, chemistry, biology, business studies	Bengali, English, history, economics, civics, higher English, physics, chemistry, biology, mathematics, computer, science, Qur'an, hadith, fiqh, Arabic	Bengali, history, Arabic, usul-i-fiqh, (explanatory law), mantiq (logic), tafsir (exegesis), faraiz (inheritance law)
4. Bachelor of arts/science/commerce	Fazil	
Bengali, English, oriental language, liberal arts, social sciences, law, business management, accounting and finance, physics, chemistry, mathematics	Bengali, English, history, political science, economics, exegesis of Qur'an, hadith, Arabic	tafsir (exegesis), usul-i-Qur'an, usul-i-hadith (explanation of the sayings of Prophet), fiqh, Arabic
5. Master's	Kamil	Taqmil
Subjects offered are similar to bachelor degree except that there are no general compulsory subjects like Bengali, English	hadith, tafsir, fiqh, Arabic, history	hadith courses (dawrah hadith), al-Qur'an, tafsir, fiqh

Source: Compiled by the author.

and another that is divided into five stages, with two additional elective stages. In the former system, students are taught a variety of religious subjects over a period of at least six years. The sequence of these subjects depends on the institution as well as the ability of the student. The objective of the teacher is to make the student proficient in subjects deemed necessary to become an authority on the Islamic lifestyle. Within this system, some institutions have a final course, successful completion of which constitutes graduation for the student. The course is called daurah. Completion of the course allows the institution to award a certificate called daurah hadith. This is akin to, if not the equivalent of, kamil in the Aliya madrassah system. A small number of Qwami madrassahs also claim to offer specialized higher courses of a two- to three-year duration. In the second strand of Qwami madrassahs, courses are sequenced in five stages: ibtedayee (primary), mutawassitah (secondary), sanu-biah ulyia (higher secondary), fazeelat (baccalaureate), and taqmeel (master's). Two elective stages are: i'imul qiraat wat taujid (higher qiraat) and hifzul Qur'an (memorization of the Holy Qur'an).

Although these two systems are widely followed, there are several other practices as well. A number of madrassahs divide their curriculum into nine stages.[11] Some madrassahs divide the entire curriculum into fifteen years. The first five years are considered as the ibtedayee stage, when the students are taught the language and the basics of the Islamic texts. This is followed by ten years of learning. The grades of the following ten years are usually named after the main text the students study. However, madrassahs name them differently.[12]

Furkania/Hafizia Madrassahs

Furkania/Hafizia madrassahs are preprimary educational institutions offering basic Islamic education for about four years, and are concerned almost exclusively with memorizing the entire Holy Qur'an. They teach Arabic language, Qur'an recitation, Bengali language, and some simple mathematics. Furkania madrassahs are commonly attached to mosques and operate as residential institutions. Students are required to stay year round. These institutions are run by the management committee of the mosque; and receive funding from local people, more often in kind than in cash. Where the madrassah is attached to the mosque, the imam of the mosque teaches the students, and where it is not attached to a mosque, a *quari* (reciter of the Qu'ran) is appointed for teaching. Students graduating from the Furkania/Hafizia madrassahs move to Qwami madrassahs for further studies.

Nurani Madrassahs and Maktabs

Nurani madrassahs and maktabs are also preprimary educational institutions. They offer literacy and basic knowledge of Islam. Typically these institutions are not residential; students are expected to spend about four to six hours a day in class, often in two segments—in the morning and afternoon. Subjects taught in the Nurani madrassahs and maktabs include holy Qur'an recitation, tafsir, hifz, hadith, and Islamic aqida (tenets of belief). In most maktabs there is only one teacher, a graduate from a Qwami madrassah.

It is clear from this description that the latter two kinds of madrassah are largely equivalent to kindergartens and act as feeders for the Aliya and Qwami madrassahs. Although these institutions influence the early childhood socialization process, whether they can in any way indoctrinate the students is debatable. What is beyond any doubt is that the children going to these schools are often without the necessary preparation to gain entrance into secular schools.

The madrassahs in Bangladesh, therefore, can be broadly categorized into three categories: maktabs or Furkania/Nurnai madrassahs, Qwami madrassahs, and Aliya madrassahs. In the eighties, with the strengthening of the Ahl-e-Hadith movement, a major shift took place within the Qwami madrassah system. Hundreds of new madrassahs designed to operate as a base of political activism flourished in various parts of the country, and close links between and among these madrassahs were established. Despite the fact that these madrassahs were part of the Qwami madrassah tradition and followed a similar curriculum, they deserve special attention.

Ahl-e-Hadith Madrassahs

The Ahl-e-Hadith movement, as we may recall, originated in the early twentieth century in India as the most conservative subsect within Sunni Islamic thought. Inspired by a puritan eighteenth-century thinker, Muhammad bin Wahhab of Saudi Arabia, Ahl-e-Hadith (commonly referred to as Wahabbis, or Salafis), came into existence as a reaction to the disagreement between the Deobandis and the Barelvis. The teachings of the Barelvis, formally known as Ahl-e-Sunnat wal Jamaat, were advanced by Imam Ahmad Reza Khan of Bareilly in 1906 as an alternative to the austere path followed by the Deobandis. The Ahl-e-Hadith movement, on the other hand, took a more orthodox stance. After 1947, adherents of the Ahl-e-Hadith school of thought established three separate committees to continue their organizational work: one in India, and two in the provinces of Pakistan. In 1948, the Pakistan Markazi Jami'at-e-Hadith was founded at Lahore. The Nikhil Banga O Assam Jami'at-e-Hadith (All Bengal and Assam Jami'at-e-Hadith) formed at Calcutta in 1946 shifted its headquarters to Pabna, a northern city in what was then East Pakistan. The Anjuman-e-Ahl-e-Hadith was formed in West Bengal in 1951, with the result that two years later, the Ahl-e-Hadith movement renamed itself East Pakistan Jami'at-i-Ahl-e-Hadith. In 1956 its headquarters was shifted to Dhaka. Followers of the Ahl-e-Hadith school maintained their presence and remained visible in what was then West Pakistan, but were organizationally weak. Until his death, Abdullahil Kafi al-Quareshi led the East Pakistan committee. Dr. Abdul

Bari, a university lecturer, assumed the leadership in 1960. After the independence of Bangladesh, like many other religious organizations, Ahl-e-Hadith disappeared from the public scene.

In the mid-seventies, particularly after the political changes instituted in 1975, the adherents of the Ahl-e-Hadith school of thought reorganized themselves and the Jami'at-i-Ahl-e-Hadith became engaged in public activities. However, differences within the leadership surfaced in 1978 when Muhammad Asadullah al-Ghalib, a young university student and a radical activist, formed the youth wing Ahl-e-Hadith Jubo Sangha (AHJS). The youth organization received a boost in 1980 when Ghalib moved to the northeastern town of Rajshahi and joined the university as a faculty member. Differences with regard to the mode of operation, particularly the issue of organizing youth for jihad, created a rift within the Jami'at-i-Ahl-e-Hadith. This resulted in the formation of a breakaway group in 1984, who later established the Ahl-e-Hadith Tablig Jamaat. Over the following decade, Rajshahi remained the base of the former organization, while its operation expanded to various parts of the country and various strata of society. The AHJS maintained a low profile until 1990, the year Ghalib left the Jamaat and established the Ahl-e-Hadith Andolon Bangladesh (AHAB, Ahl-e-Hadith Movement Bangladesh). This move came after Ghalib succeeded in creating a financial base for running an independent organization. The funding came under the guise of a welfare organization—the Tawhid Trust. Ghalib also established a publication wing—the Hadith Foundation Bangladesh. Both the trust and the foundation began to receive funds from external sources to assist the running of the vast network of madrassahs the AHAB had established in the previous decade.[13] During the later part of the eighties, the primary conduit of the external funds was an Indian Islamist named Abdul Matin Salafi. Salafi, a self-styled *muballig* (preacher), was expelled in 1988 by the Bangladesh government for anti-state activities. However, Salalfi left a huge fund to his disciple Ghalib, presumably generated from a number of Saudi sources.

The leaders of the Ahl-e-Hadith Jami'at, after their initial failure to keep the organization intact, began an effort to regain lost ground in 1994 through establishing new madrassahs. Significantly, the Ahl-e-Hadith Jubo Sangha (AHJS), the rival organization to the Jami'at, throughout the eighties, established the madrassahs with a political goal: to engage the students in jihad against Islamic failings, including treating shrines with respect. This was the central point of contention when Ghalib left the Jami'at-i-Ahl-e-Hadith and created his own organization.

The Qawmi madrassahs established by the AHJS and the AHAB were intended primarily to recruit activists and create a support base for their political objectives, instead of providing Islamic education.[14] The modus operandi of these madrassahs bears out this statement. The *Daily Star*, quoting a student of the Salafi madrassah, remarked that activism is an essential part of the education provided in these madrassahs: "Every student of the nearly 700 Ahab madrasas across the country must work with a suitable front organisation of Ahab, sources said yesterday. For example, students up to class seven work with Sonamoni, the children's wing of Ahab, while students of upper classes are usually involved with Ahl-e-Hadith Jubo Shangha, Ahab's youth wing, until they are mature enough for Ahab membership, said Hussain, an Alim student at Salafi Madrasa."[15] The newspaper further mentioned that "Ahab has its own process of recruiting imams and muezzins for its mosques. 'Just anybody can't be an imam at our mosques. Our imams are trained on how to bring about a social revolution through preaching and know how to recruit new members,' said a teacher at Salafi Madrasa."

THE PROLIFERATION OF MADRASSAHS

The growth of the madrassahs of the Ahl-e-Hadith persuasion in the eighties received very little attention because this was consistent with the long-term trend. Available statistics in regard to Aliya madrassahs bears testimony to the phenomenal growth of madrassahs in Bangladesh since the mid-seventies. The rate of growth of the postprimary madrassahs documented in table 4.2 shows that over a period of thirty-two years (1972–2004), they have grown about 732 percent. Madrassahs have grown at an average annual rate of 6.8 percent. Over the decade between 1983 and 1993, the growth was almost 100 percent; in the following eleven years (1993–2004), the overall increase was about 111 percent. The most significant growth has taken place at dakhil (secondary) level. In the first decade after the creation of the state of Bangladesh (1972–1983) the annual rate of growth was 7.2 percent; in the second decade (1983–1993), the rate was 8.8 precent; and in the third decade (1993–2004), the rate was 8.3 percent. Over the thirty-two year period 1972–2004, the growth of dakhil madrassahs has been astounding: 1,103 percent. The annual rate of growth has been 8.1 percent.[16] The increase in the number in institutions has been matched by the number of students enrolled in these institutions. In terms of absolute numbers, the growth is phenomenal: from 400,000 in 1972 to 3.43 million in 2003. The number of teachers has grown to 128,000 from a meager 14,000 (table 4.3).

The reported number of ibtedayee madrassahs has varied enormously. However, we can glean data for a seven-year period between 1995 and 2002 (table 4.4). In contrast to the trend in the postprimary stage, ibtedayee madrassahs (and primary classes attached to high madrassahs) have declined sharply from 13,951 in 1995 to 7,017 in 2002.[17] The decline can be attributed to two factors. First, between 1996 and 2003, despite a nominal increase in the number of satellite and community schools, the total number of primary schools of all types decreased from 80,818 to 79,883. This downward trend affected the ibtedayee madrassahs

TABLE 4.2

GROWTH OF SECONDARY AND POST-SECONDARY MADRASSAHS IN BANGLADESH, 1972–2004

Types of madrassah	No. of institutions					Growth rate in percentage									
						1972–1983		1983–1993		1993–1999		1993–2004		1972–2004	
	1972	1983	1993	1999	2004	OVER 11 YEARS	ANNUAL	OVER 10 YEARS	ANNUAL	OVER 6 YEARS	ANNUAL	OVER 11 YEARS	ANNUAL	OVER 32 YEARS	ANNUAL
Dakhil	765	1,645	3,825	4,865	9,206	115.0	7.2	132	8.8	27.2	4.1	140.7	8.3	1103.4	8.1
Alim	302	508	806	1,090	1,180	68.2	4.8	58.6	4.7	35.2	5.2	46.4	3.5	290.7	4.4
Fazil	300	591	831	1,000	1,180	97.0	6.4	40.6	3.5	20.3	3.1	42.0	3.2	293.3	4.4
Kamil	54	61	97	141	180	12.9	1.1	59.0	4.8	45.4	6.4	85.6	5.8	233.3	3.8
Total	1,412	2,805	5,561	7,096	11,746	98.6	6.1	98.3	7.1	27.6	4.2	111.2	7.0	731.9	6.8

Sources: 1972: Government of Bangladesh, *Education Commission Report 1974*, 81. 1983, 1993, and 1999: Bangladesh Bureau of Education, Information and Statistics, and Government of Bangladesh, *Education Commission 2003 Report*. 2004: Government of Bangladesh, *Education Commission Report 2003*, 271. The growth rates were computed by the author.

TABLE 4.3

ALIYA MADRASSAHS IN BANGLADESH: ENROLLMENT AND TEACHERS, 1970–2005

	1970	1972	1975	1977	1978	1980	1981	1985	1990	1992	1995
No. of institutions	1,518	1,412	1,830	1,976	2,329	2,684	2,466	3,739	5,793	5,959	5,977
Students	283,380	400,000	291,191	375,000	423,000	380,013	388,000	638,926	996,996	1,278,240	1,837,013
Teachers	16,015	14,000	18,728	21,579	22,643	28,499	22,969	31,945	81,636	83,761	85,351

	1999	2000	2001	2002	2003	2004	2005 (est)
No. of institutions	7,096	7,279	7,651	7,820	8,410	8,410	8,897
Students	2,935,348	3,112,205	3,299,107	3,398,043	3,438,707	3,499,035	3,597,453
Teachers	100,800	108,491	109,993	113,810	128,380	123,744	128,084

Sources: Data for the years 1970, 1975, 1980, 1985, 1990, 2000, 2001, and 2002 are provided by Bangladesh Bureau of Education Information and Statistics (BANBEIS). The 1972 data are from the education commission report headed by Qudrut-i-Khuda, commonly referred to as the Khuda Commission report. The 1978 data does not include Kamil madrassahs and the students enrolled at Kamil level (A.Z.M. Shamsul Alam, *Madrassah Sikhsha*, provides a different set of numbers for madrassahs, students, and teachers for 1978. Quoting an official account, Alam (p. 5) suggests that the numbers are: 1,622 madrassahs, 350,000 students, and 17,624 teachers. 2003 figures used here are from the BANBEIS, but the Madrassah Board claims to have 15,661 institutions, 2.82 million students, and 133,445 teachers. 1999, 2004, and 2005 (estimated) data gathered from the *Bangladesh Economic Survey 2005*, Ministry of Finance, Government of Bangladesh.

TABLE 4.4

IBTIDAYEE MADRASSAHS IN BANGLADESH, 1995–2002

	1995			1996			1997		
	INSTITUTIONS	ENROLLMENT	TEACHERS	INSTITUTIONS	ENROLLMENT	TEACHERS	INSTITUTIONS	ENROLLMENT	TEACHERS
Ibtedayee	10,788	7,01,293	41,954	9,499	6,14,160	37,943	8,231	5,42,039	32,316
Percentage	9.21	3.39	11.71	8.11	3.24	10.44	6.91	2.78	9.03
Attached to high madrassahs	3,163	253,095	12,919	2,759	233,934	11,332	2,850	243,517	11,742
Percentage	2.70	1.37	3.60	2.36	1.23	3.11	2.40	1.25	3.28
Total percentage		4.76			4.47			4.03	

	1998			2000			2002		
	INSTITUTIONS	ENROLLMENT	TEACHERS	INSTITUTIONS	ENROLLMENT	TEACHERS	INSTITUTIONS	ENROLLMENT	TEACHERS
Ibtedayee	7,173	438,715	28,196	3,710	417,411	14,760	3,443	417,000	
Percentage	5.74	2.20	7.95	4.8	2.4	4.8		2.3	
Attached to high madrassahs	2,948	2,45,096	11,498	3,437	403,621	14,318	3,574	403,000	
Percentage	2.36	1.23	3.24	4.5	2.3	4.6		2.2	
Total percentage		3.43			4.7			4.5	

Sources: 1995–1998 data are from CAMPE-UPL, *Hope Not Complacency: State of Primary Education in Bangladesh*, 80. Figures for 2000 are provided by Ministry of Primary and Mass Education and cited in ADB-World Bank, *Bangladesh Public Expenditure Review 2001*, Table 1.3. Other sources provide a different set of numbers; the UNESCO report of 2000 put the total figure at 12,350; ibtidayee institutions: 3,843; enrollment: 438,957; teachers: 15,774; primary-level classes attached to high madrassahs: institutions: 3,574; enrollment: 417,383; and teachers: 14,885; UNESCO, *EFA 2000 Assessment Country Reports Bangladesh* 2000. Figures for 2002 are provided by the Ministry of Primary and Mass Education in 2004, also quoted in Global March—ICCLE, *Review of Child Labor, Education and Poverty Agenda: Bangladesh Country Report 2006*, 7. Other sources suggest a total (both ibtidayee and attached to high madrassahs) of 6,423 institutions, 1,552 million students (with 310,000 in attached madrassahs), and 26,778 teachers.

in particular. Second, there has been a major increase in the total enrollment, thanks to a combination of centralized policy making and pluralist provision. This increased number has been largely absorbed by the mainstream government schools. But a significant number also enrolled in ibtedayee madrassahs. The number of students in 2003 is documented in table 4.5.

The primary education sector in Bangladesh, however, provides an enigmatic picture. The country has been rightly applauded for its success in "expanding access to primary and to some extent degree secondary, education for the poor and for the girls."[18] The gross primary enrollment rates, which were only 61 percent in 1980, increased to 72 percent in 1990 and to 96 percent by 2000. In 2002, national gross enrollment rate was 106.34. In terms of absolute numbers, between 1991 and 2003, enrollment increased from 12.36 million to 17.46 million. On the other hand, at least 2.4 million children aged six to ten years have remained outside the schools.[19] In some ways, these children become the vast pool of potential madrassah students, particularly of Qwami madrassahs.

There are no official figures regarding the Qwami madrassahs. These madrassahs drew scant attention from researchers and perhaps policy makers until they appeared on the political scene in the nineties. A report from Bangladesh Bureau of Education, Information and Statistics (BANBEIS) in 1992 maintained that the number was three thousand, and boasted that "some of them are functioning as [the] highest seat of Islamic learning attracting foreign students to pursue Islamic studies and research."[20] In 1998, government sources claimed that the number was 2,043.[21] A study conducted in 2004, however, estimates the number as around four thousand.[22] In 2003, the Befakul Madarisil

TABLE 4.5

NUMBER OF ALIYA IBTIDAYEE (PRIMARY LEVEL) STUDENTS BY GRADE
AND DIVISION IN BANGLADESH, DECEMBER 2003

Division	Class 1	Class 2	Class 3	Class 4	Class 5	Total
Barisal	83,233	66,715	56,477	51,473	45,812	303,710
Chittagong	65,016	54,823	54,889	54,955	54,392	284,075
Dhaka	134,947	95,530	83,518	74,756	73,272	462,023
Khulna	58,629	40,018	37,107	35,736	36,990	208,480
Rajshahi	186,603	137,205	119,244	108,824	103,304	655,180
Sylhet	13,956	9,980	9,359	9,048	9,612	51,955
Total	542,384	404,271	360,594	334,792	323,382	1,965,423

Source: Asian Development Bank, "People's Republic of Bangladesh: Preparing the Secondary Education Sector Improvement Project—II," 184.

Arabia Bangladesh (Bangladesh Qwami Madrassah Education Board), one of the umbrella organizations that claim to represent the Qwami madrasssahs, put the total figure at forty-three thousand.[23] In early 2006, the secretary general of the organziation, Abdul Jabbar, claimed the board has a list of fifteen thousand madrassahs. The list, he acknowledged, is incomplete, as a large number of institutions did not register with the board. He also mentioned that in 2005, in an application to the prime minister seeking official recognition to these madrassahs, the board estimated the number of Qwami madrassahs at 15,250 with 1.85 million students and 132,150 teachers.[24]

The variation in number is due to the fact that these institutions do not have to register with any government agencies or local administration. They remain outside the purview of the government, as they do not receive any financial aid from it. The number of Furkania and Nurani madrassahs is equally staggering, and there is no way to reach a reliable figure. In 1965–1966, the education department reported a total of 2,929 Furkania and 188 Nurani madrassahs. In 1972, soon after independence, a government report put the combined figure at 6,601.[25] About twenty years later, a survey by BANBEIS estimated that there are at least one hundred thirty thousand madrssahs attached to mosques and sixty thousand independent maktabs.[26] Abdalla et al. quoted an official of the Madrassah Education Board saying that there are 58,124 maktabs/Nurani madrassahs.[27] This number does not include the Furkania madrassahs. According to a UNESCO report, government sources reported the number of maktabs/Hafezia/Furkania madrassahs as 78,821.[28] According to a primary survey of the Qwami Madrassah Education Board, there are about one hundred thousand Furkania maktabs.[29]

These statistics, as I mentioned previously, document a long-term trend. The data for four years (2001–2005) support this trend. Since the BNP-led alliance government came to power in 2001, madrassah education has received increased state support, and madrassahs have grown faster than other educational institutions. The Bangladesh Economic Survey 2004–2005, an annual document published by the Finance Ministry, states that between 2001 and 2005 madrassahs increased by 22.22 percent while general educational institutions grew 9.74 percent.[30] Conversely, during Awami League rule between 1996 and 2001, madrassahs grew 17 percent while general educational institutions grew 28 percent. It is interesting that during 1996–2001 there had been a surge in the number of students in madrassahs. There was an increase of 58 percent compared to 33 percent in general education. Special attention should be given to this figure, because apparently it indicates that the society at large was becoming receptive to and inclined toward religious education. The enrollment figures, particularly their share in total enrollment, should help us to find out whether Bangladeshi society acquiesces in this proliferation of religious education.

Enrollment in Madrassahs

In 2002, primary education was delivered through 78,363 schools serving about 17.6 million children. Of these, 48 percent of the schools were Government Primary Schools (GPS), while the remainder were registered nongovernmental schools partly funded by the government. In terms of enrollment, a significant proportion—39 percent—of students were enrolled in nongovernment schools (table 4.6). Yet primary-level madrassahs, which constitute more than 9 percent of the educational institutions, had a less than 5 percent share of the total enrolled students aged between five and seventeen. This is equally true for the years 1995, 1996, 1997, 1998, and 2000 (table 4.4). However, a survey conducted in ten *upazillas* (the lowest administrative unit) covering 3.2 million people with a primary-school-age population of 512,000 shows a higher level of madrassah enrollment. According to the survey, out of 2,452 educational institutions, 400 were madrassahs, accounting for 9 percent of the students.[31] Interestingly, in 2002 the share of the nonformal schools operated by NGOs was far smaller than generally perceived: about 4 percent

TABLE 4.6

SCHOOLS AND ENROLLMENTS IN BANGLADESH, 2002

Type	Schools		Enrollments	
	NUMBER	%	NUMBER	%
GPS	37,671	48	10,832	61
RNGPS	19,428	25	4,170	24
Community	3,225	4	454	3
HSAPS	1,576	2	499	3
NGPS	1,792	2	307	2
IM	3,443	4	417	2
HMAPS	3,574	5	403	2
Satellite	4,823	6	209	1
NGOs and others	2,831	4	376	2
Total	78,363	100	17,677	100

Source: Government of Bangladesh, *Education Commission Report 2003.*
Note: GPS: government primary schools; RNGPS: registered nongovernment primary schools; HSAPS: high school attached primary schools; NGPS: nongovernment primary schools; IM: ibtedayee madrassahs; HMPAS: high madrassah attached primary schools; NGOs: nonformal schools run by nongovernmental organizations.

of total primary educational institutions were operated by NGOs, and these schools had about 2 percent of the total enrolled students. CAMPE reported the share of nonformal instututions at 1.1 percent in the ten upazillas they surveyed in 2004.

The situation at the secondary level is remarkably different. As noted before, secondary education in Bangladesh covers five academic years, from grade six through grade ten, and concludes with a public examination—the Secondary School Certificate (SSC). Secondary schooling is not compulsory. The local communities run a large proportion of the existing secondary schools. The government provides 90 percent salary support for the teachers of nongovernment schools and a bridge grant for maintenance and construction. In madrassah education, the equivalent stage is the dakhil. At the secondary level there are specialized educational institutions called Cadet colleges which offer secondary and higher secondary education (from grade six through twelve). At the secondary level, students can also pursue two other curricula: a trade certificate, and artisanal courses (that is, ceramics). Additionally, children from affluent families have the option to go to English-medium schools and complete British GCE (General Certificate of Education) courses. The availability of these options makes it difficult to ascertain the exact share of the dakhil students in total secondary-level enrollment figures. Available government statistics show that in 2003, the secondary school-age population in Bangladesh was 17.98 million and a total of 206,557 institutions were offering junior secondary and secondary level general education to 8.12 million students, while 5,995 dakhil madrassahs educated 2.19 million students. These statistics demonstrate two important points: that the gross enrollment rate at the secondary level is about 45 percent, meaning close to 8 million school-age children remain without any formal schooling; and that of the enrolled students, about 20 percent attend madrassahs. The share of secondary-level madrassahs is significantly higher compared to madrassahs at the primary level, but is consistent with the growth of dakhil-level institutions over the last thirty-two years, particularly between 1999 and 2004 (table 4.2). A sample taken recently supports these general observations. A survey of 2,400 households and 600 secondary-level educational institutions throughout the country conducted by Education Watch in 2005 reveals that about 14 percent of students attend madrassahs—close to 11 percent attend dakhil madrassahs and the remainder higher madrassahs.[32] There are an additional 2 percent of students who attend nongraded madrassahs. The survey also found that there is a variation between rural and urban areas. In the rural areas the share of the madrassahs is slightly higher, at 16 percent of total enrollment.

The above statistics related to Aliya madrassahs demonstrate a general trend: that both the number of madrassahs and their share of enrolled students are increasing at a significant rate. As for the Qwami madrassahs, reliable numbers—of institutions and of students—are nonexistent. In early 2006, at least twelve groups claimed to have established separate Qwami madrassah boards and have provided varying numbers of students enrolled in these institutions. I have previously referred to the comments of Abdul Jabbar, who claimed that about 1.8 million students are currently enrolled. Fazlul Hoq Aminee stated on many occasions, including in an interview with the author, that there are at least twenty thousand institutions and 2 million students. Since 1992, the semi-government Islamic Foundation has offered three cycles of one-year maktab or mosque-based Islamic education to 2.41 million students.[33]

The combined figure for the students enrolled at various levels of madrassah education—from preprimary to master's level—estimated to be at least six million is a testimony to the fact that madrassah education is now a major component of the Bangladeshi education system, and that the examination of the causes of and conditions for the proliferation of madrassah education is well overdue. Add to this the growth of the youth population, and it becomes imperative to look at the picture closely. Despite a reduction in the population growth rate from 3 percent to 1.6 percent, the Bangladeshi population is expected to reach or exceed 170 million by 2020. Currently, adolescents and youths (ten to twenty-four years) form the biggest segment of the population of Bangladesh. According to the 2001 census, nearly one-third (32 percent) of the country's population (total 132 million) is in this age group, and 45 percent is below fifteen years. The growth in madrassahs provides an indication of what kind of education these children will be receiving in the future.

WHY ARE THE MADRASSAHS GROWING?

The spectacular growth of madrassahs took place within a sociopolitical context that has also included the rise of Islamism as a political ideology and proliferation of Islamist organizations—both social and political. Understanding this phenomenon demands examination of several equally significant factors, such as the sectoral priorites in funding education, changes in state ideology and Islamization of the society, changes in global politics, particularly the rise of political Islam as an ideology, and Bangladesh's interaction with the global economy.

Allocation of Resources: Misplaced Priorities

One can say without hesitation that over the last decades educational opportunities have expanded in Bangladesh. But it also true that "the expansion of the entire system . . . was not enough to draw in all of the poorest."[34] The Education Watch 2004 survey confirms that the most prominent factor related to differences among groups of children with respect to enrollment, repetition, dropout, and participation in primary education was the socioeconomic category of the child. For example, a child from an "always in food deficit" family had a 30 percent lower chance of being enrolled in a school and five times greater chance of dropping out compared to a child from a "surplus" family. In the six-to-fourteen age group in the poorest economic category, one-third of the children were nonstudents and at work or unemployed, and 30 percent were students and working at the same time. In the "surplus" group, there was about the same proportion of both students and working students; but only 7.5 percent of the children were nonstudents, either working or without any work.[35] Similarly, in 1999, Education Watch found that of the 23 percent of children not enrolled in schools, 79 percent were poor compared to 66 percent of those enrolled.

The failure of public education to reach the poorest section of the society, particularly in the rural areas, has paved the way for the expansion of madrassah education. The government allocation for education in general has remained very low throughout the entire history of Bangladesh. Government expenditure on education was 0.73 percent of total GDP in the seventies, 1 percent in the early eighties, 1.3 percent in the late eighties, and no higher than 2.4 percent in the nineties (table 4.7). Allocation to education in the five-year plans also demonstrates that education has remained a low priority (table 4.8). This has had a devastating effect as the population has grown. Additionally, the urban bias of planning and allocations made education opportunities unavailable to a section of the rural population. This created a void prompting the community to find local solutions. In a society where "primary education had been entirely a local effort" until the nationalization of community-based primary schools in 1973,[36] it is not surprising that local people came forward with an indigenous solution, that is, to establish schools with limited resources and based on available infrastructure, which often meant mosques and orphanages. The situation, however, began to change in the early nineties as NGOs increasingly became partners in providing nonformal education. While the education projects of the NGOs have facilitated the extension of opportunities to the rural population, it has also engendered a conflict between the conservative elements of rural society and the NGOs, as these new educational institutions appeared to challenge the authority of the local mullahs and Islamists.[37]

While successive governments, under pressure from international donor communities, extended support to the NGOs in their efforts to expand primary education, they appeased the Islamists by increasing the allocation to madrassah education. The increase of allocations for madrassahs at the expense of secular primary educational institutions has made the situation worse. Between 1973 and 2000, for example, the number of primary schools grew by 165 percent while the dakhil madrassahs grew by 767 percent. Between

TABLE 4.7

TRENDS IN THE LEVEL OF GOVERNMENT EXPENDITURE ON
EDUCATION IN BANGLADESH, 1973–2000
(percentage of GDP)

Fiscal year	Revenue expenditure	Development expenditure	Total expenditure	Expenditure on primary education
1973–1980 average	0.63	0.27	0.9	
1981–1985 average	0.73	0.23	1.0	
1986–1990 average	1.03	0.30	1.3	
1991	1.06	0.16	1.2	0.9
1992	1.14	0.21	1.4	1.1
1993	1.34	0.47	1.8	1.2
1994	1.36	0.66	2.0	1.4
1995	1.30	1.06	2.4	1.5
1996	1.30	0.83	2.1	1.3
1997	1.30	0.90	2.2	1.3
1998	1.34	0.73	2.1	1.2
1999	1.35	0.80	2.1	1.2
2000	1.37	0.84	2.2	1.2

Source: Data provided by the Ministry of Finance, Government of Bangladesh, and
Naomi Hossain, *Access to Education*, 10.

1991 and 1998, even after the government made primary education compulsory,
the number of public primary schools remained unchanged at 38,000. At the
same time, the government increased its expenditure for madrassahs from taka
180.12 crores in 1994–1995 to taka 295.00 crores in 1998–1999.

One can ask whether the decision to increase funding for madrassahs
was guided by pragmatism or, in other words, are these institutions more
efficient in delivering the services? Five indicators are commonly used to
assess the efficiency levels of educational institutions; they are: promotion,
dropout, repetition, retention, and attendance rates. Studies have revealed
that madrassahs have the lowest rate of promotion, retention, and attendance,
and the highest rate of dropout and repetition compared to state-managed

TABLE 4.8

ALLOCATIONS IN THE FIVE-YEAR PLANS AND EDUCATION SECTOR IN BANGLADESH
(in crores taka)

Plans	Total allocation	Allocation to education	% allocation to education
First Five-Year Plan (1973–1978)	4,455	316	7.1
Two-Year Plan (1978–1980)	3,861	186	4.81
Second Five-Year Plan (1980–1985)	16,060	836	5.20
Third Five-Year Plan (1985–1990)	38,600	1,370	3.54
Fourth Five-Year Plan (1990–1995)	67,230	3,289	4.89
Fifth Five-Year Plan (1997–2002)	203,422.9	128,680.15	6.32

Source: Compiled from various Five-Year Plans of Bangladesh.

TABLE 4.9

UNIT COSTS IN EDUCATION BY LEVEL IN BANGLADESH, 1999

Level	Annual cost per student ($)	Cost per student as percent of GNP per capita	No. of student years to produce a graduate	Cost per graduate ($)
Primary	12.7	3.6	8.7	110.5
Secondary				
Government	67.9	19.4	13	882.7
Non-gov't	16.3	4.7	13	211.9
Madrassah (gov't)	161.6	46.2	18	2,909.0
Gov't college	88.6	25.3	3.3	292.0
Technical	300.0	85.7	NA	NA
Degree college	93.0	26.5	NA	NA
University	731.1	210.0	NA	NA

Source: Estimated by World Bank, *Bangladesh Education Sector Review* 1, 68.

and nonformal general schools. For example, Titumir and Hossain note that the attendance rate is 87.5 percent in nonformal schools, 58.8 percent in government schools, and 46.1 percent in madrassahs; and the dropout rate is 7.8 percent in madrassahs as opposed to 3.3 percent in nonformal schools and 4.7 percent in government schools.[38] Lack of resources or overcrowding cannot be blamed for the poor performance of the madrassahs. The 2001 data shows that madrassahs have the most favorable teacher-student ratio—1:28 as opposed to 1:70 in government schools, 1:47 in private schools, and 1:31 in nonformal schools.[39] The larger number of teachers in madrassahs has obviously driven up the per capita unit cost and per capita rearing cost in madrassahs (table 4.9 and table 4.10). In other words, although madrassah education has been expensive compared to secular public education, successive governments have continued funding these institutions.

The lack of funding for the public education sector and the implicit bias of successive governments toward religious institutions provide us with some clues to the causes of growth of Aliya madrassahs, but they also raise two

TABLE 4.10

PER STUDENT GOVERNMENT RECURRING COST BY TYPE OF
INSTITUTION IN BANGLADESH, 2003–2004

Type of institution	Per student cost (taka)
Govt. primary school	1,238
Non-govt. primary school (registered)	470
Govt. secondary school	4,938
Non-govt. secondary school	1,174
Govt. madrassah	5,695
Non-govt. madrassah	1,480
Govt. college	4,722
Non-govt. college	4,019
Govt. polytechnic institute	13,536
Govt. vocational training institute	13,810
Govt. primary training institute	12,949
Teacher's training college (govt.)	10,655
Cadet college	67,546
University (public)	34,115

Source: Interview with an official of the Bangladesh Bureau of Education, Information and Statistics (BANBEIS), 2006.

questions: first, why has government shown a predilection for religion-based education? Second, how have the Qwami madrassahs, which did not receive government support, thrived? Answers to these questions can be found in contemporaneous changes in domestic politics, particularly in the ideological shift of the Bangladeshi state.

Shifts in the Sociopolitical Environment

A watershed in the history of Bangladesh is 10 October 2001. The four-party coalition government led by the Bangladesh National Party (BNP) that came to power on that day epitomized the transformation of the sociopolitical environment of Bangladesh, and the ideological shift of the Bangladeshi state over three decades. For the first time in the history of Bangladesh, the Jamaat-i-Islami, which had opposed independence, found its way into the cabinet as a partner of the alliance. A nation that had emerged in 1971 on the basis of secular-socialistic principles and whose constitution—framed in November 1972—banned the use of religion in politics saw the phenomenal rise of the most prominent Islamist party of the country from the political wilderness to the seat of power. It is this transformation that has played a pivotal role in the growth of madrassahs in Bangladesh and that therefore needs to be examined thoroughly.[40]

At independence, Bangladesh declared secularism to be one of its founding principles and banned all religious political parties.[41] The Awami League, which played a pivotal role in the struggle for national independence and became the first ruling party of the country, soon began to undercut the spirit of secularism. The regime's growing tilt toward religious rhetoric can be attributed to the rupture of its ideological hegemony over the masses established during the struggle against Pakistani colonial rule. The relevance of nationalism as the hegemonic ideology was lost and attempts to fill the void with a new ideology (that is, Mujibism) failed. The crisis accelerated after the demise of the Awami League (AL) regime following a coup d'état in 1975. Over the following fifteen years, military regimes faced a crisis of legitimacy in addition to a lack of moral leadership. The military regimes, which usurped power through coups in 1975 and 1982 and ruled the country until 1990, pursued policies of Islamization as a means to gain much-needed political legitimacy. This provided the previously banned religion-based parties with the opportunity to resurface in the political arena.

The military regime led by General Zia-ur Rahman took several steps beginning in 1978 that revealed an intent to make Islam the focal point of the regime's ideology. Although they appeared initially to be more symbolic than substantial, these steps proved to be long lasting. Two of them involved education. In 1977, the government appointed a "syllabi committee," which declared that "Islam is a code of life, not just the sum of rituals. A Muslim has to live his personal, social, economic and international life in accordance with Islam from childhood to death. So the acquiring of knowledge of Islam is compulsory for all Muslims—men and women."[42] In 1978, the government established a separate directorate within the Education Ministry and set up the Madrassah Education Board to oversee madrassah education. The board's responsibilities included standardization of madrassah curricula and tests. The board was entrusted with the task of making madrassah education equivalent to secular education. This entailed creating opportunities for madrassah-educated students to enter university. The second change was the introduction of Islamiat—a course on Islamic studies—at primary and secondary levels (that is, grades one to eight). This course was made mandatory for all Muslim students. The government established a new Ministry of Religious Affairs. Soon afterward, Eid-e-Miladunabi—the Prophet Muhammad's birthday—was declared a national holiday. The state-controlled electronic media began broadcasting Azan—the call for prayers—five times a day and to carry programs on Islam's role in daily life. At one level, this seemed at best tokenism, yet taken together the measures signaled a clear shift in policy with long-term implications. The cabinet and the newly established ruling party were composed of defectors from various political parties and people who had collaborated with the Pakistani regime in 1971. But, more important, those who had close ties with religious organizations became more visible within the cabinet. Maulana Abdul Mannan, leader of the Jamaat-i-Mudarresin (Association of Madrassah Teachers), for example, became a close confidant of Zia-ur Rahman.

General Zia's regime, which lasted from 1975 through 1980, when he was assassinated in an abortive coup, created a new ideological terrain with religion, territoriality of identity, and national security at its center. The new political party, the Bangladesh Nationalist Party, formed under the leadership of Zia-ur Rahman in 1978, emphasized the role of Islam in daily life and as a guiding political ideology. Constitutional changes, including the deletion of secularism as a state principle and the inclusion in the constitution of "absolute trust and faith in the Almighty Allah" and "Bismillah-ar-Rahman-ar-Rahim" (In the name of Allah, the Beneficent, the Merciful) marked a decisive move away from a secular nationhood.

This was taken further by the regime of General Ershad during his military rule, which spanned 1982 to 1990. Like his predecessor, General Ershad turned to Islamization to legitimize his rule. In late 1982, he declared in a religious gathering that Islam would be the basis of the new social system and would be given its due place in the constitution. On 15 January 1983, Ershad declared that making Bangladesh an Islamic country was the goal of his struggle.[43] He also stated his intention to introduce Islamic principles into the cultural life of Bangladeshi Muslims. The announcement was made at a gathering of madrassah teachers organized by Maulana Abdul Mannan, head of the Association of Madrassah Teachers and a former minister in the Zia cabinet. In the face of strong opposition from political parties and periodic popular uprisings, Ershad utilized Islam as a tool to its fullest extent. In June 1988, the constitution was amended to declare Islam the state religion.[44]

The secularist political parties, at the same time, pursued a policy of expediency and befriended the religiopolitical forces that had accorded them recognition as legitimate political actors. Between 1982 and 1990, the year the Ershad regime was toppled in a popular urban uprising, opposition political parties, including secularists, worked closely with the Islamists, thus providing the latter with political legitimacy while idioms and icons of religion became central to the political discourse of Bangladesh. For example, the Awami League, which once took pride in its secular identity, made a remarkable change in its approach toward religion and religion-based political parties. By the early nineties, it preferred to be portrayed as a party that valued Islam as an integral part of the culture of Bangladesh. Beginning in 1991, the statements of party leaders and party publicity materials showed that the Awami League was eager to present itself as a suitable custodian of Islam in Bangladesh.

In the new democratic era of Bangladeshi history (1991–January 2007), the two main political parties have sought the support of Islamists, particularly the Jamaat-i-Islami, either to achieve power or to topple a democratically elected regime. The BNP, for example, courted the Jamaat in 1991 to form a cabinet when it lacked the necessary votes in the Parliament.[45] This "marriage of convenience" was over within two and half years, after which the Awami League succeeded in wooing the Jamaat into the fold to unseat the BNP regime through popular agitation. The Jamaat went back to the BNP camp again in 1998 and became a partner of a coalition that came to power in 2001.

Pursuing the politics of expediency is not the sole preserve of the two major political parties; the action of the Jatiya Party led by General Ershad in 2001 demonstrates that others are equally adept in this exercise. In 2001, when Ershad left the opposition alliance under pressure and tacit threats from the ruling Awami League, he formed an Islamist alliance called the Islami Jatiya Oikya Front (IJOF, Islamic National United Front) with the Islami Shashontontro Andolon (Islamic Constitution Movement). The pir of Charmonai, Syed Fazlul Karim, leader of the Islamic Constitution Movement (ICM), declared that the IJOF would establish an Islamic government in the country if voted to power. Meanwhile, the Jatiya Party's election manifesto, especially on issues pertaining to religion, inferred that the ICM was dictating terms. The JP election manifesto stated that, if the party was voted to power, "existing laws would be brought in line with the principles of the Quran and Sunnah, . . . laws contrary [to the] Quran and Sunnah shall be amended; . . . Shariah laws would be followed as far as possible; . . . special laws would be made for punishing those making derogatory remarks against the Prophet and the Shariah; . . . religious education would be made compulsory at all levels."

All this shows that within three decades of Bangladesh's independence, Islamists had emerged as a formidable political force, Islam had become a prominent political ideology, and religious rhetoric occupied a central position in political discourse.

These developments reflect an Islamization process—a process of ideological shift of the state—with the acquiescence of the secularists. Concomitant to these political changes there has been a gradual shift at societal level, especially in attitudes toward the possible fusion of religious ideology and social practices. Despite some resistance from civil society, there is a growing trend within Bangladesh society of tolerating and accepting a particular interpretation of Islam that is being continually redefined by the state and the socioreligious organizations linked to the Islamists.

These sociopolitical developments indeed provided an environment for the growth of madrassahs, but their operations needed money and moral support, especially in the rural areas. These much-needed resources largely came from Bangladeshi migrants in the Gulf, and the Islamic NGOs operating within the country.

The Migrant Connection

Since the oil boom of 1974, countries in the Gulf region have attracted a large number of short-term migrants for contractual jobs from relatively poor countries. Bangladesh is no exception. Since 1976, exporting unskilled, semi-skilled, and skilled labor to these countries has increasingly become one of the main sources of the country's foreign revenue. Labor migration has impacted positively on the nation's economy in at least two ways: first, it has kept the unemployment rate low, and second, it has brought a flow of remittances, often in the face of dwindling exports. Studies have shown that the contribution of migrant worker remittances to Bangladesh's GDP has risen from 1 percent in 1977–1978 to 5 percent in 1982–1983. In the nineties, the rate continued at the level of 4 percent.[46] Data from the Bureau of Manpower Employment and Training (BMET), a government agency in Bangladesh, show that between 1976 and January 2002 the number of Bangladeshis who migrated on short-term employment contracts was about 3 million. Although Bangladesh also exports migrant workers to some Southeast Asian countries, seven Middle Eastern and North African countries have been the main destinations. They account for more than 82 percent of migrant workers from Bangladesh. These countries are Saudi Arabia, Kuwait, Qatar, Iraq, Libya, Bahrain, and Oman. Saudi Arabia alone accounts for half of the workers who migrated from Bangladesh during this period. These workers are mostly male and young, overwhelmingly unskilled with little education, and are drawn from rural areas. Usually the length of their stay abroad is about four years.

While the economic impact of the migration has been enormously positive for the country, there have been major social costs. The migrant workers have been exposed to a set of retrogressive social values, and a less tolerant version of Islam in the host countries. Lack of education provided them with a notion that Islam practiced in its birthplace is more authentic than that practiced anywhere else. Thus upon returning home the migrants try to emulate the lifestyle and values they have been exposed to and share them with their communities. In poorer rural communities, the returnees also assume a social status that allows them to become authority figures. This has contributed to the deepening of social conservatism in the name of Islam and has played a crucial role in the Islamization process Bangladesh has been undergoing since 1975. To maintain the newly earned social status of the returnee migrants, these values and norms needed to be reproduced in the society. This is where the madrassahs, especially Qwami madrassahs, became relevant and necessary institutions—as guardians of orthodoxy and propagators of a certain version of Islam akin to Wahabbism of Saudi Arabia. The migrants have contributed to the Qwami madrassahs, because the management structure of madrassahs, especially their autonomy from the government, allows patrons to have more control over the institution. The other motivation of the members of this new social stratum has been the "act of piousness." They often contributed to local mosques which in turn maintain Furkanai and/or Nurani madrassahs.

One neglected aspect of the philanthropic attitude of the returnee migrants is their desire for upward mobility. As most of the migrants come from very poor backgrounds they have generally encountered social exclusion and often humiliation at the hands of the socially powerful segments of the society during most of their lives. They lack education or other necessary assets to be counted in the society and to facilitate upward social mobility. Upon returning from abroad they discover that although they have moved upward in terms of wealth they still face social exclusion. The job provided them with wealth, yet they remain at the bottom of the social hierarchy. It is commonly perceived by the returning migrants that involvement with educational and religious institutions will help them move upward in the social hierarchy. Interestingly, such perceptions are not wrong. There are ample examples in rural Bangladesh that these acts of philanthropy have provided individuals with the opportunity to interact with local government officials and political leaders and move in socially powerful circles.

Contributions of the Islamic NGOs

South Africa is far away from Bangladesh and events there have little impact on the South African press. Yet on 31 January 1999, the *Sunday Times*, a prominent newspaper of Durban, published a news item on Bangladesh that attracted the attention of many.[47] The headline, "Priest in Terror Probe," was not a catchy one but the subhead grabbed readers' attention: "Held SA moulana suspected of links with America's enemy number one." The report read: "A South African Muslim high priest arrested this week in Bangladesh is under police investigation for alleged links to a notorious international terror." It continued, "Port Elizabeth moulana and popular Islamic scholar, Ahmed Sadiq, 60, and a Pakistani, Mohammad Sajid, are suspected of having ties with Saudi dissident and terrorist mastermind, Osama bin Laden." For many in South Africa this came as surprise, because they knew Sadiq as a registered fund-raiser, and to his friends he was "a champion of poor." The reporter revealed that Sadiq had opened about 500 madrassahs in Bangladesh after collecting funds from various countries including South Africa. The story in Bangladesh, however, was not an uncommon one. Sadiq, Sajid, and forty-five others were arrested in Dhaka for their alleged connection with a militant organization called Harkat-ul-Jihad. Two of its members had been apprehended when they had tried to kill the most reputed poet of the country two weeks earlier. Harkat-ul-Jihad, a network of militant Islamists, was yet to become a familiar name. But fingers were pointed toward some madrassahs as their recruiting and training grounds. Rumors circulated that Osama bin Laden had given $4 million for training and recruiting members of extremist groups to carry out a reign of terror in Bangladesh. The alleged recipients included Mohammad Sadiq and his madrassah network located in the port city of Chittagong and in the rural areas of the district. The news of Mohammad Sadiq's arrest reached South Africa on 28 January, three days after police took him to custody, through a reporter of the *Sunday Times*. The reporter contacted the organization called Servants of Suffering Humanity (SOSH) to which Sadiq belonged to verify a Reuters report, saying that the two foreigners arrested in connection with the attempt on the life of poet Shamsur Rahman had confessed that they received funds from Osama bin Laden for running the training camps. Quoting police sources, the Bangladeshi media reported that Sadiq's organization, the SOSH, had set up 421 madrassahs in various parts of the country. The police also claimed that one of the madrassahs funded by the SOSH in Lalkhan Bazar in Chittagong had been used as a military training camp for fourteen years and had trained about twenty-five thousand young men. While these claims were being debated in the press, the arrests of two foreigners involved in madrassah education brought to light a fact that was not known to most Bangladeshis— the involvement of international Islamic nongovernment organizations in local madrassah education.

Since independence, NGOs have grown substantially in Bangladesh due to the failure of the state to assist the poor and reduce poverty, particularly in rural areas. The NGOs came to the fore as agents of development in the late eighties. Supported by Western funding agencies, NGOs embarked on income-generating micro-credit projects and projects such as health services, education, human rights, and advocacy. While the role of NGOs became pivotal in the development efforts of the nation, they also drew criticism from various sections of the society.[48] Islamists have been critical of these NGOs, saying that the NGOs aided by Jews and Christian conspirators were undermining Islamic cultural values, spreading atheism, converting people to Christianity, and trying to create an aggressively feminist, impure society. In the early nineties, Islamist organizations devised a two-prong strategy: one was to attack the secular NGOs.[49] The other was to establish Islamic NGOs with the help of foreign Islamist NGOs such as Rabita al-Alam al-Islam, the World Assembly of Muslim Youth, the al-Haramain Islamic Foundation, the International Islamic Relief Organization (IIRO), the Revival of Islamic Heritage Society (RIHS), and the Ishra Islamic Foundation, to name but a few.[50] The Islamic NGOs placed education at the top of their agenda and became involved in setting up madrassahs in various parts of the country.

The rise of the Islamic NGOs was also facilitated by events beyond the southeastern border of Bangladesh in 1977 and in 1991. In 1977, Burmese immigration and military authorities conducted what they called Operation Nagamin (Dragon King), a national effort to register citizens and deport foreigners prior to a national census. Consequently, by May 1978, more than two hundred thousand Rohingya (Muslims from the northern Burmese state of Arakan) fled to Bangladesh alleging widespread army brutality, rape, and murder. The International Committee of the Red Cross and the Bangladeshi government supplied emergency relief but were quickly overwhelmed. The Bangladeshi government requested assistance from the United Nations, and soon thirteen camps for refugees were established along the border. The government allowed some NGOs to work with the refugees. Rabita al-Alam al-Islami was prominent among them. Although most of the refugees were repatriated within a year, the networks developed by Rabita in the southeastern part of the country remained intact. The areas were close to the site of an ongoing tribal rebellion. This made the region a restricted area and inaccessible to many government agencies. In late 1991, Bangladesh saw another influx of Rohingya refugees, when more than two hundred fifty thousand people fled forced labor, rape, and religious persecution at the hands of the Burmese army. With the assistance of the UN High Commisioner for Refugees (UNHCR) and nongovernmental relief agencies, the Bangladeshi government sheltered the refugees in nineteen camps in the vicinity of Cox's Bazar. Funds for the refugees from international sources soon dried up, and the repatriation process progressed at a slow pace, leaving the Bangladesh government in a precarious situation. By 1997, some two hundred thirty thousand refugees were repatriated. But throughout the process Rabita al-Islam and al-Harmain acted as the principal NGOs working in the refugees' camps. This enabled them to establish unrestrained control over some sections of the hill areas.[51]

The activities of well-known international Islamic NGOs like Rabita have not only helped gather momentum in establishing local Islamic NGOs and soliciting funds from international sources but also provided opportunities to radical international organizations to expand their operations in Bangladesh. The Servants of Suffering Humanity (SOSH) exemplifies this phenomenon. SOSH, based in South Africa, began its operation in Bangladesh in 1996 after registration with the NGO Bureau. The principal objective of the organization is to fight the "onslaught of [the] Christian missionary in poor countries." The organization states that "This vicious Octopus of Kufr has extended its deadly tentacles to a network of outlying villages in Muslim countries to mislead unwary and uninformed Muslims and entrap them in the web of dark kufr. It is said that in Bangladesh alone they are operating in over 800 villages."[52]

SOSH insists that "the ultimate objective of the numerous mission organizations and agencies operating in Bangladesh is the evangelization of the people of Bangladesh. The organization strongly feels that jihad against apostasy has now become a moral duty for the Muslims." SOSH even went so far as to criticize the Taliban, during their heyday, for not being Islamic enough and to reprimand Usama bin Laden for not being radical enough to face the Western conspiracy. Their operations in Bangladesh, as elsewhere, include establishing madrassahs, as part of what they called the Maktab Struggle initiated by their parent organization Mujlisul Ulama of South Africa. The rationale for the struggle: "Hundreds of thousands, if not millions, of the Ummah's children are completely deprived of the very basic and elementary teachings of Islam. All over the world, especially in Muslim countries, children in their thousands are growing up like non-Muslims. Innumerable thousands have already been alienated from Islam and have in the process become cheap fodder for the kufr machine operating under the auspices of the conspirators of the Western world." As for their success, the organization states:

> By the fadhl (grace) of Allah Ta'ala, the Mujlisul Ulama has embarked on this struggle in its own small way. More than a thousand Maktabs (small Madrassahs) with a role of approximately a hundred thousand children have been established in a number of countries. More than 600 of these Maktabs are located in Bangladesh. This number is only a drop in the ocean. In Bangladesh alone there is an urgent need to establish another thousand Maktabs in such villages where the forces of the kuffaar are operative and where there are absolutely no facilities for providing elementary Deeni education to the children.[53]

The SOSH case illustrates three important aspects of madrassah education, particularly Qwami madrassahs: first, the involvement of international nongovernment organizations; second, the presence of radical Islamists in madrassah education; and third, the existence of networks among the madrassahs.

Some of the Islamic NGOs involved in madrassah education had dubious records from the outset, and the questionable track records of some others became known after 2001. The Kuwait-based Revival of Islamic Heritage Society (RIHS, Jam'iyyat Ihya' al-Turah al-Islami) is a case in point. Founded in 1992, the RIHS established branches in various parts of the world within five years "to improve the condition of the Muslim community and develop an awareness and understanding of Islam amongst the non-Muslim communities, by concentrating on youth and education."[54] Significantly, the activities of the RIHS showed a pattern: "a special interest in Islamic or partially Islamic states where a certain level of turbulence prevails, where stagnant economies and governmental corruption can be assailed from a broadly populist viewpoint—and, notably, where there is no historical tradition of Arab Salafi worship."[55] The United States administration included the RIHS in its terror list in February 2003.

The foregoing description clearly shows that the common perception that madrassahs are run purely on public donations and alms is far from true. People certainly do give generous donations to madrassahs, orphanages, and shrines to atone for their sins and to suppress guilty consciences. But a significant number of madrassahs in Bangladesh no longer depend on contributions from *zakat* (almsgiving) and *sadaka* (charity/donations), especially since the Islamic NGOs have begun operating in the country. The scope of the Islamic NGOs and the size of their purses can be understood from the amount of money they receive from donors through legitimate channels. It is estimated that thirty-four major Islamic NGOs, fifteen of which are very active, annually receive about taka 200 crores (approximately $40 million).[56] These NGOs include the International Islamic Relief Organization (IIRO), al-Marakajul Islami, Ishra Islamic Foundation, Ishlahul Muslimin, and al-Forkan Foundations, among others. The funds come from various international organizations and governments. In addition to the organizations mentioned before, Jamia Toras Islami, the Kuwait Joint Relief Committee, and the Nahian Trust based in Abu Dhabi are important contributors.[57] On occasion donors have formed a consortium from which donations are made. These NGOs also receive funds from abroad through personal channels. Often their leaders travel abroad and obtain funds from institutional sources and receive personal donations. Expatriate Bangladeshis and their friends living in Europe, the United States, and the Gulf states donate generously to these NGOs. For example, the Ishlahul Muslimin (IM), which has branches in various countries, raised 50,000 British pounds (approximately $95,000) for its projects in Bangladesh from the Indian Muslim community of Leicester in England in June 2000. Its sympathizers reported in an internet forum that between 1997 and 2000 the organization had raised 3 million pounds (approximately $5.75 million) from England.[58] Sources within the NGO bureau, the government arm for monitoring the activities of NGOs, informed the press that the IM also received 15 million taka in 2004. The IM started its operation in Bangladesh in 1997 and had established a network reaching fifty-four districts of the country by 2005. Al-Haramain Foundation reportedly spent approximately $40 million for the construction of eighty madrassahs and four orphanages between 1992 and 2004.[59] According to their annual report, between 1997 and 2001 AHF brought in taka 20 crores (about $3.2 million). When it was closed down in July 2004, the AHF had been operating in thirty-eight districts and had a five-year grant of taka 19.27 crores (about $3 million dollars) in the pipeline.

Although the presence of militant groups in Bangladesh and the connections between the Islamic NGOs and militancy were reported in the Bangladeshi press, the government did not take any steps until early 2005. On 23 February 2005, the government, in a dramatic departure from its earlier stance, acknowledged the presence of militant Islamist organizations within the country and banned two of them. Alleging that the Jagrata Muslim Janata Bangladesh (JMJB, the Awakened Muslim People of Bangladesh) and the Jamaatul Mujahedin Bangladesh (JMB, the Organization of the Holy Warriors of Bangladesh) had been engaged in subversive activities throughout the country, the government announced its determination "to take action against anyone involved in destroying peace and discipline, and instigating anarchic activities in the name of any organization."[60] Asadullah al-Ghalib, chief of the Ahl-e-Hadith Andolon Bangladesh (AHAB), was arrested on the same day; and scores of supporters were taken into custody within days.[61]

Within less than six months, Bangladesh was rocked by nearly simultaneous blasts of about five hundred bombs in sixty-three districts. The JMB claimed responsibility for these well-orchestrated attacks of 17 August. This was followed by four incidents of suicide attacks. Following the 17 August bombing, intelligence agencies reported that an orphanage funded by the AHF was being utilized to provide training to about five hundred militants of the Jamaatul Mujahedin Bangladesh (JMB, the Organization of the Holy Warriors of Bangladesh) in how to manufacture and use bombs.[62] AHF's involvement with militancy beyond the Chittagong Hill Tracts had been well known to the government for almost three years. On 24 September 2002, seven foreign staff members of the organization including its country director, Sudanese national Hasan Adam, were arrested from its headquarters in an upscale neighborhood of Dhaka. They were, however, secretly put on a plane at the request of a Middle Eastern country.

These Islamic NGOs share not only the ethos but also the same networks and staff. For example, the AHF orphanage used to train the militants was supported by the RIHS after the AHF ceased to operate in Bangladesh. The RIHS itself is also under close scrutiny since the 17 August bomb attacks, because the investigators believe that the organization has funded militant activities.[63] As with the AHF, the government was aware of the shady activities of RIHS and had expelled five officials of the organization in July 2005 for residing illegally and assisting Islamist militants.[64] But expulsion of the staff did not put an end to the activities of the RIHS or their practice of employing people with questionable track records. Four of the former staff of the AHF returned to Bangladesh and joined the RIHS without the approval of the government.[65]

NETWORKS OF QWAMI MADRASSAHS

Relationships among various madrassahs, let alone the existence of a network, stand in complete contrast to the common perception of Qwami madrassahs, which are often described as autonomous institutions managed by local communities with little support from the outside. But closer examination reveals that contrary to the common perception, most of the Qwami madrassahs in Bangladesh are part of large networks. Ikra, a network of fourteen madrassahs established by the Ishlahul Muslimin (IM) under the stewardship of Maulana Fariduddin Mashud, is a case a point. Fariduddin Mashud, a graduate of Deoband Madrassah and a former director of the state-run Islamic Foundation, has established the network in less than five years. Ikra, however, is a very small network compared to the other networks that have been in existence for decades.

In many cases, hundreds of madrassahs operate under the supervision of one large madrassah. For example, Jamia Qu'arania Madrassah, established in 1950, located in Lalbagh at Dhaka controls about 70 small madrassahs; in Patiya district of Chittagong, 300 madrassahs are under the management of Ittehadul Madrassah; in the northeastern district of Sylhet, Azad Deeni Education Board is in charge of 90 madrassahs. In Mymensingh, Sawatul Hera madrassah has authority over 50 madrassahs. Often these large madrassahs perform roles similar to the Madrassah Education Board, but in most cases they provide funds gathered from external sources, exert control over the employees, and use the madrassah infrastructures and students for specific political objectives. The largest networks are controlled by three large madrassahs located in Chittagong and adjacent districts. These three madrassahs are reported to control more than seven thousand smaller madrassahs located throughout the entire country. Activities of these madrassahs—al-Jamiah al-Islamia located in Patiya district, Darul Uloom Mainul Madrassah located in Hathazari, and Darul Uloom Madrassah located in Lalkhan Bazar of Chittagong—are closely coordinated and they appear to be the core institutions of a larger network.

The significance of these networks, especially their implications for radical Islamist politics, can be understood from events that took place in Brahmanbaria, a small southeastern town in December 1998, September 1999, and February 2001, and which serve to demonstrate how these networks are utilized for a specific political agenda. These are just the tip of the iceberg, however.

On 7 December 1998, a gathering of rural poor women, largely beneficiaries of the NGOs, was attacked in Brahmanbaria for not heeding the Islamists' warning not to join the gathering organized by an NGO called Proshika. Throughout the day, the militants unleashed a reign of terror while the local administration remained a silent spectator. At the end of the day, the militants blamed the NGOs for the destruction and called a dawn-to-dusk general strike on the next day to protest against what they claimed to be the partisan role of the police. During the general strike, they set fire to a number of NGO offices, attacked the residences of high-ranking officials of the local administration, and damaged the state-run TV relay station. The NGO activists were practically forced to flee the city. Journalists and eyewitnesses reported that most of the militants who reigned in the city for two consecutive days were young boys of local madrassahs and were led by organizers of the Islami Oikya Jote (IOJ).

Although conflict between the NGOs and the Islamists had been brewing since 1994 and various projects of the NGOs were attacked in several parts of the country, the Brahmanbaria incident was the most dramatic showdown of force by the militants. The place was chosen for several reasons. The most prominent among them was the relative strength of the Islamists. Over the years, madrassahs, under the influence of the militant Islamist party IOJ, proliferated, while various projects of the NGOs were trying to neutralize their influence. According to a government report, Brahmanbaria had 1,645 madrassahs of various kinds—more than 1,400 of which can be classified as Qwami madrassahs; about 2,640 teachers were teaching more than 77,000 students.[66] Some fifty-eight NGOs were engaged in various development projects, most of which targeted poor women. Most of the madrassahs in the area had been under the control of the Jamia Islamia Yunusia Madrassah, the base of Boro Huzur (Elderly Cleric), the spiritual leader of the local IOJ. At that time, at least fifty-four smaller madrassahs were under the direct command of local IOJ leaders associated with the Jamia Islamia Yunusia Madrassah.

The cleric and his supporters insisted that they protested against the celebration organized by the NGO because that would allow thousands of women to mingle with unknown men, which is forbidden in Islam. They also argued that as the guardian of morality it was incumbent on them to resist un-Islamic acts. But there was more to it. The political actions of the NGOs during the previous general election had angered the local Islamists. During the 1996 general elections, NGOs in the region had attempted to influence the voters against the IOJ candidate. The party had already created a large support base through various means. The incumbent member of Parliament of the locality used all the resources at his disposal to strengthen that support base. As the lone member of his party in Parliament, he did not have to compete for resources with other party members. Additionally, as a member of Parliament, he had access to government grants and certain other resources that he utilized fully for the benefit of his organization. Thus, the local IOJ decided to settle the score and used the madrassah students as their foot soldiers.

In late September 1999, local Islamists flexed their muscle once again and gave an ultimatum to all NGOs in Brahmanbaria district to wind up their activities or else face the Islamists' wrath. This time around the government intervened, but only as a deal broker. On October 9, the militants and Proshika reached an agreement in a meeting organized and presided over by the minister of law, Abdul Matin Khasru. The government initiative signaled that, if any misapprehension remained, it had no intention of facing up to the Islamists. The understanding collapsed within six months. Citing an allegedly offensive comment by the head of Proshika about Boro Huzur, the group called a general strike in Brahmanbaria on 19 April 2000. The local wings of the major political parties joined the fray. Addressing a rally during the general strike, the secretary general of IOJ, Fazlul Hoq Amini, called upon the public to kill on sight the Proshika chief Kazi Faruque Ahmed.[67] Although incitement to killing is a criminal offense under Bangladesh law, neither Amini nor anyone else who shared the podium with him was ever charged.

This militant brand of Islamism reappeared with more strength during early 2001, in the so-called pro-fatwa movement. Following a court verdict in January 2001 declaring fatwas illegal, the Islamists with IOJ at the helm launched violent demonstrations in the capital and elsewhere over the following month. The wrath of the militant Islamists erupted on 2 February. During the general strike on the next day, a police constable was lynched. One of the severest clashes between the police and the demonstrators took place a few days later in Brahmanbaria, where seven people died. The student wing of the Islamist alliance, the Islamic Constitution Movement, described the deceased as martyrs of jihad and vowed that "no power on earth can stop the Jihad for Islamic rule in this country."[68]

The strengths of the madrassah network were indeed displayed in the events of Brahmanbaria, yet this organization is small compared to the nexus of militants, madrassahs, and Islamic NGOs developed in the hilly districts of Chittagong in the early nineties and throughout the country over decades. These networks, particularly that developed by the Jamaat ul-Mujaheedin Bangladesh (JMB) in conjunction with the AHAB and with the support of external funds came to light after the bomb attacks on 17 August 2005.

The Dangerous Liaison: Madrassahs, Militancy, and NGOs

When police in the port city of Chittagong arrested a forty-five-year-old man named Salumullah Selim on 22 January 2001, they were unaware of his identity and had no clue as to what they were about to unearth. Police records showed that he had been arrested previously and released. Interrogation revealed that he was the army chief of an Arakan militant group called Arakan Rogingya National Organisation (ARNO).

> More quizzing brought out further startling information. He admitted to police that he trained local madrasa students in armed combat. According to him, more trainers from African and Middle Eastern countries frequently visit Bangladesh to train local Islamist militants. Away in the forest of Bandarban, police followed a narrow trail through rows of betel nut trees. The forest, about twenty-five kilometers from the town, was dense and dark. One had to walk for two and a half hours and cross two streams and hillocks to reach a thatched structure. The hut is a madrasa. Boys take religious lessons during the day; night turns it into a militant camp to train the same madrasa students in arms and explosives. This was one of the many madrasas that militants use as training centres. Three of them were sealed by the government after police raids found dummy rifles for training.[69]

Although the discovery of the training camps was disquieting, it was not an exceptional event in that part of Bangladesh. Local people, and perhaps local officials, were aware of the existence of these training camps established under the guise of madrassahs. This had been in the making since 1977 with the arrival of the refugees from neighboring Burma and the Internal Islamic NGOs who landed soon afterward.

The relationships between militants, madrassahs, and Islamic NGOs began when Rohingya refugees crossed the border, and the government allowed only selected NGOs to work with the refugees. Local NGOs were not permitted, and the Rabita-al Islami became the primary nongovernment organization with unrestricted access to the region where the local tribal population, aided by neighboring India, was waging a war.[70] As a long-term strategy to combat tribal insurgency, the government also sponsored migration of Bengali settlers into the Chittagong Hill Tracts, providing land grants and cash. The settlers, with the connivance of the almost totally Bengali administration, have been able to take over land and even whole villages from the local Jumma population. It is alleged that the government also supported the forcible conversion of the local Buddhist population. As for the Rohiyanga refugees, although the government was unwilling to accept them, it had tacitly supported arming them. After the refugees were repatriated, the NGO in question continued its operations. The nexus solidified in 1992–1993 with the second influx of refugees.

This time around, other Islamic NGOs followed Rabita's lead: the Saudi-based al-Haramain Foundation, the Arab Emirates-based welfare association popularly known as al-Fujira, the Dubai-based organization al-Ansar al-Khairiah, the Kuwait-based organization Dawlatul Kuwait, the Bahrain-based NGO Dawlatul Bahrain, and the International Islamic Relief Organization (IIRO) became visible within a short span of time. Most of these organizations started their operation in the southeastern region and then moved to other areas. Al-Haramain Foundation, for example, opened its first office in Cox's Bazar in 1992. Three years later, in 1995, it opened an office in Dhaka. Their operations outside the southeast include four orphanages in Uttara (a suburb of Dhaka), Nilphamari (a northern district), and Gazipur (a city on the outskirts of Dhaka) and sixty mosques across the country.[71] Another Islamic NGO, the Dubai-based organization al-Ansar al-Khairiah, has headquarters in a remote location in Chittagong.

In the following years, these NGOs worked closely with rebel organizations such as the Rohingya Solidarity Organization (RSO) and the Arakan Rohingya Islamic Front (ARIF) and built hundreds of infrastructures—operating as madrassahs—to train rebels. An investigation by a Bengali newspaper, *Prothom Alo*, revealed that not only do these institutions lack the basic amenities of an educational institution but hardly any students are seen in these places. Local people told the reporter that often young people visit these places in groups and participate in "physical education" during the night. The numbers of madrassahs in these remote parts also make them suspicious. In one hilly upazilla, Ramu, five madrassahs are located within a radius of fifty yards.[72]

In the nineties, the government tacitly supported these developments, as these organizations were used to counteract the tribal rebels. A number of other Burmese rebel organizations, such as the Arakan Rohingya National Organization (ARNO) and the Rohingya National Army (RNA) began moving their headquarters to these areas. Subsequently, some of the rebel Rohingyas managed to get certificates of citizenship from the local authorities, and militant outfits from other parts of the country joined them. Their so-called madrassahs soon became training centers of various militant organizations. The most disturbing development has been the tie between the Rohingya rebels and Islamist militants from other parts of the country. The relationship between the Harkat-ul-Jihad al-Islam (HUJI) and Rohingya rebels is a case in point. The Harkat-ul-Jihad al-Islam Bangladesh was formed under the leadership of Shafiqur Rahman in 1992 when a group of militants returned from Afghanistan after participating in the anti-Soviet war. The organization soon moved to the Chittagong Hill Tracts to help the Rohingya refugees. Subsequently, HUJI and RSO fostered a close relationship acknowledged by HUJI activists arrested in 1998, in 2000, and in 2001. Arrested militants have also acknowledged the existence of various training camps in Chittagong and Cox's Bazar districts centered on Qwami madrassahs established with foreign funds.

An alliance with the RSO not only gave HUJI a footing in the southeastern hilly areas but also protection as Rohingya rebels were receiving the blessings of the government. This alliance was far more than tactical; it was driven by the ideological position of the HUJI—to initiate a struggle for Muslim rights in non-Muslim countries. In this context, Burma was high on the priority list of the HUJI's international organizers. But having the tacit support of the government allowed them to work with impunity. Making the most out of government patronage, it gradually crept into other parts of the country in the nineties and made its presence felt on many occasions. To understand how the network spread throughout the country, we must follow the trail of HUJI both in Pakistan, its birthplace, and in Bangladesh. Although the organizational structure of the HUJI-Bangladesh organization was put together in 1992, the conditions for its emergence began in 1984 when a volunteer corps was organized to join the "jihad" in Afghanistan at the height of the anti-Soviet war. Some three thousand people under the leadership of Abdur Rahman Faruki were motivated to travel in several batches to Afghanistan and fight alongside other volunteer mujahideen. In the following four years at least twenty-four of them died and ten became disabled. In 1988, a delegation of ten self-proclaimed ulama from Bangladesh visited Afghanistan. Among them was Muhammad Sultan Jawak, the founding director of Darul M'Arif al-Islamia, a madrassah located in Chittagong. The returnees of the Afghan war maintained close contacts and were jubilant when the mujahideen captured Kabul in 1992. By then Shafiqur Rahman, a returnee of the Afghan war, had already established contacts with a Pakistani Islamist organization called Harkat-ul-Jihad al-Islami (HUJI). In Pakistan the organization started spontaneously in 1980 when three students of Jamiat ul-Uloom Islamia madrassah in Karachi began their journey to join the Afghan resistance. Initially called Jammat ul-Ansar of Afghanistan, the organization renamed itself Harkat-ul-Jihad al-Islami in 1988. In the meantime they were joined by a small number of militants and began receiving the support of the Pakistani intelligence agency, the ISI (Inter-Services Intelligence).

The HJI [HUJI] was pan-Islamic, and its intention was, by means of a renewed jihad, to combat the worldwide oppression of Muslims by infidels. Its objective was to give the Muslims back their past glory, and it placed special emphasis on the liberation of occupied Muslim territory, such as Kashmir and Palestine. It also aimed at launching a struggle for Muslim rights in non-Muslim countries, such as the Philippines and Burma. In due course, its activists fought in Bosnia, where the first group arrived in 1992, and in Tajikistan—as well as in other places. However, from 1980 to 1988 it restricted its activities to Afghanistan.[73]

It was between 1988 and 1992, during the expansion phase of the organization, that Shafiqur Rahman was contacted and the Bangladesh chapter began its clandestine operation. On 30 April 1992, a week after the mujahideen emerged victorious in Afghanistan, the Bangladeshi participants in the war expressed their delight in a press conference at Dhaka, where some of the speakers identified themselves as members of HUJI-Bangladesh. In the first four years HUJI-B's activities were largely restricted to the southeastern hills close to the border with Burma, which suggests that their initial objective was to use Bangladesh as a launching pad to influence the Rohingya movement. However, changes in the domestic politics of Bangladesh in the early nineties, particularly the results of the elections of 1991, which brought Jamaat-i-Islami to the forefront of constitutional politics and elevated them to kingmaker position, inspired the HUJI militants to work for an Islamic revolution in Bangladesh.

The presence of camps in the remote parts of the southeastern districts run by HUJI to provide training to Bangladeshis came to light on 19 January 1996, when forty-one militants with a huge arms cache were arrested in a village in Cox's Bazar district. Of those arrested, only one was a Rohingya rebel, four came from the vicinity, and the remainder from various parts of the country. This list of participants evidently shows that the camp was not meant to train the Burmese rebels, and that HUJI had already started recruiting trainees from other districts. The arrest exposed HUJI, and therefore it was time for them to move out of the region, at least for a while. They immediately moved to districts in the northern and northwestern parts of the country, particularly poverty-stricken border areas, and adopted the name Qital fi Sabililalah (Fighting in the Way of Allah). A huge pool of unemployed youth became potential new recruits. But further expansion was dependent on finding places to house their camps and getting support from influential local people.

The HUJI found the ally it was looking for when contact was made with Abdur Rahman, son of a deceased Ahl-e-Hadith leader. Rahman, who graduated from an Ahl-e-Hadith madrassah and received his higher education at Medina University in Saudi Arabia, had visited Afghanistan and allegedly received military training. He had been advocating jihad for a number of years. Rahman had made contacts with various Middle Eastern diplomatic missions when he worked for the Saudi Embassy in Dhaka and later as a translator for a small company in Dhaka. Utilizing these contacts, he gathered funds and established two madrassahs in villages in the northeastern Jamalpur district, his adopted home. The funds for these two madrassahs reportedly came from Rabita-al-Alam-al-Islami. Rahman, a student activist of the Jamaat-i-Islami (JI) in his youth, tried his political luck with the Jami'at-i-Ahl-e-Hadith for some time, but was expelled in 1986 for extremist views. Rahman, however, used his own madrassahs, particularly the Medina Cadet madrassah, to preach violence. It is allegedly still used as a training camp. Rahman, in an exclusive interview on 9 April 2004, told a reporter: "this is not the Bangladesh we want. The constitution [of Bangladesh] is contrary to Islam and irrelevant. We want [an] Islamic state and if necessary Taliban [-style] rule."[74] Rahman knew Ghalib and extended his support to Ghalib's organization. Ghalib, by then, had not only established hundreds of madrassahs in the northeastern districts, but also received funds from the Revival of Islamic Heritage Society (RIHS) and another Saudi-based NGO, Hayatul Igachha. Abdur Rahman and Asadullah Ghalib joined forces in 1998 and established the Jamaat ul-Mujaheddin Bangladesh (JMB).

Asadullah Ghalib was a mysterious character, as well. "After getting stationed in Rajshahi, Galib visited Afganistan, India and Pakistan with fake travel documents. He had close relations with Islamist militants in Kashmir. He visited India in 1998 with a business passport, for which he had to face interrogation by the Rajshahi University (RU) authorities." There was, however, no mystery in regard to his views on Islamic revolution.

> Ahab Amir Galib advocates armed struggle to bring about an Islamic revolution in the country, according to a book on jihad authored by him that The Daily Star obtained yesterday. The book titled *Daoat O Jihad* (invitation and crusade) is a transcription of a speech Galib delivered at an Ahab conference in 1991. At its end, he said, "At every village, there will be a team of mujahids committed to reconstructing the society and reforming their personal, family and social lives according to the dictums of the Holy Qur'an and Hadith. . . . We want pure Islamic politics, not political Islam." In the speech, he named many past and present-day mujahids and narrated their heroic deeds to inspire his audience for an armed uprising.[75]

The youth front—the AHJS and the madrassahs. commonly known as Kuwaiti madrassahs in the northwestern districts established by the AHAB with funding from the RIHS—became centers of training and operation. In the southern districts, the HUJI activists who were operating under the name of Qital fi Sabililah decided to rename themselves al-Jamaat ul-Jihad. This network was assimilated into the JMB in early 2000.

As the tentacles of these networks spread to other parts of the country, concern was raised in some quarters of the government in early 2002. In March 2002, the Ministry of Home Affairs instructed the local police to take action against the three madrassahs (al-Jamiah al-Islamia located in Patiya district, Darul Uloom Mainul Madrassah located in Hathazari, and Darul Uloom Madrassah located in Lalkhan Bazar of Chittagong) for suspected links to militants. Local authorities, however, disregarded the instruction. The connection became obvious after a police raid in 2004. Two persons arrested in a police raid on a militant training center in Hathazari, thirty-two kilometers north of the port city of Chittagong, on 1 June, confided that the training center was patronized by HUJI and had been used to train madrassah students. They revealed that the madrassah students who arrived there were trained "Taliban style" in the hilly areas, adding that some trainees planned to go abroad for further training while many others went to Sylhet and Mymensingh. Intelligence sources informed the press that the center—operated by Mir Anis, cousin of a state minister and teacher of a local women's madrassah—used to provide training to madrassah students in batches. At least twenty-four madrassah students in each batch subsequently fanned out across the country to carry out subversive activities, police discovered.[76] Mir Anis graduated from Patiya's al-Jamiah al-Islamia Madrassah before moving to this madrassah. The madrassah authority has never denied that some students of the madrassah are HUJI activists.[77]

The spread of the HUJI network to other districts has been confirmed by press reports. In Gopalgonj, thirty-eight Qwami madrassahs under the control of the Tungipara Gohardanga Madrassah were reported to have been used by this outfit in 2000. On 13 February 2003 in Dinajpur, a northern city, a high-powered bomb went off inside the staff residence of a local girls' madrassah. Soon afterward, police recovered revolvers, explosives, bomb-making equipment, maps, training manuals, and documents related to the Jamaatul Mujahideen Bangladesh (JMB). On 20 September the same year, eighteen extremists were arrested at Boalmari in western Faridpur. Audiocassettes, mobile phone sets, and literature in Arabic promoting militancy were also recovered. The arrested persons confessed that they came to Faridpur from the Jamia Islamia Nurul Uloom Qwami Madrassah of Bhaluka in Mymensingh district to raise funds for an armed revolution against the "enemies of Islam." "Maulana Abdur Rashid, the leader of the group, confessed that he had received arms training in Pakistan and fought for four years in Afghanistan against the Soviet forces."[78] Rashid also claimed that he had been educated in Deoband Madrassah.

The arrests made between 2000 and 2003 demonstrate that the nexus between madrassahs and the militants has reached an alarming level. But the government was not only reluctant to admit this but also went to great lengths to hide the fact. This led to the release of some militants from custody and others to be released on bail by higher courts. In the latter cases, on many occasions the public prosecutor did not oppose the bail petitions. Examples abound, but perhaps the most dramatic is the case mentioned above, involving forty-one militants arrested in Cox's Bazar in 1996. Despite the discovery of seditious documents during the raid, the militants were charged with possession of illegal arms, a lesser charge allowing them a lenient sentence. The accused were tried by a special tribunal and after two years of hearings, were sentenced to life imprisonment. But as part of the appeal process they were granted bail, and all of them escaped. As of May 2007 no measures have been taken to apprehend them. Similar actions have been repeated on a regular basis throughout the country over the years, sending a clear signal to the militant Islamists that they can act with impunity.[79] The meek response of the government, resulting from a combination of lack of political will and the inability to clamp down, gave the militants a sense of invincibility. This is what led to the countrywide show of strength on 17 August 2005.

Following the hundreds of simultaneous blasts, as the law-and-order agencies were given the green light to act, they found that the facilities of various Qwami madrassah networks located throughout the entire country had been used to recruit, plan for, and train the militants. The law enforcement agencies discovered scores of instances, and arrested suspected militants have also made signed confessions. For example, newspaper reports quoting local and police sources revealed that in Satkhira, a stronghold of the militants in the south, forty-nine madrassahs established by the Ahl-e-Hadith group were used for training purposes.[80] Arrested suspected militants confirmed these reports.[81] The Ramdeb Forkania Rahmania Madrassh, established by the AHAB in 1993, in the northern district of Lalmonirhat, had raised suspicions among local people from the outset and was found to be one of the places where planning meetings took place.[82] The Mahadut Tarbialtil Islamia Madrassah located in the rural areas of the Tangail, about 110 miles northwest of the capital, had been used as transit camp and provided training to several batches of militants.[83] The intelligence agencies, in their initial assessment, identified 233 madrassahs where training took place.[84]

Jamaat, the IOJ, and the Madrassahs

It is often argued that the rise of militant Islamist organizations in Bangladesh, and particularly the use of madrassahs as their bases, is not in the best interests of the Jamaat-i-Islami (JI), the largest Islamist party of Bangladesh. The JI leaders have argued this on many occasions. The chief of the JI and then industries minister, Matiur Rahman Nizami, insists that it is a democratic organization and has no involvement in any sort of fanaticism. "It believes in lawful movement," he said in a press conference after the bomb blasts of August 17.[85] Prime Minister Khaleda Zia not only concurred but also defended the Jamaat and other Islamist organizations belonging to the ruling four-party alliance in a speech to the Parliament saying that "the religion-based parties in the ruling alliance believe in democracy and constitutional politics."[86] Yet the name of Jamaat-i-Islami keeps reappearing in discussions on the nexus of madrassahs and militancy. The political background of a large number of individuals arrested in charges of being involved in militant activities between 2001 and 2005 show both connections.[87]

Among the Islamists who are participating in mainstream politics, the Jamaat-i-Islami is at the forefront, but not alone. During the general election of 2001, more than fifteen Islamist parties filed candidates for parliamentary seats.[88] Although the existence of a large number of these parties is limited to their own letterheads, some of them have gained significant power and influence, not to mention mobilizational capacity. Although they have not succeeded in garnering large-scale support from the electorate, they have built up enough manpower to organize street agitations. On occasion they have flexed their muscles. The frightful events in early 2001 demonstrated the strengths of the Islami Oikya Jote (IOJ), a coalition partner. The IOJ was founded in 1990 with seven smaller groups to work for an Islamic state with the ideals of the Khilafat. In the initial years the alliance drew very little attention from political analysts despite the fact it won a parliamentary seat in 1991 election. However, since the mid-nineties the alliance has practically acted like a political party and made its presence felt in the political scene. In the mid-nineties its support appeared to be limited to a few areas in the southeast and northeast, and was almost nonexistent in other areas. The alliance retained its seat in the 1996 election. When the BNP took the initiative to form a center-right alliance in the late nineties, the IOJ joined the four-party alliance.[89]

Nevertheless, in early 2001 it was made clear to the public at large that the IOJ had the means to create havoc, if it wanted to, and as mentioned previously, one of the principal sources of their strength was their control over the madrassah networks in that city. Although Brahmanbaria has proven to be the citadel of the IOJ, their control over madrassah networks is not limited to this city. Instead, the party has established control over a large number of networks. The three largest Qwami madrassah networks of Chittagong that I have referred to earlier are also under the control of the IOJ and like-minded organizations such as the Islamic Constitution Movement (ICM), and the Khilafat Movement. Jamaat-i-Islami, on the other hand, has tried to establish control over the Aliya madrassahs either through establishing new madrassahs or through their student organization, the Islami Chattra Shibir. In 1995, a Jamaat leader confided that they have established control over 500 mosques, 256 Aliya madrassahs, 82 kindergartens, and 32 colleges in major cities.

There is a need to acknowledge here that there are ideological differences between the more orthodox radical organizations, the IOJ and the JI. While both of them aim to establish an Islamic state, they disagree on various issues, including the ideal disposition of the Islamic state. The differences are both ideological and strategic. Jamaat has shown a degree of moderation for the sake of political legitimacy and social acceptance, and has been in favor of using the existing rules, regulations, laws, and conventions to achieve its ultimate objective. The orthodox Islamists, on the contrary, have tried to work under the radar screen and have looked for ways to capture state power by force. Jamaat's strategy enabled it to work with various political forces including the Awami League, and garner support in urban areas, while the IOJ and their ilk have appealed to the rural population. In the eighties and early nineties, these organizations openly criticized each other for being un-Islamic and have been engaged in occasional turf fights. But in the nineties they have come closer together, thanks to the BNP. The first term of the BNP (1991–1996) created an environment conducive to these forces and later the four-party alliance led by the BNP provided them with a platform to work closely.

In July 2005 the Jamaat initiated a vigorous effort to increase its influence over the madrassahs—both government-supported and privately operated. The JI has established a national organization of teachers of the Aliya madrassahs. The existing organization, the Bangladesh Jamiatul Modaresin has remained under the leadership of rival groups since its reemergence in 1976. Differences between the JI and their rival organizations, especially the IOJ, with regard to the madrassahs involve the recognition of the degrees conferred by the Qwami madrassahs and the institutional control of the Aliya madrassahs. Presently the Madrassah Education Board supervises the completion examination of the Aliya madrassahs, and their degrees are considered equivalent to the secular educational institutes, allowing the successful students to enroll in colleges and universities. IOJ demands include upgrading madrassah education, recognizing the status of fazil, which is equivalent to a degree from the general university, and kamil, which is equivalent to a master's degree. While the JI has very little disagreement on this issue, they want these institutions to be a part of the national university, the central authority of graduate and postgraduate collages in Bangladesh, while the IOJ and like-minded organizations, with the support of the current leadership of the Jamiatul Modaresin, demand an Islamic Arabic university.

CONCLUSION

The foregoing discussion has shown that madrassah education in Bangladesh has undergone a dramatic transformation over the last two decades—both in terms of numbers and its role in the society. The madrassahs have long been part of the education system of Bangladesh, and like any other society have been the "social sites for the reproduction of social orthodoxy,"[90] but these changes have taken some of the madrassahs far beyond reproducing orthodoxy; they have become a menace to society: the nature of Bangladeshi society is under threat, as well as the security of the country. The social fabric is now being torn apart by one variety of madrassah. These are not due to changes in the curriculum of the madrassahs but largely due to the political environment of the country. The nonchalant attitude of the government and the official promotion of the ruling parties and coalition have contributed to the making of this situation. Without the ideological shift of the Bangladeshi state and the subsequent political developments, such dramatic changes would have been impossible. External connections have expedited the process in an unprecedented manner.

Discussions on madrassah education often center on curriculum, and for good reason. It is indeed important to know what lessons these institutions are imparting and how they are being presented to the students. While the relevance of the curriculum and courses of Aliya madrassahs can be debated and questions can be raised as to what roles the graduates of these institutions would play in the socioeconomic life of the country, it is urgent to address the future of the Qwami madrassahs, especially in the context of the nexus between madrassahs, militants, and foreign charities. It is also imperative that Bangladeshis examine the future roles of these madrassahs as sociopolitical institutions as much as educational institutions. The gravity of the situation cannot be understood through abstract doctrine and tradition, but only through looking at the hard realities on the ground. Looking at the curriculum of madrassahs, one can conclude that "there is absolutely nothing in the madrassa curriculum that can be deemed as promoting or encouraging militancy, not to mention terrorism,"[91] but that can also breed complacency, the time for which has passed in Bangladesh—on 17 August 2005, to be precise.

CHAPTER 5

INDIA

DIVERSITY AND CHANGES IN MADRASSAHS

The region that constitutes present-day India was the heartland of Muslim revivalism during colonial rule (1757–1947). One of the key institutions that contributed to this revivalism was the madrassah. The fountainhead of one of the most discussed strands of madrassah education, the Deobandi tradition, began and is still located in Uttar Pradesh, India. Nearby, the Darul Uloom Nadwatul Ulama in Lucknow, is still an educational institution revered by Muslims across South Asia, despite the fact that it no longer commands the political influence it had during the nineteenth century. Likewise, the Darul Uloom of Sharanpur, established in the late nineteenth century, is still engaged in imparting education to the community, as is the Jamia Arusiyya of Kilak-karai in Tamil Nadu. Hundreds of prominent madrassahs dotted the country before independence, and thousands have emerged over the last half century. The glory that once marked these institutions has faded, and their importance has declined over time; but the tradition has not died out, because these institutions are yet to become obsolete.

Limitations notwithstanding, madrassahs play a distinctive role in contemporary India, and it is difficult to understand the present role of the Muslim community in India without examining the importance of madrassahs in Indian society. The madrassahs in India play a fundamentally different role from similar institutions in Pakistan and Bangladesh. For instance, while madrassahs in Pakistan have taken an overt political role, the Indian madrassahs have maintained a safe distance from political activism, although the number of madrassahs is significantly higher in India. This is not to say that there are no similarities between Indian madrassahs and their counterparts in neighboring countries. For example, in common with the Bangladeshi education landscape, where some madrassahs are integrated into mainstream education and some remain outside, madrassahs of both kinds are easy to find in

India. This diversity is a result of the geographical vastness and the historical richness of the country, on the one hand, and the different paths of development traversed by these institutions, on the other. Therefore, there cannot be a homogenous, archetypical Indian madrassah. I refer to Indian madrassahs in this chapter on the basis of some common characteristics of those institutions that offer Islamic education, and the common understanding reflected in popular discourse. This is by no means an attempt to disregard variations based on sectarian and denominational differences, both of which are very important to the understanding of madrassahs; neither do I intend to say that there is an ideal type of madrassah in India.

For a proper appreciation, discussions on madrassahs in India must be located within the wider context of the socioeconomic-political status of the Muslims, and the political economy of the Indian education system.[1] The former is needed because, unlike Pakistan and Bangladesh, these institutions are located in a society where Muslims are a minority community. The socioeconomic conditions of the community that madrassahs primarily serve influence the nature of institutions as much as, if not more, than other factors such as their historical lineage. Consideration of the political economy of the Indian education system is vital because some intrinsic features of the system rationalize the existence and growth of the madrassahs.

Indian Muslims: A Profile

India is the home of the third largest Muslim community of the world; about 150 million Indians are Muslims. They comprise about 14 percent of the total population, which makes them the largest minority within the country. Equally important is the fact that Muslims account for two-thirds of all religious minorities in India. Despite such overwhelming numbers and thereby enormous importance, Muslims are the most deprived population of India. The available statistics reveal that widespread illiteracy, low income, irregular employment, and consequently a high incidence of poverty are all pervasive among Muslims. The appropriate description of the conditions faced by the Muslims in India, therefore, is of social exclusion, when social exclusion means "the multiple and overlapping nature of the disadvantages experienced by certain groups and categories of the population, with social identity as the central axis of their exclusion."[2]

The socioeconomic status of Muslims has been an issue of discussion in India for some time, and social researchers and Muslim activists have argued that Muslims have been subject to systemic discrimination since independence. There is no dearth of data to prove the point, although the Hindu chauvinist parties allege that all secularist regimes have appeased the Muslim community. Their miniscule political representation and the virtual absence in the administrative and security structures of the state confirm that in this case there is no correspondence between share of the population and representation. The endemic poverty in India consigns almost a quarter of its population, irrespective of religion, to the margin of the society. For Muslims this is one of two faces of marginalization, because their social identity as Muslims marginalizes them at another level. This is why "doubly marginalized" is an oft-used term in describing the Muslim populations' relative place in Indian society.

Documented in the fifty-fifth round of the nationwide survey in 2001, conducted by the National Sample Survey Organization (NSSO), is the fact that 29 percent of rural Muslims live in absolute poverty, with monthly consumption expenditure per head of Rs. 300 or less. Of rural Muslims, 51 percent (as compared to 40 percent of rural Hindus) are landless. In urban areas, 40 percent of Muslims (as compared to 22 percent among Hindus) belong to the absolute poor category.[3] Extensive statistics in regard to health, education, and employment of the Muslim community and their access to physical and social infrastructure are documented in the 425-page report of the Prime Minister's High Level Committee on the Socio-Economic and Educational Status of the Muslim Community in India (headed by Rajinder Sachar, hereinafter Sachar Committee Report) published in late 2006.[4] The scope of this chapter does not allow discussion of these data in detail, but salient features in regard to education and employment illustrate the situation.

The literacy rate among Muslims in 2001 was 59.1 percent, well below the national level of 65.1 percent. In urban areas, the gap between the Muslims and the national average is 11 percentage points. Among the age group of 6–13 years, 90.2 percent of the population as a whole is literate, while the corresponding figure for Muslims is 74.6 percent. This means that more than 25 percent of Muslim children in this age group have either never attended schools or have dropped out. In terms of the completion of elementary education, 44 percent of Muslim children on average are likely to move on to middle school, while the rate is 62 percent among upper-caste Hindus. In higher education the proportion of Muslim students is remarkably low. Muslims aged twenty years and above are 11 percent of the population, but their share of graduates is 6 percent.

In the key civil service structures of India, that is, the Indian Administrative Service (IAS), the Indian Foreign Service (IFS), and the Indian Police Service (IPS), Muslims are virtually absent. Their shares are: 3 percent in IAS, 1.8 percent in IFS, and 4 percent in IPS. In the security agencies (Border Security Force, Central Reserve Police Force, Central Industrial Security Force, and Sashastra Seema Bal) the share is as low as 3.6 percent at the higher level and 4.6 percent at the lower level. Among the workers engaged in "Public Order and Safety Activities" (police and fire protection, administration and operation of law courts, and prison administration and operation), Muslims constitute only 6 percent.

Consistent with the employment rate in the civil service, the number of Muslims in public sector or government jobs is abysmally low: fewer than 24 percent of Muslim regular workers are employed in the public sector. The number is the lowest among all socioreligious groups. Of Scheduled Castes/ Scheduled Tribes regular workers, 39 percent are employed in the public sector, as are 30 percent of Hindu Other Backward Class workers. The Hindu Upper Castes' share is 37 percent.

The picture of Muslim participation at various levels of public service at the state level is no different from that of the central government: "In no state does the representation of Muslims match their population share. Instead, they are falling far behind."[5]

The social exclusion of the community is matched by real, symbolic, and potential violence. Violence perpetrated against Muslims is now naturalized: riots are "well-known and accepted transgression of routine political behavior in India."[6] Therefore, a constant threat of persecution looms large. Members of the community have not only experienced incessant vilification and demonization but have also been subjected to pogroms. The demolition of the centuries-old Babri Mosque in Uttar Pradesh by Hindu militants in 1992, followed by violence in Bombay that killed hundreds, and the Gujarat massacre in 2002 that cost thousands of lives, have received some media coverage.[7] But few in the international community know that "Hindu-Muslim riots and anti-Muslim pogroms have been endemic in India since independence." These pogroms, as Paul Brass has correctly pointed out, are "classified in the press, by the authorities, and by the public as riots," and hence blame is equally portioned between victims and perpetrators, creating an environment of impunity to the instigators.[8] This engenders a culture of fear under which the victims have to live.

As I have explained elsewhere, the demolition of Babri Mosque in December 1992 by the Sangh Parivar was neither an isolated event nor a spontaneous act, but something that had been in the making for long time.[9] Privileging majoritarian arguments in political discourse, succumbing to political expediency by the so-called secular parties, demonization of Muslim difference, and peripheralization of Muslim voices all came together to activate the pickaxes that demolished the sixteenth-century mosque. It is well to bear in mind that the Sangh Parivar's planned attack on the mosque and the violence in Bombay in December and in the following month were conducted with the complicity of the state machinery.[10] The Saffron Brigade's marching song did not end in Ayodhya;[11] electoral politics has delivered central power to the Bharatiya Janata Party (BJP) twice since, and Indian Muslims once again became victims in Gujarat in 2002. Thus the rise of Hindu militancy with a distinct anti-Muslim agenda should not be seen as an aberration of Indian democracy, but intrinsically connected to the Indian political discourse and process.

Economic deprivation, social exclusion, and persecution inform part of the Muslim community's situation, while another element is determined by changing intracommunal sociopolitical dynamics, particularly since the rise of Hindutva politics.[12] The community's reactions have thus far included reassertion of religious identity, conscious withdrawal from politics to act as a community group, efforts to build an independent communal political platform, and underscoring a shared subaltern identity.[13] Except for some elements of the last, these reactions have further isolated the Muslims from the wider political processes, thereby causing more harm than good. The profound relationship between the Muslims' plight and the struggle for social justice and secularism in India has been largely ignored by the community. The internal reforms, necessary for adapting to the transformed political landscape, remain in abeyance.

THE POLITICAL ECONOMY OF INDIAN EDUCATION

The Indian education system, the second largest in the world, is diverse and complex. But the most important characteristic of the Indian education system, particularly at the primary and secondary level, is that it is plagued with exclusion and marginalization along the social, geographical, and gender lines that characterize Indian society. This means that education remains out of reach of the poorest, of socially marginalized groups, of people in the rural areas, and of a vast number of girls, irrespective of their socioeconomic condition. India, in this respect, is not different from its neighbors, Pakistan and Bangladesh.

The fact that at least 30 million children are out of school is of itself remarkable, because this is the highest absolute number of children out of school in any country in the world.[14] The fact assumes greater significance when one takes into account that the constitution promised to provide free universal education to all children up to the age of fourteen half a century ago.[15] Additionally, the 86th amendment to the constitution, passed in December 2002, made free and compulsory education a fundamental right for all children in the age group six to fourteen years. Thus, the nonavailability of education to almost 18 percent of children of school-going age is nothing less than a violation of a fundamental right that merits more attention than it usually receives in popular discourse.

In recent years, however, the Indian government has taken steps to "universalize" education. The program for universalization comprises four components: universal access, universal enrollment, universal retention, and universal quality of education. The flagship program under the plan is the

Sarva Shiksa Abhiyan. Despite success in increasing the number of schools in rural areas, it is far from achieving its aim to universalize primary education (up to grade five) by 2007 and elementary education (up to grade eight) by 2010. The fundamental problems of education in India linger on.

The education system in India is divided into preprimary, primary, middle, secondary (or high school), and higher levels. Reading and writing skills are developed in the preprimary level. There is no minimum age to enter this stage, but a wide range of institutions, mostly private, provide the service. The National Policy on Education of 1986 and its subsequent modification in 1992 have increased the government's involvement in the preprimary stage of education. In 1996, the Sixth All India Education Survey found that only 25 percent of the total number of children of qualifying age were receiving any kind of preprimary education.[16]

Primary grades include grade one through five, comprising children ages six to eleven. The secondary level—often referred to as middle and upper primary—usually covers sixth through tenth grades. In some cases this stage is divided into two: sixth through eighth grades, and ninth and tenth grades. The students sit for their first standardized tests after completion of tenth grade. Successful completion of the tests allows the student to join a two-year college, after which there is another set of standardized tests leading to higher education. Both public examinations are administered by the state boards of secondary and higher secondary education.

The school and college curricula are centralized at the federal level: the National Council for Educational Research and Training (NCERT) is responsible for proposing the national curricula, while the detailed syllabi and prescribed texts are chosen by the Central Board of Secondary Education (CBSE). In addition to the CBSE, there are forty-two state boards of examination throughout the country, which are responsible for the standardized public examinations. Other boards such as the Indian Certified School Examination (ICSE), Matriculation Board of Education (MBE) also exist. "Apart from the CBSE, each state has an independent role in defining the details of education offered in its school[s]."[17]

Since 1968, the government has adopted a three-languages formula for educational institutions. The three languages taught at schools are the regional language, Hindi or English, and a modern Indian language. It is worth pointing out that eighteen languages are recognized as national languages in India. At the primary and upper primary level (up to eighth grade), English and Hindi languages and literatures, a third language, mathematics including algebra and geometry, science subjects including physics, chemistry, and biology, among other subjects, are taught. Within the secondary education system students can opt for one of two major streams: academic or vocational. The academic stream offers the opportunity to move to higher education, while the vocational stream is geared toward offering job opportunities. Within the academic stream, courses are grouped into science courses, commerce courses, and humanities courses.

The foundation of the post-Independence Indian education policies, particularly policies toward primary and secondary education, can be traced back to the Kothari Commission Report on Education of 1966. The report, named after the head of the commission D. S. Kothari, not only proposed free universal education for all but also insisted on common education for all children, and for making the mother tongue the medium of instruction at primary level. Subsequent education policies, such as the 1986 National Policy on Education and the 1992 update of the National Policy, have endorsed the basic principles espoused by the Kothari report, but in reality neither has the Indian education system become accessible to all children nor has a common system been created.

The Acharya Ramamurthy Report of 1990 sponsored by the Central Advisory Board of Education opined that "socio-economic disparities resulted in richer families sending their children to private schools with better infrastructure, higher teaching standards, and teachers who were better qualified. Government schools were less sought after and consequently less invested in."[18] Fifteen years later, in her study on the Indian education system, Marie Lal echoed these words:

> There is no common school system; instead children are chanelled into private, government-aided and government schools on the basis of their ability to pay and social class. At the top end are English-language schools affiliated to the upscale CBSE (Central Board of Secondary Education), CISCE (Council for the Indian Schools Certificates Examination) and IB (International Baccalaureate) examination Boards, offering globally recognized syallabuses and curricula. Those who cannot afford private schooling attend English-language government-aided schools, affiliated to state-level examination boards. And on the bottom rung are poorly managed government or municipal schools, which cater for the education of the poor majority.[19]

For the poor who are doubly marginalized either because of their geographical location (such as a remote rural area) or because of their minority status (such as Muslim or Scheduled Caste) there remains no option but to rely on institutions that can offer literacy to their children. It is not unknown to observers of the Indian education scene that the inadequacies of educational facilities—from poor infrastructure to lack of teaching materials to teacher absenteeism—are more prevalent in poor rural areas, particularly in Muslim-dominated villages. This is where the madrassahs play a pivotal role in making opportunities available in the most modest way. Resources for madrassahs are wanting as well, because madrassahs depend on the local members of the community, who are often the poorest of the poor. In other words, "it [the madrassah] is a feasible recourse for those whose lack of resources leaves them little room for manoeuvre in planning their children's educational careers."[20] Therefore, the failure of the state to provide education to the community is indeed a vital factor in understanding why parents choose to send their children to madrassahs. The Sachar Committee Report has acknowledged the failure of the state eloquently: "very often one finds that madrassas have indeed provided schooling to Muslim children where the state has failed them."[21]

The cost of education is another crucial factor in this regard. Despite the official pronouncements of free education, education is not free in India—it has both direct and indirect costs. The Public Report on Basic Education (PROBE), published in 1999 revealed that the average annual cost of sending a child to school is about 318 Indian rupees in rural areas.[22] The Probe Report mentions that according to the 1994 study of the National Council for Applied Economic Research (NCAER), the cost is about 378 Indian rupees. The National Family Health Survey II in 1998–1999 showed that cost is a significant barrier to education, particularly with regard to nonenrollment and dropout rates. Although the survey did not provide information about different social, economic, and religious groups, members of the Muslim community are expected to be disproportionately affected by this barrier due to their general economic underdevelopment.

Both the social exclusion and persecution faced by Muslims as a community, discussed at the beginning of this chapter, become factors, often subconsciously, in parental choice of schools. As Muslim majority areas are deprived of good schools, usually the only option left is to send the child to a school away from home. But many parents, especially in states where anti-Muslim violence has taken place, are afraid to do so. This affects girls more than boys, particularly when the former have to use public transport. At another level, a sense of resignation with regard to future opportunities influences which kind of school the child ends up at. Parents settle with local madrassahs because they do not want to "waste" the meager resources they have sending their children to general schools.

This is not to say that parental choice is guided only by the nonavailability of educational institutions nearby; other factors such as the linguistic content of the curriculum, the Hindu bias of the syllabi, and above all, the desire to provide basic religious education, particularly *adab* (etiquette or basic rules of conduct), play a part in the decision making. The curricula of government schools have not only removed Urdu as a language of study, even in states where there is a substantial Muslim community, but have also adopted a highly Sanskritized form of the Hindi language. The adoption of Sanskritized Hindi is actually encouraged by the constitution (Article 351), and thus has the approval of the political establishment in general.

Many Muslim scholars believe that the absence of Urdu in schools has contributed to the educational backwardness of the Muslim community.[23] As Urdu is considered an important element of Indian Muslim identity, particularly for north Indian Muslims, Muslim parents send their children to madrassahs where Urdu has remained the medium of instruction. The extent of the problem is highlighted by the Sachar Committee: "the provisioning of education through Urdu medium is precarious in Uttar Pradesh, Jharkhand, Andhra Pradesh and Bihar."[24] The dismally low number of children enrolled in Urdu-medium schools in Uttar Pradesh is due not to parents being unwilling to teach Urdu to their children but to the nonavailability of schools offering instruction in Urdu. The Deeni Talim Council's success in Uttar Pradesh is testimony to the fact that parents still feel that there is a need to learn Urdu.[25] However, it should also be borne in mind that overemphasis on Urdu by some segments of the Muslim community has been detrimental to the community interest, as it has contributed to the isolation of the community from the mainstream.[26]

In addition to the use of a Sanskritized form of the Hindi language, Hindi linguistic texts with an anti-Muslim bias have been allowed to be used in schools. The elitist version of the Hindi language marginalizes the rural poor, while at the same time inserts a Hindu element into the educational content. The latter is due to Sanskrit's close association with the Hindu scriptures.[27] Inserting an overt Hindu bias into the curricula, or the so-called "saffronization" of education, became the principal educational agenda of the Sangh Parivar between 2001 and 2004. Space and the scope of this chapter will not allow us to go into detail, but in broad strokes, during the BJP rule, under the banner of "Indianize, Nationalize, and Spiritualize," the government launched a massive assault on the secular content of textbooks, on certain narratives of history, and on the fundamentals of science education.

Changes in the school textbooks were one element of the two-prong strategy of the Sangh Parivar in regard to education. The other involved founding educational institutions to indoctrinate students with their worldview. This began in 1952 with the establishment of the first RSS (Rashtriya Swayamsevak Sangh)-backed school called Shishu Mandir under the umbrella of the Vidya Bharati, a voluntary organization. By early 2002, the Vidya Bharati chain had founded about 14,000 schools at the primary, middle, and secondary levels and had over 1.8 million students under its tutelage. About 80,000 teachers were employed in these schools. The Vidya Bharati chain also controlled at least sixty colleges, which offer graduate and postgraduate degrees, and twenty-five other centers of higher learning, of which two are educator-training institutes. In practice, the Sangh Parivar has created a parallel education system that produces supporters of the radical Hindutva ideology and activists of the party machines. This development has encouraged some members of the Muslim community to develop an education system capable of countering the influence of the Hindutva ideology. Strengthening of the madrassah system was one response.

In large measure, the BJP regime's blatant communal actions brought forth the debate on the content of school curricula, but for the Muslim population the Hindu ambiance of educational institutions including the communal contents of texts had been a matter of concern for a long time. These features of the mainstream educational system create a dispiriting environment for the Muslim community and encourage Muslims to search for alternative institutions of education where they feel more at home. Occasionally overt discrimination faced by children in school has a determining effect as well. The Sachar Committee Report maintains that when trying to get admission for their children Muslim parents face discrimination from school authorities in the form of rude questioning and lack of civility in behavior. Children are also treated as second-class citizens in the schools.[28]

The drawbacks of the educational system—structural and ideological, deliberate and accidental—not only drive the message home to the Muslim community that they are unwelcome in the education arena but also reproduce social exclusion and reinforce Muslims' sense of alienation. But do these factors result in the mass exit of Muslims from mainstream educational institutions in favor of madrassahs? The answer to this question lies in the number of madrassahs and their share of school-age Muslim children.

THE MURKY WORLD OF NUMBERS

The total number of madrassahs in India, as in the other two South Asian countries discussed in preceding chapters, is shrouded with mystery. Due to the absence of a centralized database and reliable sources, reported numbers have varied widely. The available figures are suspect due to two factors, first, the presence of a significant number of unregistered institutions. Although there are large numbers of madrassahs registered with the state governments or other madrassah boards in various states, many operate without any government support or formal recognition. Many of these institutions are small in size and limited in terms of their geographical reach, but some are medium-sized and cater to a large number of children. Whether big or small, they affect the total picture provided by the government sources. The official data, therefore, show a smaller number than that which truly exists.

The second problem with regard to reliable figures lies in the absence of any effort to conduct a comprehensive survey of religious educational institutions in India. No census of madrassahs has been conducted in India. After 9/11, as elsewhere, the issue became so politically charged that the numbers have been caught up in the polemics, particularly because of the anti-Muslim leanings of the then-ruling alliance led by the BJP. The party leaders and cabinet ministers made comments regarding the number and roles of madrassahs often without any empirical basis; at times these comments were detrimental to the relationship between the majority Hindu community and the minority Muslim community. In public discourse the number widely varies and is often referred to as "thousands."

According to the Third All India Educational Survey conducted by the National Council for Educational Research and Training (NCERT), in December 1973, the number of madrassahs was 1,033. In the directory of madrassahs published in 1985 by the Center for Promotion of Science, an institution affiliated with the Aligarh University of Delhi, a total of 2,890 madrassahs were listed. Contemporaneously, the Institute of Objective Studies based in Delhi produced a list of only 500 institutions. The list was undoubtedly an incomplete one and the number was too low to be accepted as reliable. No explanations were forthcoming as to why madrassahs, which were numbered in thousands prior to independence, would decline after 1947. According to one account, in 1946–1947 at least 169 madrassahs existed in West Bengal alone. In 1969, Bihar had 186, and Uttar Pradesh had 170 madrassahs.[29] Syed Maqbool Ahmad, in an article published in 1969, asserted that at least 4,000 madrassahs provide education to children in India.[30] In 1998, Mohammed Shoyeb Ansari estimated the number at "more than 8000."[31] Thus, inconsistency in available numbers is striking.

There is a general agreement that in the eighties, India like its neighbors experienced a rise in the number of madrassahs. Yoginder Sikand insists that both the number and power and influence of madrassahs grew during the decade.[32] The rise in numbers can be attributed to the growing sense of disenfranchisement among the Muslim population, and the gradual rise of the Hindu chauvinist parties and their front organizations. By the mid-nineties, as the Sangh Parivar––that is, the combination of BJP, the Rashtriya Swayamsevak Sangh (RSS), the Bajrang Dal, the Viswa Hindu Parishad (VHP), and the Shiv Sena––assumed a pivotal position within mainstream politics, the Muslim community began adopting an inward-looking stance. This is reflected in their growing affiliations with institutions that help preserve their Muslim identity, and continue Islamic traditions. The events in 1992, particularly the demolition of Babri Mosque and subsequent atrocities against the Muslim community, sent a clear signal to the Muslim community that secularism in India was on the wane. While empirical data are wanting to draw a causal relationship between the events of the early nineties, the tendency of Muslims to withdraw from public spaces, and the growth of madrassahs, this observation is nonetheless pertinent. Thus when Madho Rao Scindhia, minister of human resources, the ministry in charge of education, stated in 1995 that 12,000 madrassahs existed in the country, it was not perceived as an inflated number. Instead, many analysts believed that the number was higher in reality, and that the government either did not have the complete picture or were unwilling to discuss an issue that in some ways touched upon religion. In 2002, Minister of State for Home Vidyasagar Rao informed the parliament that the number of madrassahs was as high as 31,850, of which 11,453 were located in border regions.[33] The statement came in a new environment; by then vilification of madrassahs was the order of the day, thanks to post-9/11 global paranoia; but it is also worthwhile to note that the BJP was in power. The number was no longer a piece of information, but a matter of political statement with a definite political agenda behind the numbers.

In 2005 a newspaper report suggested that the total number of registered madrassahs was 27,518 throughout the country.[34] According to a government statement made to the parliament on 18 August 2005, six states (that is, Arunachal Pradesh, Meghalaya, Mizoram, Nagaland, Pondicherry, and Jammu and Kashmir) did not have any madrassah. This was of some surprise, because for many it was hard to believe that Jammu and Kashmir, the only Muslim majority region of India, did not have any madrassah. The State Waqf Board of Jammu and Kashmir (J&K) stated that they ran 86 private schools. But according to Badiuzzaman, Jammu and Kashmir had 122 institutions with more than eight thousand students.[35] Table 5.1 culls the figures from information provided by the Home Ministry and other sources. These numbers are accepted by some as reliable; for example, Naqvi Bhaumik estimates the number at around 25,000.[36] On the other hand, Sikand maintains that the number should be somewhere between 30,000 and 40,000, and elsewhere he quotes a leading Islamic scholar who claims that there are 125,000 madrassahs with 3 million students.[37]

A significant number of madrassahs located in various states are, as mentioned before, registered with the state boards. These boards came into existence in the eighties and the nineties. One account of 1998 show that madrassah boards in Assam, Bihar, Orissa, Uttar Pradesh (UP), and West Bengal were effectively coordinating the activities of the madrassahs in their respective states. In Bihar, about 1,800 madrassahs were affiliated with the madrassah board and in Orissa 79 madrassahs registered with the state madrassah board. Numbers registered with comparable boards were 375 in UP and 400 in West Bengal.[38] In some instances the madrassahs registered with the state board of secondary and senior secondary education, which allowed the students of these institutions to sit for state-approved standardized examinations and receive certificates that are accepted by higher educational institutions and employers. By 1998, some madrassahs in Assam and Maharashtra took this route to serve their students. Often registration with the state boards has benefited the institutions and the students alike. For example, in 2001, the overall results of the standardized tests of the students of madrassahs in Rajasthan were better than those of the government-supported schools.[39] But the boards have their

TABLE 5.1

NUMBER OF MADRASSAHS AND STUDENTS IN INDIA BY STATE

State	No. of madrassahs	No. of students
Andhra Pradesh	721	72,258
Andaman and Nicobar Islands	54	
Assam	2,002	120,000
Bihar	3,500	
Delhi	1,161	3,722
Gujarat	1,825	120,000
Jammu and Kashmir	122	8,515
Karnataka	961	84,864
Kerala	9,975	738,000
Madhya Pradesh	6,000	400,000
Maharashtra	2,435	20,397
Rajshathan/ Rajasthan?	1,780	25,000
Uttar Pradesh	10,000	
West Bengal	506	200,000

Sources and Notes: Figures for Assam, Bihar, Gujarat, Karnataka, Kerala, Madhya Pradesh Rajasthan, and West Bengal are quoted from Amir Ullah Khan, Mohammad Saqib, and Zafar H. Anjum, "To Kill the Mockingbird," 2003, available at http://www.chowk.com/articles/6216 (accessed 4 January 2005). Although the article cites the Home Ministry as the source of these data, a different set of numbers for some of the states was provided by the government in August 2005 in the Parliament. They are: Andaman and Nicobar 54, Bihar 4102, Gujarat 1,727, Kerala and Madhya Pradesh 6,000 each, Rajasthan 1,985, Uttar Pradesh 4,292; Gilani, "India's Madrassas 3 x Pakistan's." According to Khan, Saqib, and Anjum, the total number of madrassahs in Assam is 721 and the number of students is 120,000, but according to Badiuzzaman, the total is 2,002 madrassahs enrolling 20,000 students (Badiuzzaman, "Hindustan ke Madrase aur Masajid Markazi Hukukmat ke Nishane par," quoted in Sikand, *Bastions of the Believers: Madrasas and Islamic Education*, 315 n. 1); in Uttar Pradesh there are about 15,000 maktabs in addition to the madrassahs. Data for Andhra Pradesh, Delhi, and Jammu and Kashmir are derived from Badiuzzaman, ibid. The number of madrassahs in Bihar is quoted as 4,000 in newspaper reports ("Girls Outshine Boys in Bihar Islamic Seminary Exams"). Of the 3,500 madrassahs in Bihar, 1,118 are government-aided, meaning that the salaries of the teaching and nonteaching staff are paid by the government. All madrassahs in West Bengal listed in the table are affiliated with the state madrassah board. The numbers for West Bengal provided by Badiuzzaman are 2,116 institutions and 90,000 students.

detractors as well. The All India Muslim Majlish-e-Mushawarat (AIMMM) complained in a letter to the Minority Commission in 2005 that the state madrassah boards have brought down the standard of education in the affiliated madrassahs.[40]

The extent to which madrassahs are not registered with the government merits further elaboration. The number of such institutions, understandably, cannot be ascertained with certainty, but the situation in West Bengal provides some clue. According to the available official statistics, 507 madrassahs are registered in the state. About 400 madrassahs are either awaiting a decision on their requests for registration or have been declined by the government. Baharuddin, a high-ranking official of the West Bengal Madrassah Board, states that additionally at least 300 institutions, commonly described as Khariji madrassahs, operate in the state. These institutions sought neither recognition nor any government support.[41] Completely dependent on community support, these institutions do not intend to be part of the state education system. According to Baharuddin, the total number of madrassahs in the state of West Bengal is at least 4,000. This figure includes the institutions, estimated at 2,060, that offer literacy and primary religious knowledge to children, mostly at the preprimary stage or, in other words, the maktabs. However, there are 702 madrassahs that offer education up to the eighth grade, although they have no formal recognition. In late 2006, these madrassahs, located in North Dinajpur, Maldah, Murshidabad, and North 24 Pargana districts, reportedly had 300,000 students.[42] These numbers alone demonstrate that the unregistered madrassahs in India play a role in providing education to many children; hence it cannot be labeled as a fringe issue.

It is important to mention that since independence steps have been taken by the ulama and Muslim educationists at both national and state level to establish madrassahs and maktabs to continue the tradition of Islamic education. The Anjuman Talimat-i-Deen (Deeni Talim Council) of Uttar Pradesh is a case in point. Founded in 1959, the council has maintained a close relationship with the Darul Uloom Nadwatul Ulama of Lucknow and established chapters throughout the state. Over the last forty years the council claims to have established 20,000 maktabs to provide education with the goal of "inculcating Islamic values and ethos" among Muslim children.[43] Similar efforts are evident in other parts of the country, including the south. In Kerala, for instance, the Kerala Nadwatul Mujahideen, an organization of Ahl-e-Hadith persuasion, has been engaged in educational and social awareness since 1950. They administer more than 500 madrassahs through their Madrasa Vidyabhyasa Board.

Although the exact number of students enrolled in madrassahs in India is difficult to ascertain, the number of madrassahs, even by a conservative estimate, is high. Many analysts, however, extrapolate from this fact that the share of madrassahs among total school-going students is higher than the reality. For example, Fahimuddin suggests that the share is as high as "around 36 percent of all school age children in the age group of six to eighteen years." He further suggests that "during initial years of schooling, more than half of the Muslim children are sent to Madrasas."[44] The common misperception that the majority of Muslim parents send their children to madrassahs is likely to arise from the failure to differentiate between maktabs and madrassahs, and from inaccurate counts of students. The first myth was debunked in 2006, when the Sachar Committee submitted its report. According to this ground-breaking report, only 3 percent of Muslim children study in madrassahs.[45] Figures from the National Council for Applied Economic Research (NCAER) indicate that only 4 percent of all Muslim students of school-going age group are enrolled in madrassahs. Estimates made from school level data by the NCERT (National Council for Educational Research and Training) show that only 2.3 percent of Muslim children between the ages of seven and nineteen study at madrassahs. The report also noted that the proportions are higher in rural areas and among males. Regional variations can be significant; for example, in Bihar 24.1 percent of rural students and 9 percent of urban students attend madrassahs, according to Abuzar Kamaluddin. [46]

Failure to differentiate between maktabs and madrassahs, as we have seen in the case of Pakistan, often inflates the number of students enrolled and thereby provides an inaccurate picture. The Sachar Committee report highlighted this difference and underscored its significance: "while madrassas provide education (religious and/or regular), maktabs are neighbourhood schools, often attached to mosques, that provide religious education to children who attend other schools to get 'mainstream education.'"[47] Unawareness of this aspect also results in inaccuracy in counting, because many students who attend both "madrassahs" and mainstream schools are often only counted as madrassah students. The report provided an example from the state of Kerala, where more than 60,000 students attend both mainstream schools and maktabs at the same time. The conclusion of Jeffery et al., drawn from extensive field study in Bijnor of Uttar Pradesh, that "schools and madrasas are not hermetically sealed from one another" is true of many parts of the country.[48]

STRUCTURES OF MADRASSAH EDUCATION

While madrassahs in India follow different *maslaks* (creeds), there are broad similarities among these institutions in terms of the structure of the education system. The typical madrassah curriculum comprises seventeen years from primary or elementary to master's level, and is usually organized into six stages. The specialization, particularly for those who intend to become ulama, takes a longer period, and they pursue their education after these six stages. This de facto standardization has been a result of the emergence of madrassah

TABLE 5.2

TYPICAL STAGES OF MADRASSAH EDUCATION IN INDIA

Stage	Period of study	Comparable stage of general education
Tahtania	4 years	primary/elementary
Wastania	4 years	middle or upper primary
Fuqania	2 years	high school
Moulvi	2 years	intermediate
Alim	3 years	bachelor's degree
Fazil	2 years	master's degree

Source: Based on curricula of various madrassahs.

boards and the attempt to make madrassah education comparable to the general education system. The similarity among madrassahs and comparability with general education allows students to make a lateral move to the general education stream, provided the student successfully completes the requirements of national standardized tests and sits for these tests.

Typical stages of madrassahs can be gathered from the structure followed by the madrassahs under the Bihar Madrassah Education Board (Table 5.2). In Uttar Pradesh (UP), although the entire period of study and the number of stages remain the same, the stages are organized in a slightly different way (Table 5.3). In the third stage of the UP curriculum study, students have to choose between Persian and Arabic streams. The former makes them munshis, while the latter

TABLE 5.3

STAGES IN MADRASSAH EDUCATION IN UTTAR PRADESH, INDIA

Stage	Period of study	Comparable stage of general education
Tahtania	5 years	primary, up to 5th grade
Fuqania	3 years	middle/upper primary
Munshi/Moulvi	2 years	secondary/high school
Alim	2 years	intermediate/senior secondary
Kamil	3 years	bachelor's degree
Fazil	2 years	master's degree

Source: Based on curricula of various madrassahs in Uttar Pradesh.

makes them moulvis. Similarly, in the fourth stage, alim students have choices to study in Persian or Arabic. Often students follow their earlier choice and thus munshis follow the Persian stream and moulvis choose Arabic.

Some of the traditional and respected institutions, while following the general pattern, have made some revisions in their own systems. The Darul Uloom Nadwatul Ulama in Lucknow is a case in point. The primary stage in Nadwa, including a preprimary level, covers a period of six years. The secondary stage comprises three years, the higher secondary stage is two years, the baccalaureate level study (*alimiyat*) is four years, and the master's level (*fazilat*) is two years. Students can then proceed to *takmil* or research level, at which stage the student specializes on a topic under the guidance of an individual scholar for two years. The Nadwa curriculum is followed by those madrassahs that maintain relationships with the Nadwa, but Ahl-e-Hadith madrassahs also divide their curriculum into similar stages, although their content differs considerably.[49] The Darul Uloom Deoband has structured its curriculum into four stages: primary, intermediate, graduate, and postgraduate. The first three stages, comprising eight years, are considered mandatory for students who enter into the system.

The Markazi Darsgah (Central School) founded by the Islamist political party Jamaat-i-Islami Hind (JIH) in 1949 in Rampur has since been replicated in many parts of the country, despite its setback in 1960. The madrassah remained closed for almost twenty-six years until 1986, but has attracted attention in recent years because of its different approach toward structuring its curriculum. The fifteen-year curriculum is divided into two stages of eight and seven years. "A number of madrasas following this curriculum prepare their students simultaneously for both a modern degree examination and for the madrasa examination for the degree of Aalimiat, Fazeelat, etc."[50] The other Jamaat-sponsored madrassah, Jamiat ul-Falah, located in eastern UP, offers a three-tier curriculum: seven years of primary education, three years of alim degree, and two years of fazil degree.[51]

The Jamiat ul-Hidaya, established in 1986 in Jaipur, has divided the period of study in a different way from others. The total period of study is nine years, and instead of enrolling children at the age of six, the Jamiat ul-Hidaya enrolls students at the age of ten or eleven. The first stage of five years is called *aali* stage and the following five year stage is called *sanwi*.[52]

The state-supported madrassahs in West Bengal have devised a three-tier system: junior high madrassahs (fifth through eighth grades), high madrassahs (fifth through tenth grades) and senior madrassahs (first through tenth grades). Some high madrassahs go up to twelfth grade and are supervised by the West Bengal Board of Secondary Education. This structure of madrassahs has, however, more to do with institutional identification than the stages of madrassahs. The madrassah board conducts the alim examination for tenth-grade students of senior madrassahs, and a regular, school-leaving exam for tenth-grade students of high madrassahs. Both of these are equivalent to the *madhyamik* examinations conducted by the West Bengal Board of Secondary Education.

THE CONTENT OF THE MADRASSAH CURRICULUM

Denominational differences and regional contexts had always contributed to the content of the madrassah curriculum in India. The most obvious example of the latter is the issue of language. Madrassahs located in the south Indian states have been using local languages since the late nineteenth century. The decline of Urdu in public life and within educational institutions has had very little effect on them, particularly in comparison to the states located in the northern region. Therefore, the curricula of southern madrassahs do not have Urdu as the main language of instruction or as one of the main subjects of study. In some southern states, particularly in Kerala, Arabic gains considerable importance. Also the trend with regard to variations has been accentuated over recent decades because of the equivalence with general education. Besides, the ulama in India have been engaged in debates to make the madrassah education relevant to the current needs of the Muslim community, thereby constantly striving for changes.

The curricula followed by the majority of the community-based madrassahs can be broadly divided into three streams: the traditional Deobandi, the traditional Nadwa, and the reformist Jamiat ul-Hidaya. The madrassahs registered with the state education boards are required to offer state-mandated courses with some additional courses on Islamic subjects.

While the foundation of the Deoband madrassah curriculum rests on the curricula of three schools of an earlier period—the Madrassah Rahimia of Delhi, Farangi Mahal of Lucknow, and madrassah of Allama Fazl-e-Huq of Khairabad—the curriculum has changed over time. Since 1995, Deoband has adopted a two-step curriculum under which students spend the first five years studying Urdu and Persian primary courses. The subjects taught at the "basic level" are listed in table 5.4. At the completion of the five years of basic-level education, students are allowed to enroll in the advanced Arabic level. The eight-year plan of study allows the students to earn degrees as alim, and as fazil. After the successful completion of this eight-year course of Arabic classes, the student becomes eligible for the graduate degree (*sanad-e-faraghat*) of Darul Uloom. The subjects taught at the advanced level are listed in table 5.5. In addition to these two levels of education, Deoband offers specialized postgraduate degrees in tafsir, theology, fiqh, literature, and calligraphy, to name but a few.

The curriculum of Nadwatul Ulama emphasizes Arabic rather than Urdu, and has incorporated some elements of general education. At the primary

TABLE 5.4

BASIC LEVEL (DARJA AFTAL) URDU/PERSIAN COURSES AT
DARUL ULOOM DEOBAND, INDIA

Grade	Name	Subjects
Basic level	darja atfal	Persian alphabet; memorization of the first creed of confession (*kalmia*); basic religious beliefs (*aqa'id*); counting to 100; basic written Urdu
Grade 1	darja avval	memorization of parts of the Qur'an; memorization the first three kalimas; Urdu grammar; written Urdu; basic religious beliefs and practices; multiplication table; prayers and ablutions
Grade 2	darja doum	memorization of parts of the Qur'an; memorization the first five kalimas; basic religious beliefs and practices; Urdu grammar; Hindi alphabet; basic geography; basic mathematics, prayers and ablutions
Grade 3	darja saum	memorization of parts of the Qur'an; basic Islamic history; religious beliefs and practices; Urdu grammar; Hindi grammar; Persian; English alphabet; local geography; basic mathematics; memorizing six kalimas; prayers and ablutions, methods of supplication (*du'a*) and burial (*janaza*)
Grade 4	daraja chaharum	memorization of parts of the Qur'an; Urdu grammar; Persian literature; Islamic history; religious beliefs and practices; local geography; basic English; Hindi; basic mathematics; basic science
Grade 5	daraja panjam	Persian literature and grammar; Urdu literature; basic Hindi; basic English; Indian history; history of the founders of the Darul Uloom, Deoband; geography of India; basic mathematics; basic science; general knowledge

Source: Interviews of and personal communication with ulama of Darul Uloom
Deoband.

stage, Nadwa follows the prescribed courses for general schools, and teaches
elementary levels of Urdu, Hindi, and English, arithmetic, geography, and
general sciences. At the three-year secondary stage, Persian and Arabic
grammar, literature, and composition are emphasized along with English.
In the higher secondary stage, Arabic, Persian, and English are taught with

TABLE 5.5

ADVANCED ARABIC COURSE (DARJA ARABIYA) AT DARUL ULOOM DEOBAND

Grade	Name	Subjects
Year 1	sal avval	biography of the Prophet; Arabic grammar; recitation of the Qur'an; memorization of parts of the Qur'an
Year 2	sal daum	Arabic grammar; translation (*tarjam*) of parts of the Qur'an; fiqh (*qaduri*); hadith; morals and manners (*akhlaq*); logic; tajwid; history of the four righteous caliphs
Year 3	sal saum	translation of parts of the Qur'an; fiqh (*qaduri*); hadith; morals and manners (*akhlaq*); logic; tajwid; history of the four righteous caliphs
Year 4	sal chaharum	translation of parts of the Qur'an; fiqh (*sharh-i-wiqaya*); principles of fiqh (*'usul al-fiqh*); tajwid; rhetoric; logic; history of the Ummayad, Abbasid, and Ottoman caliphs; world and Arabian geography
Year 5	sal panjam	translation of the Qur'an; fiqh; adab; beliefs (*aqa'id*); tajwid; logic; history of the Muslim rulers in India
Year 6	sal shasham	Qur'anic commentary (*jalalayn*); fiqh (*hidaya*); principles of tafsir (*'usul-i-tafsir*); principles of fiqh; tajwid; biography of the Prophet; Arabic literature; philosophy
Year 7	sal haftam	hadith; fiqh (*hidaya*); *'aqa'id*; different schools of Islamic law
Year 8	sal hashtam (also called daura-i-hadith sharif)	specialized study of hadith (Bukhari, Muslim, Tirmidhi, Abu Da'ud, Nisa'i, Ibn Maja, Tahavi, Shama'il Tirmidhi, Muwatta Imam Malik, Muwatta Immam Muhammad)

Source: Interviews of and personal communication with ulama of Darul Uloom Deoband.

"religious sciences" and Islamic history. The courses included in the four-year graduation level (*alimiyat*) stage are commentary of the Qur'an (*tafsir*), traditions (*hadith*), Islamic jurisprudence (*fiqh*), Arabic literature, and other branches of Islamic learning. At this level Nadwa ensures that students have a stronger grasp of Arabic literature, while knowledge of English is equivalent to the intermediate standard of the Uttar Pradesh Board of High School and Intermediate Education. At the master's level (*fazilat*), Arabic literature, tafsir, hadith, fiqh, and Sharia, are studied. In addition, students have to conduct intensive study on one of the subjects. Writing a thesis at this stage is mandatory for all students. Courses on comparative religions and Islamic *d'awah* (lit., invitation; in Islamic context, inviting to the way of submission and surrender to Allah) have been introduced in recent years. Among the new additions to the Nadwa are a Department of Islamic Thought and Comparative Religions, and an institute of teacher training.

Despite inclusion of some secular subjects, particularly in the Nadwa curriculum, the traditional curriculum of both the Deoband and the Nadwa schools are overwhelmingly fiqh-centric. Many consider this a serious weakness, especially because of the use of outdated books. Recent madrassah graduates also underscore this point. The perceptive comments of Naseem ur-Rahman, a graduate of the Jamiat ul-Falah Madrassah in Azamgarh, eastern UP, and a doctoral student at the department of Islamic Studies at the Jamia Millia Islamia, New Delhi, is worth quoting at length:

> For instance, the old fiqh books that continue to be used in most madrassas discuss in great detail such issues as: What should you do to purify a well if a cat or lizard falls inside it? How much water should you remove from the well in order to restore its purity? Is it legal to eat a bird that has been shot while flying? And so on. Now, these issues, many of which are purely hypothetical, are not really such pressing questions that madrassa students should have to spend weeks upon weeks studying and thinking about them.
>
> I think madrassas must radically reform the fiqh component of their curriculum, and in place of these outdated things should teach their students about fiqh perspectives on issues of contemporary concern, from organ transplants and cloning to insurance and banking. Almost no madrassa in India arranges for these issues to be taught to its students. Although there are a number of books on fiqh issues of contemporary relevance [*jadid fiqhi masa'il*], these are not taught in the madrassas as part of the classroom curriculum.[53]

There are also debates among ulama, madrassah teachers, policy makers, and students as to what kinds of secular disciplines should be included in the madrassah curriculum. This debate is not limited to India, but is going on in other countries as well. In Pakistan, reformers have insisted on introducing science and computer teaching. Similar efforts are being made in Bangladesh. Inclusion of science is viewed as a means to make the madrassah students aware of, and prepare for, the outside world. Naseem Rahman insists that madrassah students cannot relate to the wider society because of their ignorance of "the problems of the real world" and consequently "they come up with completely unrealistic solutions to the problems of the community." But he is of the opinion that madrassahs should be teaching modern social or human sciences (*uloom al-insani*) rather than teaching physics, biology, or chemistry because the students would find these "useful in their future roles as religious leaders." Rahman underscores the need to teach English "to understand global and national developments and also . . . to relate to others and communicate your views to them."[54]

Rahman's comments, although personal, reflect the essence of the trend adopted by the Jamiat ul-Hidaya and similar madrassahs. The Hidaya curriculum attempts to balance between theological content and general subjects. Other courses offered at Hidaya include various diplomas and degrees in computer applications, mechanical engineering, electrical engineering, accounts and business management, communication, refrigeration, leather/footwear technology, air-conditioning, and offset printing, besides others that include pharmacy, journalism, and automobile engineering. Understandably, there is opposition to the curriculum of Jamiat ul-Hidaya. The All India Muslim Majlish-e-Mushawarat (AIMMM), in 2005, for example, voiced its concern saying that combining madrassah and CBSE syllabi creates a "heavy load" for students. Additionally, the organization expressed skepticism as to "how theologically good and acceptable are the Alims produced by this institution in keeping with the essential objects and purpose of Madrasas."[55]

To many observers of Indian madrassahs, the revised curriculum heralds a new era in madrassah education in India: "The new type of Islamic scholars that these institutions seek to create are thought of as more capable of responding to the challenges of contemporary life in what is seen as a 'truly' Islamic fashion, reflecting a certain form of 'Islamic modernity.' They are regarded as possibly more socially engaged, 'modern,' and as better able to represent the community and Islam than the traditional ulama."[56] But it is well to bear in mind that this new initiative, represented by Jamiat ul-Hidaya, Jamiat ul-Falah madrassah, and the like, comes from a politicized organization—the Jamaat-i-Islami Hind (JIH). Although, unlike its counterparts in Pakistan and Bangladesh, the JIH is a cultural and religious organization, it has the same ideological bent and subscribes to the ideas of Abu Ala Maududi (one of the prominent Islamist ideologues), among others. It is, therefore, pertinent to ask whether these institutions are vehicles of political Islam in India, and if so, what future that might herald for the Muslim community.

THE INDIAN GOVERNMENT AND THE MADRASSAHS

The Indian government's involvement with madrassahs is at two levels: at the state level and at central government level. At the state level the primary interaction is through the madrassah boards. These boards operate as coordinating bodies for the madrassahs, organize the terminal examinations, and issue diplomas. Additionally some madrassahs, as discussed previously, are registered with the state-level general educational boards that allow the students to sit in nationally accepted standardized tests. This level of interaction involves curricular issues, and the madrassahs receive financial support from the state, primarily in the form of salaries for the teachers and staff.

At the state level, some governments have taken a more active stance than others. In West Bengal, where Muslims comprise more than a quarter of the population, the state government is extensively involved with the madrassahs. Madrassahs registered with the government follow the curricula of the general schools, and madrassah diplomas are recognized by all. The teachers are appointed to these madrassahs by the West Bengal School Service Commission in common with teachers at all government schools. As part of the equivalence with general education, madrassah teachers are given the same salaries and pensions as teachers in government colleges. The West Bengal Madrassah Education Board is considered analogous to forty other general education state boards, and thus the West Bengal Madrassah Board Certification is nationally recognized. The amount spent by the West Bengal government on madrassah education is greater than that spent by the central government for madrassah modernization of the entire country. These steps have resulted in the appointment of non-Muslims as teachers in the madrassahs and community participation in managing madrassahs. Local madrassah committees, for instance, are composed of Hindus and Muslims alike. But the most noticeable change has taken place in the student composition of these institutions: it is estimated that 12 percent of about 329 thousand students enrolled in the madrassahs are non-Muslims, and 85 percent of students completing madrassah courses enter into the general stream of education. [57]

The central government's involvement with madrassah education is primarily through its modernization project. The project has its roots in a panel set up by the government in the eighties to review the education of the minorities, which recommended the modernization of madrassahs among others. The process began in 1986, and the central government embarked on a voluntary modernization scheme in 1992–1993. Under the scheme, madrassahs and maktabs introducing subjects like science, math, English, and Hindi receive financial support from the government. The scheme allows an institution to receive ad hoc grants-in-aid to appoint two teachers for general subjects like language, math, and science. Additional grants are available to purchase scientific instruments and kits for mathematics instruction, and for book-banks to strengthen libraries.

Initial reactions of the ulama and managers of madrassahs to the modernization scheme were predictably negative. Many madrassahs refused to cooperate, wary of the state's hidden agenda and the possible adverse effects of interference. Some ulama seriously objected to the label, particularly inclusion of the word "modernization." But over time some madrassahs have signed up. The madrassah modernization scheme has gradually increased its reach, but as of 2006 the scheme was only effective in seven states (Assam, Bihar, Madhya Pradesh, Orissa, Rajasthan, Uttar Pradesh, and West Bengal). In the Tenth Five-Year Plan (2002–2007), the government merged two major schemes aimed at the minority community and created a unified program called Area Intensive and Madrassah Modernization Program (AIMPP). This merger expanded the scope of the scheme and now allows the central government to allocate funds for infrastructural development of madrassahs. In 2006, funds were allocated to the states of Uttar Pradesh and Andhra Pradesh. In 2005–2006, a total of 1,831 madrassahs received funds under the scheme. The modernization scheme, however, is fraught with many problems; the teachers assigned to teach general subjects are often poorly trained, they are poorly paid, and the curricula are not revamped to give the general subjects due importance, to name but a few.

Over the years, the central government has become involved in some other projects concerning the madrassah sector. These projects are primarily organized jointly with Muslim socioreligious organizations. For example, the Human Resources and Development Ministry sponsored a program with the Hamdard Education Society to provide training to madrassah teachers. The project had two aims: to strengthen the values of education and to introduce modern pedagogy. As for the latter, the project intended to encourage teachers to replace rote memorization with comprehension and understanding of the subject.

One perennial issue of madrassahs for the central government is the establishment of a central madrassah board. The idea of a central board has been on the table for long time but it has gained salience in recent years. Politicians of various shades and academics of different persuasions have insisted on founding a central board to oversee the madrassahs. Conversely, this has elicited emotional reactions from some ulama and different segments of the society. The government report entitled *Reforming the National Security*, authored in February 2001 under the BJP-led government, insisted on the founding of a board to counter the "security threat" posed by the growth of madrassahs (see the next section). Although this security-centric approach was bitterly criticized not only by the Muslim community but also by many members of the public, it rekindled the debate about the madrassah board.

The principal arguments in favor of a centralized board, at that time, were that it would make the madrassah sector transparent and would help integrate the sector into mainstream education. The latter has been the main argument in almost all reform measures in South Asia since 1947 (see chapter 6). Even those who were suspicious of the government's intention owing to its anti-Muslim political agenda opted for an open debate on this issue. But the opposition to the proposal was fervent. The All India Muslim Personal Law Board

(AIMPLB) argued passionately that it was a ploy to defame the institutions and a contravention of the constitution.[58] The government backed down, and the BJP-led alliance was thrown out of power in the general election in 2004.

The debate, however, continued in the media and within academia.[59] The All India Muslim Majlish-e-Mushawarat (AIMMM) raised concerns in April 2006 saying that the government's modernization scheme had failed to make any impact, and argued that further government intervention would also be ineffectual. It insisted that an alternative or informal or private system of education is no solution to the educational backwardness of the community; instead the AIMMM demanded that the government should establish regular schools under the Sarva Shiksa Abhiyan (SSA).[60]

In the wake of the Sachar Committee report submitted in late 2006, the issue has gained new steam. Government began reconsidering the proposal, although the approach changed, as they suggested that affiliation with the proposed board would be voluntary. The initial reaction of the ulama was predictably one of opposition. The All India Muslim Personal Law Board (AIMPLB), an Islamic organization; the Jamiat Ulema-e-Hind; and the Darul Uloom Deoband continued their opposition. The opposition of the AIMMM indicates that the Nadwa is also opposed to the move. The All India Milli Council (AIMC), a sociopolitical platform of Muslims established in 1992, was divided on the issue. But letters to the editor of a Muslim newspaper revealed support from common members of the community. Some argue that with fewer than 4 percent of Muslim children attending madrassahs there is very little need to have a centralized body to oversee these institutions, while others insist that the central madrassah board will pave the way for the uniformity of the curricula and thereby make it easier for government universities to recognize the degrees of the madrassahs. As of May 2007, press reports suggest that the government is heading for the establishment of the board through an act of the parliament.[61]

MADRASSAHS AND MILITANCY

Although the classified government report entitled *Reforming the National Security System*, prepared in February 2001 and released in May 2001, was the first official report portraying madrassahs as citadels of anti-Indian activities and dens of foreign agents,[62] attacks on madrassahs by Hindu militants were not new; they began in the nineties. Involvement of some madrassahs in militant activities in Pakistan and Bangladesh gave impetus to the virulent attacks, while no specific and verifiable information was forthcoming from the propagandists; but the foundation of these assaults rested on the anti-Muslim Hindutva ideology of the BJP and its ilk.

The concerted effort to vilify the madrassahs took a great leap forward after 9/11 when BJP leaders began making inflammatory statements. In March

2002, as mentioned previously, the minister of state for home, Vidyasagar Rao, informed the parliament that more than 30,000 madrassahs were in existence and that almost one-third were located along the country's borders. The statement also added that Pakistani Inter Services Intelligence (ISI) was actively misleading the students of these institutions. Subsequently, Rao insisted that madrassahs in Kerala were engaged in terrorist activities, and later threatened to take legal action against madrassahs indulging in such illegal activities. The government began considering laws to curb foreign funding to the madrassahs. In May 2002, an official secret memo from the government was sent out to all chief secretaries and education secretaries of the state governments and union territories to verify the antecedents of the madrassahs applying for financial assistance from the government.[63] Attacks on the parliament building in New Delhi on 13 December 2001, and on the American Information Center in Calcutta on 22 January 2002, were used as excuses to link the madrassahs with terrorist acts. Shortly after the second incident, Buddhadeb Bhattacharya, the chief minister of West Bengal, joined the fray, suggesting that antinational activities were being conducted in madrassahs along the Indo-Bangladesh border and threatened to shut down all unregistered madrassahs.[64] Contemporaneously, a senior police official in UP asked the police to keep track of newly constructed madrassahs in the state because of the suspected connection between the madrassahs and the Pakistani-funded terrorists, despite the admission by the director general of UP police that in his entire career as an intelligence official he had not seen any instance of the ISI using madrassahs as training camps.[65]

The madrassahs in border regions, targeted by BJP activists since the mid-nineties, attracted the attention of the central government from 2002. Madrassahs near the Nepal border were asked to provide proof that they were not engaged in any anti-state activities. Allegations were brought by the media that madrassahs were mushrooming along the Indo-Nepal and Indo-Bangladesh borders. The statistics provided in support of these allegations were 367 madrassahs established within a ten-kilometer belt on the Indian side of the Indo-Nepal border and 195 on the Nepal side. Similarly on the Indo-Bangladesh border, 445 madrassahs operated in twenty-two bordering districts of West Bengal while 156 madrassahs were operational on the Bangladesh side.[66] A fervently anti-Muslim Web site, quoting "studies" without sources, provided a more extensive picture of the "mushrooming."

Studies conducted along the Indo-Nepal border show that there are 343 mosques and 367 madrasas in the bordering districts on the Indian side and 291 mosques and 195 madrasas in corresponding Nepal side. In Nepal many madrasas are fully or covertly indulged in anti-India activities. The Indo-Bangladesh border has 955 mosques and 445 madrasas in 22 bordering districts of West Bengal on the Indian side and 976 mosques and 156 madrasas in

28 districts on Bangladesh side. 57 mosques and 88 madrasas have been constructed on the Indian side in West Bengal, Assam, Meghalaya and Tripura during the last five years. Although the populations of Muslims in Himachal Pradesh is very negligible, there are extremely disturbing reports about the activities of 29 madrasas operating in seven districts of the State. Even in the Western border of the country, Rajasthan to Gujrat, the situation is deteriorating as can be seen from the fact that in border district of Jaisalmer only, madrasas and muktabs are now more than 100 in number, which was not even in double figure in 1980.[67]

TABLE 5.6

LOCATIONS OF MADRASSAHS IN THE BORDER AREAS OF INDIA
(by area)

On the Indian side		On the Nepali side		On the Indian side of West Bengal-Bangladesh	
Siddharthnagar	54	Rupendehi	24	Jalpaiguri	26
Maharajganj	55	Kapilavastu	29	North Dinajpur	34
Bahraich	18	Nawalparsi	18	Makla	55
Sarawasti	18	Bardia	18	Murshidabad	28
Balrawasti	27	Banka	16	Nadia	12
Champawat	07	Dang	01	North 24 Parganas	18
Udham Singh Nagar	07	Kanchannager	01	South 24 Parganas	04
Pilibhit	05	Kailai	05	Cooch Behar	12
Pithoragarh	05	Monatiari	30	South Dinajpur	16
Lakhmppur Kheri	24	Sirha	06		
West Champaran	24	Dhanaura	02		
East Champaran	24	Sarlah	14		
Sitamarhi	47	Parsa	03		
Madubani	27	Bara	01		
Gopalganj	27	Saptari	05		
Araia	22	Sunsari	07		
Darjeeling, WB	04	Morang	14		
		Jhapa	01		
Total:	384		195		208

Source: Fahimuddin, *Modernization of Muslim Education in India*, 97.

Various organizations and media, such as the *Milli Gazette*, the Indian Social Institute, and the *Week*, investigated the allegations.[68] None of these investigations found any evidence to suggest that there had been an unusual growth of madrassahs in border regions in recent years; neither did they find any connections between the extant madrassahs and the terrorist organizations. On the contrary, information provided by the *Week* revealed that the actual number of madrassahs was far lower than the figures being publicized in certain quarters (table 5.6).

Since the Congress-led government took power in 2004, the government's position in regard to the allegation of a madrassah terrorism nexus has changed. In July 2006, Union Home Minister Shivraj Patil stated that madrassahs are not the center of terrorism.[69] The Human Development Resources Minister Arjun Singh echoed the position in December 2006, saying that the allegation that madrassahs were a breeding ground of terrorists was untrue. But the BJP and its ilk continued with their claims and the campaign to demonize the madrassahs goes on.

CONCLUSION

The dominant trend within madrassah education in India is one of dynamism. Madrassahs have experienced changes since the country emerged as an independent nation in 1947, and they are still undergoing transformation. While some institutions have embraced change, others have preferred to continue their past practices. The changes have taken different paths and some changes are experimental; whether these new institutions will create new possibilities for the Muslim community is an open question. A note of caution should be sounded here that politicized educational institutions should not be the only alternative to orthodoxy. The small proportion of Muslims dependent on madrassah education confirms the fact that Indian Muslims do not consider madrassahs as their only path for upward social mobility even when they face social exclusion, political marginalization, and brutal persecution. But this may not remain the same if hatred against the Muslims and the madrassahs promoted by the radical Hindutva ideologues and their militant supporters continues, or the state continues failing to address the problems of access to education. Tendencies for a communalist response to these social injustices are already present and perhaps gaining ground within the Muslim community. Delaying the immediate and sustained actions necessary to address the issues of secularism, equality, and human dignity will only help these communalist forces in the long run, and thereby further isolate the community from the Indian society at large. It is impossible to disassociate the future trajectories of madrassahs in India from these wider issues.

CHAPTER 6

REFORMING MADRASSAHS

In recent years, reform has become one of the central elements of discussion concerning madrassahs. Media analyses and policy discourses, especially in the West, present a simple and linear equation—the problem is security threats, the causes are the madrassahs, and reform is the panacea. Whether or not they subscribe to this perceived causal relationship, governments and civil societies in countries with substantial Muslim populations have also emphasized the need for reform. In a similar vein, some of the scholars of Islamic history and contemporary Muslim politics, portrayed as "Muslim modernists," insist that reform of the madrassahs, particularly in South Asia, is long overdue. These discussions both explicitly and implicitly provide an impression that madrassahs in South Asia have remained unchanged for centuries, and that no reforms have been implemented since these madrassahs began emerging in the nineteenth century. The implied immutability of these institutions is at times linked to the absence of an Islamic reformation, with little regard to the fact that "many of the religious practices and legal principles that constitute Islam evolved over time and as the product of constant reform and adjustment."[1]

The experiences of Pakistan and Bangladesh over more than a half a century show that efforts to reform the madrassahs have been ongoing for some time in South Asia. Success or failure aside, there have been policy interventions from the governments and initiatives from the societies to change the madrassahs. These reforms have been diverse and occasionally contradictory. Despite adopting different approaches, they have, however, some common features, the integrationist mindset being the most important. The goals of these changes—proposed and implemented—have been to create equivalence between general education and that offered by the madrassahs; to introduce nonreligious, occasionally described as "useful," subjects to the latter, thereby rendering the madrassah students more employable in jobs; and to establish control over the sources of funding. All these features (except the last) are perceived to be characteristics of modern education. Thus reforms and modernization are seen as one and the same. At the same time, the experiences of these two countries are also indicative of the complexities of the reform process. The Bangladeshi experience particularly serves as a reminder that the heterogeneity of madrassahs cannot be overlooked in devising measures to address these institutions, for reform purposes or otherwise.

Although it is necessary to recognize that madrassah reform is not an externally induced post-9/11 phenomenon, it must also be acknowledged that, particularities notwithstanding, the successes of state-sponsored reform measures have been limited at best. Therefore, it is necessary to reflect on those reform measures, but also to suggest a pathway for future endeavors.

Pakistan: A Circular Path of Reform

Since the inception of Pakistan in 1947, three organized efforts have been launched to reform the madrassahs: in 1962, in 1979, and in 2001. These efforts have been planned, initiated, and implemented by the government with and without the help of the ulama. All of these endeavors are closely tied to politics in Pakistan, not only because they were initiated by military rulers (General Ayub Khan, General Zia-ul Huq, and General Pervez Musharraf, respectively), but also because political considerations shaped the contents and contours of these reforms, as much as the outcomes. It is fair to say that these initiatives were driven as much by the need of the military rulers to carve out a space within the political landscape as for the purpose of addressing deep-seated concerns about general or Islamic education. Equally important is that the issue of Islamic education and, by extension, the issue of interpreting Islam are fundamentally connected to Pakistani nationhood and thereby themselves constitute a political issue.

The First Step—Reforms under Ayub Khan

In 1959, within a year of his assumption of power, Ayub Khan (1958–1969) embarked on a plan to make changes in the curriculum and restrict the funding sources of the madrassahs. The primary motivation of the reform measures was to tame the potential opponents of the new regime.

The coup d'état that brought Ayub Khan to power was engineered against the backdrop of an intense tussle between those who favored the role of Islam in political life and those who wanted to keep religion outside the realm of politics. The debate with regard to the role of Islam in Pakistani politics and governance had ensued soon after independence in 1947 as the nation's Constituent Assembly began formulating the fundamental principles of the newly established state.

The untimely demise of the founding leader of Pakistan, Muhammad Ali Jinnah in 1948, not only deprived Pakistan of a guide who could steer the nation through a difficult phase but also opened the door for conflicts between various social forces. The Objective Resolution passed by the Constituent Assembly in March 1949 pointed to a public role for Islam without forsaking the idea of a pluralist society. The Objective Resolution stated that Pakistan would be a state "wherein the principles of democracy, freedom, equality, tolerance and social justice, as enunciated by Islam, shall be fully observed"; "wherein the Muslims shall be enabled to order their lives in the individual and collective spheres in accordance with the teachings and requirements of Islam as set out in the Holy Qur'an and Sunnah"; and "wherein adequate provision shall be made for the minorities freely to progress and practice their religions and develop their cultures."[2]

The Objective Resolution was followed up by a twenty-four-member committee called the Basic Principles Committee (1949–1952) entrusted with the responsibility to formulate the guidelines and principles of the future constitution of Pakistan. Among the committee's propositions were that the head of the state would have to be a Muslim, and that a board of ulama was to examine the lawmaking process to ensure that no law was passed that went against the principles of the Qur'an and Sunnah.[3] Although these propositions received the immediate approval of a section of the population, a large number of Pakistani citizens were not happy to see that a body was to be created outside the jurisdiction of the parliament to oversee the lawmaking process.

Two years later, when the first constitution was adopted by the second Constituent Assembly, this provision was discarded. But by then Pakistan had already seen the rise of the Jamaat-i-Islami (JI) as a political organization under the leadership of Abul Ala Maududi. The JI, which opposed the establishment of an independent Muslim homeland in India, not only became the mouthpiece of an Islamic Pakistan during the constitutional debate in the period between 1947 and 1954 but also flexed its muscle through organizing the virulent anti-Ahmadiyya campaign leading to the riots in 1953 in Punjab.[4]

The first Pakistani constitution empowered the president to appoint a committee to bring the "existing law into conformity with the Holy Qur'an and Sunnah." The "directive principles of the state policy" stated that "the state shall endeavor ... to make the teachings of the Holy Qur'an compulsory for all Muslims; to promote the unity and observance of moral standards," among other things.[5] Although these provisions had very little practical implication, their inclusion demonstrated the clout of the political forces who were far removed from Jinnah's ideal Pakistan, where "Hindus would cease to be Hindus and Muslims would cease to be Muslims, not in the religious sense, because that is the personal faith of each individual, but in the political sense as citizens of the State."[6] For them, Pakistan was to be an Islamic state.

Against this backdrop, the coup of October 1958 brought General Ayub Khan, then chief of the Pakistani Army, to power. The coup was not planned to "resolve many of the anomalies that had confounded state formation" as Nasr has claimed, or to prevent Islamist takeover, as its protagonists have insisted, even if those turned out to be the results of the military intervention.[7]

Marginalizing the political forces was the primary objective of the coup, but it was also designed to ensure the preeminence of the military-bureaucratic oligarchy in the policy-making apparatuses. The chaos and political instability between 1954 and 1958 provided the immediate justifications and the pretext for martial law, but political developments, particularly the inability of the ruling party to resolve the conflict between two propertied classes (that is, the landed aristocracy and the entrepreneurial class) allowed the bureaucracy to emerge as the mediator and later usurp state power.[8] To begin with, the Pakistani state, like any other postcolonial state, was "overdeveloped," to borrow Hamza Alavi's term, and consequently highly interventionist in nature.[9] Owing to the capitalist agenda of the state and the absence of a strong endogenous capitalist class, state interventions were blatant, to say the least. Necessitated by the interventionist nature of the state (in conjunction with the global power game), the military-bureaucratic oligarchy took power in 1958.

Thus the primary goal of the military regime of Ayub Khan was "to strengthen state institutions, and to expand their control over the society, economy and politics."[10] In so doing, at the beginning, the military regime opposed the traditional sectors, including the ulama, the shrines, and the socioeconomic institutions, including the mosques, that support the ulama and their interpretations of Islamic rituals, practices, and traditions.

The most significant attempt to bring these institutions under the direct control of the state was the nationalization of *awaqaf* (sing. *waqf*) or Islamic endowments (property that cannot be transferred and that is therefore inalienable) in 1960. Nationalization of the Islamic endowments, to establish control over the autonomous ulama and undermine the traditional religious institutions, was nothing new. Egypt, Turkey, and Iran under Reza Shah are the most obvious examples in this regard.

In the case of Egypt, Muhammad Ali (1805–1848) was the first to take steps in this direction in 1812. He reorganized land ownership and nationalized waqf lands that used to finance the schools and mosques and were the foundations of the power of the ulama. Similarly, Gamal Abdul Nasser's land reform measures in 1952 included the establishment of a new Ministry of Endowment (Wizarat al-Awqaf) and placing the waqf lands under its control. In similar vein, almost all Egyptian governments since Muhammad Ali have tried to control the traditional religious institutions, including mosques and the famous al-Azhar University.[11]

In the regions that comprised the modern state of Pakistan, the waqf system prevailed through British colonial rule because of the ambiguous policies of the colonial administration with regard to the law of inheritance within the Muslim community.[12] In the postindependence era, as much as during colonial rule, waqf properties were the primary sources of finance for the *pirs* (founders of sufi orders), *mujawirs* (persons administering a heritage), *sajjadah nashins* (holders of a shrine), and the ulama. A portion of these resources were used for the maintenance of mosques, shrines, and madrassahs (often attached to mosques).

The "West Pakistan Waqf Properties Rule" of 1960 was passed, citing examples of how these endowments were being misused by a small number of people and had been misappropriated from their original purposes of ensuring the economic welfare of the Muslim community. The government was less interested in the revenue it would generate than in challenging the authority of the traditional religious institutions and individuals whose legitimacy rested on their involvements with these institutions.

This administrative action had profound impacts at various levels; it weakened the traditional institutions, most of which were located in the rural areas, forced a change to the ulama's cognitive environment, and posed a threat to their political vitality, to name but a few results of the policy. Follow-up ordinances delinked the administrators of awaqaf properties and their religious credentials, thus making the awaqaf properties secular institutions.

What followed the takeover of the religious endowments by the state was the attempt to establish control over the religious educational institutions, namely deeni madrassahs, with a view of changing their curricula. A committee, formed in 1961, to examine the curricula and make recommendations as to how the students of the madrassahs could be prepared to meet the demands of employers, suggested the introduction of new subjects, but also the substitution of "unnecessary non-religious subjects" with "religious subjects based on undisputed sources of knowledge."[13]

The report of the "Committee set up by the Governor of West Pakistan for recommending an improved syllabus for the various Darul Uloom and Arabic Madrsas in West Pakistan" was submitted in 1962. Among its recommendations were that the madrassah curriculum be extended to fifteen years, of which five years would be primary education (ibtidayee), that the new school system be divided into five stages, that Arabic and/or English be the medium of instruction at secondary and higher level while Urdu be the language of instruction at primary level, that new subjects such as mathematics be introduced to the curriculum, and that students who complete the highest stage of the madrassah education take five exams on hadith, astronomy, and euclidian mathematics. Interestingly, the committee felt that logic and philosophy should be excluded from the madrassah curricula, because they were "not essential in achieving

TABLE 6.1

PROPOSALS AND CHARGES OF THE COMMITTEE OF 1960/61, PAKISTAN

	Primary secondary	Lower secondary	Middle secondary	Upper secondary	Highest level
Arabic	ibtidayee	thanawi tahtani	thanawi wastani	thanawi fawqani	al'la
Duration	5 years	3 years	2 years	2 years	3 years
Grades	1–5	6–8	9–10	11–12	13–15
Suggestions and modifications by the committee	According to directions of the Ministry of Education	More Koran and hadith; Prophet's tradition; Islamic law; modern Arabic literature; English; mathematics; social sciences; sports; Urdu	Islamic history; alternative books; English; Sports; optional subjects (preferably Urdu)	principles of tafsir; more hadith; modern Arabic literature; English; less philosophy; less logic	history of hadith compilation; fatwa; modern philosophy

Source: Jamal Malik, *Colonization of Islam*, 127.

the objective of religious education."[14] The proposed changes, as summarized by Jamal Malik, are presented in table 6.1.

It was evident by 1962 that the regime had adopted a two-pronged strategy—to control, if not eliminate, the sources of funding of the madrassahs, and to bring about changes in the curriculum of these institutions. The government achieved considerable success in dealing with the funding issue, but the curriculum issue remained unsettled. The controversy surrounding the curriculum was far greater than appears at first sight. It was not only a matter of the books to be read at various grades, and whether or not the teachers of the madrassahs were to go through the "reorientation" courses at the Teachers Training College but, more important, who would define the meaning and role of Islam in the Pakistani society and polity.[15] In short, this was the question of authority: who would define the meaning of Islam, and the role of Islam in society and politics. The regime's efforts were intended to undermine the ulama's authority and therefore privilege the state's interpretations of religion and religious education.

Within this frame of reference, the ulama are seen as ossified institutions, they "represent a millennium-old tradition of Islamic learning," which should be replaced with a modernist agenda, the paradigm set forth by the state. Although the ulama do not deny that their authority is based on their connections to the Islamic tradition, what is important is their ability to "[mobilize] this tradition to define issues of religious identity and authority in the public sphere."[16] Thus their relevance lies with defining the current state of the community and providing direction for the future. The state's decision to intrude into this realm troubled the ulama, and pitted them against the regime and its plan for reform. This was predestined in the sense that each felt challenged by the other, as they were battling for control over the meaning of religion.

Impacts of the 1962 Reform Efforts

A debate on the issue of authority in regard to the Islamic tradition and education was one of the results of the reform measures initiated by the Ayub regime. The institutionalization of sectarianism and doctrinal differences in Pakistan was another.

The sectarian divide along Sunni–Shi'a lines had existed in Pakistan before the partition of 1947 but did not feature prominently in sociopolitical life for two reasons; first, the Shi'a population was relatively small (about 15 percent), and second, the folk Islamic tradition in the rural areas was accommodative of different rituals and practices as well as various sects and subsects. This is true of prepartition India in general. Similarly, doctrinal differences between the four madhabs (schools of thoughts, that is, the Hanafi, the Maliki, the Shafi'i, and the Hanbali) within the Sunnis were confined to juridico-legal discourses rather than matters of public life until the mid-nineteenth century.

However, the divergence between Sunnis and Shi'as, within the Sunni community, and within the adherents of Hanafi madhab, became an issue of intense debate after the establishment of the Darul Uloom madrassah in Deoband in 1867, thanks to the establishment of a number of madrassahs representing these divergent beliefs. Madrassahs, in essence, became the conduit of these doctrinal positions. The rise of the Barelwis in 1906 as a distinct subsect is a case in point (see chapter 2). Although these madrassahs maintained an affiliation to a central madrassah (for example Deoband, in case of Deobandi madrassahs) they remained organizationally autonomous. The number of madrassahs grew as they spread throughout India, yet the concept of being part of a nationwide, organized network was absent.

In Pakistan, the situation changed in the late fifties, primarily as a response to the reform measures. Following the lead of the Ahl-e-Hadith school, who brought their madrassahs under the umbrella organization Markaz-e-Jamiat Ahl-e-Hadith in 1955,[17] other subsects organized similar boards in 1959. The Deobandis created Wafaq al-Madaris al-Arabiya, Barelwis set up Tanzim al-Madaris al-Arabiya, and the Shi'as were grouped under the Majlis-e-Nazarat-e-shiah Madaris-e-Arabiah.[18]

The rise of madrassah boards along sectarian lines brought conflicting impulses to the fore. On the one hand, their creation fostered a hostile relationship between the adherents of these doctrinal subgroups while, on the other hand, mosque leaders and board members experienced a new sense of power, recognizing that together they wielded influence over a large number of young people. The reorganization of the Tanzim al-Madaris al-Arabiya in 1974 bears testimony to the fact that madrassah boards were ready to work together for common causes such as opposition to the interference of the government.

This newly found power was exercised during the Bhutto regime (1972–1977). These networks succeeded in thwarting the government initiative to "nationalize" the madrassahs at a time when the government took control of the entire education sector. The regime's self-contradictory stance on the role of Islam in politics—declaring Pakistan an Islamic Republic, Islam a state religion, Ahmadiyyas non-Muslim, and frequently using Islamic rhetoric on the one hand, while trying to contain political activism of the religiopolitical forces on the other—gave the Islamist political parties enough reason to mount a strong opposition to the regime. This created opportunities for the marginalized ulama to return to the limelight through the political parties.

The ulama-political parties' confluence became the core of the postelection antigovernment alliance in 1977. The movement pressed not only for democratization but also for Islamization of the society, as the declared aim of the alliance was to achieve Nizam-e-Mustapha (the system of Prophet Muhammad). The madrassah networks of the Deobandi persuasion (affiliated with the political party Jamaat ul-Ulama-i-Islam—JUI), and those affiliated with

Jamaat-i-Islami Pakistan (JIP), allegedly provided foot soldiers for the street agitation.

The Bhutto regime, although it did not have a plan to reform the madrassah system, was not oblivious to the presence and roles of these institutions. For example, in 1975/1976 the government initiated an assessment of the future of an Islamic system of education,[19] introduced religious subjects in the general education curriculum in 1975, and attempted to integrate the madrassah graduates into mainstream education through recognition of the *sanads* (certificates) of the Wafaq al-Madaris al-Arabia.

The demand for the recognition of the diploma came from the Tanzim al-Madaris in 1973. But it took almost two years for the government to act on the proposal presented to the parliament. The National Assembly agreed to recognize the higher diplomas of the madrassahs as equivalent to a master's degree in Islamiyat (Islamic studies), provided the students could qualify for a bachelor's in English. Due to the conditionality attached to the recognition of these degrees, madrassah boards, particularly of the Deobandi strand, rejected the proposal. In 1976, the Ministry of Education agreed to comply with the parliamentary resolution, but only up to the bachelor's degree. Not all universities agreed to this regulation, and therefore the changes were ineffective.[20]

Whether these measures were half-hearted or driven by political expediency is an open question, but they do demonstrate that the regime's mindset was no different from that of its predecessor—that madrassahs needed to be integrated into mainstream education, that madrassah education was inadequate for the students to secure jobs in the existing economic system, and that the state should shape the nature and roles of madrassahs.

Reforms under Zia-ul Huq (1979–1982)

The most far-reaching and consequential reform of madrassah education in Pakistan was carried out by the Zia-ul Huq regime between 1979 and 1982. General Zia, like Ayub Khan, came to power through a military coup, lacked constitutional legitimacy, and initiated the Islamization of Pakistani society.[21] Zia's Islamization project was both a matter of political expediency and ideological conviction. Although Zia-ul Huq is known for his support for the institutions labeled madrassahs that have been at the forefront of Afghan war, his initial reform plan was in many ways identical to the plan initiated by Ayub Khan. It is no coincidence that the committee nominated to draw up the reform plan in 1979, in light of a pilot survey conducted in previous year, was headed by Dr. A.W.J. Halepota, the person who was largely responsible for the 1962 report.

The striking similarity between the 1962 initiative and the 1979 report lies in the primary goal of the reform—"integrating them [madrassahs] with the overall educational system in the country."[22] Like previous initiatives, the reform proposals of 1979 contended that madrassah education was failing to prepare students for the requirements of the modern age and for careers, particularly in the public sector.

The report suggested introduction of new subjects including Urdu, arithmetic, and general science at the primary level; English, general mathematics, and Pakistan studies at the secondary levels; political science, political economy, and English as optional subjects at the baccalaureate and master's level; and comparative religious sciences as a mandatory subject at the master's level. The committee proposed an autonomous National Institute of Madrassahs to compile and revise madrassah curricula, supervise these institutions, administer standardized written tests, and award diplomas to the students. The proposed national institute, the committee recommended, was to have an equal number of members from all four subsects within the madrassah education system, and representatives from the government.

Despite such elaborate suggestions with regard to the curriculum, and the proposal for a supervisory institution, the report and thereby the government maintained that it had no intention of "interfering" in the internal affairs of the madrassahs. One can easily conclude that in essence the 1979 report was a replication of the 1962 report. This is not to imply that there were no dissimilarities, in appearance if not in content, and in the processes.

The 1962 reform proposals came from a committee that did not consult with the ulama and therefore was disconnected from the religious community from the outset. The 1979 committee, on the other hand, had significant numbers of ulama as members, demonstrating that their participation was more than tokenism. But the ulama did not constitute the majority nor did an alim head the committee. Therefore, the ulama could not sway the focus away from the government's design.

This reflected the regime's strategy of cooptation instead of confrontation. In similar vein, the implementation of the proposed reforms was put on hold in 1980–1981, changes were made to the proposed structure of the National Institute for Dini Madaris Pakistan (NIDMP) to accommodate more ulama in deciding the curricula of the madrassahs, and in reviving the 1976 proposal for recognition of madrassah qualifications as equivalent to bachelor's and master's degrees in regular universities.

Where these two reform measures apparently differed was in the sources of funding for the madrassahs. In contrast to the 1962 measure of establishing government control over the waqf (endowment), and therefore removing the possible sources of funding for the madrassahs, the government in 1979 offered various means, including unconditional financial aid to these institutions. Additionally, the government established a system of providing regular financial support to madrassahs from the zakat fund.[23] While the latter move demonstrated that the government understood the need of funding to sustain the madrassahs and showed that the government did not intend to deprive them of their resources, it also, in the long run, paved the way to influence the madrassahs, for both political and educational reasons. One can say that the difference is more of a method, for the goal remains the same—to make the madrassahs increasingly dependent upon the government for financial resources.

The government initiative with regard to the madrassahs was welcomed by the ulama at an early stage (for example when the committee was formed), but it did not take long for opposition to grow. The ulama of the Deobandi persuasion were the first to express serious reservations, and then to call for a boycott of the committee. Madrassahs of all other schools of thought, with the exception of those with close connections to the Jamaat-i-Islami Pakistan (JIP), became vocal critics of the reforms recommended by the committee. The ulama affiliated with the JIP-supported madrassahs welcomed most of the suggested changes, including extending the madrassah curriculum to sixteen years from eight years, as these ideas mirrored their own agenda.

The recognition of their degrees, the availability of the zakat fund, and the potential of increasing influence within the government and secular sectors changed the tone of the criticisms over succeeding years, particularly after 1982. Two of the four umbrella organizations made changes in their curricula by 1984, mostly at the secondary and higher levels.[24] Recommendations in regard to the primary level, however, were largely ignored. The changes, or in fact additions of some new subjects, in curricula of various grades had very little impact because "there was . . . no essential alteration of the classical DM [Dini Madaris] course of instruction."[25]

In Jamal Malik's view, this was a no less than a quid pro quo between the government and the ulama; the Zia regime secured "acceptance of his leadership by the ulama" and "an 'Islamic legitimation of his rule,'" while the ulama achieved "social recognition"; these changes demonstrated their ability to "meet the demands of innovation and pragmatism without acting against their own interests."[26]

Notwithstanding the above-mentioned factor, political changes in the atmosphere within the country and in the region also influenced the course of action. By then Pakistan had become the frontline state in the war in Afghanistan against the Soviet Union. An elaborate infrastructure under the guise of madrassahs was built to provide training to the mujahideen, leaving no room for insisting on the curriculum and sources of funding. Thus, the initiative to reform the madrassahs in Pakistan came to an end, until it was resurrected in 1998 by a committee and followed up by the Musharraf regime in 2001.

Déjà vu in Pakistan: Reforms under Pervez Musharraf

On 12 January 2002, Pervez Musharraf, the military ruler of Pakistan, addressed the nation in a televised speech. The speech came at a time when the government of Pakistan was under intense pressure from the European Union and the United States with regard to militant groups within Pakistan, especially their involvement in violence in Indian-administered Kashmir. Musharraf, who was also facing domestic pressure for his unqualified support for the U.S. "war on terrorism" and military operations in Afghanistan, announced that his government would no longer tolerate extremism in the name of Islam, "no organization will be allowed to indulge in terrorism in the name of Kashmir," and his government would soon rid the madrassahs of extremist elements.[27]

General Musharraf's speech received widespread acclaim from the international community, and has been described in international media as a bold and unprecedented step in the history of Pakistan. The tone and tenor of the media coverage of the speech is best reflected in the words of Uwe Parpart, editor of the *Asia Times*: "No civilian Pakistani leader has ever seen fit or dared to put the country's choices in such clear and uncompromising terms."[28]

Contrary to common belief, however, Musharraf's initiatives were not new by any standards. Reforming madrassah education had been on the agenda of the military regime of Musharraf since it took power in 1999. Besides, as we have already discussed, his predecessors in Pakistan had already attempted to bring changes to the madrassahs. In his first speech as head of the government on 17 October 1999, Musharraf warned against the use of religion, saying that "Islam teaches tolerance not hatred, universal brotherhood and not enmity, peace and not violence, progress and not bigotry. I have great respect for the Ulama and expect them to come forth and present Islam in its true light. I urge them to curb elements which are exploiting religion for vested interests and bringing a bad name to our faith."[29] This set the Musharraf regime's tone toward the madrassahs, militancy, and the role of Islam in Pakistani politics.

Commensurate with the position outlined in Mushrraf's 1999 speech, the government promulgated the "Pakistan Madrassah Education (Establishment and Affiliation of Model Deeni Madaris) Board Ordinance 2001" on 18 August 2001. One can trace the genesis of this ordinance to the recommendations of a committee appointed in 1998 by the Ministry of Education. The committee, headed by S. M. Zaman, outlined a model curriculum for the madrassahs and suggested the establishment of a board to oversee the madrassahs. The ordinance of 2001 was aimed at bringing the madrassahs into the mainstream by introducing secular subjects in the curricula taught at these schools. Three model institutions were subsequently established: one each at Karachi, Sukkur, and Islamabad. One of these was for girls while the two others were for boys. Their curricula include English, mathematics, computer science, economics, political science, law, and Pakistan studies. But even before the new ordinance came into full force and the model madrassahs were established, the events of 9/11 took place and Pakistani madrassahs came under intense scrutiny and immense criticism.

These criticisms led to the second and more comprehensive legal measure regarding the madrassahs. On 19 June 2002, the government announced the Madrassah Registration Ordinance of 2002, which went into effect immediately. Under the ordinance, all madrassahs were required to register with the Pakistan Madrassah Education Board and provincial boards. Madrassahs failing to do so were to be fined or closed. The ordinance prohibited madrassahs from accepting grants or aid from foreign sources, while madrassahs offering courses in science, math, Urdu, and English would be eligible for government funding in these subjects. Foreign madrassah students were to be required to obtain no objection certificates (NOCs) prior to admission. Madrassahs were given six months to comply with the ordinance.

Two Approaches, Two Sets of Goals

These two attempts signal two different approaches toward the madrassahs. The pre-9/11 approach was to modernize the institutions without the imposition of particular standards. The model madrassahs designed under the 2001 ordinance were intended to provide examples of how the madrassahs could be utilized in training a new generation of liberal-minded religious scholars. The implicit expectation was that these "model" institutions would set an example and thus draw other madrassahs into the stream of changes. On the other hand, the Madrassah Registration Ordinance of 2002 was designed to be restrictive and bring the whole madrassah sector under the direct control of the state. The goals of the post-9/11 measures, heralded as "reform," have all the hallmarks of an interventionist state. The focus of this legal measure was on the management of the institutions. The three-year plan also promised to train 28,000 teachers on subjects related to sectarian issues.

One common point shared by both measures was the integrationist mindset. The Pakistani policy makers and their international supporters worked under the assumption that the problems of the madrassahs, the total number of which was anybody's guess at that time, stemmed from their autonomous existence, particularly because they existed parallel to the secular general educational system of the nation. Therefore, if these institutions were integrated into the system the problems would be easier to address, if not eliminated altogether.

In comparison to the ordinance of 2001, the Madrassah Registration Ordinance of 2002 was ambitious and elaborate; yet there was an obvious contradictory element in it: the registration of the madrassahs with the government was voluntary. Even before the intense struggle between the various actors involved with the madrassahs came to the fore, there was serious bureaucratic wrangling involving four ministries (foreign, education, religious, and interior) resulting in an absence of a central authority in charge of the implementation of the program. On the one hand, the government was claiming that tough enforcement of the new law would enable it to obtain a reliable figure of the number of madrassahs within the country and closely monitor their activities and sources of funding, while on the other hand the president promised that no action would be taken against the madrassahs.[30] With the promulgation of the ordinance, the focus shifted from curricula to the management of these institutions, particularly their external connections.

The Crux of the Reform

Notwithstanding the popular media's obsession with the registration of madrassahs, there was more to the reform measures. These came under a different project in mid-2002. The five-year plan (2002/03–2007/08) of the government, interchangeably referred to as madrassah reform and mainstreaming madrassah education, is aimed to "facilitate 8,000 willing Deeni Madaris of Pakistan through teaching of English, Mathematics, Pakistan Studies/Social Studies and General Science from Primary to Secondary levels and English, Economics, Pakistan Studies and Computer Science at Intermediate level to integrate religious education with formal education system."[31] The objectives of the project have been:

> 1. To teach formal subjects in 8,000 Madaris to bridge the gulf between Madrasah Education and Formal Education system; 2. to open the lines of communication with the Ulama who run the Madaris to impart formal education in addition to religious education for spreading of Islamic values at national and international levels; 3. to improve and update knowledge of their teachers in formal subjects through workshops at different parts of the country; 4. to provide incentives as costs of equipments (computers, printers, apparatus etc) for teaching of Computer Science, costs of textbooks, sports and other facilities to Madaris; 5. one-time grant to the Madaris for improvement of their libraries and equip their buildings.

Thus, there are three elements to the project: changes in the curricula through introduction of formal subjects, training for the teachers, and improvement of the infrastructure. The latter two, however, are intrinsically linked to the first.

Buried in the details of the plan is an important element of the proposed changes in the curriculum: control over the content. The plan states, "The Ministry of Education will develop textual and instructional material as and when required." Juxtaposing these with the provision of registration under the Madrassah Registration Ordinance of 2002, one can see that, the proposed reform is taking an integrationist approach, which means that the madrassahs are to become part of a uniform education system.[32] It is significant that the authority to decide the curriculum rests with the state instead of ulama and the institution.

Progress of and Reactions to the Reform, 2002–2006

The new measures came at a time when the international media began portraying the Pakistani madrassahs as the citadel of global terrorism, and U.S. leaders insisted that the Pakistani government make serious efforts to bring these institutions under control. Obviously these pressures gave the clearest indications that the government was acting at the behest of the U.S. administration, if not on their behalf. In an environment where the regime's relationship with the ulama was already tense due to Musharraf's statements in 1999, this could not be a positive development. In 2000, as a reaction to the Musharraf regime's initial declaration of intent to clamp down on militancy and institutions associated with militancy, the ulama formed a coalition called Ittehad-e Tanzimat-ul Madaris-e-Deenia (ITMD) and vowed to resist the implementation of any laws that would curb their autonomy.

The opposition to the proposed reforms came from two quarters: first, the ulama and individuals involved with the religious educational institutions, particularly madrassahs; and second, from within political circles.

For the individuals belonging to the first category, the principal motivating factor was the autonomy of these institutions—both in terms of management and determining the content of the curriculum. "To the ulama, governmental initiatives towards integrating madrasas into the educational mainstream are but a thinly veiled effort to undermine their status as bastions of what the ulama call 'an unadulterated Islam' in society and politics."[33] From the perspective of the ulama, the government is not only trying to take away the control of these institutions but also striving to transform the fundamental characteristic of madrassahs. Madrassahs, as viewed by the ulama, are the means of transmission of religious knowledge to the next generation, and thus the creation of religious authority figures. This aspect of madrassah education, in the view of the ulama, is under threat in the proposed reform, particularly when the ulama's ability to decide the texts and instructional materials is being restricted by the government.

For political opponents, the measure is a hegemonic project of the West, particularly the United States, to undermine Islam and Islamic society. Often the rhetoric of these two groups overlapped, but distinctions can be made on close examination of their arguments.

Comments made by Qari Hanif Jallundhari, secretary general of the Wafaq al-Madaris al-Arabia Pakistan, the Madrassah Education Board for the Deobandi school of thought, are instructive in this regard. He said that "the Madaris Reform Project is not a sincere offer to help Islamic institutions and is actually a part of a global conspiracy to deviate us from our basic purpose to teach Qur'an and Hadith." Maulana Abbas Naqvi said, "we have resisted all such moves [government control] in the past and will continue to resist any attempt aimed at curtailing our independence." Pir Saifullah Khalid also said that all madrassahs are completely united on this platform and would abide by its joint decision.[34]

The Madrassah Registration Ordinance 2002 was seen by the ITMD and their supporters as an assault on Islam and Pakistani culture. The daily newspaper with the second largest circulation in the country, *Nawa-i-Waqt*, in its editorial on 21 June 2002 articulated this position in a scathing criticism of the proposed reform: "the aim [of the reform] is to indoctrinate the students with material pursuits. It seeks to replace the spirit of Jihad and love for Islam with material objectives. . . . The madrassah culture is part of the Pakistani tradition." Additionally, the newspaper insisted, this measure is part of a global anti-Islamic design: "[Pakistan] is facing a threat from the US, Israel and India, which is primarily anti-Islamic. . . . The US is backing Israel and India in an anti-Islamic campaign. Since the government is a part of an international coalition against terror, therefore it is targeting religious schools."[35]

In similar vein, the Islamist political parties reacted sharply to the proposed changes. For example, the Muttahida Majlis-i-Amal (MMA, United Action Forum), an alliance of Islamist parties, emphatically rejected the new law and the reform plan, labeling it a foreign-sponsored plan to corrupt the Islamic values of Pakistan. Munawar Hassan, secretary general of the Jamaat-i-Islami, was infuriated by the ordinance, as he insisted that it was a command from Washington D.C., since the United States offered $35 million dollars to Pakistan to reform its schools.[36]

Thus by the end of 2002, although about 1,200 madrassahs had registered with the government, a vast number of madrassahs decided not to follow suit. They chose not subscribe to the government-sponsored reform of the curriculum, and not to divulge their sources of funding. The government's policy of providing funds to the registered madrassahs therefore failed in its objective of bringing them on board. Except for denying government assistance to 115 madrassahs due to their alleged links to militancy, there was very little progress in making changes in the madrassah sector. Besides, the scope and nature of the reform remained contentious. With major domestic political developments— the referendum in February and parliamentary elections in July—the reforms reached a stalemate. It is suspected that the rise of the MMA and the victory of these allied parties in elections to provincial assemblies slowed down the process significantly.[37] In the following year, the government offered new textbooks and training to teachers who would specialize in secular subjects, yet it did very little to assuage the critics of the reforms; instead there were growing criticisms that the United States was behind the move, to "suppress the growing Islamic influence which is resiliently rising after the U.S. aggression on Afghanistan and has now gained momentum after recent war on Iraq," according to Sarfas Naeemi, the secretary general of the board for the Barelwi madrassahs.

The issue of reform continued to haunt the Pakistani government in 2004 as the media, at home and abroad, became vocal due to lack of progress. Many analysts questioned Musharraf's sincerity and opined that he had no intent of following through on his promise.[38] The tone of the Congressional Research Office's 2004 brief on Pakistan's educational reform indicates that the patience of the U.S. administration began to run out, as well. The report stated, "Despite Musharraf's repeated pledges to crack down on the more extremist madrassahs in his country, there is little concrete evidence that he has done so." Quoting two analysts, the report further states, "most of the madrassahs remain unregistered, their finances unregulated, and the government has yet to remove the jihadist and sectarian content of their curricula. Observers speculate that Musharraf's reluctance to enforce reform is rooted in his desire to remain on good terms with Pakistan's Islamist political parties, which are seen to be an important part of his political base."[39]

The media reports after the bombing in London on 7 July 2005 that three of the bombers visited Pakistan and may have spent some time in local madrassahs brought the issue of reform, once again, to the forefront and placed the Pakistani government in a difficult situation. President Musharraf, in a deft move, called for the expulsion of all foreign students enrolled in Pakistani madrassahs, numbering 1,400 in July 2005, and made the registration of the madrassahs mandatory.[40] The leaders of the alliance of the madrassahs refused to adhere to any of these demands. After prolonged negotiations, representatives of the grouping of five associations of madrasshas, Ittehad-e Tanzimat-ul Madaris-e-Deenia (ITMD), finally agreed in September to register, while the government had to drop the provision of disclosing the sources of the funding of these institutions.[41] The order to expel the foreign students fizzled out in the face of resistance from the madrassahs.[42]

The voices of opposition were louder, but support for reform was also expressed by many. Backing for reform came mainly from those who were least connected to the religious realm including religious education, and who can be characterized as Western-educated elites, but some support did come from those involved with religious education.

One of the most important arguments of the secularists was that these "antiquated" institutions are ineffective in producing a workforce necessary for the modern state and economy. Put bluntly, the essence of the arguments is as follows: "All education is to prepare the alumni for life—and better and ever improving life at that. Education has to be purpose orientated. At a certain stage, it has to be career-related. What kind of career [do] these Madaris prepare their students for?"[43]

Such arguments have been challenged by the ulama, saying that it reflects a belief in the supremacy of the values of Western liberal capitalism, and an understanding that a relevant curriculum is one that prepares a student to fit in to the contemporary capitalist economic system. On the contrary, the relevance of a certain curriculum is to be judged according to the extent to which it prepares students to be "good" Muslims and also to prepare them for life after death, and the fact that the curriculum may not equip students to function "well" in a capitalist economy is of secondary or of no importance to them. The ulama argued that madrassahs do provide their students with the skills necessary to become active participants in society, as the students go on to become religious specialists in various capacities and this, the ulama believe, is the best way for Muslims to become "active participants in society." Furthermore, they insist that the state must create new career options for madrassah graduates.

Such debates notwithstanding, supporters of madrassah education also voiced the need for reform, especially the need for introducing new subjects in the madrassah curriculum. For example, Najma Najam, vice chancellor of the Fatimah Jinnah Woman University in Pakistan, who believes that madrassahs are "the best form of educational institution you can have, because they take care of the child's need as clothing and food and residence as well as education," opined that "this education needs to be expanded. I think the child needs to be ready for the twenty-first century; it needs subjects such as math, computer science, and English. This is a good system, but it needs to be elaborated to meet the modern needs."[44] Similarly, "the scholars representing the Madaris nevertheless acknowledged that in spite of rendering important service for the society from the religious and educational perspective, the REIs [Religious Education Institutions] education system suffers from shortcomings which have made it difficult for them to produce the desired manpower." It was duly emphasized that "neither the students nor the teachers of these institutions had a proper awareness about the academic, social, political and cultural needs and demands of the contemporary times."[45]

Criticisms of the reform measures from the political perspective abound, but they bear the same tone and tenor. For them the central question is: why does the West want a reform in the madrassah system? To them the answers are intrinsically connected to growing anti-U.S. sentiment in the Muslim world: "Finding it impossible to totally eliminate the institutions of religious learning throughout the length and breadth of Muslim World, it was stressed to introduce far-reaching reforms in their operation. The purpose was to alter the education system in such a way that REIs may remain neither religious nor 'extremist' in character, but become modern, liberal and secular. This is how it decided to forestall the growing anti-US and anti-West threat."[46] Echoing this sentiment, Abid Ullah Jan writes in 2002, "madrassa are not the only targets. Eyes are set on every kind of institute that focuses on Islam in its curriculum—no matter how well it may mix it up with secular education. There is no end to compromise on Islam."[47] The following excerpts from Jan's essay, originally published in a local newspaper named the *Balochistan Post* in

September 2002 as a reaction to a report of the International Crisis Group and soon copied into many Web sites, represent this stance.[48] "A consensus has now emerged throughout the European and American capitals that their imaginary threat of Islam can never be neutralised as long as these Madaris are not eradicated altogether. Efforts are underway to tear down the established systems in these Madaris. Whatever was happening in the beginning of twentieth century at local level under British colonial rule is happening on global scale under American colonial rule."

Abid Ullah Jan argued that the crux of the anti-madrassah campaign is the fear of jihad. He quotes the ICG report: "Its rationale of existence remains virtually unchanged and as emotive as ever: to defend the faith of Islam—if need be through Jihad." Jan goes on with his criticism, saying that "actually this is the best form of Jihad. Not every war in which Muslims are involved is Jihad, but the one for defending the faith of Islam certainly is. It is good that reports from organizations such as ICG admit the reality that these Madrassa 'do not necessarily conduct military training or provide arms to students,' and that only 'few' who went to fight in Kashmir and Afghanistan 'had ever been to a traditional madrasa.'" The central point of Jan's criticism is that the Western opposition to madrassahs is "against the message of Jihad in Islam."

The objectives of the reform, argued Rahman and Bukhari, are threefold: modernization of the Muslim societies in a manner to render them no longer a threat to the West and Western systems, bringing the West and the Muslims closer, and eventually assimilating the Muslims into Western cultures to achieve the West's "Civilizing Mission."[49]

Although more than five years have passed since the latest effort to "modernize" the Pakistani madrassahs was launched, one can point to little success. Neither the government officials nor the ulama are happy with the achievements to date. Looking back at these three initiatives, one can observe that the reform measures in Pakistan are moving in a circle.

BANGLADESH: SUCCESS AND FAILURE AT ONCE

If reform is to be understood as the state's control over the curriculum, particularly the inclusion of "nonreligious" subjects in the madrassah curriculum, increase in the employability of the madrassah students within the current economic system, and the state's control over the resources available to the madrassahs, Bangladesh can claim astounding success and abject failure at the same time. The Aliya madrassahs represent the former while the Qwami madrassahs the latter.

Even a cursory glance at the Aliya madrassahs in Bangladesh leaves little doubt that the government has enormous control over these institutions. Highly dependent on the government for their revenues, these institutions follow a standardized curriculum formulated by a government-appointed board, and the degrees of the Aliya madrassahs are considered equivalent to those of the general education stream. As mentioned in chapter 4, Aliya madrassahs, especially the secondary and the postsecondary madrassahs, are now integral parts of the Bangladeshi education system. Conversely, the government has no control over the curriculum and the funds of the Qwami madrassahs.

The integration of Aliya madrassahs into general education took place in the eighties. They faced little resistance from the ulama or the secularists. Unique historical developments, earlier reform initiatives, and the particular nature of the Bangladeshi education sector should be credited for the success in mainstreaming the Aliya madrassahs. The same factors, however, have contributed to the increase in Qwami madrassahs, and have made organized reform of the Qwami madrassahs difficult.

The Reform Begins, 1915–1947

With the encouragement and support of the colonial administration, three madrassahs were founded in 1873 in the areas that constitute present-day Bangladesh. These madrassahs in Chittagong, Dhaka, and Rajshahi were modeled after the Calcutta Madrassah. The model was further replicated throughout eastern Bengal in the late 1800s and the early 1900s. By 1915, a total of 214 madrassahs came into existence.[50] These madrassahs not only maintained close connections with the Calcutta Madrassah but also followed its curriculum. But the reform of 1915 that replaced Farsi with English and introduced, among other subjects, mathematics, geography, history, and physical education in the curriculum created a rift between the Calcutta Madrassah and the madrassahs in eastern Bengal. While the Calcutta Aliya madrassah was exempted from these changes, other madrassahs had to make the choice, and 240 madrassahs in eastern Bengal accepted the changes.

Both financial considerations (that is, the government's decision to provide funds to the reformed madrassahs) and enthusiasm for change within the Muslim middle class played a part in the decision to adopt the changes. The extent of the enthusiasm can be appreciated from the comments of the Moslem Education Advisory Committee, appointed about fifteen years after the reform measures were initiated. The report states that this reform created "unprecedented educational awakening among a large section of the community."

Many ulama, however, decried this as the colonial administration's machination to isolate the Calcutta Madrassah from the Muslim community at large, and remove the religious disposition of the madrassahs. Ulama who opposed these changes founded new madrassahs that would follow the old curriculum. Consequently two streams within the Aliya madrassah tradition emerged—the new-scheme madrassahs, and the old-scheme madrassahs. It also accelerated the proliferation of Khariji (Qwami) madrassahs.[51] The ulama's fear that the reform would dissolve the madrassahs came partially true when some of the new-scheme junior madrassahs became schools and some senior madrassahs were converted into colleges. The Dhaka madrassah and Chittagong madrassah are cases in point. The former became a college in 1919, and the latter was converted into a college in 1927.[52]

The reform of 1915 created schisms within the ulama community, and those who insisted on the continuation of the old curriculum severed ties with the new-scheme madrassahs. Many ulama felt that the tradition of Islamic education could only be continued through Deoband-style madrassahs, and therefore became engaged in founding Khariji madrassahs in various parts of the country.

Forging a common ground between these two streams of Aliya madrassahs became a major concern of various education commissions and committees appointed between 1915 and 1947.[53] These commissions and committees recommended a variety of measures to bring changes in the education system as a whole, not only to the madrassahs, ranging from curriculum to infrastructure. But two questions remained central to their endeavors—how to make the madrassahs responsive to the ongoing changes while maintaining the theological character of these institutions, and how to coordinate the two systems so as to serve the Muslim community best.

These commissions, without any exceptions, emphasized the weaknesses of madrassahs, particularly the old-scheme madrassahs; but none supported the idea of abolishing these institutions altogether. For example, the Momen Committee commented in 1934 that, the old-scheme madrassahs are "very poorly equipped, the teachers are ill-paid, and the teaching is extremely inefficient, with the result that they turn out men who are generally a burden on society and a drag on the educational progress of the community"; and that "the students who are turned out by them are very deficient in general knowledge and in vernacular. The maulvis who pass out of these institutions are often unable to express themselves in their own mother tongue, it said, and lack even rudimentary knowledge in history, geography, and mathematics." However, the commission emphatically stated that the members do not subscribe to the idea that these (old-scheme) madrassahs "be swept clean out of existence," because "[the Muslim community] cannot be satisfied with a system of education which aims at providing a modicum of Islamic education and culture along with secular training, but want a system which would turn out savants and religious preceptors who will devote themselves to the acquisition of theological knowledge and diffusion of religion and serve as guides and final authorities in all theological matters."[54]

Therefore, the commission recommended establishing small numbers of theological colleges to meet these needs. The members contended that huge numbers of old-scheme madrassahs were not necessary; instead the Calcutta

Madrassah and a few others could serve these needs. The commission was of opinion that standardization was imperative to make madrassah education effective and recommended a separate board—"Board of Control of Madarssahs"—to conduct examinations, grant diplomas, and prescribe textbooks for the new-scheme madrassahs.

The latter recommendation was implemented in 1936 and revised in 1939 with elaborate processes of various standardized examinations and their syllabi. The Board of Central Madrassah Examinations, Bengal, was established through government orders.[55] Thus a mechanism for the centralization of supervision was in place by 1937. Changes were brought in the curriculum of the new-scheme madrassahs. Some changes affected the curriculum of the old-scheme madrassahs as well.

Although the Maula Bakhsh Committee (1939–1941) opined that both systems must be retained, and that total abolition of the madrassah system "will not lead to the appreciable increase in the number of Muslim pupil in secondary schools," the committee was also of the opinion that there was a need to coordinate between these two systems, particularly at the primary level, in order to allow students to move from one system to the other should they choose to do so.[56]

There were some dissenting voices within the committee in regard to the retention of the old scheme, changes in the old-scheme curriculum, and the proposal for coordination up to primary level. Zobair Siddiqi, head of the department of Arabic, Persian, and Islamic Studies of Calcutta University, and S. M. Hossain, head of the department of Arabic, Persian, and Islamic Studies of Dhaka University, took two different positions. For the former the recommended changes were not enough, while the latter was worried that the committee was going too far.

On the issue of old-scheme madrassahs, Siddiqi argued that "if Muslim masses are to be influenced and improved," "learned Muslim divines" are needed, and they can only be "nurtured in the cradles of time-honoured madrassahs of olden type," but the old-scheme madrassahs have "miserably failed." Siddiqi stated, "as they are, they produce neither educated men well qualified for the keen struggle for existence, nor great savants, well versed in the Religious sciences of Islam."[57] On the other hand, S. M. Hossain and his colleague Serjaul Haque disagreed with the proposal to introduce, at junior-level madrassahs, English as a mandatory subject. They argued that having six secular subjects out of nine subjects at the junior level, and having both optional subjects from secular subjects at alim and fazil examinations, would "defeat the object" of imparting "religious education of a high order."[58] Siddiqi also contended that the coordination with general education must not end at the junior stage but should be extended to the end of the senior stage of the madrassah (up to grade 12 or 14).[59]

One of the recommendations of the Maula Bakhsh Committee deserves special attention. For the first time, a specific proposal with regard to the equivalence between the university system and the degrees of the old-scheme madrassah was put forward. The committee recommended that Calcutta University permit the candidates of the fazil examinations to take English examinations held for the matriculation degree (at the end of tenth grade), and that successful candidates be granted a matriculation degree. If the university refused to do so, the committee suggested that the Madrassah Examination Board should organize an English examination "equivalent to the Matriculation Examination in English." Similar suggestions were made in regard to the intermediate degree (after twelfth grade) and baccalaureate degree.[60]

The suggestion that a few old-scheme madrassahs with high standards could serve the needs of the Muslim community in Bengal was echoed in the report of the Syed Moazzamuddin Hosain committee, which finalized its report in the wake of partition. The Hosain committee also underscored that these institutions should "correspond to the best known theological centers in India and abroad."[61]

The support for the new-scheme madrassahs, although widespread among the members of various commissions, was not unanimous. There were criticisms of these madrassahs; at times the condemnation came from those who favored integration. Maulvi Muhammad Muzammel Huq, a member of the Maula Bakhsh Committee, for example, commented, "the education in reformed madrassahs also neither makes the students sufficiently fit for the ordinary vocation of life, nor gives them sufficient knowledge of Islamic laws as to make them useful as religious guides."[62]

The recommendations of the commissions and consequent actions during colonial rule demonstrate that the integrationist approach dominated the mindset of the educationists, ulama, and administrators in devising the reform proposals. Standardization of examinations, centralization of the overseeing authorities, and bringing consistency to mandatory texts within the madrassah sector have been at the forefront of the reform measures, while coordination with the general education system and equivalency between madrassah education and general education always loomed large in their deliberations.

Despite the fact that the 1915 reform measures created two different strands within the madrassah sector, the members of the committees and commissions did not see these two strands as mutually exclusive; instead they viewed them as complementary to each other. This stems from the recognition that the madrassah, as a center of theology, has a place within society and within the realm of education. But to serve this function madrassahs had to be intellectually vibrant and well equipped. The sorry state of the old-scheme madrassahs, both intellectually and structurally, made them prime candidates for reforms, whether or not they became integrated into the secular education system.

Reforms Slow Down, 1947–1971

The partition of Bengal in 1947 affected the madrassahs in East Bengal at three levels; first, the Bengal Madrassah Board with all its staff and facilities remained in Calcutta, therefore madrassahs in East Bengal were left without any centralized supervision authority; second, the most venerated madrassah of Bengal, the Calcutta Madrassah, was partitioned and only the Arabic department "migrated" to Dhaka. This tarnished the standing of this historical institution, while giving a boost to the old-scheme madrassahs. Third, a large number of ulama associated with the Calcutta Madrassah decided to migrate not to Dhaka but to West Pakistan.

It took almost two years to reconstitute the Madrassah Board and organize standardized examinations for alim, fazil, and kamil degrees.[63] In 1950, implementing the recommendation of the Moazzamuddin Hosain committee, the board introduced a standardized examination for students who completed the fourth year in junior madrassahs. The examination was later named the dakhil examination.[64]

The new political reality (that is, the emergence of Pakistan) warranted an examination of the education system in general, particularly madrassah education. What role should madrassahs play in a society where an Islamic state is being established? In the following two decades, commissions appointed to frame the education policy, committees to reform the education system, and advisory committees to make recommendations on madrassah education tried to grapple with this question. While changes were called for, a continuation of the present education system was also needed. As for madrassahs, the challenge was monumental and choices were stark, as articulated by the East Bengal Educational System Reconstruction Committee in 1952: "Now the question before us is whether, under the present changed conditions, we are to retain the two systems of Madrasah education undisturbed or one of them or to combine them or to liquidate them both with a view to unifying our educational system." At the end, the verdict was in favor of continuity—to maintain the two systems. Considering "the public opinion, the needs of an Islamic state and sound educational principles," the committee recommended further integration of the reformed madrassahs to the general education (saying "public opinion also favors it").[65] It also recommended introduction of more secular subjects in the curriculum (as mandatory rather than optional subjects), and to recognize what already exists ("integration between the two systems already exists in fact though not in name").[66]

As for the old-scheme madrassahs, the committee concluded that the introduction of secular subjects such as trigonometry, chemistry, and physics would defeat the purpose of these institutions (that is, to produce future spiritual guides proficient in the various Islamic branches). But the committee did suggest introduction of some "useful" secular subjects (arithmetic, history, geography, elementary science, and economics) on a mandatory basis, and some as optional (civics and English).[67]

Equivalence between the general education and madrassah education systems, an issue raised by the Maula Bakhsh Committee in 1941, received further attention. Changes in the duration of junior (dakhil) and alim stages of madrassah education were suggested to harmonize the two systems. In similar vein, the committee recommended that fazil and kamil (commonly known as "title") degrees from the old-scheme madrassahs should be considered equivalent to bachelor of arts and master of arts degrees, respectively, particularly for jobs that require Islamic education such as teaching Islamic studies.

The tone and tenor set by the Reconstruction Committee largely prevailed through the Pakistani era (1947–1971), although quite a few committees came after this.[68] Recommendations by the Akram Khan Commission in regard to the duration of various grades of madrassah were revisited by others, and new suggestions were advanced. For example, the 1956 Advisory Committee for Madrassah Education recommended that the dakhil be six years, alim two years, and fazil two years, as opposed to the Akram Khan Committee's suggestion of dakhil three years, alim five years. Four groups of subjects (that is, hadith, fiqh, tafsir, and Arabic) at the kamil stage was suggested, with the addition of comparative religion as well as Islamic history and culture as mandatory subjects to be taught.[69] As for inclusion of secular subjects, the 1959 Commission on National Education insisted that at the higher-level madrassahs, science, philosophy, economics, and contemporary history should be included so that these institutions could present "Islam as a dynamic and progressive movement which can endure through changing time."[70]

Proposed changes did not remain only on the books as recommendations, but were being implemented at various levels of madrassahs. The incentive of grants-in-aid provided by the government, and the requirements of the Madrassah Board for allowing students to take part in standardized examinations of dakhil, fazil, amil, and kamil ensured compliance, at least on paper. The increase of madrassahs affiliated with the board (from 590 in 1952 to 1,091 in 1962) bears testimony to the compliance.[71] The absence of rigorous inspections, however, prevents us from reaching to any conclusions as to the effectiveness of these changes.

In some ways, by the mid-sixties the differences between old- and new-scheme madrassahs became blurred, because by then a large number of the old-scheme madrassahs had adopted many facets of curriculum reforms, and few new-scheme madrassahs were established. Besides, a large number of reformed madrassahs were converted into schools.

Reformists took comfort in these developments, and remained oblivious to a major shift within the madrassah education system, that is, the growth of

Khariji (or Deobandi-style Qwami) and Furkania madrassahs. The growth of these unsupervised madrassahs indicates that at one level reforms were failing.

Ahmad Hussain, an official of the Education Directorate of the government, observed in 1967 that 1,265 old-scheme and 86 reformed madrassahs were listed with the Madrassah Board; on the other hand, at least 3,328 Furkania and 37 Hafizia madrassahs were in existence (table 6.2). Little was known about these institutions except that they were "under no obligation to follow any uniform course of studies." Hussain described the central features of these madrassahs in the following manner:

> Many of them are well-founded and residential to a large extent. They are wholly dependent on public charity. Their students bear a special stamp in dress . . . and . . . appear to be under a tighter control. It is said that in determining the progress of students these madrasahs go by books read through, rather than by the number of regimented classes crossed over [that is, completed]. They seem to have no faith in selected chapters of any text books. Greater attention is perhaps paid to [Qirat-]i-Quran Majid [recitation of the Holy Qu'ran] in these madrasahs.[72]

Hussain's account of these madrassahs is illustrative of either the failure of the reform measures to reach a growing number of madrassahs, or an unintended consequence of helping the spread of the Deobandi-style madrassahs. In either case, two streams within the madrassah sector—Aliya and Khariji—became evident.

Concentrating on the madrassahs that voluntarily subscribed to the reform process, and ignoring the impact on the other madrassahs, reflected the myopic nature of the reform measures and thereby increased the possibility of failure. The lack of funding for the madrassahs registered with the board

TABLE 6.2

REFORMED AND OTHER MADRASSAHS IN BANGLADESH, 1967

Geographical locations (division)	Old-scheme madrassahs	Reformed madrassahs	Furquania madrassahs	Hafizia madrassahs	Total
Dacca	317	17	1,306	12	1,652
Chittagong	439	33	1,746	18	2,236
Khulna	237	19	84	5	345
Rajshahi	272	17	192	2	483
Total	1,265	86	3,328	37	4,716

Source: Ahmed Hussain, "Madrassah Education," 115.

exacerbated the situation.[73] Together they not only undermined the process but raised questions with regard to the sincerity of the authorities.

The shortcomings of the policy interventions may be important, but it is impossible to ignore the changes in the sociopolitical environment that contributed to the growth of the unregistered madrassahs. Discussions of these factors would take extended space. But worth noting here, in brief, is that urbanization, economic differentiation, and the rise of Bengali nationalism were the three main dynamics of these changes. The first two factors required the Bengali middle class to send their children to secular schools in order to take advantage of opportunities that were opening up; Bengali nationalism shrank the social space for religion-based identity, Islamic social institutions, and Islamic discourses.

The ulama who viewed these as challenges to their authority resorted to madrassahs of the Deobandi style as a means to "preserve" an Islamic identity. They found a sympathetic community in rural areas, because rural Islamic practices have been often identified with rusticity and obscurantism, and mullahs have been depicted in liberal discourse as nefarious. The new economic opportunities allowed the middle class, largely of urban and semiurban areas, to make use of secular schools—private and public—while the rural community had very few similar opportunities. The growing number of Qwami madrassahs provided a modicum of education to the children in rural areas and thus began to gain popularity within the rural poor community.

New Lease of Life to Reform, 1972–Present

Although after August 1975 political expediency and the Islamization projects of the military rulers provided the impetus for mainstreaming the Aliya madrassahs (see chapter 4), the need for change was highlighted by the first education commission, appointed in 1972. Actions were being taken in line with the recommendations of the commission since publication of their report in 1974. For example, the Madrassah Board, reorganized after independence, began recommending texts and arranging standardized tests in early 1975.[74]

By late 1975, the board took initiatives to revise the syllabi of the fazil and kamil degrees; included the text books published by the National Curriculum and Text Books Board in madrassah syllabi; and introduced separate science sections in both alim and fazil degrees in selected madrassahs.[75]

The most momentous change in madrassah education came in 1978, when the government recognized the Bangladesh Madrassah Board and reconstituted the board as an autonomous body for the "organization, regulation, supervision, control, development and improvement of Madrassah education in Bangladesh."[76] With the recognition of the board, Aliya madrassah education was brought under the control and supervision of the government, which ensured its future equivalence to the general secular education system.

In some areas, dakhil and alim degrees were already being considered equivalent to the secondary and higher secondary levels of general education when durations of these stages of madrassah were harmonized with those of general education in the mid-seventies. But official recognition of these degrees was wanting. The students completing the dakhil degrees were not allowed to enroll in higher secondary-level colleges, and similarly alim students could not continue on to university education. The recognition came in 1985 as the government, after a series of discussions with the University Grants Commission, decided that from 1985 on the dakhil degree would be considered equivalent to the Secondary School Certificate (SSC) degree, and from 1987 on the alim degree would be considered as equivalent to the Higher Secondary School (HSC) degree.[77] This was a watershed event in the history of madrassah reform in Bangladesh.

The fazil and kamil degrees have yet to be formally recognized by the government, although in 2005 the government agreed in principle to recognize them.[78] In August 2006, Prime Minister Khaleda Zia informed a gathering of Islamist political leaders that the last step to recognize these degrees was expected soon.[79] The recognition would allow the madrassah graduates to sit for examinations for public service jobs, and thus would open newer possibilities for madrassah students.

Qwami Madrassahs: The Absence of Organized Reform

The success in standardization, integration, and mainstreaming of Aliya madrassahs over the last three decades in Bangladesh is built upon the earlier efforts beginning in 1915. The changes have been incremental and inclusive of people involved with the madrassah sector and the general education sector. During this period an organized effort to reform the Qwami madrassahs on a national scale has remained conspicuously absent.

The lack of reform measures within the Qwami madrassah sector is due to the reluctance of the ulama associated with these madrassahs on the one hand, and the neglect of the government and the civil society, on the other. As discussed earlier, the growth of the Qwami madrassahs has been fueled by the suspicion about the government's intention with regard to the madrassahs. In addition, the perceived duty to maintain the "integrity" of Islamic education and to preserve the "pristine" form of transmission of Islamic heritage has produced a mindset inimical to change in the Qwami madrassahs in Bangladesh.

This is not to say that there has been no effort to standardize the Qwami madrassah curriculum. Sporadic and regional efforts to establish education boards of Qwami madrassahs are indicative of endeavors to synchronize the syllabi and examinations of these institutions. Efforts of this nature have drawn attention in recent years, but one can trace the source of inspiration to the establishment of the Assam Provincial Azad Deeni-Edraye Talim in 1924.[80] The Befakul Madarrisil Arabia (Qwami Madrassah Board), established in 1978, is at the forefront of the recent attempt to organize a national-level body to oversee the curriculum and examinations of the Qwami madrassahs. It claims to have two thousand madrassahs as members who follow the board's prescribed syllabi and texts. Thus, standardization is not an alien concept to ulama associated with the Qwami madrassahs.

Variations in years spent to attain degrees, mandatory texts, and the order in which these texts are used also suggest that Qwami madrassahs have not remained entirely unchanged, as many ulama claim. Some of the Qwami madrassahs have made changes in their curriculum to complete the degrees in a shorter time period and some have introduced new religious texts.[81]

These sporadic changes notwithstanding, Qwami madrassahs have remained outside the supervision of external entities, be it the state or other sectors of the society. Also missing is an effort to integrate these institutions within the education system of the country. Integration is often equated with recognition of the degrees by the government and, by extension, the society at large. The ulama associated with the Qwami madrassahs have been pressing for recognition since the early 2000s, but on condition that the government will not infringe on their autonomy in terms of curriculum or resources, and will not attempt to mainstream the Qwami madrassahs. In discussions on these issues, many ulama bring up the experience of the reforms of 1915 and the eventual demise of the high madrassahs. They also insist that the Aliya madrassahs have lost their Islamic character, thanks to mainstreaming.[82] Critics, on the other hand, insist that the extant curriculum of the Qwami madrassahs needs an overhaul before mainstreaming is even considered.

These debates became more intense in 2006, when the prime minister of the center-right coalition government made a politically expedient move and announced the decision to recognize the dawra-i-hadith (the highest degree of Qwami madrassah) as equivalent to a master's degree in Islamic Studies or Arabic.[83] The decision was made without any consultation with the University Grants Commission, the national accreditation body for higher education, with no rigorous examination of the curriculum, and above all, even before formulating any policy guidelines in regard to the implementation mechanism.[84] That the government has decided to recognize the highest degree without considering the other degrees conferred by the same institution demonstrates an inconsistency and the absence of a planned measure to reform the Qwami madrassah sector. Islamist politicians, who have been pressing the government for the recognition, and a section of the ulama are euphoric about the recognition, but also stated unequivocally that they would not allow any government "interference" in these madrassahs even if public funds were provided to them.[85]

THE FUTURE OF REFORMS

What emerges from the preceding discussion is that reforms of madrassahs in Pakistan and Bangladesh centered on the question of control of these institutions, both in terms of resources and curriculum, particularly the latter. In regard to the revision of the curriculum, the point of departure has been the needs of the society and economy. Or, in other words, the usefulness of the knowledge imparted by the subjects taught in madrassahs. Whether madrassah education prepares students to serve the society, and makes them a workforce appropriate to the economic system, has been the central focus of these efforts. This is reflected in the recommendation to introduce "useful" subjects in madrassahs. In fact, the word "useful" has been used in various reports, including the East Bengal Educational System Reconstruction Committee report in 1952 and the report on madrassah education in West Pakistan in 1962. Subsequent reports have echoed this concern in many ways. Although such an approach in comprehending the role of educational institutions in a society is reasonable, whether madrassahs should be judged by this standard is a matter of debate, and is seriously questioned by many ulama throughout South Asia. Yoginder Sikand quoted the late Qari Muhammad Tayyeb of the Deoband madrassah, who discussed the issue eloquently: "When people criticize the madrasa syllabus, they forget that the aim of the madrasa is different from that of modern school. . . . The only way to pass judgment on the madrasa is to see how far they have been able to achieve their own aims, such as inculcating piety, promoting religious knowledge, control over the base self (*tahzib-i nafs*) and service of others." In similar vein, a number of ulama in Bangladesh asked, if ulama do not judge the students of general education by the standards of madrassah education, why should the madrassah students be judged by the standards of secular education?[86]

Muhammad Qasim Zaman traced the application of categories such as "useful" and "religious," and situated them in opposition to the colonial administration in India, but also underscored that the notions featured in the discourses of medieval Muslim scholars.[87] But they are used not only in two different contexts but also with two different meanings and with different goals.

It is a fair summation that the lack of usefulness of madrassah education has served as the premise of madrassah reform throughout South Asia during and since the colonial era. But the reformists have not engaged themselves in a robust and informed debate with the ulama on the purposes of madrassahs. The fundamental point here is whether there is an understanding and an appreciation of the purpose of madrassah education. To determine the scope, the nature, and the efficacy of the reforms this debate can no longer be avoided.

Recommendations of various reform measures are intrinsically related to this debate. Take, for example, the introduction of secular subjects in madrassahs.

This is an issue of the perceived dichotomy between knowledge about din and duniya (spiritual and temporal, in the words of the 1962 Report in Pakistan: Deeni Uloom and Duniavi Uloom) as much as an issue of equivalence with general education. Should religious knowledge be separated from temporal knowledge? Or can these two be separated at all? The history of madrassahs in South Asia informs us that in the early days the curriculum of the most respected madrassahs was balanced between manqulat (revealed/transmitted knowledge, such as morphology and syntax; also described as *al-uloom an-naqliya*) and maqulat (rational sciences, such as logic, philosophy, astronomy, medicine; also described as *al-uloom al-aqliya*). This was intended to impart a broader base of knowledge.

The fusion of these two aspects of knowledge was embraced by leading ulama closely attached to madrassah education in colonial India. Francis Robinson, in his seminal tome on the Farangi Mahall, quoted Maulana Abd-al Bari of Farangi Mahall: "It is wrong to assume that the study of modern philosophy promotes atheism. It is bad society that does this. Most of those with atheistic leanings are quite ignorant of ancient or modern philosophy or metaphysics. It has now been definitely proved that the idea that study of material sciences and metaphysics promotes atheism is ill founded and quite wrong."[88] Similarly, Farhat Hassan points out that Maulana Manazir Ahsan Gilani, a leading alim of Deoband, not only advocated a fusion between dini and duniyavi knowledge but also devised a reformed course to teach at Deoband.[89]

Bearing this tradition in mind, one can legitimately ask why a disjuncture between these two is necessary today. Indeed, some of the ulama will insist on the separation as it involves protecting their authority to define and interpret the teachings of Islam. On the other hand, there will be voices from within the ulama community who would favor reforms and balancing these two aspects of knowledge. Maulana Muhammad Aslam Qasmi, a teacher at a Deoband madrassah, is a case in point; he insists that Muslims must take to both modern as well as Islamic education.[90] Yoginder Sikand's study on Indian madrassahs documents the reformist voices within various madrassahs in India.[91] He mentions that the magazine published by the alumni association of Deoband, *Tarjuman-i Dar ul-'Ulum*, has become a forum for discussions on reforms. Waris Mazhari, the editor of the magazine, opined that "in many respects, the syllabus [of Deoband] is irrelevant and is unable to meet the challenges of modern life."[92] Some of the Deoband alumni feel that the ulama's opposition to inculcating modern knowledge to students is "against the original vision of the founders of Deoband."[93] The desire for reform is very much present within a group of ulama and people involved with the madrassahs. Two surveys in India, one nationwide and another in Delhi, have clearly demonstrated that a majority want change to take place in the madrassah curriculum and the inclusion of modern subjects.[94] These debates, in India and elsewhere in South

Asia, will create the environment and the space for discussions on the modus operandi of inclusion of "secular subjects" in the curriculum, and by extension reforms of the madrassahs in their entirety.

The history and tradition of madrassahs in South Asia, therefore, provides enough precedents and arguments for reexamination of the current madrassah education. The reformists—whether those with a secular background or members of the ulama community—should harness them in making a stronger case for reform. Additionally, there are at least two other sources that should also be engaged. One is Islamic theology, particularly the Islamic concept of *islah* (reform). The idea of *al-islah wa al-tajdeed* (reform and renewal) is not a foreign concept to Islamic thought, but flows from the Qur'an. It has often been argued that islah is both *fard ayan* (individual obligation) and *fard kifaya* (collective obligation).[95] It is not too difficult to emphasize that madrassah reform is deeply grounded within the philosophy of reform (*islah*) and renewal (*tajdeed*), two important elements of Islamic teachings. The second source that could be utilized is the insights from rich and diverse discussion on education by early Islamic scholars such as al-Jahiz (ca. 776–868), Abu Nasr al-Farabi (d. 950, known as Avennasar in medieval Europe), Ibn Sina (980–1037, known as Avicenna), Abu Hammid al-Ghazali (1058–1111), to name but a few. All of them emphasized "the intimate relationship between knowledge, theoretical and practical wisdom, logical reasoning, ethics and aesthetics of learning, loving and caring, and spirituality" as the most important elements of education.[96] These could well serve as the guide to examine the contents and pedagogy of madrassahs.

The final point that needs to be addressed with regard to the reforms is the necessity of engaging the ulama as indispensable actors. Many authors, for example Malik, Zaman, Sikand, and Hartung, have argued that the engagement of the ulama is a precondition for the legitimacy and success of reforms.[97] Although I do not intend to question the validity of their arguments, for it is true that the ulama comprise an integral part of the madrassah sector, and that their participation will provide reassurance that any reform is not a Western design, I would like to interrogate the indispensability of the ulama. Does reserving to the ulama the decisive position make the reform hostage to the wishes of a segment of society? The authority of the ulama as the only qualified source for leading the reform can be undermined if reformists harness the Islamic tradition, and frame the reform with theological underpinnings. While the state can be a part of this endeavor, this is primarily a task for scholars of Islamic theology. The democratic nature of Islam, particularly the absence of a hierarchy within the Sunni denomination, would provide a supportive environment.

CHAPTER 7

WHERE TO?

Four major issues have emerged out of the discussion on madrassahs in general and particularly the South Asian madrassahs: transmission of religious knowledge to the next generation, addressing the problems of curricula, stemming the proliferation of unregulated madrassahs, and decoupling the nexus of madrassahs and militancy. These four issues dominate the madrassah scene and demand the attention of anyone interested in South Asian society. For madrassahs, the principal challenge is how to transmit religious knowledge yet remain relevant and adaptive to ongoing changes. They have a dual role to play: "the ability to accommodate curricular changes and concurrently maintain long-traditional ways of education exemplifies the dual roles of change and preservation."[1] Their success or failure depend on the ulama, the institutions themselves, and the society within which they are located.

The discussions in the preceding chapters demonstrate that state and politics are central to an understanding of the nature and role of these institutions in all three countries. It is the failure of states that assists the rise of and provides an environment in which madrassahs can thrive in all three countries. If constitutions are the guide, in some form or other these states have not only failed in their primary responsibility but have also engaged in outright human rights violations by not providing adequate educational opportunities to their citizens. To date, the Bangladeshi state may claim some credit for improving this situation, but progress has been too limited to allow for any complacency and has clearly proved to be less than effective. In essence the education system in Bangladesh is still divided along class lines—the poorer you are, the less likely you are to have the opportunity to go to school or remain in school. The laudable role of nongovernmental development organizations in the education sector is also a testimony to the failure of the state and a policy of franchising responsibility. India, where the largest number of children remains unschooled, reveals another disturbing dimension—the children of minority community bear the brunt of this abject failure of the state. The fragmented education system in Pakistan reflects the deep-seated division within the society. In both instances the privatization of education might have given a gloss to the education statistics, but has done little to help the poorer segments of the society.

The contours and contents of madrassahs, as our discussions have demonstrated, were and still are shaped by the politics of the respective countries. This is particularly pronounced in Pakistan and Bangladesh. The Islamization drive of the military regimes of Zia ul-Huq of Pakistan (1977–1986), and Zia ur-Rahman of Bangladesh (1975–1981), carried out to legitimize their unconstitutional rule, provided impetus to the growth of madrassahs. The democratic hiatus propelled the orthodox schools of thought and Islamists to the political forefront and shaped societal norms, including socioeducational institutions like madrassahs. Once the Islamists assumed a prominent position within politics there was no attempt to reverse their position; instead all secularist parties befriended them. The alliances and coalitions with Islamist parties that emerged in the postauthoritarian era made it impossible to bring about any substantive changes. On a general note, once the deployment of religion in politics begins, politics will traverse a certain trajectory unless determined efforts are launched to change that course. In all three South Asian countries discussed in this book, this determined effort has been shown to be wanting.

The national dynamics play a pivotal role, but international political dynamics loom large—this is evident directly in the case of Pakistan, and less so in the case of Bangladesh. The former is well documented in discussions on war in Afghanistan, the rise of the Taliban, and the rise of the MMA political alliance that has dominated the domestic political landscape, particularly in two provinces; but as our discussion has demonstrated, it is true of Bangladesh as well. The militant groups that have emerged since the mid-nineties have been inspired and organized by those who joined the Afghan war. The so-called the "War on Terror" helps them gain sympathy and gives them some semblance of legitimacy, which is then reproduced through various means including measures taken inside the madrassahs. This aspect has implications beyond the boundaries of South Asia. The lesson is plain: the potential impact of international dynamics cannot and should not be ignored anywhere because, however clichéed it sounds, we live in a globalized world, and Islamists are prominent political actors in many Muslim countries.

One can hardly contest or ignore the call for reform in madrassahs, particularly in their curricula. Similarly, two questions are unavoidable: reform for what? And why is the reform necessary now? Reform cannot be merely for its own sake; instead it should be linked to the intrinsic role of the madrassahs in the contemporary world. Often proponents of madrassah reform argue that these institutions fail to train students to enter a workforce with skills necessary to become active participants in society. The validity of the arguments cannot be questioned, but one can challenge the premise of the question, as many ulama in South Asia have. For them the issue is whether the madrassahs should be imparting these skills. The goal of madrassahs, in short, is to train Islamic scholars. The question then should be posed: can the extant curricula of traditional madrassah produce scholars capable of dealing with the contemporary world? Barring a few exceptions, the answer is indisputably negative. Additionally, discussions should be launched concerning the numbers of madrassahs: why should a society need so many "Islamic scholars"? Perhaps the ulama should examine seminaries of other religions, their curricula and roles in society, to offer a balance between "worldly" and "other-worldly" subjects.

To suggest that reforming madrassahs is a new or externally induced idea is a dangerous proposition, and grossly inaccurate. Any social institution must undergo reform to remain relevant to the society it serves. The Muslim community in South Asia, as elsewhere, is dynamic, and therefore Muslim institutions must reflect the changes that occur. This is by no means a new realization; the history of the madrassah since its inception in the eighth century validates this argument. In the South Asian context, the emergence of various denominational schools of thought indicates that there were attempts to make this institution pertinent to societal needs. Scholars who initiated the Nadwatul Ulama in the late nineteenth century recognized the dangers of an emphasis on denominational differences and isolating the community from mainstream educational trends. This rings equally true today. Thus the spirit of reform, present within the Muslim community, must be revived with new vigor. The voices for reform need not be invented but must be nurtured.

Since their creation, nation-states in South Asia have played a significant role in bringing about change within madrassah education. Often the states took leading roles. However, frequently their initiatives were overbearing and consequently counterproductive. Above all, states have lacked political will to sustain the process. Perhaps Pakistan is the best example in this regard: a policy of one step forward two steps back has done great damage, owing to other considerations. The Musharraf regime is treading the same path as its predecessors. In this context, many analysts have questioned the prudence of the state's heightened involvement in reform measures; they argue that the state should only provide an enabling environment. Although a predatory state is less likely to achieve much because of the lack of stakeholder involvement, the state cannot remain oblivious to the madrassah sector, because education is too important to be left to the vagaries of market economy and the whims of the private sector, especially in a region where youth comprise the majority of the population.

When it comes to the issue of reform, it is well to bear in mind that the madrassahs are the site of contestation between Islamists and traditionalists; the former see the madrassah as ideological weapons while the latter view them as institutions to maintain tradition. This contestation has implications for the local Muslim community and domestic politics as much as for Muslims worldwide and for global politics. This is in some ways part of conflicting ideas about the need for a homogenous Muslim identity, a "true" meaning of Islam, and the representation of the global Muslim community. This is why Islamists insist on reform as much as do the Western media. To be truthful, it must be stated that the Islamists were more vociferous before the security-centric cacophony of reform began after 9/11. The madrassahs established under the auspices of the Jamaat-i-Islami in Pakistan and India since 1947 represents a vision of reform. Two features are evident in the curricula of these madrassahs: first, they do not overtly profess any sectarian agenda, although their syllabi reflect the teachings of Sunni Hanafi tradition. Second, they endeavor to make these institutions equivalent and alternative to the extant general education. Not so conspicuous in these developments is the politicized role of the madrassahs and their graduates. The traditional madrassahs are obscurantist but the new ones have a clear political agenda.

The close relationship between madrassah and sectarianism or denominationalism is a matter of grave concern, not only to Western observers but also for Islamic scholars. It is well known that the principal source of the unabated sectarian violence in Pakistan is the nature of the madrassahs, particularly the way madrassah boards are organized. Sectarianism in Pakistan, indeed, has many dimensions. But one cannot evade the fact that sectarianism is fundamentally related to Islamic jurisprudence or fiqh. Fiqh is essentially sectarian, therefore the madrassahs that focus on fiqh are bound to teach a narrow and parochial version of religion and thus contribute to intolerance. The intolerance can be expressed through violence, as we have seen in case of Pakistan. Sectarian teachings are not the sole preserve of the Pakistani madrassahs, however, but are prevalent across South Asia. Take for example India, where sectarian differences have yet to erupt into major violent confrontations. Madrassahs that belong to Barelwis, commonly known to be less radical than Deobandis, teach the global supremacy of Islam, the duty to defend Islam against all enemies, and to combat Wahhabis; the Ahl-e-Hadith madrassahs teach that Muslims should insulate themselves from the poisonous influence of the unbelievers.[2] Involvement of Qwami madrassah students in the anti-Ahmadiyya movement in Bangladesh, a country that had never experienced sectarianism before the phenomenal rise of madrassahs in recent years, also bears testimony to the sectarian impact of traditional madrassah education. This is where the Islamists find space to present themselves as the alternative: their madrassahs are suprasectarian. The madrassahs under the control of the Jamaat-sponsored board in Pakistan, the Aliya madrassahs in Bangladesh, and madrassahs like Jamiat ul-Hidaya and Jamiat ul-Falah in India are the most glaring examples. While these madrassahs transcend, at least apparently, sectarian divides, they present a political agenda that has the potential to transcend geographical borders. What is common to both the sectarian madrassahs and the politicized madrassahs is that they compromise the universal message of Islam.

Media and policy makers, particularly after 9/11, often ask the question: what can be done in regard to the madrassahs? Even if the misplaced urgency of recent years recedes, the need to understand madrassahs and to engage in bringing changes within these important institutions of Muslim societies will not. However, any response to this question must begin with the acknowledgment that there is no ready-made answer; a cookie-cutter solution to a complex phenomenon only makes the situation worse. The issue of the madrassah is multidimensional, and socioeconomic and political contexts are more than backgrounds—they have serious implications. The international community must take serious note of these elements before devising any policy, as must Muslim scholars and social activists. Emboldening those who look at the global scene in binary frame—us versus them, believers versus "infidels," good versus evil, the West versus Islam, and so forth—creates insurmountable roadblocks toward understanding and progress.

Within the region much is left to be done. Civil societies in these three countries have shown very little interest in madrassah education except for scathing criticisms and polemical debates. Their bias and predisposition have isolated them from the madrassahs and the reformers within. The millions of children who now attend these educational institutions, and the many more in years to come, deserve better. These institutions cannot be wished away. Therefore, it is imperative that members of the civil society engage them in understanding these institutions. National particularities notwithstanding, the commonalities among the three South Asian countries should encourage policy makers, particularly educationists and members of civil society, to discuss and formulate a concerted approach. The borders of the countries are too porous and the linkages between madrassahs are too strong to be ignored.

NOTES

INTRODUCTION: WHY STUDY MADRASSAHS?

1. Sageman, *Understanding Terror Networks*; Bergen, "The Madrassa Scapegoat"; Evans, "Understanding Madrasahs."

2. On 7 July 2005, bombs were detonated in three crowded subway trains and aboard a London bus. At least fifty-six people died, along with four bombers, and seven hundred were injured. Two of the four suspected bombers were identified as British citizens of Pakistani origin. Media reports suggested that one of them briefly attended a madrassah in Pakistan during a four-month trip in 2004–2005. All of the suspected bombers had been educated in the public schools in England from childhood. The ringleader of the plot was a schoolteacher in an elementary school.

3. Ahmed and Stroehlein, "Pakistan: Still Schooling Extremists."

4. While Jeffery et al. ("Islamization, Gentrification and Domestication: 'A Girls' Islamic Course' and Rural Muslims in Western Uttar Pradesh," 39), agree that madrassah education is exclusionary and parochial, drawing on their survey of twenty madrassahs in Uttar Pradesh, they insist that "bigotry and militancy are not the inevitable companions of piety." Also they "saw little indication that madrasah staff deliberately foster religious intolerance and arrogance" in Uttar Pradesh, but my observations of a wide variety of madrassahs in Bangladesh point to the opposite direction. A large number of mullahs in Bangladesh often engage in bigotry in their formal and informal interactions with their students and others. Demonization of unbelievers, particularly Hindus, are very common in privately operated madrassahs, called Qwami madrassahs.

5. Denoeux, "The Forgotten Swamp."

6. Marty and Appleby, eds., *Fundamentalisms Comprehended*.

7. Denoeux, "The Forgotten Swamp."

8. Ismail, *Rethinking Islamist Politics: Culture, the State and Islamism*, 26.

9. Denoeux, "The Forgotten Swamp."

10. Bubalo and Fealy, *Between the Global and the Local: Islamism, the Middle East and Indonesia*, 2.

11. Sivan, *Radical Islam: Medieval Theology and Modern Politics*, 137.

12. Ismail, *Rethinking Islamist Politics*, 16.

13. Aziz al-Azmeh, "Reconstituting Islam."

14. Burgat, *Face to Face with Political Islam*, 183.

15. Riaz, *God Willing: The Politics of Islamism in Bangladesh*; Ismail, *Rethinking Islamist Politics;* Burgat, *Face to Face with Political Islam*; Sayyid, *A Fundamental Fear.*

16. Asad, "The Idea of an Anthropology of Islam."

17. I do not mean to imply that there can only be two strands within the Muslim community in a given country. There can be, and usually are, varieties of groups. In the context of Bangladesh, for example, Taj I. Hashmi ("Islamic Resurgence in Bangladesh: Genesis, Dynamics and Implications," 39) suggests four. They are: (a) the fatalists/escapists, (b) the Sufis/pirs, (c) the militant reformists ("fundamentalists"), and (d) the Anglo-Mohammedan (opportunist/pragmatists). I focus on the two groups who are relevant to the issues at hand.

18. Ismail, *Rethinking Islamist Politics*, 57.

19. The clearest articulation of this ideology comes from Sayyid Qutb (1906–1966) of Egypt. Qutb, leader of the Muslim Brotherhood (al-Ikhwan al-Muslimun) was tried and executed for his alleged involvement with an abortive coup to overthrow Gamal Abdel Nasser but became a primary source of inspiration for the Islamists after his death. Sayyid Qutb saw jahiliya everywhere: "Humanity today is living in a large brothel! One has only to glance at its press, films, fashion shows, beauty contests, ballrooms, wine bars, and broadcasting stations! Or observe its mad lust for naked flesh, provocative postures, and sick, suggestive statements in literature, the arts and the mass media! And add to all this the system of usury which fuels man's voracity for money and engenders vile methods for its accumulation and investment, in addition to fraud, trickery, and blackmail dressed up in the garb of law." "Today we are in the midst of a jahiliya similar to, or even worse than the jahiliya that was 'squeezed out' by Islam. Everything about us is jahiliya: the concepts of mankind and their beliefs, their customs and traditions, the sources of their culture, their arts and literature, and their laws and regulations. [This is true] to such an extent that much of what we consider to be Islamic culture and Islamic sources, and Islamic philosophy and Islamic thought is nevertheless the product of that jahiliya."

20. See Mowdudi, *The Islamic Law and Constitution*. Militant Islamists and transnational terrorists subscribe to this position. Aymen al-Zawahari, the ideologue of the transnational terrorist group al-Qaeda, in his biography *Knights under the Prophet's Banner*, writes, "Democracy is *shirk-u-billah* (assigning partners with God). The distinction between democracy and *tawhid* (monotheism), is that tawhid renders legislation the sole prerogative of God whereas democracy is the rule of the people for the people.... The legislator in democracy is the people while the legislator in tawhid is the Almighty God.... Hence, democracy is *shirk* (idolatry) because it usurps the right to legislation from the Almighty and offers it to the people."

21. Hansen, *The Saffron Wave: Democracy and Hindu Nationalism in Modern India.*

22. Talabani, "Pedagogy, Power and Discourse: Transformation of Islamic Education," 66.

23. Eickelman and Anderson, "Preface to the Second Edition," x, xi.

24. The word comes from the Latin word *educere* which means "to educe, to lead away, and to disengage from." See Dupont, "Language and Learning in a Visayan Community," 70.

25. Foucault, *Discipline & Punish: The Birth of the Prison*, 27.

26. Althusser, Lenin and Philosophy and Other Essays, 103–104.

27. Moyser, "Politics and Religion in the Modern World: An Overview," 14.

28. In the case of Bangladesh, for example, the Islamists allege that the non-governmental development organizations, commonly referred to as NGOs, are a blatant example of the imposition of Western ideologies in the Muslim societies. For the Islamist arguments see Riaz, *God Willing*, 121–131.

29. Ismail, *Rethinking Islamist Politics*, 57.

30. Gross enrollment means the total enrollment in a specific level of education, regardless of age, expressed as a percentage of the official school-age population corresponding to the same level of education in a given school year. This is why the percentage can be higher than 100 percent. Gross Enrollment Ratio (GER) is widely used to show the general level of participation in a given level of education. It indicates the capacity of the education system to enroll students of a particular age group. In 2002, 106.34 percent GER of secular schools in Bangladesh demonstrates that the existing schools were capable of accommodating all school-age children. Therefore, insofar as the capacity is concerned, there was no need for madrassahs. GER is typically used as a substitute indicator to net enrollment ratio (NER) when data on enrollment by single years of age are not available. However, the principal weakness of using this indicator is that it does not tell whether the children of the school-going age are attending the schools, because there are over-aged and under-aged enrollments.

31. Bangladesh Bureau of Statistics (BBS) 2001 Census report estimates the figure at 4.47 million, while BBS 2002–2003 survey of child labor estimates the figure at 2.4 million.

32. Jeffery et al., "Islamization, Gentrification and Domestication," 34–36.

33. European Commission, Draft National Indicative Program (NIP): Pakistan 2003–2005.

34. Dreze and Gazdar, "Uttar Pradesh: The Burden of Inertia," 71.

35. Hossain, "Access to Education for the Poor and Girls: Educational Achievements in Bangladesh," 8.

36. CAMPE (Campaign for Popular Education), *Education Watch 2001*. The relationship between food security and school attendance is well documented in the context of Bangladesh and elsewhere. For Bangladesh, see Ahmed and Ninno, "Food for Education Program in Bangladesh: An Evaluation of Its Impact on Educational Attainment and Food Security." Similar results can be found in studies related to the school feeding programs in other countries. See Rosso, "School Feeding Program: . . . A Guide for Program Managers."

37. Candland, "Madaris, Education and Violence."

38. Dalrymple, "Inside the Madrasas."

39. Ahmad, "Urdu and Madrasa Education"; Jeffery et al., "Islamization, Gentrification and Domestication," 37.

40. Malik, "Welcome Address."

41. Hindutva refers to the right-wing political ideology which insists on Hindu identity as the principal social marker and calls for the establishment of a Hindu state (*Hindu rashtra*) in India. The term was first coined by Vinayak Damodar Savarkar (1883–1966), a political activist who was allegedly involved with the assassination of Gandhi. The ideology was introduced to the Indian political arena by the Rashtriya

Swayamsevak Sangh (RSS, National Volunteer Corps) in the 1920s and is espoused by the Bharatiya Janata Party (BJP) and its affiliate organizations.

CHAPTER 1 — MADRASSAHS: LITTLE KNOWN, MUCH DISCUSSED

1. Friedman, "In Pakistan: It is Jihad 101."

2. "Worldwide Threat—Converging Dangers in a Post 9/11 World." Testimony of Director of Central Intelligence George J. Tenet before the Senate Armed Services Committee, 19 March 2002, http://archive.infopeace.de/msg00942.html (5 June 2004).

3. Rumsfeld also asked, "How do we stop those who are financing the radical madrassa schools?" For the full text of the memo, see http://www.usatoday.com/news/washington/executive/rumsfeld-memo.htm (23 October 2003). Rumsfeld underscored the issue of the madrassah in an interview with Fox television on 2 November 2003. In response to a question from Brit Hume in regard to the memo, especially the lack of a matrix for measuring how well the war on terror was going, Rumsfeld replied, "And probably [the matrices] will always be lacking. In other words, it's probably not knowable how many people are being recruited. Somewhere in a jail in America, in a madrasa school that's taught by a radical cleric somewhere in one of twenty other countries of the world. We can't know how many there are, but what I do know, I think, is that we need to engage in that battle of ideas. We need to be out there encouraging people not to do that. Rather, they should be learning things like language or math or things that they can provide a living from." For full transcript of the interview, see http://www.dod.mil/transcripts/2003/tr20031102-secdef0837.html (4 September 2004).

4. International Crisis Group, *Pakistan: Madrasas, Extremism and the Military.*

5. Rashid, *Taliban: Militant Islam, Oil and Fundamentalism in Central Asia.* This is not to say that all Taliban leaders have studied in madrassahs. Many of them studied in ramshackle schools along the Pakistan-Afghanistan border that were funded by the Saudis and backed by the United States, and that were not madrassahs in the conventional sense of the word, although they might have been so termed in order to give them respectability and funds. They were more in the nature of military camps that also taught a particular version of Islam—very different from traditional madrassahs in South Asia.

6. Fathers, "At the Birthplace of Taliban."

7. Coulson, "Education and Indoctrination in the Muslim World: Is There a Problem? What Can We Do about It?," 3.

8. From the mid-nineties "Islamic fundamentalism" began to appear as the principal concern of the United States and its allies. See, for example, Khalilzad, "The United States and the Persian Gulf: Preventing Regional Hegemony"; Yost, "Nuclear Debates in France"; Palmer, "French Strategic Options in the Nineties," 3. For Islamic fundamentalism as a central concern of French foreign policy, see Kipp, "Key Issues Confronting France, French Foreign Policy, Franco-US Relations, and French Defense Policy."

9. Krauthammer, "The New Crescent of Crisis: Global Intifada."

10. "The Islamic Threat," *Economist,* S 25.

11. John Trumpbour has rightly noted that it would be hard to imagine a similar symposium on a rival world religion, "Is Christianity a Threat?" "Is Judaism a Threat?" or "Is Buddhism a Threat?" See Trumpbour, "The Clash of Civilizations: Samuel P. Huntington, Bernard Lewis, and the Remaking of Post-Cold War World Order," 93.

12. Lewis, "The Roots of Muslim Rage."

13. Krauthammer, "The New Crescent of Crisis," A25.

14. Huntington, "The Clash of Civilizations," and Huntington, *The Clash of Civilizations and the Remaking of the World Order.*

15. Lewis wrote in 1964 that "the crisis in the Middle East . . . arises not from a quarrel between states but from a clash of civilizations." Lewis, *The Middle East and the West,* 135.

16. Fukuyama, "The End of History."

17. Barber, *Jihad vs. McWorld.*

18. For the strongest statement of this threat, see Pipes, "There Are No Moderates: Dealing with Fundamentalist Islam." For a small sample of articles discussing such perspectives, see Judith Miller, "The Challenge of Radical Islam," and Robin Wright, "Islam, Democracy and the West."

19. Kramer, "Is Sharansky Right? Does Everyone Want to Be Free?"

20. Spencer, *Onward Muslim Soldiers,* and Timmerman, *The Preachers of Hate.*

21. Spencer, *Onward Muslim Soldiers,* 28, 212.

22. Timmerman, *The Preachers of Hate,* 60.

23. Weaver, "Blowback"; Johnson, *Blowback.*

24. Said, "Islam and the West Are Inadequate Banners."

25. Kellner, "Theorizing September 11: Social Theory, History, and Globalization," 3.

26. Said, "Islam and the West."

27. Poole, *Reporting Islam: Media Representations of British Muslims,* 43.

28. Ibid., 47.

29. Mamdani, *Good Muslim, Bad Muslim: America, the Cold War, and the Roots of Terror,* 24.

30. Esposito, "Political Islam: Beyond the Green Menace."

31. Pipes, "The Muslims Are Coming! The Muslims Are Coming!"

32. At the same time, critical and more balanced views were also being presented. For example, see Fuller and Lesser, *A Sense of Siege: The Geopolitics of Islam and the West;* Husain, *Global Islamic Politics;* Mayer, *Islam and Human Rights: Tradition and Politics.*

33. Three academic studies (Metcalf, *Islamic Revival in British India: Deoband 1860–1900;* Malik, *Colonization of Islam: Dissolution of Traditional Institutions in Pakistan;* and Robinson, *The 'Ulama of Farangi Mahall and Islamic Culture in South Asia*) published between 1982 and 2001 have not been connected to the policy environment within which other studies have appeared; thus they are discussed separately.

34. Roy, *Islam and Resistance in Afghanistan;* see also Roy, "The Origin of Islamist Movement in Afghanistan."

35. Roy, *Islam and Resistance in Afghanistan,* 45–50. In 1867 in Deoband, a small town about a hundred miles north of Delhi, a madrassah called Darul Uloom was founded by Maulana Muhammad Qasim Nanautawi (1833–1877) and Maulana Rashid Ahmed Gangohi (1829–1905). This is commonly referred to as the Deoband madrassah. This became the citadel of the most orthodox school of thought within Sunni Islam. The history of this madrassah and its influences are discussed in chapter 2.

36. Roy, "Modern Political Culture and Traditional Resistance," 112. To illustrate the point, Roy quotes from *Arab News* (14 September 1985, 9): "The Muslim scholars in the world have a great role to play in enlightening the ignorant Afghans. Un-Islamic customs and traditions have found their way into their lives." Wahhabism is a movement

within Islam that began in the mid-eighteenth century, calling for a renewal of the Muslim spirit, with a cleansing of morals, and removal of all innovations from Islam (Arabic: *bida'*). It is named after Muhammad ibn Abd al-Wahhab, an Arabian cleric. He drew his inspiration from the Muslim thinker Ibn Taymiyya. The movement played an important role in the founding of Saudi Arabia. Wahhabism is known for its conservative regulations which affect all aspects of life. The term *wahhabism* is not used by its followers. The term they use is *muwahhidun* (Unitarians) and they call their movement Salafism. Although Wahhabism is often portrayed as a monolithic idea, it is necessary to remember that there are many variants of Wahhabism.

37. Rashid, "Pakistan and Taliban"; Rashid, *Taliban: Militant Islam, Oil and Fundamentalism in Central Asia.*

38. Quote from Rashid, *Taliban: Militant Islam, Oil and Fundamentalism in Central Asia,* 22.

39. Huntington, *The Clash of Civilizations and the Remaking of the World Order,* 120, 112.

40. "The Road to Koranistan."

41. "The Battle for Uzbekistan."

42. Evans, "Islam's Rising New Force," *Guardian,* 8 April 1995, 1, 15.

43. Mary Ann Weaver, "Children of the Jihad," 40, 44. In similar vein, Weaver followed the footsteps of another mastermind of the bombing of the WTC, Omar Abdul-Rahman, in her article "Blowback" in the *Atlantic Monthly* in June 1996.

44. "Pakistani Religious Groups Vow to Resist Government Interference."

45. "Islamic Seminary Has Strong Ties to Bin Laden."

46. Pervez Musharraf took over the power through a coup d'état on 12 October 1999.

47. "Pakistani Father Laments His Teenaged Son Sent to Fight in Afghanistan."

48. "Pakistani Government Not Planning Crackdown on Islamic Schools."

49. "Pakistan Religious Schools under No Threat of Takeover."

50. Judith Miller, "Pakistan Outlines Plan to Curb Militant Networks."

51. BBC Summary of World Broadcasts (BBC SWB), 22 October 1999, part 1 Former USSR; Tajikistan; SU/D3672/G, "Authorities Close Religious School Suspected of 'Training Religious Extremists.'" Source: Khabar TV, Almaty, in Russian 1110 gmt 20 Oct 1999.

52. BBC Summary of World Broadcasts (BBC SWB), 6 July 2000, Thursday, part 1 Former USSR; Russia; Internal Affairs; SU/D3885/B, "Russian Mufti Says Some Islamic Schools 'Breeding Grounds for Terrorists.'" Source: Interfax news agency, Moscow, in English 1643 gmt 4 July 2000.

53. Stern, "Pakistan's Jihad Culture," 120.

54. "Madrassas Breeding Terrorists, Says Powell."

55. Schumer, "Letter to Saudi Ambassador."

56. Schumer, "Schumer: Saudis Are Suffering from Arafat Double Talk Syndrome."

57. Schumer. "Growing Influence of Wahhabi Islam over Military and Prisons Pose Threat."

58. Stern, "Preparing for a War on Terrorism," and Stern, *Terror in the Name of God.*

59. Stern, *Terror in the Name of God.*

60. Stern, *"Preparing for a War,"* 356.

61. Stern, *Terror in the Name of God,* 259.

62. Benjamin and Simon, *The Age of Sacred Terror*, 172.

63. Ibid., 174, 201.

64. Friedman, "In Pakistan."

65. It is also pertinent that while there is a growing body of literature trying to identify the "causes of terrorism," some authors are averse to this line of enquiry. Alan Dershowitz is perhaps the most vocal representative of this school of thought. Dershowitz argues strongly against any reflection upon the root causes of terrorism. He states, "We don't address the root causes of a bad marriage that may have led a man to murder his wife—we hunt down the murderer and punish him." He insists that we should not allow terrorism to motivate an internal debate that amounts to appeasement. Dershowitz, *Why Terrorism Works*.

66. Gold, *Hatreds Kingdom*, 3.

67. Hoffman and McCormick, "Terrorism, Signaling, and Suicide Attack," 251.

68. National Commission on Terrorist Attacks, *The 9/11 Commission Report*, 54, 63, 367.

69. Singer, "Pakistan's Madrassahs: Ensuring a System of Education Not Jihad"; Robert Looney, "A U.S. Strategy for Achieving Stability in Pakistan: Expanding Educational Opportunities"; and Looney, "Reforming Pakistan's Educational System: The Challenge of Madrassa."

70. Singer, "Pakistan's Madrassahs," 2, 3.

71. Looney, "A U.S. Strategy," 1.

72. Riaz, *Unfolding State: The Transformation of Bangladesh*.

73. Bergen and Pandey, "The Madrassa Myth."

74. Ibid.

75. Sageman, *Understanding Terror Networks*, 74, 75.

76. Brokaw, "Reforming Pakistan's Madrassas: Musharraf Determined to Change Muslim Schools' 'Indoctrination'"; Quraishi, "Pakistan's Religious Schools under Fire"; Landay, "Pakistan to Rein in Religious Schools, President to Sign Law Following U.S. Pressure"; "Pakistan Targets Religious Schools That Preach Violence."

77. Hundley, "In Pakistan: Schools Indoctrinate Young Radicals."

78. Anderson, "Classes, the Koran and Jihad: Religious Schools in Pakistan Teach Extremist Islam."

79. Hundley, "In Pakistan: Schools Indoctrinate Young Radicals"; Anderson, "Classes, the Koran and Jihad: Religious Schools in Pakistan Teach Extremist Islam"; Ahmed-Ullah and Barker, "Schooled in Jihad."

80. Ahmed-Ullah and Barker, "Schooled in Jihad."

81. Ibid.

82. Ibid.

83. Lamb, "Rounding Out the Seminary Curricula."

84. Ibid.

85. Ibid.; Lamb and Watson, "Pakistan Pledges to Curb Militants"; Mohan, "Radical School Reform"; and Kraul, "Dollars to Help Pupil."

86. Kraul, "Dollars to Help."

87. Marquand, "The Tenets of Terror."

88. Baldauf, "Pakistan's Two Schools of Thought."

89. Smucker, "School Fighting Brewing"; Tohid, "Pakistan, US Take on the Madrassahs."

90. Paul Blustein, "In Pakistan's Squalor, Cradles of Terrorism."

91. John Lancaster, "Lessons in Jihad for Pakistani Youth: Religious Schools Resist Law to Curb Extremism."

92. Hardy, "Pakistan's 'Culture of Jihad.'"

93. Benett-Jones, "Afghanistan's Scholarly Soldiers;" Benett-Jones, "Support for Musharraf's War on Extremism."

94. Price, "Pakistan Religious Schools Deadline"; Anderson, "Pakistan Call for Extremist Curb."

95. Rashid, "The 'University of Holy War.'"

96. Benett-Jones, "Afghanistan's Scholarly Soldiers."

97. ABC News, "A Reporter's Notebook: A Booming Voice."

98. Moraeu, Yousafzai, and Hussian, "Holy War 101."

99. Dajani and Michelmor, "Islam and Time, 1944–1994."

100. Said, *Covering Islam: How the Media and the Experts Determine How We See the Rest of the World.*

101. See Ghareeb, "A Renewed Look at the American Coverage of the Arabs: Toward a Better Understanding"; Ghareeb, "The Middle East in the U.S. Media"; Shaheen, *Arab and Muslim Stereotyping in American Popular Culture*; Poole, *Reporting Islam: Media Representations of British Muslims*; Karim, *Islamic Peril: Media and Global Violence.*

102. Martin and Phelan, "Representing Islam in the Wake of September 11," 265, 267.

103. Ibid., 268.

104. "Trainees Eager to Join 'Jihad' against America."

105. Bressler.org, http://bressler.org/forum/showthread.php?t=202 (16 November 2005).

106. Little Green Footballs, "Eager Little Killers," http://www.littlegreenfootballs.com/weblog/?entry=1236 (16 November 2005).

107. "Ex-USA TODAY Reporter Faked Major Stories."

108. "Islamic Seminary Has Strong Ties to Bin Laden."

109. "Austere Muslim Colleges That Turn Young Minds to Militancy."

110. Rick Bragg, "A Nation Challenged: Shaping Young Islamic Hearts and Hatreds," *New York Times*, 14 October 2001, 1.

111. Friedman, "In Pakistan: It Is Jihad 101."

112. Anderson, "Classes, the Koran and Jihad: Religious Schools in Pakistan Teach Extremist Islam."

113. Mohan, "Radical School Reform."

114. Lancaster, "Lessons in Jihad."

115. Lamb, "The Pakistan Connection."

CHAPTER 2 — THE GENESIS AND THE TRAJECTORIES

1. *'Ilm* is mentioned 750 times in the Qur'an, more than any other word except Allah (2,800 times) and *rabb* (950 times). The point is noted in Rosenthal, *Knowledge Triumphant*, 20–21, and Boyle, "Memorization and Learning in Islamic Schools," 484–485. The importance attached to 'ilm (knowledge) assumes further significance if we take note that the obligatory prayer is mentioned only about 200 times in the Qur'an.

2. The year 610 CE is taken as a benchmark because it was then that the Prophet Muhammad began receiving revelations. Perhaps a history of education in Islam will

be able to connect various forms of institutions and thus provide a comprehensive history allowing us to understand the larger picture. This book does not intend to attempt such a monumental task.

3. Hisham, *Siratun Nabi*, 2: 77. The original text in Arabic, in several volumes, by Ibne Hashim was composed in the early ninth century and has been translated in various languages. I have used the Bengali translation.

4. These meetings and discussions were not described as *halqa* at that time, but were identified as such in later years.

5. According to A. L. Tibawi, four centuries (seventh through tenth) of practice show that these majilsh were "for *ahl al-'ilm* (tradition or religious sciences in general) or *ahl al-adab* (literature) or later *ahl al-hikmah* (philosophy), etc. according to the accomplishments and needs of teachers and pupils"; Tibawi, "Origin and Characteristics of 'al-madrassah,'" 226.

6. Sattar, *Aliya Madrassahar Itihash*, 17. The original text was written in Urdu. I have used the Bengali translation.

7. On his way to Medina, the Prophet established a mosque in Quba (Masjid al-Quba), outside Medina. Many historians consider this the first structure ever built specifically as a mosque. The Medina mosque, built by the Prophet, is considered the first mosque in Medina. But some accounts suggest that there were at least two other mosques, and nonformal educational institutions centered on these two mosques were established before the Prophet's migration. Sattar, *Bangladeshe Madrassah Shikhya o Shomoaj Jibone tar Probhab*, 45–50.

8. After the death of the Prophet Muhammad in 632, four of his companions, revered as the "rightly guided Caliphs" (al-Khulafa-ur-Rashidun), led the community. They are: Abu Bakr (632–634), Umar (634–644), Uthman (644–656), and Ali (656–661).

9. The most recent example of such historical narrative is Kadi, "Education in Islam: Myths and Truths," 314.

10. Maulana Shibli Numani, *Majmun Musalmanu ki Gujasta Talim* (in Urdu), quoted in Sattar, *Bangladeshe Madrassah*, 78.

11. Tibawi, "Origin and Characteristics," 236.

12. Kuldip Kaur, *Madrasa Education in India: A Study of Its Past and Present*, 15, n 37.

13. Numani, *Majmun Musalmanu*, quoted in Sattar, *Bangladeshe Madrassah*, 80, and Kaur, *Madrasa Education*, 15, n 37.

14. Sikand, *Bastions of the Believers: Madrasas and Islamic Education in India*, 26.

15. Arjomand, "The Law, Agency, and Policy in Medieval Islamic Society," 269.

16. Tibawi, "Origin and Characteristics," 227.

17. Arjomand, "The Law, Agency, and Policy," 270.

18. Tibawi, "Origin and Characteristics," 226.

19. Ibid.

20. Nakosteen, *History of Islamic Origins of Western Education: A.D. 800–1350*.

21. Arjomand, "The Law, Agency, and Policy," 269.

22. On Shi'a-Sunni rivalry, see Tibawi, "Origin and Characteristics," and Arjomand, "The Law, Agency, and Policy."

23. Tibawi, "Origin and Characteristics," 234.

24. Arjomand, "The Law, Agency, and Policy," 284.

25. Sourdel, "Reflexions sur la diffusion de la madrasa à Alep," quoted in Arjomand, "The Law, Agency, and Policy," 284.

26. Sikand, *Bastions of the Believers*, 34.

27. In recent days, with growing interest in ijtihad, discussions abound. For a brief introduction and consideration of its relevance to the contemporary political situation, see Smock, "Ijtihad: Reinterpreting Islamic Principles for the Twenty-first Century." Among the earlier works, two are notable: Schacht, *An Introduction to Islamic Law*, and Coulson, *A History of Islamic Law*.

28. Makdisi, "Muslim Institutions of Learning in Eleventh-Century Baghdad," and Makdisi, *The Rise of Colleges Institutions of Learning in Islam and the West*. Establishment of the Muntasariya by Abbasid Caliph al-Muntasir to bring four schools together is interpreted by some scholars as an effort to bring unity and solidarity among the Muslims to counter the growing threats of the Mongols (Sourdel, "Refelexions," quoted in Arjomand, "The Law, Agency, and Policy," 284).

29. Armstrong, *A History of God: The 4,000-Year Quest of Judaism, Christianity and Islam*; Martin, Woodward, and Atmaja, *Defenders of Reason in Islam: Mu'tazilism from Medieval School to Modern Symbol*, and Ess, *The Flowering of Muslim Theology*.

30. Saklain, *Bangladesher Sufi Sadhak*, 3. Richard Eaton, however, suggests that the earliest contact was in the eleventh century with the arrival of Sufis of Turkish-speaking origin; Eaton, *The Rise of Islam and the Bengal Frontier, 1204–1760*.

31. According to some accounts, the city was built by Amr, the son of bin Qasim. The city became one of the flourishing cities in Sind within a short time. By 957 it occupied a prominent position.

32. Kaur, *Madrasa Education*, 17.

33. Ibid., 18; Sikand, *Bastions of the Believers*, 33.

34. Iqtidar Husain Siddiqui, "Madrasa-Education in Medieval India," 8.

35. Ahmad, "Muslim Tradition in Education," 44; Kaur, *Madrasa Education*, 21; Sikand, *Bastions of the Believers*, 33.

36. Nayyar, "Madrasah Education Frozen in Time," 219. Some scholars insist that the trend of emphasizing the rational sciences, such as rhetoric, logic, and theology, in the curriculum began during Sikandar Lodi's reign (1489–1518); Sufi, *Al Minhaj: The Evolution of Curriculum in the Muslim Educational Institutions of India*, 33.

37. Sikand, *Bastions of the Believers*, 33.

38. Kaur, *Madrasa Education*, 24.

39. Law, *Promotion of Learning in India during Muhammadan Rule by Muhammadans*, 19.

40. Islam, *Prosohongo: Shiksha*.

41. Kaur, *Madrasa Education*, 30.

42. Rahim, *Banglar Samajik o Sangskritk Itihash*, 1: 164.

43. Sikand, *Bastions of the Believers*, 34. Traditionally, Islamic educational theory divides knowledge into two categories: *manqulat* (revealed/transmitted knowledge, such as morphology and syntax, also described as *al-uloom an-naqliya*) and *maqulat* (rational sciences, such as logic, philosophy, astronomy, and medicine, also described as *al-uloom al-aqliya*).

44. Metcalf, *Islamic Revival in British India: Deoband, 1860–1900*, 18–19.

45. Law, *Promotion of Learning in India*, 190.

46. Ikram, *Muslim Civilization in India*, 154.

47. Khafi Khan, *Muntakhabul-Lubub*, pt. 1, 249 and *Tarikhi-Akbari*, 66—both manuscripts are available at the Asiatic Society of Bengal, Calcutta; also quoted in Law, *Promotion of Learning in India*, 175.

48. Jan Jahan Khan, *Tarikhi-Jan-Jahan*, manuscript available at the Asiatic Society of Bengal, Calcutta.

49. Law, *Promotion of Learning in India*, 190.

50. Some scholars, however, disagree with the claim that education was patronized by the royal courts. Saiyid Naqi Husain Jafri, for example, opines that "there were only sporadic efforts at establishing institutions of learning by the rulers, perhaps this was not the priority of the nobility unlike their counterparts in Europe" (Jafri, "A Modernist View of Madrasa Education in Late Mughal India," 49).

51. Metcalf, *Islamic Revival*, 21–22.

52. Jafri, "A Modernist View of Madrasa Education," 46.

53. Ibid., 47.

54. Ibid.

55. Law, *Promotion of Learning in India*, 160.

56. For details of Akbar's rule, see the three volumes of Beveridge, trans., *The Akbarnama of Ab-ul-Fazl*.

57. Robinson, *The 'Ulama of Farangi Mahall and Islamic Culture in South Asia*, 14.

58. Faruki, *Aurangzeb and His Times*, 117, quoted in Ikram, *Muslim Civilization*, 199.

59. Lane-Poole, *Aurengazeb and the Decay of the Mughal Empire*.

60. This was documented by French traveler François Bernier. who was present at the royal court during the period. Bernier, *Travels in the Mogul Empire A.D. 1656–1668*, 156.

61. Allami, *Ain-i-Akbari*, vol. 1, chap. 202, Ain 25, "The Regulation of Education."

62. Sufi, *Al Minhaj*, 53; Law, *Promotion of Learning in India*, 161–162.

63. Azad Bilgrami, quoted in Husain, "Mir Fathullah Shirazi's Contribution for the Revision of the Syllabi of Indian Madrasas during Akbar's Reign," 25; Ikram, *Muslim Civilization*, 238.

64. Ikram, *Muslim Civilization*, 189.

65. The most authoritative study of Farangi Mahall to date is authored by Robinson, *The 'Ulama of Farangi Mahall*. For a succinct description of the institution and its intellectual tradition, see Metcalf, *Islamic Revival*, 29–34.

66. Robinson, *The 'Ulama of Farangi Mahall*, 14–15.

67. Ibid., 71.

68. Nayyar, "Madrasah Education Frozen," 223.

69. Metcalf, *Islamic Revival*, 31.

70. Robinson, *The 'Ulama of Farangi Mahall*, 53, 23; Metcalf also noted, "preparing quazis and muftis, the legal officials required by Muslim courts, was the specialty of Farangi Mahall" (Metcalf, *Islamic Revival*, 30).

71. The madrassah in question bore no name until its closure in 1890. During its existence the madrassah was known by the name of its head (*sadr muddarris*); for example, during the days when Shah Waliullah headed the madrassah, it was known as *madrassah-i-Shah Waliullah* and when it was headed by his son Shah Abd al-Aziz, it was known as *madrassah-i-Shah Abd al-Aziz* (Ashraf, "Madrasa-i-Rahimiah: Growth and Pattern of Educational Curriculum, Origin and Character of Islamic Education," 63–64).

72. For the life and work of Shah Waliullah, see: Jalbani, *Teachings of Shah Waliyullah of Delhi*; Rizvi, *Shah Wali-Allah and His Times*; Baljon, *Religion and Thought of Shah Wali Allah Dihlawi, 1703–1762*; and Ghazi, *Islamic Renaissance in South Asia (1707–1867): The Role of Shah Wali Allah and His Successors*. For a shorter discussion, see Metcalf, *Islamic Revival*, 35–43.

73. It is important to note that Muhammad ibn Abd al-Wahhab (1703–1787), the eighteenth-century Islamic scholar commonly known as the founder of Wahhabism, was also a student of Haya al-Sindi. Some researchers have insisted that this demonstrates the intellectual connection between Shah Waliullah and Abd al-Wahhab; see John O Voll, "Muhammad Hayya al-Sindi and Muhammad ibn Abd al-Wahab: An Analysis of an Intellectual Group in Eighteenth-Century Medina."

74. Dallal, "The Origins and Objectives of Islamist Revivalist Thought, 1750–1850."

75. Concerned with the plight of the Muslims and their vulnerability under non-Muslims, he requested a number of Muslim rulers of India to take the leadership of the community, and invited Ahmed Shah Abdali of Afghanistan to come as its savior. The latter did accept his invitation and invaded India, but instead of being the sort of ruler Waliullah envisioned, Abdali turned out to be a warrior with no scruples and killed thousands—Muslims and Hindus alike.

76. Metcalf, *Islamic Revival*, 36.

77. Jafri, "A Modernist View of Madrasa Education," 51.

78. Although the East India Company emerged as the ruling power after the Battle of Plassey in 1757, it was not officially recognized by the empire centered in Delhi. In 1765, the Company was awarded the Diwani, the right to collect revenues on behalf of the Mughal emperor, in Bengal, Bihar, and Orissa. This provided both the official power and the recognition to the Company as the political authority of the region. Control over other parts of India took a long time. Delhi, for example, came under the control of the East India Company in 1803. Regions in the north and northwest of the subcontinent were annexed in the mid-nineteenth century: Balochistan in 1840, Sindh in 1843, and Punjab and the region now known as the North Western Frontier Province (NWFP) in 1849.

79. Islam, *Prosohongo: Shiksha*, 27.

80. Ali, *The Bengali Reaction to Christian Missionary Activities 1833–1857*; Laird, *Missionaries and Education in Bengal 1793–1837*.

81. Seth, "Secular Enlightenment and Christian Conversion: Missionaries and Education in Colonial India," 27, 28.

82. Quoted in Naik and Nurullah, *A Students' History of Education in India: 1800–1973*, 30.

83. In 1772, Hastings ordered that "in all suits regarding inheritance, marriage, caste and other religious usages and institutions, the laws of the Koran with respect to the Mohammedans and those of the Shaster with respect to the Gentoos [Hindus] shall be invariably adhered to; on all such occasions the Moulvies or Brahmins shall respectively attend to expound the law, and they shall sign the report and assist in passing the decree"; quoted in Rudolph and Rudolph, "Living with Difference in India: Legal Pluralism and Legal Universalism in Historical Context," 390. This was initially known as Bengal Regulation Law 1772. In 1793, it was amended to Mohammedan Law and Hindu Law.

84. The Rudolphs argued that Hastings and Jones "treated Sanskrit and Persian civilizations as equivalent to those of Greece and Rome. Their sense of being local rulers

led them to do what they thought local rulers did, rely on the laws of the peoples under their authority to administer justice" (Ibid., 39).

85. The Sanskrit College was established by Jonathan Duncan. He obtained the permission from the authorities "to establish a college in the holy city for the preservation and alleviation of laws, literature and religion of Hindus, for recovering and collecting books on the most ancient and valuable general learning and tradition now existing in perhaps any part of the globe"; Prashad, *The Progress of Science in India during the Past Twenty-five Years*, vii–viii.

86. Garg, *Charles Grant: The Forerunner of Macaulay's Educational Policy.*

87. The debate was multifaceted and involved a number of issues. For discussions and documents related to the debates, see Zastoupil and Moir, eds., *The Great Indian Education Debate: Documents Relating to the Orientalist–Anglist Controversy, 1781–1843.*

88. Macaulay's Minute on Education, 1835, in *The Report of the Saddler's Commission*, 14.

89. Resolution of the Governor-General of India in Council in the General Department, no. 19 of March 7, 1835, India General Consultations P/186/88 (2), India Office Records, British Library, London.

90. Basu, *Reports on the State of Education in Bengal 1835 and 1838*; Islam, *Prosohongo: Shiksha*, 47.

91. The dispatch also proposed appointing five regional departments of public instruction to oversee government initiatives in regard to educational institutions, and founding three universities in Calcutta, Madras, and Bombay.

92. Langohr, "Colonial Education Systems and the Spread of Local Religious Movements: The Case of British Egypt and Punjab," 162.

93. The impact was also felt in the traditional secular educational institutions such as pathshalas in Bengal. For a succinct discussion on the nature of the changes in pathshalas, see ibid., 170–171. The scope of the impact of the colonial system on indigenous educational system has been an issue of debate among scholars, and some disagree that it completely marginalized local educational practices. For example, Nita Kumar (*Lessons from Schools: The History of Education in Banaras*) argues that the conflict between two competing hegemonies—British and Banarasi—is unresolved and ongoing.

94. Seth, "Secular Enlightenment," 30.

95. Quoted in John Clive, *Macaulay: The Shaping of the Historian*, 411.

96. Vishwanathanan, *Masks of Conquest: Literary Study and British Rule in India*, 55.

97. Sikand, *Bastions of Believers*, 65.

98. Hasan, "Madaris and the Challenges of Modernity in Colonial India," 61.

99. Langohr, "Colonial Education Systems"; and Langohr, "Educational Sub-contracting and the Spread of Religious Nationalism: Hindu and Muslim Nationalist Schools in Colonial India," 42–49.

100. Langohr, "Colonial Education Systems," 172.

101. For detail of various revivalist Muslim movements, see Reetz, *Islam in the Public Sphere, Religious Groups in India, 1900–1947*, 52–81. Similar responses can be found within the Hindu community in India. The Arya Samaj, founded in 1875 as a response to missionary activities, is a case in point.

102. Sikand, *Bastions of Believers*, 74.

103. Reetz, *Islam in the Public Sphere*, 83.

104. Rahman, "The Madrassa and the State in Pakistan."

105. Ibid.

106. Qasmi, *Recounting Untold Histiry, Darul Uloom Deoband: A Heroic Struggle against the British Tyranny.*

107. Metcalf, *Islamic Revival*, 135.

108. For an authoritative account of the emergence of the Ahl-e-Sunnat movement in British India, and the instrumental role of Ahmed Riza Khan, see Sanyal, *Devotional Islam and Politics in British India: Ahmed Riza Khan Barelwi and His Movement 1870–1920.*

109. Reetz, *Islam in the Public Sphere*, 91.

110. Metcalf, *Islamic Revival*," 296.

111. For a detailed discussion on Nadwatul Ulama, see Metcalf, *Islamic Revival*, 335–347; for the Darul Uloom Nadwatul Ulama, see Hartung, "The Nadwat al-'ulama: Chief Patron of Madrasa Education in India and a Turntable to the Arab World."

112. Hartung, "The Nadwat al-'ulama," 141. Salafism is the the self-disignating term used by Wahhabis; see chapter 1 note 36.

113. Reetz, *Islam in the Public Sphere*, 275.

CHAPTER 3 — PAKISTAN: THE MADRASSAH AS A MIRROR OF SOCIETY

1. The University Grants Commission is the accreditation body for university degrees. For recognition of the shahadah al-alamiyaah degree, see UGC notification 8-418 /Acad/82/ 128, 17 November 1982. Referred to in the Supreme Court of Pakistan in the case of "Civil Petitions for Leave to Appeal no 1569-L, 1579-L, 1597-L, 1600-L, 1622-L and 1624-L of 2005," Lahore 16 August 2005. For a copy of the judgment see: http://www.manupatra.com/downloads/2005-data/pakistan%20judgement.htm (5 December 2007).

2. Shah, "A Case Study of Madrassahs—Ahmedpur East (Bahawalpur), Pakistan," 14.

3. International Crisis Group, *Pakistan: Karachi's Madrasas and Violent Extremism*, 7. SITE (Sindh Industrial Trading Estate) Town is a densely populated area of western Karachi.

4. Rahman and Bukhari, "Pakistan: Religious Education and Institutions," 327.

5. Ibid.

6. Rahman, "Language, Religion and Identity in Pakistan: Language-Teaching in Pakistani Madrassas," 200.

7. Ibid., 200–201.

8. "The US and South Asia: Challenges and Opportunities for American Policy," Hearing before the Subcommittee on Asia and the Pacific of the Committee on International Relations, House of Representatives, 104th Congress, March 20, 2003. Serial no. 108–15 (Washington, D.C.: US Government Printing Office, 2003), 31.

9. The lowest figure is drawn from Rocca's statement and the highest figure is drawn from a press report in the *Financial Times* on 8 February 2003. Neither actually represents an informed guess.

10. International Crisis Group, *Pakistan: Madrasas, Extremism and the Military.*

11. Andrabi, Das, Khwaja, and Zajonc, "Religious School Enrollment in Pakistan: A Look at Data," 33. The study insisted that nearly 70 percent of school-going children attend public schools and 30 percent private schools.

12. Candland, "Pakistan's Recent Experience in Reforming Islamic Education."

13. Ibid., 152.

14. The most notable exceptions to this are the seminal studies of Jamal Malik, *Colonization of Islam: Dissolution of Traditional Institutions in Pakistan*, and Muhammad Qasim Zaman, *The Ulama in Contemporary Islam: Custodians of Change*.

15. Fair, "Islamic Education in Pakistan."

16. On Ayub Khan's secular outlook, see Nasr, *Islamic Leviathan: Islam and the Making of State Power*.

17. Jamal, "Religious Schools: Who Controls What They Teach?"

18. Rashid, *Taliban: Militant Islam, Oil and Fundamentalism in Central Asia*.

19. Nayyar, "Madrassah Education Frozen in Time," 232.

20. Andrabi et al., "Religious School Enrollment in Pakistan: A Look at Data," 20, 33.

21. The figure for the total population is extrapolated from the 1998 census, the last one conducted to date. This estimation is based on Economic Intelligence Unit Yearbook.

22. Government of Pakistan, *Economic Survey 2003–04*, 122. The breakdown is as follows: 23.108 million students in grades one through ten, and 846,000 in grades eleven and twelve.

23. World Bank, "Pakistan Country Overview."

24. Husain, "Education, Employment and Economic Development in Pakistan," 37.

25. Rahman, "Reasons for Rage: Reflections on the Education System of Pakistan with Special Reference to English," 89; and Husain, "Education, Employment and Economic Development," 35.

26. Quoted in International Crisis Group, *Pakistan: Reforming the Education Sector*, 13.

27. Cadet colleges are special educational institutions modeled after a military academy, offering education from grades eight through twelve.

28. Rahman, *Denizens of Alien Worlds: A Study of Education, Inequality and Polarization in Pakistan*, 147–148.

29. Rizvi, *The Military and Politics in Pakistan, 1947–1977*, 57–58, quoted in International Crisis Group, *Pakistan: Reforming the Education Sector*, 4.

30. Social Policy and Development Centre (SPDC), *Social Development in Pakistan 2002–03: The State of Education*, 1.

31. Saleem, "Against the Tide: Role of the Citizens Foundation in Paksiatni Education," 72.

32. Talbot, "Understanding Religious Violence in Contemporary Pakistan: Themes and Theories," 155.

33. Ahmadiyyas, also called Qadianis, are a small Muslim sect. They are the followers of reformist Mirza Ghulam Ahmad (1835–1908), who hailed from Qadian, in Punjab, India. Ahmadiyyas claim to practice the Islam that was taught and practiced by the Prophet Muhammad and his companions. Some Muslim groups from both Sunni and Shi'a sects insist that the Ahamdiyyas are non-Muslims. The acceptance of Prophet Muhammad as the last prophet has been cited as the main source of contention between the mainstream Muslim sects and the Ahmadiyyas. In 1973 the Pakistani government declared Ahmadiyyas non-Muslims.

In 1972, soon after assuming office, Bhutto embarked on a series of land and labor reforms that challenged deeply entrenched landed interests and the industrial community. He nationalized thirty-one large companies in ten basic industries. In 1973, the government nationalized the vegetable oil industry, the domain of middle-class entrepreneurs, which caused damage to the government's support base.

In addition to the Islamic tone of the constitution drafted in 1973, the foreign policy of the Bhutto regime revealed its slant toward the Islamic world. In 1974, Pakistan hosted the Islamic Summit, and Bhutto, as the chairman of the summit, made a passionate appeal to establish a "Muslim Commonwealth"—a bloc of Muslim states.

34. Martial Law Order no 5 issued on 5 July 1977, quoted in Abbas, *Pakistan's Drift into Extremism: Allah, the Army and America's War on Terror*, 100.

35. Quoted in Nayyar and Salim, eds., *The Subtle Subversion: The State of Curricula and Textbooks in Pakistan*, 3.

36. Discussions on the role of the United States in the Afghan war abound, especially after 9/11. But the point was being made long before the tragic incidents of 11 September 2001; for example, Rashid, "Pakistan and Taliban"; Cooley, *Unholy Wars: Afghanistan, America and the International Terrorism*; Weaver, "Blowback."

37. Riaz, *Unfolding State*, 41–42.

38. "A close security relationship with Pakistan has been a cornerstone of U.S. policy in South Asia for more than three decades. Beginning with the Eisenhower administration, Washington regarded Pakistan, together with Iran, as an essential obstacle to Soviet expansionism toward the Indian Ocean and the oil fields of the Persian Gulf"; Carpenter, "A Fortress Built on Quicksand: U.S. Policy Toward Pakistan." The U.S.-Pakistan relationship has affected the domestic politics of Pakistan in favor of a military-bureaucratic axis that has ruled the country most of its independent existence. For details of the political impact on Pakistani politics, see Jalal, *State of Martial Rule: The Origins of Pakistan's Political Economy of Defense*.

39. Nixon made two trips to Pakistan as vice president, and one as a private citizen in 1967. Toledano, *One Man Alone: Richard Nixon*, 45–46. See also Rostow, *Eisenhower, Kennedy, and Foreign Aid*, 90–91. The other important factor in U.S. policy was the wish to counter the perceived Soviet expansion. Secretary of State John Foster Dulles reported to Congress in 1953 that he was impressed with Pakistani leaders' desire to resist communism "as their strength permits." Within a year Pakistan joined the South East Asian Treaty Organization (SEATO) and Central Treaty Organization (CENTO). In 1959, much to the annoyance of India, the United States signed a bilateral defense treaty with Pakistan.

40. The ceasefire agreement between these two countries after the war of 1965 was signed at Tashkhant.

41. For declassified documents related to U.S. policy decisions, see United States Department of State (USDS), *Foreign Relations of the United States*, 11, and companion electronic volume, *Foreign Relations, 1969–1976*, volume E–7, Documents on South Asia, 1969–1972. For discussion on these polices, see Hollen, "The Tilt Policy Revisited: Nixon-Kissinger Geopolitics and South Asia"; Kux, *The United States and Pakistan, 1947–2000: Disenchanted Allies*. For U.S. policy toward the Bangladesh Movement, see Riaz, "Beyond the 'Tilt': US Initiatives to Dissipate Bangladesh Movement in 1971."

42. The amendment to the 1961 act adopted in Congress in 1976 prohibits most U.S. economic and military assistance to any country delivering or receiving nuclear enrichment equipment, material, or technology not safeguarded by the International Atomic Energy Agency (IAEA).

43. Burt, "US Will Press Pakistan to Halt A-Arms Project: Series of Steps Considered for a Last Ditch Effort"; Abbas, *Pakistan's Drift into Extremism*, 96.

44. Contrary to the official narrative that the United States began helping the Afghan rebel forces in 1980 after the Soviet invasion (December 1979), the covert operation began in July 1979. This was confirmed by president Carter's National Security Adviser, Zbigniew Brzezinski, in an interview with a French weekly magazine in 1998 (*Le Nouvel Observateur*, 15–21 January 1998, 76). Brzezinski told the *Le Nouvel Observateur*, "According to the official version of history, CIA aid to the mujahideen began during 1980, that is to say, after the Soviet army invaded Afghanistan on December 24, 1979. But the reality, closely guarded until now, is completely otherwise: Indeed, it was July 3, 1979, that President Carter signed the first directive for secret aid to the opponents of the pro-Soviet regime in Kabul. And that very day, I wrote a note to the president in which I explained to him that in my opinion this aid was going to induce a Soviet military intervention." When asked whether he regretted these actions, Brzezinski replied: "Regret what? That secret operation was an excellent idea. It had the effect of drawing the Russians into the Afghan trap and you want me to regret it? The day that the Soviets officially crossed the border, I wrote to President Carter, essentially: 'We now have the opportunity of giving to the USSR its Vietnam War.'"

45. Roy, "The Taliban: A Strategic Tool for Pakistan," 152. Roy notes the later aim was not formulated in 1979, but the Pakistani military quickly understood the weaknesses of the Soviet Union.

46. Brzezinski's interview with the French weekly magazine *Le Nouvel Observateur*, 15–21 January 1998, 76.

47. Abbas, *Pakistan's Drift into Extremism*, 110, 16; and Rashid, *Taliban*, 129–130.

48. Roy, *Islam and Resistance in Afghanistan*, 45.

49. Davis. "'A' is for Allah, 'J' is for Jihad," 90.

50. There were, however, sporadic incidents of attacks on the Shi'a community. For example, in June 1963, Shi'a villages were attacked in Sindh and more than hundred Shi'as were killed.

51. Zakat (alms) is an annual mandatory tax rated at 2.5 percent. The purpose of zakat is to redistribute wealth among the less privileged. In Pakistan, however, the zakat fund is a mandatory tax that is collected by the government in addition to secular governmental taxation. The zakat fund was established in Pakistan under Ordinance XVIII issued in 1980. This made government agencies responsible for collecting the zakat from all Muslim individuals. Due to objections raised by the Shi'a population, the government exempted them from paying zakat to government funds. The implementation and administration of this ordinance is supervised by the Central Zakat Council, which provides policies, and supervises the provincial zakat council, and the local zakat fund, which enforces the policies, collects funds, and redistributes them. Zakat is one of the five pillars of Islam and therefore there is no difference on the issue of zakat per se; however significant differences exist between the major madhabs (jurisprudence schools of thought) on how to realize zakat, use the fund, and the role of the state on this matter. According to the Malikite doctrine, zakat should be paid to the public treasury, whereas the Hanifite doctrine states that zakat should be kept outside of the public treasury.

52. Zahab, "The Regional Dimension of Sectarian Conflicts in Pakistan"; and Nasr, "Islam, the State, and the Rise of Sectarian Militancy in Pakistan."

53. Nasr, "Islam, the State, and the Rise of Sectarian Militancy in Pakistan," 92.

54. Since August 2001, the Pakistan government has imposed an official ban on various militant organizations on four occasions (14 August 2001, 12 January 2002, 15 November 2003, and 20 November 2003). But proscribed organizations rename themselves and reemerge under different names with the same agenda. The SSP, for example was banned in 2001; but soon appeared under the banner of Millat-i-Islami.

55. The rise of the SSP is also explained as a reaction to the Shi'a landed aristocracy in the Jhang district of Punjab. It is argued that the SSP represented the middle-class Sunni population of the local area.

56. For details on the creation of the Sipha-i-Shahaba, the Lashkar-i-Jhangvi, and the Lashker-i-Tayeba, see Abbas, *Pakistan's Drift into Extremism*, 204–216.

57. International Crisis Group, *The State of Sectarianism in Pakistan*, 14.

58. Jamal, "Religious Schools."

59. *Dawn*, "126 Madaris Involved in Militant Activities: Report," 16 May 2000, 1.

60. Please note that Binori Town madrassah is different from the Jamia Binoria, SITE Town, Karachi, which is referred to earlier in this chapter.

61. Safqat, "From Official Islam to Islamism: The Rise of Dawat-ul-Irshad and Laskar-e-Taiba."

62. International Crisis Group, *Pakistan: Karachi's Madrasas and Violent Extremism*, 10.

63. Ganguly, "Explaining the Kashmir Insurgency: Political Mobilization and Institutional Decay." For background of the Kashmir crisis, see Human Rights Watch, *Everyone Lives in Fear: Patterns of Impunity in Jammua and Kashmir*.

64. Ganguly, *The Crisis in Kashmir: Portents of War, Hopes of Peace*, 92–112.

65. Kohli, "Can Democracies Accommodate Ethnic Nationalism? Rise and Decline of Self-Determination Movements in India."

66. International Crisis Group, *The State of Sectarianism in Pakistan*, 14.

67. Safqat, "From Official Islam to Islamism," 131–148, 138–139.

68. Rahman, "The Madrassa and the State in Pakistan."

CHAPTER 4 — BANGLADESH: A TALE OF TWO SYSTEMS

1. Editorial, *Moinul Islam* (magazine) 4, no. 11 (2005), 7.

2. Jamia Yunusia, *Annual Souvenir Booklet*, 1993, 6; Jamia Yunusia, *Annual Souvenir Booklet*, 1997, 9.

3. Ahmad, "Madrassa Education in Pakistan and Bangladesh"; and Rashid, "The Politics and Dynamics of Violent Sectarianism."

4. Sattar, *Bangladeshe Madrassah.*

5. The word *khariji* literally means "rejected or invalidated." However, this was meant to denote that they had remained outside the Calcutta Madrassah system. Later, cognizant of the pejorative implication of this categorization, these madrassahs were referred to as Qwami madrassahs or national madrassahs. It should be also noted that although most of them claimed to follow the Dars-i-Nizami curriculum, quite a few were modeled after the Madrassah Nizamia of Baghdad.

6. Murshid, *The Sacred and the Secular: Bengal Muslim Discourses, 1871–1977*, 410.

7. For a detailed analysis of the political situation and the relationship between the government and the Islamists in post-independence Bangladesh, see Riaz, *God Willing: The Politics of Islamism in Bangladesh*, 28–34.

8. The concept of nonformal schooling initiated by the leading Bangladeshi NGO, the Bangladsh Rural Advancement Committee, has received significant international

attention as a model for children who are otherwise not served by the public school system. Initially the schools were one-room/one-teacher centers; each center took a cohort of about thirty-five children who were eight years or older, beyond the entry age for regular primary school, and taught them for three years to bring them up to the level of fourth or fifth grade of primary school, so that they could join and continue in formal education. Gradually, the model has developed into a full primary education program, offering the equivalent of five-year formal primary education in four years. Almost 700 NGOs have adopted this model and are involved in providing educational services in Bangladesh.

9. Bangladesh Qwami Madrassah Education Board, *Introduction*, 39.

10. Ibid., 15.

11. These stages are called: 1) ibtedayee awual; 2) ibtedayee sani; 3) ustani awual; 4) ustani sani; 5) sanubi awual; 6) sanubi sani; 7) nehari awual; 8) nehari sani; 9) takmil.

12. They are: grade six: the main text—*Azizul Mobtadi*, called by some madrassahs *Safela Awual*; grade seven: the main text—*Mijanussaraf*, called *Safela Duam*; grade eight: the main text—*Nahube Mir*, called *Safela Suam*; grade nine: the main text—*Hidayatunnahu*, named *Safela Chaharam*; grade ten: the main text—*Kafia*, called *Aliya Awual*; grade eleven: the main text—*Sharhe Jami*, called *Aliya Duam*; grade twelve: the main text—*Mokhtasarul Mayani*, named *Aliya Suam*; grade thirteen: the main text—*Jalalain*, named *Aliya Saharam*; grade fourteen: the main text—*Meshkat*, named *Aliya Panjam*; grade fifteen—the main text *Siah Sittah*, called *Daurah Hadith* (Sattar, *Bangladeshe Madrassah*, 37–380).

13. In 2002, when the AHAB faced a split, opponents of Ghalib took control of the trust and the foundation. But most of the sources continued funding his operations as opposed to those of the trust and the foundation.

14. The AHAB faced another split in 2002, when a small group of people established another organization with the same name. But the section under the influence of Ghalib retained the larger segment of the organization and most of the madrassahs.

15. "Ahab Men on the Run, JMJB Flouts Ban."

16. Two sets of data are worth mentioning here. According to A.Z.M. Shamsul Alam, *Madrassah Shiksha*, 5 the total number of madrassahs in 1978 was 1,622. The number of madrassahs in 1983, as documented in table 4.1, was 2,805. This means that in five years 1,183 new madrassahs had come into existence.

17. The number of ibtedayee madrassahs reported by UNESCO in 2000 is far higher than the ones reported by the government sources. According to UNESCO, there were 12,350 ibtedayee madrassahs in 2000; UNESCO, *EFA 2000 Assessment Country Reports Bangladesh 2000*. A government report on educational policy suggests a higher figure for 2004: 18,268; Government of Bangladesh, *National Education Commission Report 2003*, 271.

18. Hossain, *Access to Education for the Poor and Girls: Educational Achievements in Bangladesh*.

19. The number is far greater, according to the 2001 census report of the Bangladesh Bureau of Statitics. The census report suggests a figure of 4.47 million.

20. BANBEIS, *Education System of Bangladesh: A Descriptive Detail*, 27.

21. Hossain and Muhammad, "Madrasah."

22. Abdalla, Raisuddin, and Hussein, *Bangladesh Educational Assessment: Pre-primary and Primary Madrasah Education in Bangladesh*, 7.

23. Khan, "Bangladesh Launches Refresher Course for Islamic Schools."

24. Abdul Jabbar, personal interview, 4 January 2006.

25. Faridi, *Madrassah Shiksha*, 79.

26. Mehdi, *Madrassah Shiksha: Ekti Porjalochona*, 35.

27. Abdalla, Raisuddin, and Hussein, *Bangladesh Educational Assessment*, 8.

28. UNESCO, *EFA 2000*.

29. "Qoumi Madrassahs under Vigil over Aug 17 Blasts." There are a number of individuals and organizations trying to bring these madrassahs under one umbrella organization. Maulna Faizullah, the head of one of these organizations called the Nurnai Talimul Quran Board, told the author in January 2006 that they have contacted about 5,000 Nurani madrassahs.

30. Government of Bangladesh, *Bangladesh Economic Survey 2004–05*.

31. CAMPE, "Quality with Equity: The Primary Education Agenda."

32. CAMPE, "Education Watch Report 2005. The State and Secondary Education: Progress and Challenges (draft)" (Dhaka: CAMPE, 2005), 9.

33. Muhammad Shahrul Hoda Sarkar, Assistant Director, Islamic Foundation, interview with author, 30 December 2005.

34. Hossain, "Access to Education," 4.

35. CAMPE, "Quality with Equity," 9.

36. Hossain, "Access to Education," 8.

37. Riaz, *God Willing*, 121–130.

38. Titumir and Hossain, *Encountering Exclusion: Primary Education Policy Watch*, 82–87.

39. Ibid., 106.

40. This section draws on Riaz, *God Willing*, 17–48.

41. Article 12 of the Bangladesh constitution reflected these secular aspirations when it stated that "in order to achieve the ideals of secularism, a) all kinds of communalism, b) patronization by the state of any particular religion, c) exploitation (misuse) of religion for political purposes, and d) discrimination against, and persecution of, anyone following a particular religion will be ended" (Bangladesh Constitution, Article 12). The constitution further stipulates, "No persons shall have the right to form or be a member or otherwise take part in the activities of, any communal or other association or union which in the name of or on the basis of any religion has for its object, or pursues a political purpose" (Bangladesh Constitution, Article 38, paragraph 2).

42. Government of Bangladesh, *Bangladesh National Syllabi and Curriculum Committee Report*, Part 2, 149.

43. "Bangladesh Will Be an Islamic Country: Ershad," *Daily Ittefaq*, 15 January 1983, 1.

44. The State Religion Amendment Bill, commonly referred to as the "Eighth Amendment of the Constitution," was introduced in parliament on May 11, 1988, and passed on June 7.

45. Out of three hundred seats in the parliament, the BNP won 140, the Awami League 88, Allies of the Awami League 11, the Jatiya Party of General Ershad 35, and the Jamaat-i-Islami 18. A total of 151 seats were necessary to claim a stake in power.

46. Siddiqui, *Migration as a Livelihood Strategy of the Poor: The Bangladesh Case*, 3.

47. "Priest in Terror Probe."

48. The importance of NGOs in the Bangladesh economy can be understood from the fact that as of 2003, 27,000 voluntary development organizations had been registered

with the Ministry of Social Affairs, and 1,600 with the NGO Affairs Bureau; in 2000 it was reported that 90 percent of the villages have an NGO; one large NGO claimed to have reached 70 percent of the villages and 70 million people. In 2003, about 10 percent of overseas development assistance was channeled through NGOs; the share was even higher in 1997–1998, about 18 percent.

49. Riaz, *God Willing*, 121–130.

50. In 2005, at least 575 registered Islamic NGOs were working in Bangladesh; "Foreign Funds Being Used for Jihad Cause: Police." However, thirty-five organizations were prominent among them and handled the lion's share of funds arriving from abroad. They distribute funds among the small organizations.

51. In 1997, violence erupted in two remaining camps. Refugees mounted resistance, reportedly with arms, to repatriation. It took a couple of months to reestablish government control.

52. SOSH, "The Menace of the Christian Missionary Onslaught."

53. "Guarding the Imaan of the New Generations of the Ummah—The Bulwark against the Kufr Onslaught."

54. Quoted by Morris, "Charities and Terrorism: The Charity Commission Response."

55. Deliso, "Has the UN Let a Blacklisted Islamic Charity Roam Free in Kosovo?"

56. "34 Islamic Ngos Get over Tk 200cr from Donors a Year."

57. "Qoumi Madrassahs under Vigil."

58. This information is found at <http://www.bangladesh.com/forums/showthread. php3?threadid=1850> (3 January 2002). Ashad posted the information on 28 September 2000. What prompted this outpouring of support can be understood from the posting: "over the last three years Islahul Muslimeen have raised about 3 million pounds but that is no where enough to fight the kuffar organisation, which are known as ngo's which has immense finaciall backing. In the DAY OF JUDGEMENT we all would be questioned, what did you do to stop this poor bangladeshi muslims becoming kuffar—what can we say then brothers and dear respected sisters—inshallah may ALLAH open our hearts and may we be able to contribute towards the effort of ISLAHUL MUSLIMEEN, according to our means, and everyone should pray for the blessing of ALLAH to decend up that organistion."

59. "Foreign Funds Being Used for Jihad Cause: Police."

60. "Govt Cracks down on Islamists."

61. Police arrested Dr. Muhammad Asadullah al-Ghalib, a professor of Arabic at Rajshahi University and chief of the Islamist organization, Ahl-e-Hadith Andolon Bangladesh (AHAB), and three of his close associates on 23 February. On the same day, three JMB operatives in Gaibandha and two in Rangpur, as well as two JMJB activists in Rajshahi, were also arrested in a police crackdown in the northern parts of the country. Eleven JMB activists were arrested in the Dinajpur and Thakurgaon districts on 24 February. On 25 February, two JMB cadres, Qaree Nazrul, a teacher at the Shibganj Hajardighi Islamia Madrassa, and Nurul Islam, a teacher at Chandpur Dakhil Madrassa, were arrested from or at Shibganj in the Chapai Nawabganj district.

62. "Al-Haramain Trained Militants on How to Make, Use Bombs."

63. "Serial Blasts Planned in April, Had Foreign Funding."

64. "Top Boss of Kuwait-Based RIHS Leaves Country in Hurry."

65. "Where Do the Militants Get the Money?"

66. The breakdown is as follows: ibtedayee madrassahs, 74; dakhil madrassahs, 27; alia madrassahs, 28; fazil madrassahs, 3; kamil madrassahs, 2; Furquania madrassahs, 1,390; Hafizia madrassahs, 59; Qwami madrassahs, 62. See "Facts about Brahmanbaria," Bangla 2000, http://www.bangla2000.com/Bangladesh/Districts/brahmanbaria.shtm (15 January 2002).

67. Acharya, "Amini Orders to Kill Kazi Faruque, AL–BNP leaders Also Demand Trial."

68. Ahmed, "The Splitting of the Jihad in Pakistan." For more than a month, street agitation gripped the country and scores of people died in the confrontations. The tension gradually died down when the Supreme Court stayed the verdict for an indefinite period.

69. Ahsan, "Extremists Get Trained in Armed Combat."

70. For details of the insurgency and recent developments, read Mohsin, *Chittagong Hill Tracts, Bangladesh: On the Difficult Road to Peace*.

71. In 2004, the U.S. government found evidence that al-Haramain is a front organization of various transnational terrorist organizations and forced the Saudis to shut it down. The Bangladesh operation of the organization was closed down in July 2004.

72. *Prothom Alo*, August 14, 2004, through August 18, 2004, 1.

73. Zahab and Roy, *Islamist Networks: The Afghanistan-Pakistan Connection*, 28. The organization faced a split in 1991, and the splinter group formed the Harkat-ul-Mujahideen (HUM). In 1993, the group merged with HUM to form Harkat-ul-Ansar, but left after three years. "Who's Who in the Kashmir Militancy"; and Ahmed, "The Splitting of the Jihad in Pakistan."

74. Ijaz. "Dateline 9 April 2004 Bagmara/Abdur Raliman Say Constitution Is Irrelevant," *Jungator* 27 August 2004, 1.

75. "Govt Finally Cracks Down on Militants; Galib Arrested."

76. "Ctg Islamic Militant Training Den Busted."

77. Maulana Nurul Islam, director general of the madrassah, acknowledged the presence of HUJI activists to the reporter of *Prothom Alo* in August 2004.

78. Habib, "The Menace of Militancy."

79. "Militants Caught Several Times, Released Again and Again" (in Bengali), *Prothom Alo*, 21 August 2005, 1; Ahsan Zayadul, "They Go Free Too Easily," *Daily Star*, 24 August 2005.

80. "Satkhira Is the Capital of the Militants."

81. "Militant Jammatul Mujahideen Is Responsible" (in Bengali), *Prothom Alo*, 19 August 2005, 1.

82. "JMB Cadres Met at Madrassah in Lalmonirhat on the Night of 16 August"; "Jaamatul Met in Aditmari the Night before the Attacks."

83. "Tangail Became the Safe Haven of the Militants" (in Bengali), *Prothom Alo*, 30 August 2005; "Militants Tested the Bomb in Tangail" (in Bengali), *Prothom Alo*, 31 August 2005.

84. "Qoumi Madrassahs under Vigil"; "Militant Training Continues in 250 Madrassahs" (in Bengali), *Jonokantha*, 29 August 2005, 1.

85. "Jaamat Blames RAW, Mosad," *Daily Star*, 21 August 2005, 1.

86. Nurul Kabir, "BNP, AL's Political Opportunism Abets Islamist Fundamentalism." This comment contradicted the spirit of her statement on 25 February. On that day she declared that her administration would not tolerate anarchy in the name of religion.

Talking to high-ranking police officers, the prime minister said that "those who have been creating anarchy in the name of religion are the enemies of the nation and the country"; "PM Orders Rooting out Islamist Militants."

87. Ahsan, "Jamaat Link to Militants Becomes Evident."

88. These parties include the Bangladesh Islami Biplobi Parishod, Bangladesh Islami Front, Bangladesh Islami Party, Bangladesh Muslim League, Bangladesh Nejam-e-Islam Party, Islami al-Jihad Dal; Islami Dal Bangladesh, Jaker Party, Jamiyate Ulama-e-Islam Bangladesh, Quran Drashan Sanghstha Bangladesh, Quran Sunna Bastabayan Parishad, Bangladesh Tanjimul Muslimin, and Taherikey Olama-e-Bangladesh. These parties are in addition to the well-known parties such as Jamaat-i-Islami, Islami Oikya Jote, Islami Shasantantra Andolon, Bangladesh Khilafat Andolon, and Freedom Party.

89. In the election of 2001, the IOJ added a seat to their previous one. Infighting within the alliance has erupted on a number of occasions, but the group avoided a split until after the 2001 election. Azizul Hoq, a self-styled Shaikul Hadith, broke away from Fazlul Hoq Aminee after the 2001 election but stayed with the alliance. Currently the IOJ has at least four factions: they are led by Aminee, Azizul Hoq, Ijaharul Islam, and Moulana Ishaq. Ijaharul Islam left the Aminee faction in early 2005 while Ishaq has named his faction Khilafat Majlish.

90. Ahmad, *Madrassa Education*, 102.

91. Ibid., 114.

CHAPTER 5 — INDIA: DIVERSITY AND CHANGES IN MADRASSAHS

1. The Muslims of contemporary India do not constitute an undifferentiated mass, and to some extent their condition varies by social class. For some upper-class Muslims their class status trumps their religious background. However, in this chapter, by Indian Muslims I mean the majority of the Muslim population who are still mired in poverty and subject to marginalization.

2. Kabeer, "Social Exclusion and the MDGs: The Challenge of 'Durable Inequalities' in the Asian Context."

3. Haque, "The 'Appeased' Indian Muslims Are Far More Deprived."

4. Government of India, Cabinet Secretariat, *Report of the Prime Minister's High Level Committee on the Socio-Economic and Educational Status of the Muslim Community in India* (hereinafter "Sachar Committee Report"), 78. The seven-member committee was appointed by the government in March 2005. In November 2006, the committee submitted its report, which was tabled at the parliament on 30 November 2006.

5. "Sachar Committee Report," 171.

6. Brass, *The Production of Hindu-Muslim Violence in Contemporary India*, 356.

7. On 6 December 1992, Hindu militant groups deliberately attacked and demolished the Babri mosque, built in the sixteenth century, located in Ayodhya in Uttar Pradesh. The incident came after years of agitations by the Sangh Parivar claiming that the mosque sits on top of the birthplace of the Hindu god Ram. The mosque was portrayed as sign of Muslim annexation of Hindu India. The "Ram Janmabhumi" movement, as it was called, was designed to propagate the ideology of Hindutva and bring the BJP to the center of Indian central politics. Leading up to the Ayoydha carnage, the BJP combine organized a symbolic religious caravan (*rath yatra*) across the country, which left behind a trail of anti-Muslim violence killing thousands in many states. Soon after the demolition, violence flared up in two phases.

In February 2002, a western state of India, Gujarat, saw the beginning of violence that continued for more than a month. In "retaliation" for the death of fifty-eight Hindu activists in a train, at least 2,000 Muslims were murdered, hundreds of women raped, thousands made homeless, and millions of dollars of property destroyed. Initial media reports and investigations conducted afterward suggest the state government and almost all law enforcement agencies were complicit in these heinous crimes. At times, the chief minister, a BJP leader, inflamed the situation with comments directed against the Muslim community.

8. Brass, *The Production of Hindu-Muslim Violence*, 6, 10.

9. Riaz, "Nations, Nation-State and the Politics of Muslim Identity in South Asia." Sangh Parivar (Sangh Family) refers to the Bharatiya Janata Party (BJP) and its affiliate organizations in India. These include Rashtriya Swayamsevak Sangh (RSS, National Volunteer Corps), the Bajrang Dal (Army of Hanuman), the Vishwa Hindu Parishad (VHP, World Hindu Forum), and the Shiv Sena (Army of Shiva), to name but a few. They are so named because Rashtriya Swayamsevak Sangh is the fountainhead of all of these organizations, including the BJP.

10. Chenoy, "Citizen's Inquiry Reports on Ayodhya and Its Aftermath."

11. The term "Saffron Brigade" is used to describe the activists of the BJP and its affiliates (Sangh Parivar). The name comes from the color commonly used by these parties in their promotional activities. Activists of the Sangh Parivar wear saffron bandanas and scarves during their rallies and public programs.

12. Hindutva refers to the right-wing political ideology that insists on Hindu identity as the principal social marker and calls for the establishment of a Hindu state (*Hindu rashtra*) in India. The term was first coined by Vinayak Damodar Savarkar (1883–1966), a political activist who was allegedly involved with the assassination of Gandhi. The ideology was introduced to the Indian political arena by the Rashtriya Swayamsevak Sangh (RSS, National Volunteer Corps) in the 1920s and is espoused by the Bharatiya Janata Party (BJP) and its affiliate organizations.

13. Alam, "Hindutva and the Future of Muslims in India."

14. The number of children out of school varies according to source. UNESCO reported in 2005 (based on a 2000 survey) that 27 million Indian children do not attend school; *Children out of School: Measuring Exclusion from Primary Education*, 21. Summiya Yasmeen reported in 2004 that the total number of students not enrolled in schools is 59 million; "Swelling Support for Common Schools." Marie Lal cites the number as between 35 and 60 million; "The Challenges for India's Education System," 4. The United States Agency for International Development suggests the lowest number. According to its account, "between eight million and 10 million Indian children are out of school"; USAID, Program Areas.

15. Government of India, *Constitution of India*, Article 45.

16. Gupta, "Schooling in India," 94.

17. Ibid., 93.

18. Quoted ibid., 90.

19. Lal, "The Challenges for India's Education System," 4.

20. Jeffery, Jeffery, and Jeffery, "Islamization, Gentrification and Domestication: 'A Girls' Islamic Course' and Rural Muslims in Western Uttar Pradesh," 37.

21. "Sachar Committee Report," 78.

22. Probe Team, *Public Report on Basic Education in India*.

23. Siddiqui, *Empowerment of Muslims through Education*.

24. "Sachar Committee Report," 81.

25. The Deeni Talim Council (Anjuman Talimat-i-Deen) is a Muslim organization that runs thousands of maktabs and schools in Uttar Pradesh. It prescribes and publishes (mainly religious) books for the schools it runs.

26. Ahmad, "Urdu and Madrasa Education," 2285–2287.

27. Jeffery et al., "Islamization, Gentrification and Domestication," 1–53.

28. "Sachar Committee Report," 12, n 3.

29. Quoted in Kaur, *Madrasa Education in India: A Study of its Past and Present*, 200, 202.

30. Ahmad, *Traditional Muslim Education in India*, quoted in Siddiqui, "Developments and Trends in Madrassa Education," 75.

31. Ansari, "Students' Perception of Teaching-Learning Process in Madrasas," 97.

32. Sikand, "Madrasas in a Morass: Between Medievalism and Muslimophobia."

33. Quoted in Qasmi, *Madrasa Education, Its Strength and Weakness*, 78. The issue of the growing number of madrassahs in the border regions was intended to demonstrate that India's Muslim neighbors were planting men to destabilize domestic politics. The issue is discussed in the later part of this chapter.

34. Gilani, "India's Madrassas 3x Pakistan's."

35. Badiuzzaman, "Hindustan ke Madrase aur Masajid Markazi Hukukmat ke Nishane par," quoted in Sikand, *Bastions of the Believers*, 315, n 1.

36. Saba Naqvi Bhaumik, "Old School Ties."

37. Sikand, "Madrasas in a Morass"; and Sikand, *Bastions of the Believers*, 95. Detractors of madrassahs have claimed the figure to be 350,000 with 1.5 million students.

38. Siddiqui, "Developments and Trends in Madrassah Education," 78.

39. "Madasas Outshine Schools."

40. All India Muslim Majlish-e-Mushawarat, "No Central Madrasa Board Letter to NMCME."

41. Baharuddin, "Does Madrassahs Mean Factories of Militants?" 5.

42. "Initiatives to Bring Unrecognized Madrassahs under Control in West Bengal," 1.

43. Qasmi cites the number of maktabs operated by the council as 37,000 (Qasmi, *Madrasa Education*, 81).

44. Fahimuddin, "Globalization and Growth of Madrasahs in India."

45. "Sachar Committee Report," 76–79.

46. Kamaluddin, "Muslims and Education in Bihar: Some Revealing Facts."

47. "Sachar Committee Report," 77.

48. Jeffery, Jeffery, and Jeffery, "Investing in the Future: Education in the Social and Cultural Reproduction of Muslims in UP," 73.

49. Qasmi, *Madrasa Education*, 89.

50. Ibid., 90.

51. Sikand, "New Forms of Islamic Educational Provision in India."

52. Qasmi, *Madrasa Education*, 90.

53. Combat Communalism, "Why Madrassas Need to Be Reinvented."

54. Ibid.

55. All India Muslim Majlish-e-Mushawarat, "Many Experiments in Madrasas and Islamic Edu."

56. Sikand, "New Forms of Islamic Educational Provision in India."

57. Mazumdar, "The Bengal Alifate." In some madrassahs the share of non-Muslim students is significantly higher than the state average. Mazumdar identified a madrassah where nearly one-third of the students are Hindus. It is also worth noting that the enrollment of non-Muslims in madrassahs is not entirely a West Bengal phenomenon. In other states, for example, Bihar, non-Muslims attend madrassahs; Sahay, "In Bihar, Even Non-Muslims Prefer Madrasas."

58. "Muslim Law Board Opposes Bill on Madrasas."

59. For example, Muhammad Mukhtar Alam in his study argued in favor of a central board; Alam, *Madrasas and Terrorism: Myth versus Reality.*

60. "Establishment of Central Madrasa Board Misconceived."

61. "Central Board to Oversee Madrassas."

62. Government of India, Ministry of Defense, *Reforming the National Security System.*

63. Memo No F3–5/99-D.III (L) dated 6 May 2002, quoted in Hasan, "The Madrassas in India."

64. Buddhadeb Bhattacharya later retracted the statement and alleged that his original comments were misreported.

65. Quoted in Fahimuddin, *Modernization of Muslim Education in India*, 106.

66. Chaddha,"Madrassas: A Centre of Education or a Nursery of Terrorism."

67. "Madrasas: Breeding Separatism."

68. Rahman, "Nepal-Border Madrasas : No Iota of 'Terrorism' or 'ISI' Activity"; Alam, *Madrasas and Terrorism.*

69. "Madrasas Not Centres of Terrorism: Shivraj Patil."

CHAPTER 6 — REFORMING MADRASSAHS

1. Gesink, "Islamic Reformation: A History of Madrasa Reform and Legal Change in Egypt," 325. Recent discussions on the "Islamic reformation" have been used by neo-conservatives in the United States to justify the Iraq invasion. For example, on the eve of the Iraq invasion Deputy Defense Secretary Paul Wolfowitz reportedly commented, "We need an Islamic reformation and I think there is real hope for one"; Lobe, "Neocons Seek Islamic 'Reformation.'" Salman Rushdie also insisted that a reformation is needed in Islamic thought; Rushdie, "Muslims Unite! A New Reformation Will Bring Your Faith into the Modern Era."

2. Government of Pakistan, *The Constitution of the Islamic Republic of Pakistan as Amended up to March*, quoted in Baxter et al., *Government and Politics in South Asia*, 177.

3. "Basic Principles Committee [1949–1952]," *Story of Pakistan.*

4. Government of Punjab, *Report of the Court of Inquiry Constituted under the Punjab Act II of 1954 to Enquire into the Punjab Disturbances of 1953.*

5. *The Constitution of the Islamic Republic of Pakistan (1956)*, Articles 25 and 28, quoted in Baxter et al., *Government and Politics*, 178.

6. Jinnah, Presidential Speech to the Constituent Assembly of Pakistan, 11 August 1947.

7. Nasr, *Islamic Leviathan: Islam and the Making of State Power*, 161; Nasr, *The Vanguard of Islamic Revolution: The Jama'at-i Islami of Pakistan.*

8. For details see Riaz, *Unfolding State*, 33–45.

9. Alavi, "The State in Post-Colonial Societies: Pakistan and Bangladesh."

10. Nasr, *Islamic Leviathan*, 61.

11. Moustafa, "Conflict and Cooperation between the State and Religious Institutions in Contemporary Egypt."

12. The British government tried to bring the control of the religious endowments into the public domain in 1894. But strong opposition to this effort, especially from the Muslim community at large, forced the colonial administration to retreat. They were returned to private control in 1913.

13. Government of Pakistan, *The Report of the Committee Set up by the Governor of West Pakistan for Recommending Improved Syllabus for the Various Darul Uloom and Arabic Madrsas in West Pakistan.*

14. Ibid., 22–23.

15. The 1962 report suggested six-month reorientation courses for the madrassah teachers in order to learn the new subjects to be introduced under the proposed changes.

16. Zaman, *The Ulama in Contemporary Islam: Custodians of Change,* 10.

17. The board was later renamed Wafaq al-Madaris-al-Salafia.

18. The board is currently known as Wafaq al-Madaris (Shi'a) Pakistan.

19. Government of Pakistan, Council of Islamic Ideology (CII), *Consolidated Recommendations of the CII Relating to the Education System in Pakistan, 1962–1982,* 20–28.

20. Malik, *Colonization of Islam*,129.

21. For a probing analysis of the Islamization projects in Pakistan, see Nasr, *Islamic Leviathan.*

22. Government of Pakistan, Ministry of Education, Islamic Education Research Cell, *Pakistan ke dini madaris ki fihrist,* 8f., quoted in Malik, *Colonization of Islam,* 132.

23. On zakat, see chapter 3, n 50.

24. The madrassahs associated with the JI formed their separate board in 1983 named Rabatul Madaris al-Islamia.

25. Malik, *Colonization of Islam,* 172.

26. Ibid.

27. Musharraf, "Address to the Nation," 12 January 2002.

28. Parpart, "Musharraf: Can This Man Change Pakistan?"

29. Musharraf, "Address to the Nation," 17 October 1999.

30. "Madrassah Registration Ordinance," 1.

31. Government of Pakistan, "Madrasa Reforms (Teaching of Formal Subjects in Deeni Madaris)."

32. Although for lack of a better expression I am using the term "uniform," I am aware of the fact that the Pakistani education system is by no means uniform. This is equally true of other countries of South Asia. The most conspicuous proof of a hierarchic system of education in these countries is the existence of private schools, often beyond the supervision of the government, with English as the medium of instruction. As noted in chapter 3, essentially Pakistan has a three-tiered education system: the elite schools for the rich, the public schools for the middle class, and madrassahs for the poorer segments of the society. Bangladesh is no different, as I have described in chapter 4.

33. Zaman, "Madrasas and Reform: Some Lessons from Pakistan."

34. Looney, "A US Strategy for Achieving Stability in Pakistan: Expanding Educational Opportunities."

35. "Madrassah Registration Ordinance." It is worth noting here the political leaning of the newspaper. Eminent Pakistani educationist Tariq Rahman described this succinctly: "The *Nawa-i-Waqt* has always been an upholder of right-wing views favouring the complete Islamization of the country; the suppression of ethnic diversity in order to promote uniform, monolithic Pakistani nationalism; making Kashmir a part of Pakistan and, therefore, support to militant policies and glorification of war and the armed forces. These policies stay intact and governments are supported in proportion to their adherence to them. Military governments are greeted with enthusiasm by this articulate section of the Urdu press but their liberal tendencies—as in Ayub Khan's (1958–1969) and Pervez Musharraf's case (1999–)—are criticized as being anti-Islam and anti-Pakistan. All liberal views are also castigated in the same scathing terms"; Rahman, "The Impact of European Languages in Former Colonial Territories: The Case of English in Pakistan."

36. Iqbal, "India/Pakistan: Cynics Doubt Law to Reform Pakistan Religious Schools."

37. One significant factor was the survival of the Musharraf regime. Political observers believe that Musharraf was coming under intense pressure for democratization and found a way out by demonstrating leniency toward the Islamists. The general election produced spectacular results in the sense that the MMA emerged as a major political force, eclipsing established parties. Additionally, for the first time in the history of Pakistan, madrassah graduates did well in the elections. Approximately sixty (25 percent) of newly elected parliamentarians are either madrassah graduates or directly involved in management of madrassahs. In the Senate the share is much higher: 35 percent. The chief minister and the cabinet in North West Frontier Province belong to religious parties dominated by madrassah graduates; in Balauchistan nine members of the provincial cabinet are madrassah graduates and were actually managing madrassahs before being elected to public office.

38. Hussain, "A Mixed Message."

39. Kronstadt, "Education Reform in Pakistan," 5.

40. Foreign students in Pakistani madrassahs had begun to leave the country in late 2003, fearing a crackdown on madrassahs. Khaild Hasan, quoting Mufti Mohammad Jamil, reported in the *Daily Times* published from Lahore on 15 September that about 500 students had already moved to South Africa during the year. Others were also planning to pack their bags. The students, most of whom hailed from Arab and African nations, were reluctant to leave Pakistan, but feared they could be arrested in the name of al-Qaeda, the report quoted Jamil saying.

41. Abbas, "Pakistan Madrassa Row 'Resolved.'"

42. The registration process faced a major bureaucratic roadblock as the compromise formula was being worked out: under what laws would the madrassahs be required to register and with which government agency? The madrassahs could be registered under two different acts in Pakistan—the Societies Registration Act 1925 to the Directorate of Industries, and the Trust Act, 1982. The Societies Registration Act 1925, an amended version of the 1860s act, did not provide any mechanism to regulate madrassahs, as the law was meant to oversee *markaz* (centers) and *anjuman* (societies) but not schools of any kind. It is also noteworthy that the law was amended under Benazir Bhutto's regime to prevent the madrassahs from registering under this law. Benazir Bhutto's government thought it would slow the growth of the madrassahs. A new section was added

to the Societies Act to accommodate the registration of madrassahs. The new section states, "a Deeni Madrassah shall not be established or operate without being registered as a society under the said act." The amendment also stipulates that no Deeni madrassah shall teach or publish any literature that promotes militancy or spreads sectarianism and religious hatred.

43. Jafri, "What and Wherefore of Madaris."

44. Interview with Deutsche Welle (German Radio), 9 March 2003.

45. Rahman and Bukhari, "Religious Education Institutions (REIs): Present Situation and the Future Strategy," 62.

46. Ibid., 57.

47. Jan, "Target: Jihad, Madrassa or Islam?" Abidullah Jan's arguments that discussion on madrassahs is an American design to undermine Muslim society is somewhat old. A similar sentiment was expressed in 1999 in the context of Bangladesh by Mohammad Jalal-Abadi. Abadi stated, "The US government's idiosyncratic outbursts that Osama has been funding the madrassahs in Bangladesh is not only untrue, unjust, unethical, unbecoming and absurd but also extremely insulting to Muslim Bengalis. Naturally, the Muslims in Bangladesh are forced to ask: What right does the US have to launch such an unwarranted assault on their integrity? The Muslims in Bengal and elsewhere would have no problem with this situation, or with any situation, if they would heed all the Qur'anic injunctions, for example the following: 'O ye who believe! Take not into your intimacy those outside your ranks: They will not fail to corrupt you. They only desire for you to suffer: rank hatred has already appeared from their mouths: What their hearts conceal is far worse. We have made plain to you the signs if you have wisdom and rationality' (Aal-e Imran [3]:118)"; Jalal-Abadi, "Campaign against Madrassahs in Bangladesh." Abadi was reacting to a report by the British Press Association that Osama bin Laden had been financing madrassahs in Bangladesh.

48. International Crisis Group, *Pakistan: Madrasas, Extremism and the Military*, 29.

49. Rahman and Bukhari, "Religious Education," 57.

50. Maulana Mumtaz Uddin Ahmed, *History of the Madrassa-e-Aliya*, 142; Sattar, *Madrassah Education*, 187.

51. Sattar, *Madrassah Education*, 187.

52. Faridi, *Madrassah Shiksha*, 61; Sattar, *Madrassah Education*, 333.

53. At least four commissions or committees were appointed between 1915 and 1947. The 1921 commission was headed by Syed Shamsul Huda, the 1931 commission was headed by Maulvi Abdul Momen, the 1939 committee was headed by Muhammad Maula Bakhsh, and the 1946 committee headed by Syed Moazzamuddin Hosain. These are commonly referred to by the chair of the committees, as Huda Commission, Momen Commission, and Maula Bakhsh Committee. The 1921 commission, also known by its official name, the Moslem Education Advisory Committee, submitted its report in 1934; the Madrassah Education Committee of 1939 submitted its report in 1941, and the 1946 committee, referred to as the Madrassah Syllabus Committee, reported in 1947, immediately before the partition of Bengal.

54. Ibrahimmy, ed., *Reports on Islamic Education and Madrasah Education in Bengal (1861–1977)*, vol. 3, 170, 171. This five-volume book has compiled the reports of various commissions and committees appointed between 1861 and 1977 with an introductory note by the editor Sekander Ali Ibrahimmy. I refer to the page numbers of these volumes in my discussions of various committee recommendations.

55. These were government orders no. 325T, Edn, dated 14 May 1936, and revised through order 719 Edn, 23 March 1939. See the details in Appendix E of the Maula Bakhsh Committee Report, reproduced ibid., 3: 501–514.

56. Ibid., 3: 396.

57. Ibid., 3: 558.

58. Ibid., 3: 567.

59. Siddiqi and Hossain's comments (cosigned by Haque) were added to the report of the committee as addenda.

60. Ibrahimmy, *Reports on Islamic Education,* 3: 399.

61. Ibid., 4: 59.

62. Ibid., 4: 580.

63. During this period Dhaka University shouldered the responsibility of organizing the examinations.

64. Ali, *History of Traditional Islamic Education in Bangladesh,* 161.

65. The committee was appointed in 1949 with Maulana Muhammad Akram Khan as the chair. The committee later appointed a subcommittee to prepare the section on madrassah education. Their suggestions and recommendations were incorporated within the report of the committee. Ibrahimmy, *Reports on Islamic Education,* 4: 67, 69.

66. The committee concluded that previous attempts to reform failed because essential subjects such as history, English, arithmetic, and so on were sought to be introduced as optional subjects in the fear that these subjects would take away from the main aim of the madrassah; ibid., 4:68–69.

67. Ibid., 4: 70–72.

68. The committees include the Advisory Committee for Madrasah Education, East Bengal, 1956 (headed by Ashrafuddin Chowdhury), the Educational Reforms Commission, East Pakistan, 1957 (headed by Ataur Rahman Khan), the Commission on National Education, 1959 (headed by S. M. Sharif), the Commission for New Education Policy, 1969 (headed by M. Nur Khan).

69. Ibrahimmy, *Reports on Islamic Education,* 4: 86–103.

70. Ibid., 4: 163.

71. These figures are drawn from the statistics provided by the board to a government-appointed committee in 1964. The committee was appointed by the provincial government after ulama demanded a separate Islamic Arabic university. An ulama conference in Dhaka in 1962 was held to discuss the inadequacy of the education system, and consequently a committee was formed in 1963 to draft a scheme for an independent Islamic Arabic university in East Pakistan. The organizing arm of the ulama-appointed committee comprised seven members, including Ghulam Azam, a leader of the Jamaat-i-Islami. Ghulam Azam, it must be recalled, later headed the East Pakistan wing of the JI, and became the amir of the Jamaat-i-Islami Bangladesh (JIB) in 1990. The report of the ulama committee compelled the government to form an official committee. For details of the reports of these two committees, see Ibrahimmy, *Reports on Islamic Education,* 4:165–550.

72. Hussain, "Madrasah Education," in *Education for All,* 117. The book contains the proceedings of a conference organized on the occasion of Education Week (4–8 March 1967).

73. Hussain (in "Madrasah Education") notes that the madrassah education sector received no funding for development expenditure in the first two five-year plans, and the third plan allocated only a meager amount.

74. Bangladesh Madrassah Board, Notification no 211/S-13, dated 20 January 1975. This notification involved ibtidayee and dakhil examinations to be held in 1976. This and similar notifications and memos were collected by the author from the relavant government offices.

75. Bangladesh Madrassah Board, Notification no. 8455/S-13, dated 29 September 1975; Notification no. 9485/S-13, dated 25 September 1975. The curriculum was approved by the Ministry of Education in December 1975; Ministry of Education, Science and Technology Research, and Nuclear Energy, Memo No. 1023/8 dated 19 December 1975.

76. Government of Bangladesh, Ministry of Law and Parliamentary Affairs, 1978: 3, The Madrasah Education Ordinance, 1978, Ordinance No. IX of 1978, Published in the *Bangladesh Gazette*, extraordinary, dated 2 March 1978. Since then the government has formulated rules and regulations delineating the requirements for the recognition of the madrassahs by the board. These include rules regarding the composition and functions of the management body, financial matters, and qualifications and salary structure of teachers and staff, to name but a few subjects.

77. Ministry of Education, Memo no. Sha/9/6-N-C-13/84/741(11) dated 5 November 1985.

78. The Cabinet Committee decided in February 2005 that supervision of these two degrees would be transferred to the National University from the Madrassah Board; see "Curriculum of Madrasa Goes under NU."

79. "Qawami Madrasa Degree Gets Master's Status." The tenure of the government headed by Khaleda Zia ended in October 2006.

80. The board intended to bring together the Qwami madrassahs in Assam and Bengal. Currently, two boards with the same name—Azad Deeni-Edraye Talim—operate in the northeastern Sylhet region. The ulama associated with one of these boards claimed that they conduct six examinations for 196 madrassahs on a regular basis; interview, Maulana Muhammad Abdus Sattar, 3 January 2006, in Dhaka. The other is said to oversee 247 madrassahs in the same region.

81. Mirpur Baitus Rashad Madrassah in Dhaka and Mekhal Madrssah in Hathazari near Chiitagong are cases in point. The later has reportedly made some changes in mandatory texts.

82. These comments are drawn from discussions with a number of ulama in January 2006. Similar points were made by Shaikhul Hadith Azizul Huq, Maulana Abdul Jabbar, and Maulana Ataur Rahman Khan.

83. The timing of the announcement clearly indicates that political, especially electoral, considerations prompted the decision. The announcement was made on 22 August 2006, exactly two months before the end of the tenure of the government. Worth recalling here is that the Islamists were part of the coalition, and they had been applying pressure on the government to make the decision for almost four years. Many analysts believe that the announcement was made to placate various Islamist parties and factions and to help them garner support in the election scheduled within six months. The gathering where the announcement was made lends credence to this assertion. The meeting was attended by all factions of the Islamist parties. See "Qawami Madrasa Degree Gets Master's Status"; for discussions on the decision, see "Playing Politics with

Education"; "Hasty Recognition of Quomi Madrassah Is Electoral Give-and-take"; and "How Long the Politics with the Madrassah Education?"

84. The prime minister later instructed the Education Ministry to form a twenty-one-member committee to devise the process to implement the decision. The fundamental problem faced by the committee was recognizing one board to oversee the examinations. Four regional boards insisted that all of them should be recognized, while the "national" board opposed the idea of recognizing four separate boards and pressed for their recognition. Finally, the president decided to establish a new board instead of recognizing any of the existing ones; "President Approves New Qwami Madrassah Board."

85. "Govt Won't Be Allowed to Exert Control."

86. Sikand, *Bastions of the Believers*, 141. This question was posed to me on many occasions during my field research in 1999 and 2006. In 1999, one of the ulama in a village in the northwestern district of Rajshahi of Bangladesh and another in a village in Hyderabad of Sindh province in Pakistan insisted that the fundamental problem is that the policy makers and the secular educationists never attempted to see the issue from the ulama's point of view.

87. Zaman, *The Ulama in Contemporary Islam*, 62–68.

88. Robinson, *The 'Ulama of Farangi Mahall and Islamic Culture in South Asia*, 163.

89. Farhat Hassan, "Madaris and Modernity in Colonial India," 66.

90. Sikand, *Bastions of the Believers*, 156.

91. Ibid., 140–193.

92. Ibid., 152.

93. Ibid., 151.

94. Ibid., 157.

95. The point is briefly discussed by Jan-Peter Hartung in "Towards a Reform of the Indian Madrassa? An Introduction," 11–36.

96. Gunther, "Be Masters in That You Teach and Continue to Learn: Medieval Muslim Thinkers on Educational Theory," 388.

97. See Malik, *Colonization of Islam*; Zaman, *The Ulama in Contemporary Islam*; Sikand, *Bastions of the Believers*; and Hartung, "Towards a Reform."

CHAPTER 7 — WHERE TO?

1. Agbaria, "Review of Quaranic Schools: Agents of Preservation and Change," 543.

2. Sikand, *Bastions of the Believers*, 245–247.

BIBLIOGRAPHY

Abbas, Hassan. *Pakistan's Drift into Extremism: Allah, the Army and America's War on Terror.* New York: M. E. Sharpe, 2005.

Abbas, Zafar. "Pakistan Madrassa Row 'Resolved.'" *BBC News,* 23 September 2005. http://news.bbc.co.uk/2/hi/south_asia/4275848.stm (1 October 2005).

ABC News. "A Reporter's Notebook: A Booming Voice." Commentary by Tina Babarovic, 25 October 2001.

Abdalla, Amr, A.N.M. Raisuddin, and Suleiman Hussein. *Bangladesh Educational Assessment: Pre-primary and Primary Madrasah Education in Bangladesh.* Washington, D.C.: USAID, 2004.

Acharya, Pijush Kanti. "Amini Orders to Kill Kazi Faruque, AL–BNP Leaders also Demand Trial" (in Bengali). *Bhorer Kagoj,* 20 April 1999, 8.

ADB-World Bank, *Bangladesh Public Expenditure Review 2001,* 2002.

Agbaria, Ayman K. "Review of Quaranic Schools: Agents of Preservation and Change," *Comparative Education Review* 50, no. 3 (August 2006): 543–545.

"Ahab Men on the Run, JMJB Flouts Ban." *Daily Star,* 26 February 2005, 1.

Ahmad, Hafiz Nadhr. "A Preliminary Survey of Madaris-e-Deeniyah in East and West Pakistan." Paper presented at the first Pakistan Oriental Conference, December 1956, Karachi.

Ahmad, Imtiaz. "Urdu and Madrasa Education." *Economic and Political Weekly* (India) 37, no. 24 (2002): 2285–2287.

Ahmad, Khurshid. "Muslim Tradition in Education," *Islamic Education* (Journal of All Pakistan Islamic Education Congress), (November-December 1968): 21–64.

Ahmad, Mumtaz. "Madrassa Education in Pakistan and Bangladesh." In *Religious Radicalism and Security in South Asia,* edited by Satu P. Lamiaye, Robert G. Wirsing, and Mohan Malik, 101–115. Honolulu: Asia-Pacific Center for Security Studies, 2004.

Ahmad, Syed Maqbool. *Traditional Muslim Education in India* (in Urdu), edited by S. A. Ali and Abid Reza Bedar. Delhi: Rampur Institute of Oriental Studies, 1969.

Ahmed, Akhter U., and Carlo del Ninno. "Food for Education Program in Bangladesh: An Evaluation of Its Impact on Educational Attainment and Food Security." Discussion paper 138. Washington, D.C.: IFPRI, 2002.

Ahmed, Khalid. "The Splitting of the Jihad in Pakistan." *Friday Times*, 19 August 2000.

Ahmed, Maulana Mumtaz Uddin. *Aliya Madrassahar Itihash* (History of the Madrassa-e-Aliya, in Bengali) Dhaka: Islamic Foundation, 2004.

Ahmed, Nizam. "Seven Dead in Bangladesh Clash over Edicts." *Reuters*, 2 February 2001, mediaislandgroup.com/~pilots/india/TOPNEWS/STORIES/topnewsstory6. htm (3 February 2001).

Ahmed, Samina, and Andrew Stroehlein. "Pakistan: Still Schooling Extremists," *Washington Post*, 17 July 2005, B07.

Ahmed-Ullah, Noreen S., and Kim Barker. "Schooled in Jihad." *Chicago Tribune*, 28 November 2004, 1.

Ahsan, Zayadul. "Extremists Get Trained in Armed Combat." *Daily Star*, 23 August 2005, 1.

———. "Jamaat Link to Militants Becomes Evident." *Daily Star*, 21 September 2005, 1.

———. "They Go Free Too Easily." *Daily Star*, 24 August 2005, 1.

Alam, Muhammad Mukhtar. *Madrase aur Dehshatgardi: Kya Afsana Kya Haqiqat* (Madrasas and Terrorism: Myth versus Reality, in Urdu). New Delhi: Indian Social Institute, 2004.

Alam, A.Z.M. Shamsul. *Madrassah Sikhsha* (Madrassah Education, in Bengali). Dhaka: Bangladesh Cooperative Book Society, 2002.

Alam, Anwar. "Hindutva and the Future of Muslims in India." In *Living with Secularism: The Destiny of India's Muslims*, edited by Mushirul Hasan, 137–153. New Delhi: Manohar, 2007.

Alavi, Hamza. "The State in Post-Colonial Societies: Pakistan and Bangladesh." In *Imperialism and Revolution in South Asia*, edited by Kathleen Gough and Hari P. Sharma, 145–173. London: Monthly Review Press, 1973.

Al-Azmeh, Aziz. "Reconstituting Islam." *CIAO Net*, 2006, http://www.ciaonet.org/wps/ala01/ (27 March 2006).

"Al-Haramain Trained Militants on How to Make, Use Bombs." *New Age*, 15 September 2005, 1.

Ali, A.K.M. Ayub. *History of Traditional Islamic Education in Bangladesh*. Dhaka: Islamic Foundation of Bangladesh, 1983.

Ali, Muhammad Mohar. *The Bengali Reaction to Christian Missionary Activities 1833–1857*. Chittagong: Mehrab Publications, 1965.

Ali, Zulfiqar. "EU Ready to Help Madrassas." *Dawn*, 2 September 2002, 1.

All India Muslim Majlish-e-Mushawarat (AIMMM). "Many Experiments in Madrasas and Islamic Edu." 5 December 2005, http://www.mushawarat.com/viewarchive. asp?issueno=22 (14 April 2006).

———. "No Central Madrasa Board, Letter to NMCME," 5 December 2005, http://www.mushawarat.com/viewarchive.asp?issueno=22 (14 April 2006).

Allami, Abul Fazl. *The Ain I Akbari*, translated by H. Blochman and H. S. Jarrett. Calcutta, Asiatic Society of Bengal, 1907; http://persian.packhum.org/persian/main?url=pf%3Ffile%3D00702051%26ct%3D0.

Althusser, Louis. *Lenin and Philosophy and Other Essays,* translated by Ben Brewster. New York: Monthly Review Press, 2001.

Anderson, Lisa. "Classes, the Koran and Jihad: Religious Schools in Pakistan Teach Extremist Islam." *Chicago Tribune*, 23 December 2001, 1.

Anderson, Paul. "Pakistan Call for Extremist Curb." *BBC,* 8 September 2004, http://news.bbc.co.uk/1/hi/world/south_asia/3637074.stm (11 November 2005).

Andrabi, Tahir, Jishnu Das, Asim Ijwaz Khwaja, and Tristin Zajonc. "Religious School Enrollment in Pakistan: A Look at Data," http://ksgnotes1.harvard.edu/Research/wpaper.nsf/32181f04b09f9d158525694d001bc47d/aa32877e356dc9eb85256fb9005430dc/$FILE/MadrassaFinal_wps3521.pdf (7 March 2005).

Ansari, Mohammad Shoyeb. "Students' Perception of Teaching-Learning Process in Madrasas." In *Education and Muslims in India since Independence,* edited by A.W.B Qadri, Riaz Shakir Khan, and Mohammad Akhtar Siddiqui, 98–107. New Delhi: Institute of Objective Studies, 1998.

Arjomand, Said Amir. "The Law, Agency, and Policy in Medieval Islamic Society: Development of the Institutions of Learning from the Tenth to the Fifteenth Century." *Comparative Studies in Society and History* 41, no. 2 (April 1999): 263–293.

Armstrong, Karen. *A History of God: The 4,000-Year Quest of Judaism, Christianity and Islam.* New York: Ballantine Books, 1994.

Asad, Talal. *The Idea of an Anthropology of Islam.* Washington, D.C.: Center for Contemporary Arab Studies, 1985.

Ashraf, Mujeeb. "Madrasa-i-Rahimiah: Growth and Pattern of Educational Curriculum, Origin and Character of Islamic Education." In *Madrasa Education in India–Eleventh to Twenty First Century,* edited by S. M. Azizuddin Husain, 59–75. New Delhi: Kanishka Publishers, 2005.

Asian Development Bank. "People's Republic of Bangladesh: Preparing the Secondary Education Sector Improvement Project—II." Unpublished. Manila, 2006.

"Austere Muslim Colleges That Turn Young Minds to Militancy." *Daily Telegraph,* 27 September 2001, 1.

Aznar, Uzma. "Islamic Education: A Brief History of Madrassas with Comments on Curricula and Pedagogical Practices." Paper presented at the international workshop, "Curricula, Textbooks, and Pedagogical Practice, and the Promotion of Peace and Respect for Diversity," organized by the World Bank, 24 March 2003, Washington D.C.

Badiuzzaman. "Hindustan ke Madrase aur Masajid Markazi Hukukmat ke Nishane par." *Basat Zikr-o-Fikr,* May-June 2002.

Baharuddin. "Does Madrassahs Mean Factories of Militants?" (in Bengali). *Ajkal* (Calcutta), 5 January 2006, 5.

Baldauf, Scott. "Pakistan's Two Schools of Thought." *Christian Science Monitor,* 3 October 2001, 1.

Baljon, J.M.S. *Religion and Thought of Shah Wali Allah Dihlawi, 1703–1762.* Leiden: E. J. Brill, 1986.

Bangladesh Bureau of Education, Information and Statistics (BANBEIS). *Education Commission 2003 Report.* Dhaka: Government of Bangladesh, 2004.

———. *Education System of Bangladesh: A Descriptive Detail.* Publication 169. Dhaka: BANBEIS, 1992.

Bangladesh Qwami Madrassah Education Board. *Introduction.* Dhaka: Bangladesh Qwami Madrassah Education Board, 1984.

Barber, Benjamin. *Jihad vs. McWorld.* New York: Ballatine Books, 1996.

"Basic Principles Committee [1949–1952]," *Story of Pakistan,* http://www.storyofpakistan.com/articletext.asp?artid=A136&Pg=2 (15 March 2006).

Basu, Anathnath. *Reports on the State of Education in Bengal 1835 and 1838.* Calcutta: Calcutta University Press, 1944.

"The Battle for Uzbekistan." *Economist,* 4 April 1992, 48.

Baxter, Craig, Yogendra K. Malik, Charles H. Kennedy, and Robert C. Oberst. *Government and Politics in South Asia.* 5th edition. Boulder, Col.: Westview, 2001.

Benett-Jones, Owen. "Afghanistan's Scholarly Soldiers." BBC, 13 October 2001, http://news.bbc.co.uk/1/hi/programmes/from_our_own_correspondent/1595806.stm (30 August 2004).

———. "Support for Musharraf's War on Extremism." BBC, 21 January 2002, http://news.bbc.co.uk/1/hi/world/south_asia/1772797.stm (30 August 2004).

Benjamin, David, and Stephen Simon. *The Age of Sacred Terror.* New York: Random House, 2003.

Bergen, Peter L. "The Madrassa Scapegoat." *Washington Quarterly* 29, no. 2 (Spring 2006): 117–125.

Bergen, Peter, and Swati Pandey. "The Madrassa Myth." *New York Times,* 14 June 2005, A23.

Bernier, François. *Travels in the Mogul Empire A.D. 1656–1668,* translated by A. Constable. London: H. Milford, Oxford Univerity Press, 1914.

Beveridge, Henry, trans. *The Akbarnama of Ab-ul-Fazl.* 3 vols. Calcutta: Asiatic Society of Bengal, 1897.

Bhaumik, Saba Naqvi. "Old School Ties." *Outlook* (India), 31 December 2001.

Blustein, Paul. "In Pakistan's Squalor, Cradles of Terrorism." *Washington Post,* 14 March 2002, 1.

Boyle, Helen N. "Memorization and Learning in Islamic Schools." *Comparative Education Review* 50, no. 3 (August 2006): 478–495.

Bragg, Rick. "A Nation Challenged: Shaping Young Islamic Hearts and Hatreds." *New York Times,* 14 October 2001, Section 1A, 1.

Brass, Paul R. *The Production of Hindu-Muslim Violence in Contemporary India.* Seattle: University of Washington Press, 2003.

Brokaw, Tom. "Reforming Pakistan's Madrassas: Musharraf Determined to Change Muslim Schools' 'Indoctrination.'" NBC *Nightly News* 13 February 2004, http://msnbc.msn.com/id/4264215/from/ET/ (26 November 2005).

Bubalo, Anthony, and Greg Fealy. *Between the Global and the Local: Islamism, the Middle East and Indonesia.* Washington, D.C.: Saban Center for Middle East Policy, Brookings Institution, 2005.

Burgat, François. *Face to Face with Political Islam.* London: I. B. Tauris, 2003.

Burt, Richard. "US Will Press Pakistan to Halt A-Arms Project: Series of Steps Considered for a Last Ditch Effort." *New York Times,* 12 August 1979, A1.

CAMPE (Campaign for Popular Education). *Education Watch 2001.* Dhaka: CAMPE, 2001.

———. *Quality with Equity: The Primary Education Agenda.* Dhaka: CAMPE, 2005.

CAMPE-UPL (Campaign for Popular Education–University Press Limited). *Hope Not Complacency: State of Primary Education in Bangladesh.* Dhaka: Campaign for Popular Education and University Press Limited, 1999.

Candland, Christopher. "Madaris, Education and Violence." In *Pakistan 2005,* edited by Charles Kennedy and Cynthia Botteron, 230–245. Karachi: Oxford University Press, 2005.

————. "Pakistan's Recent Experience in Reforming Islamic Education." In *Education Reform in Pakistan Building for the Future*, edited by Robert M. Hathaway, 151–165. Washington, D.C.: Woodrow Wilson International Center for Scholars, Asia Program, 2005.

Carpenter, Ted Gallen. "A Fortress Built on Quicksand: U.S. Policy Toward Pakistan." *Policy Analysis* 80. Washington, D.C.: Cato Institute, 1987.

"Central Board to Oversee Madrassas." *Times of India*, 22 April 2007, 1.

Chaddha, Rajendra. "Madrassas: A Centre of Education or a Nursery of Terrorism." *Organiser*, 3 March 2002, http://www.hvk.org/hvk/articles/0302/16html (19 April 2002).

Chenoy, Kamal A. Mitra. "Citizen's Inquiry Reports on Ayodhya and Its Aftermath." *South Asia Bulletin* 14, no. 2 (1994): 1–9.

Clive, John. *Macaulay: The Shaping of the Historian*. Cambridge: Harvard University Press, 1987.

Cohen, Stephan P. "Pakistan's Fear of Failure." *Asian Wall Street Journal*, 23 October 2000, 1.

Combat Communalism. "Why Madrassas Need to Be Reinvented." *Combat Communalism* 11, no. 101, September 2004, http://www.sabrang.com/cc/archive/2004/sep04/education.html (11 January 2005).

Cooley, John L. *Unholy Wars: Afghanistan, America and the International Terrorism*. London: Pluto, 1999.

Coulson, Andrew. "Education and Indoctrination in the Muslim World: Is There a Problem? What Can We Do about It?" *Policy Analysis* 511, 11 March 2004.

Coulson, N. J. *A History of Islamic Law*. Edinburgh: Edinburgh University Press, 1964.

"Ctg Islamic Militant Training Den Busted." *Daily Star*, 2 June 2004, 1.

"Curriculum of Madrasa Goes under NU." *Daily Star*, 14 February 2005, 1.

Dajani, Karen F., and Christina Michelmor. "Islam and Time, 1944–1994." *Studies in Popular Culture* 22, no. 1 (1999), http://pcasacas.org/SPC/spcissues/22.1/dajanimichelmor.html (3 January 2005).

Dallal, Ahmad. "The Origins and Objectives of Islamist Revivalist Thought, 1750–1850." *Journal of the American Oriental Society* 113, no. 3 (July-September 1993): 341–359.

Dalrymple, William. "Inside the Madrasas." *New York Review of Book* 52, no. 19 (1 December 2005), http://www.nybooks.com/articles/18514#fnr10 (22 January 2006).

Davis, Craig. "'A' is for Allah, 'J' is for Jihad." *World Policy Journal* 19 no. 1 (Spring 2002): 90–94.

Deliso, Christopher. "Has the UN Let a Blacklisted Islamic Charity Roam Free in Kosovo?" 2005, http://antiwar.com/deliso/index.php (16 September 2005).

Denoeux, Guilian. "The Forgotten Swamp." *Middle East Policy* 9, no. 2 (June 2002), mepc.org/public_asp/journal_vol9/0206_denoeux.asp (21 April 2003).

Dershowitz, Alan. *Why Terrorism Works*. New York: New Republic, 2002.

Dreze, J., and H. Gazdar. "Uttar Pradesh: The Burden of Inertia." In *Indian Development: Selected Regional Perspectives*, edited by J. Dreze and A. Sen, 33–128. Delhi: Oxford University Press, 1997.

Dupont, Jean-Paul. "Language and Learning in a Visayan Community." In *Shaping Local Worlds: Formal Education and Cultural Change in Rural Southeast Asia*, edited by Charles F. Keyes, 70–86. New Haven: Yale Center for International and Area Studies, 1991.

Eaton, Richard M. *The Rise of Islam and the Bengal Frontier, 1204–1760.* Berkeley: University of California Press, 1993.

"Editorial." *Moinul Islam* (magazine) 4, no. 11, 2005.

Eickelman, Dale F., and Jon W. Anderson. "Preface to the Second Edition." In *New Media in the Muslim World*, ix–xv. Bloomington: Indiana University Press, 2003.

Esposito, John. *The Islamic Threat: Myth or Reality?* New York: Oxford University Press, 1992.

———. "Political Islam: Beyond the Green Menace." *Current History* 93 no. 579 (January 1994): 19–24.

Ess, Josef van. *The Flowering of Muslim Theology*, translated by Jane Marie Todd. Cambridge: Harvard University Press, 2006.

"Establishment of Central Madrasa Board Misconceived." *AIMMM*, 4 April 2006, http://www.mushawarat.com/viewnews.asp?isno=24&newsno=241 (10 May 2007).

European Commission. "Draft National Indicative Program (NIP): Pakistan 2003–2005." 2003, http://www.delpak.cec.eu.int/WHATSNEW/NIP-Pakistan-173b.pdf (12 April 2006).

Evans, Alexander. "Understanding Madrasahs." *Foreign Affairs* 85 no. 1 (January/February 2006): 9–16.

Evans, Kathy. "Islam's Rising New Force." *Guardian*, 8 April 1995, 1, 15.

"Ex-USA TODAY Reporter Faked Major Stories." *USA Today*, 19 March 2004, http://www.usatoday.com/news/2004–03–18–2004–03–18_kelleymain_x.htm (16 November 2005).

Fahimuddin. "Globalization and Growth of Madrasahs in India." Paper presented at the G2002: Globalizations: Cultural, Economic, Democratic conference, College Park, Md., 11–14 April 2002, http://www.bsos.umd.edu/socy/conference/newpapers/uddin.txt (4 January 2005).

———. *Modernization of Muslim Education in India.* Delhi: Adhyayan Publishers, 2004.

Fair, C. Christine. "Islamic Education in Pakistan." Washington, D.C.: United States Institute of Peace, 2006, http://www.usip.org/events/2006/trip_report.pdf (19 July 2006).

Faridi, Abdul Huq. *Madrassah Shiksha* (Madrassah Education, in Bengali). Dhaka: Bangla Academy, 1982.

Faruki, Z. *Aurangzeb and His Times.* Bombay: D. B. Taraporevala Sons, 1935.

Fathers, Michael. "At the Birthplace of Taliban." *Time Online Edition*, September 21, 2001, http://www.time.com/time/nation/article/0,8599,175913,00.html (15 September 2002).

"Foreign Funds Being Used for Jihad Cause: Police." *New Age* (Dhaka) 6 September 2005, 1.

Foucault, Michel. *Discipline & Punish: The Birth of the Prison*, translated by Alan Sheridan. New York: Vintage, 1979.

Friedman, Thomas. "In Pakistan: It Is Jihad 101." *New York Times*, Op-ed, 13 November 2001, A17.

Fritsch, Peter. "Religious Schools in Pakistan Fill Void—And Spawn Warriors," *Wall Street Journal* (Eastern edition) 238, no. 65 (2001), A1.

Fukuyama, Francis. "The End of History." *National Interest* 16 (Summer 1989): 3–18.

———. *The End of History and the Last Man.* New York: Free Press, 1992.

Fuller, Graham E., and Ian O. Lesser. *A Sense of Siege: The Geopolitics of Islam and the West*. Boulder, Col.: Westview, 1995.

Ganguly, Sumit. *The Crisis in Kashmir: Portents of War, Hopes of Peace*. Washington, D.C.: Woodrow Wilson Center for Peace and Cambridge University Press, 1997.

———. "Explaining the Kashmir Insurgency: Political Mobilization and Institutional Decay." *International Security* 21, no. 2 (Fall 1996): 76–107.

Garg, B. R. *Charles Grant: The Forerunner of Macaulay's Educational Policy*. Ambala Cantonment, India: Associated Publishers, 2003.

Gesink, Indira Falk. "Islamic Reformation: A History of Madrasa Reform and Legal Change in Egypt." *Comparative Education Review* 50, no 3 (August 2006): 325–345.

Ghareeb, E. "The Middle East in the U.S. Media." *Middle East Annual Issues and Events* 3 (1984): 185–210.

———. "A Renewed Look at the American Coverage of the Arabs: Toward a Better Understanding." In *Split Vision, the Portrayal of Arabs in the American Media*, edited by E. Ghareeb, 157–194. Washington, D.C.: American Arab Affairs Council, 1983.

Ghazi, Mahmood Ahmad. *Islamic Renaissance in South Asia (1707–1867): The Role of Shah Wali Allah and His Successors*. New Delhi: Adam Publishers, 2004.

Gilani, Iftikhar. "India's Madrassas 3x Pakistan's." *Daily Times*, 19 August 2005, 7.

"Girls Outshine Boys in Bihar Islamic Seminary Exams." IANS, 2004, http://in.news.yahoo.com/060804/43/66fcv.html (4 April 2007).

Global March–International Center on Child Labor and Education (ICCLE). *Review of Child Labor, Education and Poverty Agenda: Bangladesh Country Report 2006*. Washington, D.C.: ICCLE, 2006.

Gold, Dore. *Hatreds Kingdom*. Washington, D.C.: Regenery Press, 2003.

Goldberg, Jeffrey. "Inside Jihad U: The Education of the Holy Warrior." *New York Times Magazine*, 25 June 2000.

Government of Bangladesh (GOB). *Bangladesh Economic Survey 2004–05*. Dhaka: Ministry of Finance, 2005.

———. *Bangladesh Economic Survey 2005*. Dhaka: Ministry of Finance, 2006.

———. *Bangladesh National Syllabi and Curriculum Committee Report*, Part 2. Dhaka: Ministry of Education, April 1979.

———. *Education Commission Report 1974*. Dacca: Ministry of Education, 1974.

———. *Education Commission Report 2003*. Dhaka: Ministry of Education, 2004.

Government of India. *Constitution of India*, Article 45. New Delhi: Legislative Department, Ministry of Law and Justice, 2007, http://indiacode.nic.in/coiweb/welcome.html (15 May 2007).

Government of India, Cabinet Secretariat. *Report of the Prime Minister's High Level Committee on the Socio-Economic and Educational Status of the Muslim Community in India* ("Sachar Committee Report"). New Delhi: Government of India, 2006.

Government of India, Ministry of Defense. *Reforming the National Security System*, 2001, http://mod.nic.in/newadditions/rcontents.htm (12 May 2007).

Government of Pakistan. *The Constitution of the Islamic Republic of Pakistan as Amended up to March 1999*. Islamabad: Ministry of Justice and Parliamentary Affairs, 1999.

———. *Economic Survey 2003–04*. Islamabad: Ministry of Finance. 2004.

———. "Madrasa Reforms (Teaching of Formal Subjects in Deeni Madaris)." *Policy Brief*, 2002, http://www.embassyofpakistan.org/pb7.php (14 March 2005).

———. *The Report of the Committee Set up by the Governor of West Pakistan for Recommending Improved Syllabus for the Various Darul Uloom and Arabic Madrasas in West Pakistan.* Lahore: Superintendent, Government Printing, West Pakistan, 1962.

Government of Pakistan, Council of Islamic Ideology (CII). *Consolidated Recommendations of the CII relating to the Education System in Pakistan, 1962–1982,* Islamabad: Government of Pakistan, 1982.

Government of Pakistan, Ministry of Education, Islamic Education Research Cell. *Deeni Madaris Pakistan ki Jam'e Report 1988.* Islamabad: Government of Pakistan, 1988.

———. *Pakistan ke dini madaris ki fihrist* (in Urdu). Islamabad: Government of Pakistan, 1984.

———. *Report of the Court of Inquiry Constituted under the Punjab Act II of 1954 to Enquire into the Punjab Disturbances of 1953,* Muahmmad Munir, Chairman. Lahore: Superintendent Government Printing, 1954.

Government of Pakistan, Ministry Of Religious Affairs Zakat And Ushr, *Year Book 2005–2006,* Islamabad: GOP, 2007.

"Govt Cracks down on Islamists." *New Age* (Dhaka), 24 February 2005, 1.

"Govt Finally Cracks down on Militants; Galib Arrested." *Daily Star,* 25 February 2005, 1.

"Govt Won't Be Allowed to Exert Control." *Daily Star,* 23 August 2006, 1.

"Guarding the Imaan of the New Generations of the Ummah—The Bulwark against the Kufr Onslaught." *Majlis* 15, no. 1, http://www.themajlis.net/Article24.html (23 December 2004).

Gunther, Sebastian. "Be Masters in That You Teach and Continue to Learn: Medieval Muslim Thinkers on Educational Theory." *Comparative Education Review* 50 no. 3 (August 2006): 367–388.

Gupta, Amita. "Schooling in India." In *Going to School in South Asia,* edited by Amita Gupta. Westport, Conn.: Greenwood, 2007.

Habib, Haroon. "The Menace of Militancy." *Frontline* 20 no. 12, 11 October 2003, http://www.frontlineonnet.com/f12021/stories/20031024000605900.htm (10 January 2005).

Hansen, Thomas Blom. *The Saffron Wave: Democracy and Hindu Nationalism in Modern India.* Princeton: Princeton University Press, 1999.

Haque, Mohammad Zeyal. "The 'Appeased' Indian Muslims Are Far More Deprived." *Milli Gazette,* 1 October 2002, http://www.milligazette.com/Archives/01102002/0110 200297.htm (1 April 2005).

Hardy, Roger. "Pakistan's 'Culture of Jihad.'" BBC, 5 August 2002, http://news.bbc.co.uk/2/hi/in_depth/world/2002/islamic_world/2173818.stm (30 August 2004).

Hartung, Jan-Peter. "The Nadwat al-'ulama: Chief Patron of Madrasa Education in India and a Turntable to the Arab World." In *Islamic Education, Diversity, and National Identity: Dini Madaris in India Post-9/11,* edited by Jan-Peter Hartung and Helmut Reifeld, 135–157. New Delhi: Sage, 2006.

———. "Towards a Reform of the Indian Madrassa? An Introduction." In *Islamic Education, Diversity and National Identity: Dini Madaris in India Post 9/11,* edited by Jan-Peter Hartung and Helmut Reifeld, 11–38. New Delhi: Sage, 2006.

Hasan, Mushirul. "The Madrassas in India." *Hindu,* 21 May 2003, 7.

Hashmi, Taj I. "Islamic Resurgence in Bangladesh: Genesis, Dynamics and Implications." In *Religious Radicalism and Security in South Asia,* edited by Satu P. Lamiaye,

Mohan Malik, and Robert Wirsing, 35–72. Honolulu: Asia-Pacific Center for Security Studies, 2004.

Hassan, Farhat. "Madaris and the Challenges of Modernity in Colonial India." In *Islamic Education, Diversity and National Identity: Dini Madaris in India Post-9/11*, edited by Jan-Peter Hartung and Helmut Reifeld, 56–72. New Delhi: Sage Publications, 2006.

"Hasty Recognition of Quomi Madrassah Is Electoral Give-and-take." *New Age*, 23 August 2006, 6.

Hisham, Ibne. *Siratun Nabi*. Vol 2. Dhaka: Islamic Foundation Bangladesh, 1994.

Hoffman, Bruce, and Gordon McCormick. "Terrorism, Signaling, and Suicide Attack." *Studies in Conflict and Terrorism* 27, no. 4 (July/August 2004): 243–282.

Hollen, Christopher Van. "The Tilt Policy Revisited: Nixon-Kissinger Geopolitics and South Asia." In *The Regional Imperative: The Administration of US Foreign Policy towards South Asian States under Presidents Johnson and Nixon*, edited by Lloyd I. Rudolph and Susanne H. Rudolph, 421–450. Atlantic Highlands, N.J.: Humanities Press, 1980.

Hossain, A.K.M. Yakub, and Balal Muhammad. "Madrasah." In *Banglapedia: The National Encyclopedia of Bangladesh* (2003), http://banglapedia.search.com.bd/HT/M_0032.htm (24 December 2004).

Hossain, Naomi. "Access to Education for the Poor and Girls: Educational Achievements in Bangladesh." Washington, D.C.: World Bank, 2004, http://www.worldbank.org/wbi/reducingpoverty/docs/FullCases/PDFs%2011–13–04/Bangladesh%20girls%20education.pdf (25 August 2005).

"How Long the Politics with the Madrassah Education?" (in Bengali). *Prothom Alo*, 23 August 2006, 1.

Human Rights Watch. *Everyone Lives in Fear: Patterns of Impunity in Jammua and Kashmir*. New York: Human Rights Watch, 2006.

Hundley, Tom. "In Pakistan: Schools Indoctrinate Young Radicals." *Chicago Tribune*, 3 October 2001, 1.

Huntington, Samuel. "The Clash of Civilizations." *Foreign Affairs* 72, no. 3 (1993): 22–50.

———. *The Clash of Civilizations and the Remaking of the World Order*. New York: Simon and Schuster, 1996.

Husain, Ishrat. "Education, Employment and Economic Development in Pakistan." In *Education Reform in Pakistan: Building for the Future*, edited by Robert M. Hathaway, 33–45. Washington, D.C.: Woodrow Wilson International Center for Scholars, Asia Program, 2005.

Husain, Mir Zohair. *Global Islamic Politics*. New York: Harper Collins, 1995.

Husain, S. M. Azizuddin. "Mir Fathullah Shirazi's Contribution for the Revision of the Syllabi of Indian Madrasas during Akbar's Reign." In *Madrasa Education in India—Eleventh to Twenty First Century*, edited by S. M. Azizuddin Husain, 24–36. New Delhi: Kanishka Publishers, 2005.

Hussain, Ahmad. "Madrasah Education." In *Education for All*, edited by Abdullah al-Muti Sharfuddin, 109–127. Dhaka: Polwell Printing Press, 1968.

Hussain, Zahid. "A Mixed Message." *Newsweek International*, 4 July 2006, http://www.msnbc.msn.com/id/8359724/site/newsweek/ (10 July 2006).

Ibrahimmy, Sekander Ali, ed. *Reports on Islamic Education and Madrasah Education in Bengal (1861–1977)*. Vol. 3. Dhaka: Islamic Foundation of Bangladesh, Dhaka, 1985.

———. *Reports on Islamic Education and Madrassah Education in Bengal (1861–1977)*. Vol. 4. Dhaka: Islamic Foundation of Bangladesh, Dhaka, 1987.

Ikram, S. M. *Muslim Civilization in India*, edited by Ainslie T. Embree. New York: Columbia University Press, 1964.

"Initiatives to Bring Unrecognized Madrassahs under Control in West Bengal" (in Bengali). *Prothom Alo*, 13 October 2006, 1.

Institute of Policy Studies (IPS). *Pakistan: Religious Education Institutions, An Overview*. Islamabad: IPS, 2002.

International Crisis Group (ICG). *Pakistan: Karachi's Madrasas and Violent Extremism*. Brussels and Islamabad: ICG, March 2007.

———. *Pakistan: Madrasas, Extremism and the Military*. Brussels and Islamabad: ICG, 2002.

———. *Pakistan: Reforming the Education Sector*. Brussels and Islamabad: ICG, 2004.

———. *The State of Sectarianism in Pakistan*. Brussels and Islamabad: ICG, 2005.

Iqbal, Nadeem. "India/ Pakistan: Cynics Doubt Law to Reform Pakistan Religious Schools." *Asia Times*, 28 June 2002, 2.

Islam, Shahidul. *Prosohongo: Shiksha* (Issue: Education, in Bengali). Dhaka: Shikshabarta Prokashona, 2002.

"Islamic Seminary Has Strong Ties to Bin Laden." *Philadelphia Inquirer*, 30 August 1998, 12, http://www.maykuth.com/Africa/pak830.htm (10 November 2004).

"The Islamic Threat." *Economist*, 13 March 1993, 25.

Ismail, Salwa. *Rethinking Islamist Politics: Culture, the State and Islamism*. London: I.B. Tauris, 2003.

"Jaamat Blames RAW, Mosad." *Daily Star*, 21 August 2005, 1.

"Jaamatul Met in Aditmari the Night before the Attacks" (n Bengali). *Bhorer Kagoj*, 22 August 2005.

Jafri, A.B.S. "What and Wherefore of Madaris." *Dawn* (Karachi), 20 January 2003, 16.

Jafri, Saiyid Naqi Husain. "A Modernist View of Madrasa Education in Late Mughal India." In *Islamic Education, Diversity, and National Identity: Dini Madaris in India Post-9/11*, edited by Jan-Peter Hartung and Helmut Reifeld, 39–55. New Delhi: Sage, 2006.

Jalal, Ayesha. *State of Martial Rule: The Origins of Pakistan's Political Economy of Defense*. Cambridge: Cambridge University Press, 1990.

Jalal-Abadi, Mohammad. "Campaign against Madrassahs in Bangladesh." *Muslimedia*, 16–31 March 1999, http://www.muslimedia.com/ARCHIVES/world99/ban-madrasa.htm (12 March 2001).

Jalbani, G. N. *Teachings of Shah Waliyullah of Delhi*. Lahore: Sh. Muhammad Ashraf, 1967.

Jamal, Nasir. "Religious Schools: Who Controls What They Teach?" *Dawn* (Karachi), 31 October 1996, Dawn Wire Services issue 02/44, http://www.lib.virginia.edu/area-studies/SouthAsia/SAserials/Dawn/1996/310c96.html#reli (8 July 2003).

Jamia Yunusia. *Annual Souvenir Booklet*. B'Baria: Jamia Yunusia Madrassah, 1993.

———. *Annual Souvenir Booklet*. B'Baria: Jamia Yunusia Madrassah, 1997.

Jan, Abid Ullah. "Target: Jihad, Madrassa or Islam?" 2002, http://archive.muslimuzbekistan.com/eng/islam/2002/09/a09092002.html (12 July 2003).

Jeffery, Patricia, Roger Jeffery, and Craig Jeffery. "Islamization, Gentrification and Domestication: 'A Girls' Islamic Course' and Rural Muslims in Western Uttar Pradesh." *Modern Asian Studies* 38, no. 1 (2004): 1–53.

———. "Investing in the Future: Education in the Social and Cultural Reproduction of Muslims in UP." In *Living with Secularism: The Destiny of India's Muslims,* edited by Mushirul Hasan, 63–89. New Delhi: Manohar, 2007.

Jinnah, Muhammad Ali. "Presidential Speech to the Constituent Assembly of Pakistan, 11 August 1947." *Dawn* (Karachi), Independence Day Supplement, 14 August 1999, http://www.pakistani.org/pakistan/legislation/constituent_address_11aug1947.html (13 July 2004).

"JMB and JMJ Are One and the Same." *New Age* (Dhaka), 5 March 2005, 1.

"JMB Cadres Met at Madrassah in Lalmonirhat on the Night of 16 August" (in Bengali). *Ajker Kagoj,* 22 August 2005.

Johnson, Chalmers. *Blowback.* London: Time Warner Paperbacks, 2002.

Kabeer, Naila. "Social Exclusion and the MDGs: The Challenge of 'Durable Inequalities' in the Asian Context." Paper presented at the Asia 2015 Conference of the Institute of Development Studies, London, March 2006.

Kabir, Nurul. "BNP, AL's Political Opportunism Abets Islamist Fundamentalism." *New Age,* 21 September 2005.

Kadi, Wadad. "Education in Islam: Myths and Truths." Guest editorial. *Comparative Education Review* 50, no. 3 (August 2006): 311–324.

Kamaluddin, Abuzar. "Muslims and Education in Bihar: Some Revealing Facts." *Bihar Times,* 15 December 2006, 7.

Karim, Karim H. *Islamic Peril: Media and Global Violence.* Montreal: Black Rose Books, 2003.

Kaur, Kuldip. *Madrasa Education in India: A Study of Its Past and Present.* Chandigarh: Centre for Research in Rural and Industrial Development, 1990.

Kellner, Douglas. *From 9/11 to Terror War: Dangers of the Bush Legacy.* Lanham, MD.: Rowman and Littlefield, 2003.

———. "Theorizing September 11: Social Theory, History, and Globalization," 2004. http://www.gseis.ucla.edu/faculty/kellner/papers/theorizing911.htm#fnB1 (15 January 2004).

Kepel, Gilles. *Jihad: A Trail of Political Islam,* translated by Anthony F. Roberts Cambridge: Harvard University Press, 2002.

Khalilzad, Zalmay. "The United States and the Persian Gulf: Preventing Regional Hegemony." *Survival* 37 no. 2 (Summer 1995): 95–120.

Khan, Jan Jahan. *Tarikhi-Jan-Jahan* (in Persian). Manuscript available at the Asiatic Society of Bengal, Calcutta.

Khan, Khafi. *Muntakhabul-Lubub* (in Persian). Pt. 1, 249. Manuscript available at the Asiatic Society of Bengal, Calcutta.

———. *Tarikhi-Akbari* (in Persian). Manuscript available at the Asiatic Society of Bengal, Calcutta.

Khan, Shahriar. "Bangladesh Launches Refresher Course for Islamic Schools." *OneWorld Report 2003,* http://www.oneworld.net/article/view/66855/1/1 (29 February 2004).

Kipp, Jacob. "Key Issues Confronting France, French Foreign Policy, Franco-US Relations, and French Defense Policy." US Army, Foreign Military Studies Office Web site, April 1995, http://leav-www.army.mil/fmso.

Kohli, Atul. "Can Democracies Accommodate Ethnic Nationalism? Rise and Decline of Self-Determination Movements in India." *Journal of Asian Studies* 56, no. 2 (May 1997): 325–344.

Kramer, Martin. "Is Sharansky Right? Does Everyone Want to Be Free?" *History News Network,* 22 August 2005, http://hnn.us/articles/13658.html (24 October 2005).

Kraul, Chris. "Dollars to Help Pupil." *Los Angeles Times,* 14 April 2003, 1.

Krauthammer, Charles. "The New Crescent of Crisis: Global Intifada." *Washington Post,* 1 January 1993, A25.

Kronstadt, Alan. *Education Reform in Pakistan.* CRS Report for Congress. RS 22009, 23 December 2004. http://www.fas.org/man/crs/RS22009.pdf (12 March 2005).

Kumar, Nita. *Lessons from Schools: The History of Education in Banaras.* Thousand Oaks, Cal.: Sage, 2000.

Kux, Dennis. *The United States and Pakistan, 1947–2000: Disenchanted Allies.* Washington, D.C.: Woodrow Wilson Center, 2001.

Laird, M. A. *Missionaries and Education in Bengal 1793–1837.* Oxford: Clarendon Press, 1972.

Lal, Marie. "The Challenges for India's Education System." London: Royal Institute of International Affairs, Asia Programme, ASP BP 05/03, 2005. Unpublished paper.

Lamb, Christine. "The Pakistan Connection." *Sunday Times,* 17 July 2005, 1.

Lamb, David. "Rounding out the Seminary Curricula." *Los Angeles Times,* 3 January 2002, 1.

Lamb, David, and Paul Watson. "Pakistan Pledges to Curb Militants." *Los Angeles Times,* 13 January 2002, 1.

Lancaster, John. "Lessons in Jihad for Pakistani Youth: Religious Schools Resist Law to Curb Extremism." *Washington Post,* 14 July 2002, A19.

Landay, Jonathan S. "Pakistan to Rein in Religious Schools, President to Sign Law Following U.S. Pressure." *Detroit Free Press,* 31 December 2001, 1.

Lane-Poole, Stanley. *Aurengazeb and the Decay of the Mughal Empire.* New Delhi: Low Price, 1990.

Langohr, Vickie. "Colonial Education Systems and the Spread of Local Religious Movements: The Case of British Egypt and Punjab." *Contemporary Studies in Society and History* 47, no.1 (January 2005): 161–189.

———. "Educational Sub-contracting and the Spread of Religious Nationalism: Hindu and Muslim Nationalist Schools in Colonial India." *Comparative Studies of South Asia, Africa and the Middle East* 21, nos. 1–2 (2002): 42–49.

Law, Narendra Nath. *Promotion of Learning in India during Muhammadan Rule by Muhammadans.* London: Longman's Green, 1916.

Lewis, Bernard. *The Middle East and the West.* Bloomington: Indiana University Press, 1964.

———. "The Roots of Muslim Rage." *Atlantic Monthly* 266 (September 1990): 47–60.

Lobe, Jim. "Neocons Seek Islamic 'Reformation.'" *Anti-War.com,* 8 April 2004, http://www.antiwar.com/lobe/?articleid=2273 (3 May 2005).

Looney, Robert. "Reforming Pakistan's Educational System: The Challenge of Madrassa." *Journal of Social, Political and Economic Studies* 28, no. 3 (2003): 257–274.

———. "A US Strategy for Achieving Stability in Pakistan: Expanding Educational Opportunities." *Strategic Insights* (Center for Contemporary Conflict) 1, no. 7 (September 2002).

"Madrasas Not Centres of Terrorism: Shivraj Patil." *Hindu*, 24 July 2006, 1.

"Madrasas Outshine Schools." *Milli Gazette*, July 2001, 1–15, http://www.milligazette. com/Archives/01072001/19.htm (3 April 2007).

"Madrasas: Breeding Separatism." *Inpride.com*, http://indpride.com/madrasas.html (12 May 2007).

"Madrassah Registration Ordinance." *Nawa-i-Waqt* World News Connection, 24 June 2002, 1.

"Madrassas Breeding Terrorists, Says Powell." *Daily Times*, 12 March 2004, http://www. dailytimes.com.pk/default.asp?page=story_12–3-2004_pg7_1 (11 November 2005).

Makdisi, George. "Muslim Institutions of Learning in Eleventh-Century Baghdad." *Bulletin of the School of Oriental and African Studies* 24, no. 1 (1961): 1–56.

———. *The Rise of Colleges Institutions of Learning in Islam and the West*. Edinburgh: Edinburgh University Press, 1981.

Malik, Jamal. *Colonization of Islam: Dissolution of Traditional Institutions in Pakistan*. New Delhi: Manohar, 1996.

———. "Welcome Address." Madrassah workshop, University of Erfurt, Germany, 20 May 2005.

Mamdani, Mahmood. *Good Muslim, Bad Muslim: America, the Cold War, and the Roots of Terror*. New York: Pantheon, 2004.

Mansoor, Hasan. "Pakistan Sees 2745 Percent Increase in Seminaries since 1947." 2 May 2003, http://www.pakistan-facts.com/article.php/20030428231558859 (8 July 2003).

Marquand, Robert. "The Tenets of Terror." *Christian Science Monitor*, 18 October 2001, 1.

Martin, Patrick, and Sean Phelan. "Representing Islam in the Wake of September 11: A Comparison of US Television and CNN Online Messageboard Discourses." *Prometheus* 20, no. 3 (2002): 263–269.

Martin, R. C., M. R. Woodward, and D. S. Atmaja. *Defenders of Reason in Islam: Mu'tazilism from Medieval School to Modern Symbol*. Oxford: Oneworld Publications, 1997.

Marty, Martin E., and R. Scott Appleby, eds. *Fundamentalisms Comprehended*. Chicago: University of Chicago Press, 1995.

"Maulana Farid Had Direct Role in Blasts: Police." *New Age*, 24 August 2005, 1.

Mayer, Ann Elizabeth. *Islam and Human Rights: Tradition and Politics*. Boulder, Col.: Westview, 1995.

Mazumdar, Jaideep. "The Bengal Alifate." *Outlook*, 30 January 2006, http://www. outlookindia.com/full.asp?fodname=20060130&fname=Madrasa+percent28Fperce nt29&sid=1&pn=1 (5 February 2006).

Mehdi, Mujib. *Madrassah Sikhsha: Ekti Porjalochana* (Madrassah Education: A Review, in Bengali). Dhaka: Bangladesh Nari Progoti Sangha, 2001.

Metcalf, Barbara Daly. *Islamic Revival in British India: Deoband, 1860–1900*. New Delhi: Oxford University Press, 1982.

Miller, Judith. "The Challenge of Radical Islam." *Foreign Affairs* 7 no. 2 (Spring 1993): 42–56.

———. "Pakistan Outlines Plan to Curb Militant Networks." *New York Times*, 10 June 2000, Section A6.

Mohan, Geoffrey. "Radical School Reform." *Los Angeles Times*, 23 March 2002, 1.

Mohsin, Amena. *Chittagong Hill Tracts, Bangladesh: On the Difficult Road to Peace*. London: Lynne Rienner, 2003.

Moraeu, Ron, Sami Yousafzai, and Zahid Hussain. "Holy War 101." *Newsweek*, 1 December 2003, 28–30.

Morris, Debra. 2002. "Charities and Terrorism: The Charity Commission Response." *International Journal of Not-for-Profit Law* 5, no. 1, http://www.icnl.org/JOURNAL/vo15iss1/ar_morris.htm (22 March 2003).

"Most Madrasas Now Registered, Says Aziz." *Daily Times*, 15 February 2007, 1.

Moustafa, Tamir. "Conflict and Cooperation between the State and Religious Institutions in Contemporary Egypt." *International Journal of Middle East Studies* 32 (2000): 3–22.

Mowdudi, Abu Ala. *The Islamic Law and Constitution*. Lahore: Islamic Publications, 1980.

Moyser, G. "Politics and Religion in the Modern World: An Overview." In *Politics and Religion in the Modern World*, edited by G. Moyser, 1–27. London: Routledge, 1991.

Murshid, Tazeen. *The Sacred and the Secular: Bengal Muslim Discourses, 1871–1977*. Oxford: Oxford University Press, 1996.

Musharraf, General Pervez. "Address to the Nation." 17 October 1999, http://www.presidentofpakistan.gov.pk/FilesSpeeches/Addresses/1020200475611AMword%20file.pdf (3 February 2005).

———. "Address to the Nation." 12 January 2002, Islamabad, http://www.presidentofpakistan.gov.pk/FilesSpeeches/Addresses/1020200475758AMword%20file.pdf (3 February 2005).

Muslehuddin, A.T.M. "Arabic." In *Banglapedia* 2003, http://banglapedia.search.com.bd/HT/A_0282.HTM (23 November 2004).

"Muslim Law Board Opposes Bill on Madrasas." *Times of India*, 23 September 2002, 1.

Naik, J. P., and Syed Nurullah. *A Students' History of Education in India: 1800–1973*. Bombay: Mcmillan India. 2000.

Nakosteen, Mehdi. *History of Islamic Origins of Western Education: A.D. 800–1350*. Boulder: University of Colorado Press, 1964.

Nasr, Seyyed Vali Reza. "Islam, the State, and the Rise of Sectarian Militancy in Pakistan." In *Pakistan: Nationalism without a Nation?* edited by Christophe Jaffrelot, 85–114. New Delhi: Monohar, 2002.

———. *Islamic Leviathan: Islam and the Making of State Power*. Oxford: Oxford University Press, 2001.

———. *The Vanguard of Islamic Revolution: The Jama'at-i Islami of Pakistan*. Berkeley: University of California Press, 1994.

Nath Law, Narendra. *Promotion of Learning in India during Muhammadan Rule by Muhammadans*. London: Longman's Green, 1916.

National Commission on Terrorist Attacks. *The 9/11 Commission Report: Final Report of the National Commission on Terrorist Attacks upon the United States*. New York: W. W. Norton, 2004.

Nayyar, A. H. "Madrassah Education Frozen in Time." In *Education and the State: Fifty Years of Pakistan*, edited by Parvez Hoodbhoy, 215–250. Karachi: Oxford University Press, 2003.

Nayyar, A. H., and Ahmad Salim, eds. *The Subtle Subversion: The State of Curricula and Textbooks in Pakistan*. Islamabad: Sustainable Development Policy Institute, 2002.

"126 Madaris Involved in Militant Activities: Report," *Dawn* (Karachi), 16 May 2000, 1.

"Pakistan Religious Schools under No Threat of Takeover." *Deutsche Presse-Agentur (DPA)*, 24 August 2001.

"Pakistan Targets Religious Schools That Preach Violence." *Fox News.com*, 1 December 2001.

"Pakistani Father Laments His Teenaged Son Sent to Fight in Afghanistan." *Agence France Presse* (AFP), 29 June 1997, http://www.timesonline.co.uk/article/0,2087–1697130,00.html (3 January 2005).

"Pakistani Government Not Planning Crackdown on Islamic Schools." *Deutsche Presse-Agentur* (DPA), 10 October 1999.

"Pakistani Religious Groups Vow to Resist Government Interference." *Agence France Presse* (AFP), 25 January 1995.

Palmer, Diego A. Ruiz. *French Strategic Options in the 1990s*. Adelphi Papers 260. London, International Institute of Strategic Studies, Summer 1991.

Parpart, Uwe. "Musharraf: Can This Man Change Pakistan?" *Asia Times*, 18 October 2002. http://www.atimes.com/ind-pak/DA18Df05.html (10 February 2005).

Pipes, Daniel. "The Muslims Are Coming! The Muslims Are Coming!" *National Review*, 19 November 1990.

———. "There Are No Moderates: Dealing with Fundamentalist Islam." *National Interest* (Fall 1995): 48–57.

"Playing Politics with Education." *Daily Star* (Dhaka), 22 August 2006, 1.

"PM Orders Rooting out Islamist Militants." *Daily Star* (Dhaka), 25 February 2005, 1.

Poole, Elizabeth. *Reporting Islam: Media Representations of British Muslims*. London: I. B. Tauris, 2002.

Prashad, B. *The Progress of Science in India during the Past Twenty-five Years*. Calcutta: Indian Science Congress Association, 1938.

"President Approves New Qwami Madrassah Board." *Jugantor* (Dhaka), 21 December 2006, 1.

Price, Susannah. "Pakistan Religious Schools Deadline." *BBC*, 19 June 2002, http://news.bbc.co.uk/1/hi/world/south_asia/2054719.stm (30 August 2004).

"Priest in Terror Probe." *Sunday Times* (Durban), 31 January 1999, www.suntimes.co.za/1999/01/31/news/durban/ndbn03.htm (9 December 2002).

Probe Team. *Public Report on Basic Education in India*. New York: Oxford University Press, 1999.

Qasmi, M. Burhanuddin. *Recounting Untold History, Darul Uloom Deoband: A Heroic Struggle against the British Tyranny*. Mumbai: Markazul Ma'arif Education and Research Center, 2001.

Qasmi, Muhammadullah Khalili. *Madrasa Education, Its Strength and Weakness*. Mumbai: Markazul Ma'arif Education and Research Centre, 2005.

"Qawami Madrasa Degree Gets Master's Status." *Daily Star*, 22 August 2006, 1.

"Qoumi Madrassahs under Vigil over Aug 17 Blasts." *New Age*, 5 September 2005, 1.

Quraishi, Ash-har. "Pakistan's Religious Schools under Fire." *CNN*, 13 September 2002, http://edition.cnn.com/2002/WORLD/asiapcf/south/09/13/pakistan.marassah/ (14 September 2002).

Rahim, M. A. *Banglar Samajik o Sangskritik Itihash* (Social and Cultural History of Bengal, in Bengali). Vol.1. Dhaka: Bangla Academy, 1982.

Rahman, Khalid, and Syed Rashad Bukhari. "Pakistan: Religious Education and Institutions." *Muslim World* 96 (April 2006): 323–339.

———. "Religious Education Institutions (REIs): Present Situation and the Future Strategy." *Policy Perspectives* (April 2005): 55–81.

Rahman, S. Ubaidur. "Nepal-border Madrasas: No Iota of 'Terrorism' or 'ISI' activity." *Milli Gazette*, 8–15 October 2001, http://www.milligazette.com/Archives/15072001/06. htm (15 January 2004).

Rahman, Tariq. *Denizens of Alien Worlds: A Study of Education, Inequality and Polarization in Pakistan.* Karachi: Oxford University Press, 2004.

———. "The Impact of European Languages in Former Colonial Territories: The Case of English in Pakistan." Paper presented at the Conference on Language Communities or Cultural Empires: The Impact of European Languages in Former Colonial Territories, Institute of European Studies, University of California at Berkley, 10–11 February 2005, http://ies.berkeley.edu/calendar/files/ (24 July 2006).

———. "Language, Religion and Identity in Pakistan: Language-Teaching in Pakistani Madrassas." *Ethnic Studies Report* 16, no. 2 (July 1988): 197–214.

———. "The Madrassa and the State in Pakistan." *Himal*, February 2004, www.himal-mag.com/2004/february/essay.htm (2 September 2004).

———. "Reasons for Rage: Reflections on the Education System of Pakistan with Special Reference to English." In *Education Reform in Pakistan: Building for the Future*, edited by Robert M. Hathaway, 87–106. Washington, D.C.: Woodrow Wilson International Center for Scholars, Asia Program, 2005.

Rashid, Abbas. "The Politics and Dynamics of Violent Sectarianism." N.d., http://members.tripod.com/~no_nukes_sa/chapter_2.html (25 March 2003).

Rashid, Ahmed. "Pakistan and Taliban." In *Fundamentalism Reborn? Afghanistan and Taliban*, edited by William Maley, 72–89. London: C. Hurst, 1998.

———. *Taliban: Militant Islam, Oil and Fundamentalism in Central Asia.* New Haven: Yale University Press, 2000.

Rashid, Haroon. "The 'University of Holy War.'" *BBC*, 2 October 2003, http://news.bbc. co.uk/1/hi/world/south_asia/3155112.stm (30 August 2004).

Reetz, Dietrich. *Islam in the Public Sphere, Religious Groups in India, 1900–1947.* New Delhi: Oxford University Press, 2006.

Report of the Saddler's Commission. Appendix 2, Vol. 6. Calcutta: Calcutta University, 1835.

Riaz, Ali. "Beyond the 'Tilt': US Initiatives to Dissipate Bangladesh Movement in 1971." *History Compass* 4, no. 1 (2006): 8–25.

———. *God Willing: The Politics of Islamism in Bangladesh.* Lanham, MD.: Rowman and Littlefield, 2004.

———. "Nations, Nation-State and the Politics of Muslim Identity in South Asia." *Comparative Studies of South Asia, Africa and the Middle East* 22, nos. 1–2, (2002): 53–58.

———. *Unfolding State: The Transformation of Bangladesh.* Ontario: de Sitter Publications, 2005.

Rizvi, Hassan Ashkari. *The Military and Politics in Pakistan, 1947–1977.* Lahore: Sang-e-Meel Publications, 2000.

Rizvi, Saiyid Athar Abbas. *Shah Wali-Allah and His Times.* Canberra: Ma'rifat Publishing House, 1980.

"The Road to Koranistan." *Economist*, 5 October 1996, 21.

Robinson, Francis. *The 'Ulama of Farangi Mahall and Islamic Culture in South Asia.* New Delhi: Permanent Black, 2001.

Rosenthal, Franz. *Knowledge Triumphant*. Leiden: E. J. Brill, 1970.

Rosso, Joy Miller del. "School Feeding Program: Improving Effectiveness and Increasing the Benefit to Education: A Guide for Program Managers." Unpublished paper. Oxford: Partnership for Child Development, 1999.

Rostow, Walt W. *Eisenhower, Kennedy, and Foreign Aid*. Austin: University of Texas Press, 1985.

Roy, Olivier. *Islam and Resistance in Afghanistan*. Cambridge: Cambridge University Press, 1985.

———. "Modern Political Culture and Traditional Resistance." In *The Tragedy of Afghanistan: The Social, Cultural and Political Impact of the Soviet Invasion*, edited by Bo Huldt and Erland Jansson, 106–113. New York: Croom Helm, 1988.

———. "The Origin of Islamist Movement in Afghanistan." *Central Asian Survey* 3 no. 2 (1984). Quoted in Gilles Dorronsoro, *Revolution Unending: Afghanistan, 1979 to Present*, translated by John King. New York: Columbia University Press, 2005, 69.

———. "The Taliban: A Strategic Tool for Pakistan." In *Pakistan Nationalism without a Nation?* edited by Christopher Jaffrelot, 149–160. New Delhi/London: Manohar/Zed Books, 2002.

Rudolph, Susanne Hoeber, and Lloyd I. Rudolph. "Living with Difference in India: Legal Pluralism and Legal Universalism in Historical Context." In *Religion and Personal Law in Secular India: A Call for Judgment*, edited by Gerald James Larson, 36–66. Bloomington: Indiana University Press, 2001.

Rushdie, Salman. "Muslims Unite! A New Reformation Will Bring Your Faith into the Modern Era." *Times* (London), 11 August 2005, http://www.timesonline.co.uk/article/0,,1072–1729998,00.html (12 December 2005).

Safqat, Saeed. "From Official Islam to Islamism: The Rise of Dawat-ul-Irshad and Laskar-e-Taiba." In *Pakistan: Nationalism without a Nation?* edited by Christophe Jaffrelot, 131–148. New Delhi: Monohar, 2002.

Sageman, Marc. *Understanding Terror Networks*. Philadelphia: University of Pennsylvania Press, 2004.

Sahay, Anand Mohan. "In Bihar, Even Non-Muslims Prefer Madrasas." *Rediff News*, 22 February 2003, http://www.rediff.com/news/2003/feb/22bihar.htm (27 March 2005).

Said, Edward. *Covering Islam: How the Media and the Experts Determine How We See the Rest of the World*. London: Vintage, 1981.

———. "Islam and the West are Inadequate Banners." *Observer* (London), 16 September 2001.

Saklain, Golam. *Bangladesher Sufi Sadhak* (Sufis and Holy Men of Bangladesh, in Bengali). Dhaka: Islamic Foundation Bangladesh, 1993.

Saleem, Ahsan. "Against the Tide: Role of the Citizens Foundation in Paksiatni Education." In *Education Reform in Pakistan: Building for the Future*, edited by Robert M. Hathaway, 71–86. Washington, D.C.: Woodrow Wilson International Center for Scholars, Asia Program, 2005.

Sanyal, Usha. *Devotional Islam and Politics in British India: Ahmed Riza Khan Barelwi and His Movement 1870—1920*. New Delhi: Oxford University Press, 1996.

"Satkhira Is the Capital of the Militants" (in Bengali). *Ajker Kagoj*, 27 August 2005.

Sattar, Abdus. *Aliya Madrassahar Itihash* (History of Aliya Madrassah, in Bengali). Dhaka: Islamic Foundation Bangladesh, 1994.

Sattar, Muhammad Abdus. *Bangladeshe Madrassah Shikhya o Shomoaj Jibone tar Probhab* (Madrassah Education in Bangladesh and Its Impact on the Social Life, in Bengali). Dhaka: Islamic Foundation Bangladesh, 1994.

Sayyid, Bobby S. *A Fundamental Fear.* London: Zed Books, 1997.

Schacht, Joseph. *An Introduction to Islamic Law.* [1979] New York: Oxford University Press, 1983.

Schumer, Charles. "Growing Influence of Wahhabi Islam over Military and Prisons Pose Threat." *Global Security* 2003, http://www.globalsecurity.org/security/library/congress/2003_h/030626_PR01819.htm (11 November 2005).

———. Letter to Saudi Ambassador on 4 December 2002, http://schumer.senate.gov/SchumerWebsite/pressroom/press_releases/PR01348.html (24 March 2004).

———. "Schumer: Saudis Are Suffering from Arafat Double Talk Syndrome." Press release, 4 December 2002, http://schumer.senate.gov/SchumerWebsite/pressroom/press_releases/PR01347.html (24 March 2004).

"Serial Blasts Planned in April, Had Foreign Funding." *Daily Star*, 3 September 2005, 1.

Seth, Sanjay. "Secular Enlightenment and Christian Conversion: Missionaries and Education in Colonial India." In *Education and Social Change in South Asia*, edited by Krishna Kumar and Joachim Oesterheld, 27–43. New Delhi, Orient Longman, 2007.

Shah, Syed Tauqir. "A Case Study of Madrassahs–Ahmedpur East (Bahawalpur), Pakistan." Unpublished paper, August 1994. Expanded version published as *Madrassahs in Pakistan: A Threat to Enlightened and Moderate Pakistan?.* Budapest: Open Society Institute and central European University Center for Policy Studies, 2006.

Shaheen, Jack G. *Arab and Muslim Stereotyping in American Popular Culture.* Washington, D.C.: Center for Muslim-Christian Understanding, History and International Affairs, Georgetown University, 1997.

Siddiqui, Iqtidar Husain. "Madrasa-Education in Medieval India." In *Madrasa Education in India—Eleventh to Twenty First Century*, edited by S. M. Azizuddin Husain, 7–23. New Delhi: Kanishka Publishers, 2005.

Siddiqui, M. Akhtar. "Developments and Trends in Madrassa Education." In *Education and Muslims in India since Independence*, edited by A.W.B. Qadri, Riaz Shakir Khan, and Mohammad Akhtar Siddiqui, 72–87. New Delhi: Institute of Objective Studies, 1998.

———. *Empowerment of Muslims through Education.* New Delhi: Institute of Objective Studies, 2004.

Siddiqui, Tasneem. *Migration as a Livelihood Strategy of the Poor: The Bangladesh Case.* London: Department for International Development, 2003.

Sikand, Yoginder. *Bastions of the Believers: Madrasas and Islamic Education in India.* New Delhi: Penguin, 2005.

———. "Madrasas in a Morass: Between Medievalism and Muslimophobia," 2006 http://india-forum.com/docs/MadrasasinaMorass.doc (3 April 2006).

———. "New Forms of Islamic Educational Provision in India." *Indian Muslims*, January 2007, http://www.indianmuslims.info/articles/yoginder_sikand/articles/new_forms_of_islamic_educational_provision_in_india.html (4 March 2007).

Singer, P. W. "Pakistan's Madrassahs: Ensuring a System of Education Not Jihad." Washington, D.C.: Brookings Institute Analysis Paper, November 2001.

Sivan, Emmanuel. *Radical Islam: Medieval Theology and Modern Politics.* New Haven: Yale University Press, 1985.

Smock, David. "Ijtihad: Reinterpreting Islamic Principles for the Twenty-first Century." United States Institute of Peace Special report no. 125, August 2004, http://www.usip.org/pubs/specialreports/sr125.html (14 January 2005).

Smucker, Philip. "School Fighting Brewing." *Christian Science Monitor*, 2 July 2002, 1.

Social Policy and Development Centre (SPDC). *Social Development in Pakistan 2002–03: The State of Education*. Karachi: SPDC, 2003.

SOSH. "The Menace of the Christian Missionary Onslaught," April 1997, http://www.jihaad.faithweb.com/Mencmis.html (12 June 2003).

Sourdel, D. "Refelexions sur la diffusion de la madrasa à Alep aux XIIe–XIIIe siècles d'après Ibn Saddad." *Bulletin Etudes Orientales* 13 (1976): 85–115.

South Asia Terrorism Portal. "Sectarianism Violence in Pakistan," 2007, http://www.satp.org/satporgtp/countries/pakistan/database/sect-killing.htm (21 April 2007).

Spencer, Robert. *Onward Muslim Soldiers*. Washington, D.C.: Regenery Press, 2003.

Stern, Jessica. "Pakistan's Jihad Culture." *Foreign Affairs* 79, no. 6 (2000): 115–126.

———. "Preparing for a War on Terrorism." *Current History* 100 no. 649 (November 2001): 355–357.

———. *Terror in the Name of God*. New York: Harper Collins, 2003.

Struck, Doug. "Pakistan Loyalty to Radical Islam Tests Crackdown." *Washington Post*, 20 January 2002, Section A1.

Sufi, G.M.D. *Al Minhaj: The Evolution of Curriculum in the Muslim Educational Institutions of India*. Lahore: Sh. Muhammad Ashraf, 1941.

Sultan, Tipu. "From Jaamat-Shibir to Militants of Jaamatul" (in Bengali). *Prothom Alo*, 28 August 2005, 1.

Talabani, Aziz. "Pedagogy, Power and Discourse: Transformation of Islamic Education." *Comparative Education Review* 40, no. 1 (1996): 66–82.

Talbot, Ian. "Understanding Religious Violence in Contemporary Pakistan: Themes and Theories." In *Religion, Violence and Political Mobilisation in South Asia*, edited by Ravinder Kaur, 145–164. New Delhi: Sage, 2005.

"34 Islamic NGOs get over Tk 200cr from donors a year." *Daily Star*, 31 August 2005, 1.

Tibawi, A. L. "Origin and Characteristics of 'al-madrassah.'" *Bulletin of the School of Oriental and African Studies* 25, nos. 1–3 (1962): 225–238.

Timmerman, Kenneth. *The Preachers of Hate*. Oxford: Crown Forum, 2003.

Titumir, Rashed al-Mahmud, and Jakir Hossain. *Encountering Exclusion: Primary Education Policy Watch*. Dhaka: Shamabesh, 2004.

Tohid, Owais. "Pakistan, US Take on the Madrassahs." *Christian Science Monitor*, 24 August 2004, 1.

Toledano, Ralph de. *One Man Alone: Richard Nixon*. New York: Funk and Wagnalls, 1969.

"Top Boss of Kuwait-based RIHS Leaves Country in Hurry." *Daily Star*, 22 August 2005, 1.

"Trainees Eager to Join 'Jihad' against America." *USA Today*, 27 September 2001, http://usatoday.com/news/nation/2001/09/27/schools.htm (2 November 2005).

Trumpbour, John. "The Clash of Civilizations: Samuel P Huntington, Bernard Lewis, and the Remaking of Post-Cold War World Order." In *The New Crusades: Constructing the Muslim Enemy*, edited by Emran Querishi and Michael A. Sells, 88–130. New York: Columbia University Press, 2003.

USAID. "Bangladesh: Education. Current Condition" USAID 2004, http://www.usaid.gov/bd/education.html (6 January 2005).

———. Program Areas, http://www.usaid.gov/in/our_work/program_areas/opportu-nity.htm (7 May 2007).

UNESCO. *Children out of School: Measuring Exclusion from Primary Education.* Montreal: UNESCO Office of Statistics, 2005.

———. *EFA 2000 Assessment Country Reports Bangladesh.* UNESCO, 2000, http://www2.unesco.org/wef/countryreports/bangladesh/rapport_1.html (26 January 2003).

United States Department of State. *Foreign Relations of the United States,* 11. Washington, D.C.: Office of the Historian, US Department of State, 2005.

Vishwanathanan, Gauri. *Masks of Conquest: Literary Study and British Rule in India.* New Delhi: Oxford University Press, 2000.

Voll, John O. "Muhammad Hayya al-Sindi and Muhammad ibn Abd al-Wahab: An Analysis of an Intellectual Group in Eighteenth-Century Medina." *Bulletin of the School of Oriental and African Studies* 38, no. 1 (1975): 32–39.

Weaver, Mary Ann. "Blowback." *Atlantic Monthly* 277 no. 5 (May 1998): 24–36.

———. "Children of the Jihad." *New Yorker* 12 June 1995, 40.

"Where Do the Militants Get the Money?" (in Bengali). *Prothom Alo,* 20 August 2005, 1.

"Who's Who in the Kashmir Militancy." *Herald Magazine,* August 2000.

World Bank. "Pakistan Country Overview," http://www.worldbank.org.pk/WBSITE/EXTERNAL/COUNTRIES/SOUTHASIAEXT/PAKISTANEXTN/0,,contentMDK:20131431~menuPK:293059~pagePK:141137~piPK:141127~theSitePK:293052,00.html> (14 April 2007).

——— . *Bangladesh Education Sector Review,* Vol. 1. Dhaka: University Press, 2000.

Wright, Robin. 1992. "Islam, Democracy and the West." *Foreign Affairs* 71 (Summer 1992): 131–145.

Yasmeen, Summiya. "Swelling Support for Common Schools." *India Together,* July 2004, http://www.indiatogether.org/2004/jul/edu-kothari.htm (5 January 2006).

Yost, David S. "Nuclear Debates in France." *Survival* 36, no. 4 (Winter 1994–1995): 114–115.

Zahab, Mariam Abou. "The Regional Dimension of Sectarian Conflicts in Pakistan." In *Pakistan: Nationalism without a Nation?* edited by Christophe Jaffrelot, 115–130. New Delhi: Monohar, 2002.

Zahab, Mariam Abou, and Oliver Roy. *Islamist Networks: The Afghanistan-Pakistan Connection.* New York: Columbia University Press, 2004.

Zakaria, Rafic. *The Struggle within Islam: The Conflict between Religion and Politics.* New York: Penguin, 1988.

Zaman, Muhammad Qasim. "Madrasas and Reform: Some Lessons from Pakistan." Paper presented at conference on "Muslim Politics and US Policies: Prospects for Pluralism and Democracy in the Muslim World," Pew Forum on Religion and Public Life, Washington, D.C. 17 September 2003.

———. *The Ulama in Contemporary Islam: Custodians of Change.* Princeton: Princeton University Press, 2002.

Zastoupil, L., and M. Moir, eds. *The Great Indian Education Debate: Documents Relating to the Orientalist—Anglist Controversy, 1781–1843.* Richmond, Surrey: Curzon, 1999.

INDEX

Italicized page numbers refer to tables.

ABOUT THE AUTHOR

ALI RIAZ is a professor and chair of the department of politics and government at Illinois State University. He previously taught at universities in Bangladesh and England, and worked for the British Broadcasting Corporation (BBC) in London. His publications include *Islamist Militancy in Bangladesh: A Complex Web* (2008), *Paradise Lost? State Failure in Nepal* (with Subho Basu, 2007), *Unfolding State: The Transformation of Bangladesh* (2005), and *God Willing: The Politics of Islamism in Bangladesh* (2004).